Sascha Hoffmann
Editor

Digital Product Management

Frameworks—Tools—Cases

Editor
Sascha Hoffmann
Professor of Online Management Fresenius
University of Applies Sciences
Hamburg, Germany

ISBN 978-3-658-44275-0   ISBN 978-3-658-44276-7   (eBook)
https://doi.org/10.1007/978-3-658-44276-7

Translation from the German language edition: "Digitales Produktmanagement" by Sascha Hoffmann, ©
Springer Fachmedien Wiesbaden GmbH, ein Teil von Springer Nature 2023. Published by Springer Fachmedien Wiesbaden. All Rights Reserved.

This book is a translation of the original German edition "Digitales Produktmanagement," 2nd edition, by
Sascha Hoffmann, published by Springer Fachmedien Wiesbaden GmbH in 2023. The translation was done
with the help of an artificial intelligence machine translation tool. A subsequent human revision was done primarily in terms of content, so that the book will read stylistically differently from a conventional translation.
Springer Nature works continuously to further the development of tools for the production of books and on the
related technologies to support the authors.

© The Editor(s) (if applicable) and The Author(s), under exclusive license to Springer Fachmedien Wiesbaden
GmbH, part of Springer Nature 2024

This work is subject to copyright. All rights are solely and exclusively licensed by the Publisher, whether
the whole or part of the material is concerned, specifically the rights of translation, reprinting, reuse
of illustrations, recitation, broadcasting, reproduction on microfilms or in any other physical way, and
transmission or information storage and retrieval, electronic adaptation, computer software, or by similar or
dissimilar methodology now known or hereafter developed.
The use of general descriptive names, registered names, trademarks, service marks, etc. in this publication does
not imply, even in the absence of a specific statement, that such names are exempt from the relevant protective
laws and regulations and therefore free for general use.
The publisher, the authors and the editors are safe to assume that the advice and information in this book
are believed to be true and accurate at the date of publication. Neither the publisher nor the authors or the
editors give a warranty, expressed or implied, with respect to the material contained herein or for any errors
or omissions that may have been made. The publisher remains neutral with regard to jurisdictional claims in
published maps and institutional affiliations.

This Springer imprint is published by the registered company Springer Fachmedien Wiesbaden GmbH, part of
Springer Nature.
The registered company address is: Abraham-Lincoln-Str. 46, 65189 Wiesbaden, Germany

Paper in this product is recyclable.

Preface to the Second Edition

Digitization is drastically changing the world in which we live. The internet, smartphones, and in recent years the Internet of Things, which is the extension of physical goods with additional digital functionalities, are constantly creating new digital products and services for us. With Apple, Alphabet (Google), Microsoft, Amazon, and Meta, the five most valuable companies now all come from the digital industry. And in addition to the big tech giants from Silicon Valley, countless other digital companies and start-ups with innovative business models are pushing into the market worldwide. As a result, traditional companies are also forced to digitally transform in order to continue to play a relevant role in the future.

The development of digital products, such as websites, apps or software in general, has thus become a core function in companies. At the same time, the way in which the development of digital products is carried out has changed significantly in recent years. No longer is there a process of working through a once established requirements catalog and project plan. Instead, an agile approach has been established to ensure a market-oriented, i.e., user-centered product development.

The agile development of digital products not only changes the way developers work. It also implies a new kind of product management. The active management of products is nothing new in itself: it has been a fixed component in business literature for decades, for example in the form of product policy in marketing. And the profession of a product manager has also existed for a long time. In the digital context, however, the range of tasks of product managers sometimes differs significantly from the primarily commercially oriented, "classic" one. Their area of responsibility ranges from the initial identification of new product ideas and the validation of their user and company potential, through the specification of requirements and the control of their implementation, to the sustainably successful further development of digital products. So product management is not just about economic optimization, but also about the technological feasibility of digital products that are really desired from the user's point of view—and for which there is a willingness to pay.

A product manager is holistically responsible for the setup and further development of "his" product. This is particularly evident in the agile Scrum framework, where the role as

"Product Owner" is explicitly provided—a designation that is sometimes also used in companies that organize their digital product development with other agile methods.

Product managers have a very responsible and versatile position in their companies, for which they must obtain a broad knowledge of methods and a great amount of interpersonal sensitivity. Product managers are sought after in the market. Due to a largely missing institutionalized education and the simultaneously very diverse requirements, the demand exceeds the available supply of qualified product managers by a multiple. Companies try to close this gap, among other things, by training communicative software developers or IT-affine business people internally to become product managers. This is where the present book comes in, describing how digital product management is used in a contemporary and successful manner.

Since the publication of the 1st edition of this book in 2020, the digital transformation of our world has continued to gain momentum. Current trends or hypes, such as the metaverse or the ever-widening application of artificial intelligence, suggest a continually growing importance of digital product management.

It is time for a 2nd edition of the book on digital product management. Most of the authors from the 1st edition are back with their updated contributions. In addition, further experts have joined with new contributions. As a result, the book has not only grown significantly in size compared to the 1st edition, but now offers both experts and beginners even more comprehensive insights into digital product management.

In the first article, I initially provide a basic classification of digital product management. To do this, the central agile product management concepts as well as selected methods and tools are presented. This gives beginners a practical overview of what to expect in the world of digital product development.

The further contributions each address a specific topic from digital product management and provide an in-depth overview. They range from strategic basics, through very operational questions, to the personal development of product managers and their interaction within product organizations.

Inken Petersen's article discusses how a user-centered product vision can be developed within a team and subsequently become truly present in everyday business life.

Christian Becker explains in his article why it is particularly important for agile product organizations to have a product strategy, what distinguishes a good strategy, and how it can be determined.

In her contribution, Cansel Sörgens explains in detail the popular Objectives & Key Results framework, which can be used to break down a long-term product strategy into typically quarterly defined goals. Among other things, she describes how meaningful OKR sets are defined and what organizations should consider when introducing OKR.

Dominik Busching and Lutz Göcke then explain how the product strategy and objectives manifest in a concrete Product Roadmap. They discuss the advantages and disadvantages of different types of roadmaps and highlight the factors that make a Product Roadmap successful.

Preface to the Second Edition

The contribution by Philip Steen and Alexander Hipp illustrates how important intensive Product Discovery is in order to understand the truly relevant user problems and to develop promising solution ideas based on this understanding.

Before the identified solutions are directly added to the Product Roadmap, their viability should still be validated. Anna Wicher describes in her contribution which aspects to consider and which tools can be usefully employed in this process.

Tim Adler reports in his contribution to Product Delivery, which small and large challenges arise in the actual product development in everyday life, and gives concrete tips that make the everyday life of a product manager easier.

Following this, Markus Andrezak explains in his contribution how omnipresent—and at the same time challenging—the demand for ever-increasing growth is for product managers, who are not only responsible for new development, but also for the successful further development of "their" products.

Rainer Gibbert points out that the further development of existing digital products can not only be difficult, but often also comes with resistance from their users. He describes how to reduce reservations about product changes and why sometimes just waiting and enduring can be a solution.

In another article, I explain how a market-relevant development of digital products can be ensured through A/B testing, what statistics are underlying, and what needs to be considered in the practical implementation.

Patrick Roelofs subsequently provides important advice on how to transform from a good to an outstanding product manager by shifting the focus from pure method and tool knowledge to a holistic view.

A particularly important skill of successful product managers is to make good product decisions, especially when the validation of product ideas does not yield clear results. For this, a deep "sense" for s product and its target group is indispensable. How this so-called Product Sense can be developed is explained by Robert Schulke and Nikkel Blaase in their contribution.

Experienced product managers often take on leadership responsibilities in product organizations. In his contribution to Product Leadership, Tobias Freudenreich explains how product managers can use the tools of lateral leadership to become effective within their product teams, and how superiors in product management can empower their product teams, rather than commanding them.

Product management always also means interface management with different stakeholders in a company. This is often not free from conflicts and personal sensitivities. Precisely for this reason, a good and trustful alignment is key as Arne Kittler shows in his contribution.

Following this, Petra Wille describes how others can be convinced of one's own product plans through skillful storytelling. Among other things, she discusses why stories have a great power of persuasion, what makes up a good story, and which kind is particularly suitable in which circumstances.

The development of digital products is teamwork. A particularly important person of trust for a product manager should be the Scrum Master. Jan Köster and Florian Meyer describe how a good, and trustful collaboration between Scrum Master and Product Owner can evolve, from which the entire product team benefits.

In her second book contribution Inken Petersen explains how important a good user experience is to the success of a digital product and she provides practical advice on how the interaction between product managers and UX experts can be successful.

Jan Martens also focuses on cross-functional collaboration, by raising awareness for numerous pitfalls that can lead to misunderstandings in the collaboration between product managers and data analytics experts in companies.

Michael Schultheiß, David Gehrke, and Lutz Göcke describe in their contribution, what characteristics successful product organizations generally exhibit, what types of organization are typical, and what needs to be considered during the transformation of a product organization.

In conclusion, Stefan Roock explains which agile frameworks are particularly promising in which phase of a product organization and can scale agile working methods within a company, thus rounding off the consideration of digital product management.

The book would not have been successful without extensive support. My special thanks go first and foremost to my co-authors, without whose great commitment alongside their actual professions the book would never have been created. In addition, I thank Stella Ruthe and Leon Sebening, who thoroughly formatted the contributions and proofread them. I would also like to express my gratitude to Imke Sander from Springer-Gabler-Verlag for the uncomplicated cooperation and careful editing.

And finally, a big thank you to my family, who supported me during the many evenings and weekends it took to bring the book to a successful conclusion in its second, significantly expanded edition.

On behalf of all authors, I wish you much joy in reading the contributions and success in applying the insights to your own work and experience world. Supplementary notes on the book and exciting news about digital product management can be found at www.digitales-produktmanagement.de.

Hamburg
in May 2023

Sascha Hoffmann

Contents

1 Introduction to Digital Product Management 1
Sascha Hoffmann
1.1 Product Management vs. Project Management 1
1.2 Basics of Agile Product Management 5
1.3 Digital Product Development According to Scrum 12
1.4 Digital Product Development with Kanban 22
1.5 Other Agile Methods in Digital Product Management 26
References 27

2 User-Centered Product Visions 31
Inken Petersen
2.1 What is a Product Vision? 31
2.2 Why a Product Vision is Needed 33
2.3 How to Recognize a Good Product Vision 34
2.4 Tools for Creating a Good Product Vision 35
    2.4.1 The Vision Statement 35
    2.4.2 The Product Vision Board 35
    2.4.3 The Product Vision Template 36
    2.4.4 The Visiontype 37
2.5 The Vision Workshop 38
    2.5.1 The Right Preparation 38
    2.5.2 The Workshop 39
    2.5.3 After the Workshop 40
2.6 How to Recognize that the Product Vision is Working 41
2.7 A Brief Outlook at the End 42
References 42

3 Product Strategy—The Foundation of Product Management 45

Christian Becker

3.1 Introduction 45

3.2 What is Product Strategy? 46

3.3 The Importance of Product Strategy 47

3.4 The Elements of Product Strategy 48

    3.4.1 The Product Playing Field 48

    3.4.2 The Starting Point 50

    3.4.3 The Future Factors 51

    3.4.4 The Goal 52

    3.4.5 The Path 54

3.5 The Formation Process of the Product Strategy 54

3.6 The Operationalization of the Product Strategy 57

    3.6.1 The Alignment Gap 57

    3.6.2 The Effects Gap 58

References 58

4 Implementing and Validating Product Strategy with Objectives and Key Results (OKR) 59

Cansel Sörgens

4.1 What are Objectives and Key Results about? 59

4.2 What Problems does the OKR Framework Solve? 61

4.3 How are Objectives and Key Results Defined? 62

    4.3.1 Mid-term Strategic Goal 63

    4.3.2 Objective 64

    4.3.3 Key Results 66

4.4 The OKR Cycle 68

    4.4.1 Workshop for OKR Definition 68

    4.4.2 OKR Alignment Workshop 70

    4.4.3 Initiative Planning 71

    4.4.4 OKR Check-ins 72

    4.4.5 Strategy Check-ins 73

    4.4.6 OKR Reflection 73

    4.4.7 Strategy Review 75

    4.4.8 OKR System Reflection 75

4.5 OKR Introduction 76

4.6 OKR Architecture 79

    4.6.1 Dynamic Networks Instead of Strict Cascading 79

    4.6.2 Types of OKR Teams 80

4.7 Roles in the OKR Process 81

    4.7.1 Executives 82

    4.7.2 Team Members 82

	4.7.3	Internal OKR Agents	83
4.8	Principles of OKR	83
	4.8.1	Finding the right balance between Top-down and Bottom-up	83
	4.8.2	Do not link OKR with Performance Management	84
	4.8.3	Do not use OKR for Everyone and Everything	84
4.9	Final Thoughts	85
References	85

5 Product Roadmaps 87

Dominik Busching and Lutz Göcke

5.1	Classification of Product Roadmaps	87
5.2	Types of Product Roadmaps	88
	5.2.1	The "Classic": The Feature-Based Roadmap	89
	5.2.2	Thinking from the End: Goal-Oriented and Outcome-Driven Roadmaps	89
	5.2.3	Packed in Boxes: Theme-Based Roadmaps	91
5.3	The Benefits of Product Roadmaps	91
5.4	The Risks of Product Roadmaps	94
	5.4.1	Risks for Stakeholder Management	94
	5.4.2	Risks for Product Development	95
5.5	Success Factors for Product Roadmaps	97
	5.5.1	Problem Focus Instead of Solution Focus	97
	5.5.2	Short Review and Update Cycles	98
	5.5.3	Avoiding Pseudo-Accuracy and Artificial Deadlines	98
	5.5.4	Not less, but better Communication	99
	5.5.5	From Product Strategy and Vision to Roadmap	100
	5.5.6	Prioritizing Data-driven and Coordinating with Stakeholders	100
	5.5.7	Different Representations for Different Target Groups	101
5.6	Product Roadmaps for Hardware or IoT Products	101
	5.6.1	Hardware versus Software Development	102
	5.6.2	Requirements for Hardware Roadmaps	102
	5.6.3	Roadmaps for IoT Products	103
5.7	Conclusion	104
References	104

6 Product Discovery 107

Philip Steen and Alexander Hipp

6.1	Goals of Product Discovery	107
6.2	Basic principles of a Product Discovery	110
	6.2.1	Outcome Orientation	110
	6.2.2	User Centricity and Problem Focus	111

	6.2.3	Iterative and Experimental Approach	111
	6.2.4	Interdisciplinarity	112
6.3	Manifestations of a Product Discovery		113
	6.3.1	Project-based Discovery	113
	6.3.2	Continuous Discovery	114
6.4	Frameworks for Structuring a Product Discovery		114
	6.4.1	Design Sprint	115
	6.4.2	Product Kata	116
	6.4.3	Opportunity Solution Tree	117
6.5	Product Discovery Toolbox		118
6.6	Practical Tips for Implementing a Product Discovery in the Company		120
	6.6.1	Consequences of a Focus on Product Delivery	121
	6.6.2	Potential Pitfalls in Implementing Product Discovery	121
		6.6.2.1 External Control of Product Teams	122
		6.6.2.2 Output Instead of Outcome	122
		6.6.2.3 No Regular Exchange with the User	122
References			123

7 Validation of Product Ideas in the Market 125
Anna Wicher

7.1	Why Validation?		125
	7.1.1	What Will This Be About?	126
	7.1.2	How Long Does Such a Validation Usually Take?	127
	7.1.3	What Kind of Team Do I Need for Validation?	128
7.2	Research—Where do We Start?		128
	7.2.1	Hypotheses—What are We Assuming So Far?	129
	7.2.2	Market Analysis and Target Group Definition—What are Our Initial Assumptions Based On?	130
	7.2.3	Qualitative Research—What does the target group say?	131
	7.2.4	Quantitative Validation—How Many Are There?	132
	7.2.5	MVP Definition and Resource Requirements—What Do We Need for Testing?	133
	7.2.6	Design vs. Technology—Where is the Focus in Creating an MVP?	135
7.3	Prototyping—What are We Building Now?		136
	7.3.1	Test Plan & Feature Definition—What Do We Want to Know and What Do We Need For It?	137
	7.3.2	UX and UI—What Should the MVP Look Like?	140
	7.3.3	Development—How and with Which Technology Will the MVP Be Implemented?	141
	7.3.4	Team—Who is Building This?	141

		7.3.5	Time Estimate—How Long will It Take?	142
	7.4	Testing—How Do We Get the Numbers?		143
		7.4.1	Launch & Marketing Plan—Who will test the MVP?	143
		7.4.2	Pivot—Everything New Again?	144
		7.4.3	KPIs & Business Plan—Are We Making Money Now?	145
	7.5	And What Happens Next?		145
	References			146

8 Product Delivery 147
Tim Adler

	8.1	Let's Get Started		147
	8.2	What You Need Before You Start		149
		8.2.1	MVP vs. MLP	149
		8.2.2	Documenting Features	149
		8.2.3	First, Make It "Pretty"—Preparing the Design	149
	8.3	Knowing in Advance What It Will Cost		152
		8.3.1	Classic Project Management FTW	152
		8.3.2	An Idea of Team Size	153
		8.3.3	Time and Cost Estimation	153
		8.3.4	What to Do If It's Too Expensive or Too Slow?	155
	8.4	Setting Up the Toolbox		156
		8.4.1	Even More Preparation, Seriously?	156
		8.4.2	Choosing a Name	157
		8.4.3	Preparing the Backlog	157
		8.4.4	Setting up a Sprint Board	159
	8.5	Running a Marathon		161
		8.5.1	Choosing Sprint Length	161
		8.5.2	Meetings, Meetings, Meetings … are the Sprint	161
			8.5.2.1 Sprint Planning	162
			8.5.2.2 Daily Standup	164
			8.5.2.3 Sprint Review	166
			8.5.2.4 Retrospective	167
		8.5.3	Are We Still on Schedule…?	167
		8.5.4	… And If Not, How Do We Get Back "On Plan"?	168
	8.6	Little Helpers in Everyday Life		168
		8.6.1	Developers Call for "Refactoring!"	168
		8.6.2	Customer Support Warns of "Bugs!"	169
	8.7	That's It		170

9 Growth 171
Markus Andrezak

	9.1	Everyone Wants Growth	171
	9.2	How Long Does Growth Take?	174

9.2.1	Henry Ford and the Model T	175
9.2.2	The iPhone	176
9.2.3	Digital "Growth Miracles"	176

9.3 Growth Happens in Two Phases ... 178
9.4 Growth Models ... 181

9.4.1	The Hockey Stick	181
9.4.2	The 3-Horizon Model	183
	9.4.2.1 Horizon 1	183
	9.4.2.2 Horizon 2	184
	9.4.2.3 Horizon 3	186
	9.4.2.4 The Interplay of Horizons	186

9.5 What Do We Need to Master to Achieve Growth? ... 187
References ... 188

10 Product Changes ... 189
Rainer Gibbert

10.1 Resistance to Change ... 189
10.2 Why Changes are Rejected ... 191

10.2.1	Users (Mostly) Don't Care About Design	191
10.2.2	Users Love Routines	192
10.2.3	Users Like Familiarity	192
10.2.4	Users Tend Towards the Status Quo	193
10.2.5	Users Prefer What They Already Own	193
10.2.6	Users Fear Loss of Control	193

10.3 Creating Acceptance for Change ... 194

10.3.1	Change Not As an End in Itself	194
10.3.2	Accompanying Changes in a User-Centered Manner	194
10.3.3	Make Changes Testable for Users in Advance	195
10.3.4	Let Users Choose	196
10.3.5	Prefer Incremental Changes	197
10.3.6	Communicate Changes and Make Them Appealing	197
10.3.7	Patience and Perseverance	198

10.4 Conclusion ... 199
References ... 200

11 A/B Testing in Digital Product Management ... 203
Sascha Hoffmann

11.1 Introduction ... 203
11.2 Basics of Hypothesis Formation ... 205
11.3 Statistics in A/B Testing ... 206
11.4 A/B Testing in Practice ... 207
References ... 208

Contents

12 Product Management Understood Holistically 211
Patrick Roelofs

12.1 The Tasks of the Product Manager. 211

    12.1.1 Result Dimension 1: User Satisfaction with the Product..... 212

    12.1.2 Result Dimension 2: Commercial Success of the Product. ... 213

12.2 The Product Manager as a Proactive Relationship Manager 214

12.3 The Product Manager as an Outstanding Communicator 215

12.4 The Product Manager as a "Decision Maker" 216

    12.4.1 Clearly Formulated Goals 217

    12.4.2 Maximum Transparency ("Connecting the Dots") 217

    12.4.3 Necessary Escalations 218

12.5 The Product Manager as a Supplier of Answers 219

12.6 The Product Manager as a Clear-Thought-Provider 220

References. 222

13 Product Sense 223
Robert Schulke and Nikkel Blaase

13.1 Introduction 223

13.2 What is Product Sense? 224

13.3 The Importance of Product Sense 225

13.4 How Product Sense Can Be Developed. 226

    13.4.1 Building Empathy 226

    13.4.2 Strengthening Product and Domain Knowledge 228

        13.4.2.1 Basic Product Knowledge. 228

        13.4.2.2 Specific Domain Knowledge. 229

13.5 Product Sense Quick Start 229

References. 230

14 Product Leadership. 233
Tobias Freudenreich

14.1 Lateral Leadership 235

    14.1.1 Lateral Leadership through Communication 235

    14.1.2 Lateral Leadership through Power. 237

    14.1.3 Lateral Leadership through Trust. 238

    14.1.4 The Interplay of Communication, Power, and Trust 239

14.2 Disciplinary Leadership. 240

    14.2.1 Clear Structures 242

    14.2.2 A Clear Goal Corridor 242

    14.2.3 Competent Product Managers 245

    14.2.4 Strong Product Teams 248

    14.2.5 Interdisciplinary Leadership. 249

    14.2.6 Final Considerations. 252

References. 252

15 Alignment 255
Arne Kittler

15.1 Why is Alignment Important in the Context of Modern Product
Development? 255
    15.1.1 Alignment Creates Trust 256
    15.1.2 Alignment Helps to Avoid Waste of Resources 256
    15.1.3 Alignment Helps to Make Decisions 257
15.2 Who Should a Product Manager Actively Align With? 258
15.3 In Which Contexts is Alignment Particularly Important? 258
15.4 When Should Systematic Alignment Ideally Take Place? 259
15.5 What Approaches Help in Alignment? 259
    15.5.1 The Right Conversation Partners in the Right Order 259
    15.5.2 Sensible Constellations and Methods for Active
Alignment. 260
15.6 Important Questions to Clarify in the Context of Alignment. 260
    15.6.1 Initial Situation from the User's Perspective 261
    15.6.2 Vision from the User's Perspective 261
    15.6.3 Hypotheses. 261
    15.6.4 Input—and Roles. 262
    15.6.5 Output—and Boundaries 262
    15.6.6 Outcome—and Limits 263
15.7 Identify Conflicts and Bring Them to Resolution 263
15.8 Alignment in Practice: "Auftragsklärung" at XING 265
    15.8.1 Origin and Development of the Mission Statement. 265
    15.8.2 Essential Artifacts and Common Practices 265
    15.8.3 Introduction, Application and Misunderstandings. 267
15.9 Limits of Sensible Alignment 267
References. 268

16 Product Evangelizing and Storytelling 269
Petra Wille

16.1 Why Storytelling is Important in Product Management 269
16.2 Why Our Brains Love Stories 271
16.3 What Stories can Achieve in a Professional Context. 273
    16.3.1 Elements of a Good Story 273
    16.3.2 Stories are the Perfect Design Tool 274
16.4 How to Conceive and Tell Good Stories 275
    16.4.1 What Does all This Have to do With Product
Management?. 275
    16.4.2 Overcoming the Fear of the Blank Page 278

Contents

xvii

16.5	How to Anchor the Message Sustainably		279
16.6	My Conclusion		282
References			282

17 Product Owner and Scrum Master ... 285
Jan Köster and Florian Meyer

17.1	More than a Role Model from a Framework		285
17.2	How Good Collaboration Can Succeed		286
	17.2.1	Start with Why	287
	17.2.2	Shared Visions	288
	17.2.3	Trust	289
	17.2.4	Agile Principles	290
	17.2.5	When do we Stop?	290
	17.2.6	Why do you do it that Way?	290
	17.2.7	Be Partners	291
	17.2.8	Shared Rituals	291
	17.2.9	Your PDCA Cycle	292
	17.2.10	Leading through Why and Transparency	293
	17.2.11	Leading through Attitude	294
	17.2.12	Shared Leadership	294
17.3	What's Next?		295
17.4	Learning Teams		296
References			297

18 Understanding User Experience ... 299
Inken Petersen

18.1	The Importance of a Positive User Experience		299
18.2	The Iterative UX Design Process		300
18.3	The Core Disciplines in the User Experience Field		302
	18.3.1	The UX Designer	302
	18.3.2	The Visual Designer	303
	18.3.3	The User Researcher	303
18.4	The Different Types of UX Teams		304
	18.4.1	The Classic UX Team	304
	18.4.2	The "UX Team of One"	304
	18.4.3	The Hybrid "UX & Visual Design Team" with Separate User Research Dimension	305
18.5	The Best Organizational Form		305
18.6	The Right Amount of UX		306
18.7	The Future of UX		307
References			308

xviii | Contents

19 Data Analytics 309
Jan Martens
19.1 Introduction 309
19.2 Roles and Organizations 310
19.3 The Pitfalls 310
    19.3.1 The Feel-Good Analysis 310
    19.3.2 The Justification Analysis 311
    19.3.3 The Symptom Analysis 311
    19.3.4 Simple Questions, Complex Answers 312
    19.3.5 Overconfidence 313
    19.3.6 Narcissism 313
    19.3.7 Simply Wrong 314
    19.3.8 "Not Significant" 315
    19.3.9 Too Demanding 315
    19.3.10 Lack of Distance—Sunk Costs 316
    19.3.11 Too Little Data 316
19.4 Conclusion 317

20 Product Organizations 319
Michael Schultheiß, David Gehrke and Lutz Göcke
20.1 What is a Product Organization? 319
20.2 Five Features of Successful Product Organizations 320
20.3 Structures, Processes, Employees 321
    20.3.1 Structure 321
    20.3.2 Processes 326
    20.3.3 Employees 328
20.4 Product Organization Archetypes 332
20.5 Change and Adaptation Processes 333
    20.5.1 Transformation into a Product Organization 334
    20.5.2 Transformation Within a Product Organization 334
20.6 Conclusion 335
References 335

21 Choosing the "Right" Agile Framework for the Company 339
Stefan Roock
21.1 Introduction 339
21.2 The Appropriate Framework for the Agile Pilot 341
    21.2.1 Scrum vs. Kanban 342
    21.2.2 The Thing About Beliefs 342
    21.2.3 Agile Approach in Startups vs. Corporations 343

21.3	Agile Work in Entire Product Development		344
	21.3.1	Minimize Dependencies	344
	21.3.2	Managing Dependencies	345
	21.3.3	Platforms	347
	21.3.4	Caution with Top-Down Standardization	348
		21.3.4.1 Resistance from Employees	348
		21.3.4.2 Loss of Agility	349
	21.3.5	Keep the Tools Away from Me	349
21.4	Agile Work throughout the Company		349
	21.4.1	Autonomy and Alignment	350
	21.4.2	Adaptable Structure	351
		21.4.2.1 Market Contact Through External References	352
		21.4.2.2 Company Adaptation with Sociocracy 3.0	353
21.5	Summary		355
References			356

Editors and Contributors

About the Editors

Sascha Hoffmann is a Professor of Business Administration and Online Management at the Fresenius University of Applied Sciences in Hamburg. He teaches subjects such as Digital Media, E-Commerce, Online Marketing, and digital product management. Previously, he held leading roles in business development and product management for companies such as XING and blau Mobilfunk. More at www.hoffmann-sascha.de. Contact: moin@hoffmann-sascha.de

Contributors

Tim Adler Hamburg

Markus Andrezak überproduct GmbH, Potsdam

Christian Becker leanproductable GmbH, Berlin

Nikkel Blaase Orbit Ventures GmbH, Hamburg

Dominik Busching tado°, Munich

Tobias Freudenreich Freelance Product Leadership Coach & Consultant, Hamburg

David Gehrke Nordhausen University of Applied Sciences, Nordhausen

Rainer Gibbert Star Finanz GmbH, Hamburg

Lutz Göcke Nordhausen University of Applied Sciences, Nordhausen

Sascha Hoffmann Fresenius University of Applied Sciences, Hamburg

Alexander Hipp Beyond, London

Arne Kittler facelift, Hamburg

Jan Köster Gruner + Jahr, Hamburg

Jan Martens Lotto24 AG, Hamburg

Florian Meyer Gruner + Jahr, Hamburg

Inken Petersen Hamburg

Patrick Roelofs Aroundhome, Berlin

Stefan Roock it-agile GmbH, Hamburg

Robert Schulke Freiburg

Michael Schultheiss McKinsey & Co, Kiel

Cansel Sörgens Cologne

Philip Steen Norderstedt

Anna Wicher MissionMe, Hamburg

Petra Wille Strong Product People, Hamburg

Introduction to Digital Product Management

Classification and Basic Concepts

Sascha Hoffmann

Abstract

The introductory article first addresses the fundamental differences between a classic, project-based and an agile development of digital products, highlighting the advantages of the agile approach. Afterwards, the individual phases of digital product development are explained. These range from the product vision and the derivation of a suitable product strategy, to the identification of the "right" products or product features from a market perspective within the framework of a product discovery, to the actual product development, the product delivery. Subsequently, Scrum, as the dominant agile development framework in practice, is explained in detail. Kanban, another very popular framework, is then described, before finally providing an overview of hybrid forms and other further developments of agile methods for digital product development.

1.1 Product Management vs. Project Management

The development of digital products (apps, websites or software solutions in general) was predominantly carried out in the traditional project form for a long time, by dividing the development process into individual phases to be completed one after the other. This approach is particularly associated with the **waterfall model** (Fig. 1.1).

In the waterfall model, a precise definition of the product characteristics to be developed takes place at the beginning of the development project. For this purpose, the

---

S. Hoffmann (✉)
Professor of Online Management, Fresenius University of Applies Sciences, Hamburg, Germany
e-mail: moin@hoffmann-sascha.de

© The Author(s), under exclusive license to Springer Fachmedien Wiesbaden GmbH, part of Springer Nature 2024
S. Hoffmann (ed.), *Digital Product Management*,
https://doi.org/10.1007/978-3-658-44276-7_1

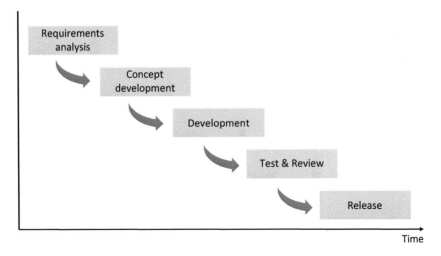

Fig. 1.1 Schematic process of a waterfall-like product development. (*Source*: Own illustration)

requirements of the targeted user group and possibly other relevant stakeholders of the new product are collected in detail during an analysis phase. Once this phase is completed, the specifications for the digital product to be developed are derived in the planning or conception phase and are written down in a detailed requirement catalog (specification sheet). This serves as requirement specifications for the developers. Subsequently the actual programming starts in the development phase, which can last several months or even years for larger projects and is often divided into sub-phases (design, implementation, etc.). Once the development is fully completed, a test or review phase usually follows before the product is launched, during which it is checked whether the product has been implemented without errors and according to the client's specification sheet. If this is the case, the product is handed over to the client or taken live (released) in the final project step (Laudon et al. 2016).

A development project in the traditional project management sense is considered successful as soon as all content requirements have been implemented within the given time and budget framework, i.e., the required **output** has been delivered. In product management, on the other hand, a product is only considered successful when it is accepted by the users and leads to the desired behavior change **(outcome),** through which the company expects a positive effect on its (monetary) success indicators **(impact).**

▶ An excellent description of what a product is in the sense of product management is given in the current Scrum Guide:

"A product is a tool to deliver value. It has clear boundaries, known stakeholders, clearly defined users or customers. A product can be a service, a physical product, or something more abstract." (Schwaber and Sutherland 2020)

1 Introduction to Digital Product Management

Whether the intended behavior change actually occurs, however, is uncertain. Especially because, presumably, environmental and market conditions are subject to constant change. This is often described as **VUCA**. This acronym stands for Volatility, Uncertainty, Complexity, and Ambiguity and describes the difficult conditions under which people or organizations must make decisions (Mack et al. 2015).[1]

In product management, the aim is to minimize the risk of developing a product that does not meet market needs. It is consciously acknowledged that no one can predict on the basis of a supposedly good product idea alone that a product will be successful later on. This is especially true in today's dynamic and complex times. Product ideas are therefore always "bets" that still need to prove themselves as correct.

The supposed planning security of traditional project management often turns out to be a delusive certainty. Even the most detailed specifications at the beginning of a product idea can only be imprecise and incomplete. Market changes, technical innovations, changes in laws, etc., regularly lead to changes in the requirements for the product to be developed during the development process. However, in traditional project management, this is only noticed at the end when the product is not accepted by the market or, for example, due to changes in regulations in the meantime, cannot go live at all. In the worst case, this means that the development project has to start all over again, by starting with a new analysis of the changed requirements.

In digital product management, on the other hand, it is accepted that not all parameters are known at the beginning of a software development project and thus new requirements can be added during development, and originally assumed ones can change or even be dropped. According to the **Cynefin Framework** by David Snowden (2000), this is a complex problem situation where cause-effect relationships are not yet clear at the beginning (see the Cynefin Framework in the context of digital product management in detail in Chap. 17 by Jan Köster and Florian Meyer).

In contrast to classical project management, with **agility** a **different kind of digital product development** has been established in product management. This means that a product is developed incrementally along the entire development process and regularly obtains feedback from stakeholders, especially the later users, to validate that the pursued solution constantly meets the actual requirements and needs of the market. The result of each feedback loop directly influences further product development (Fig. 1.2).

---

[1] As a variation of VUCA, the world is now also characterized with the acronym **BANI**, which stands for brittle, anxious, non-linear, and incomprehensible. Both concepts describe the challenge of being successful in a rapidly changing environment. While the VUCA model emphasizes the complexity of decisions and consequences of actions, the BANI model assumes increasingly chaotic and thus unpredictable influencing factors, especially in connection with exponential technological progress (Cascio 2020).

Fig. 1.2 Schematic process of agile product development. (*Source*: Own illustration)

The agile approach in digital product management is not entirely new: For example, Tom Gilb (1988) developed a model called "Evolutionary Project Management" in the 1980s, which anticipated many basic principles of agile development. Similarly, Kent Beck (2000) developed the Extreme Programming (XP) methodology in the 1990s, which already included agile concepts such as Test-Driven Development (TDD) and Continuous Integration (CI).

In 2001, the **Manifesto for Agile Software Development** (www.agilemanifesto.org) was written, which serves as conceptual framework for modern digital product development. It established four fundamental values and derived twelve principles on how digital products should be developed.

▶ The four fundamental values of the Agile Manifesto are

1. Individuals and interactions over processes and tools.
2. Working software over comprehensive documentation.
3. Customer Collaboration over contract negotiation.
4. Responding to change over following a plan.
Beck et al. (2001)

The primary goal is to provide a working product that is truly accepted in the market. To achieve this, a close, trustful cooperation with the customers or the internal stakeholders of a company and obtaining market feedback are necessary. Therefor the basic prerequisite is a sincere willingness to be open to requirement changes in the development process at all times (Cagan 2018).

1 Introduction to Digital Product Management 5

Of course, this does not mean that agile development proceeds without a plan or structures. However, these are not an objective in themselves, but are only used if they contribute to improving product development.

▶ "The Agile movement is not anti-methodology [...]. We embrace modeling, but not in order to file some diagram in a dusty corporate repository. We embrace documentation, but not hundreds of pages of never-maintained and rarely-used tomes. We plan, but recognize the limits of planning in a turbulent environment." (Beck et al. 2001, p. S.)

While projects are usually implemented with temporary, project-specific teams, digital product management prefers to work with long-term responsible teams (Dedicated Teams) that are responsible for a specific product or product area (Neuberger 2018). To give these product teams real "ownership" for their product or the user problem to be solved, their members should be allowed to organize themselves, work in an inspiring environment, and ensure through personal conversations that there is maximum transparency within the team regarding the project goals, the current status quo, and the derived requirements. In addition, the team should regularly reflect on its processes and behavior in order to continuously improve its collaboration and ensure technical excellence (Epping 2011; Beck et al. 2001).

For the concrete implementation of agile product development, different frameworks or methods have been developed, which are all based on these fundamental agile principles.

1.2 Basics of Agile Product Management

Regardless of the individual framework or the specific method, the general goal is to release working software on the market as early and regularly as possible. Therefor, digital products are developed incrementally, i.e., in consecutive versions, to integrate market feedback into further product development. Thus, the forecast accuracy of a subsequent market success can be increased and the risks in product development can be controlled better (Cagan 2018).

The first product increment released to the market is often referred to as a **Minimum Viable Product (MVP)**[2] and should focus on the most necessary product features in order to incorporate real market feedback into further product development as early as possible (Krasadakis 2019; Gibbert 2014a).

---

[2]There are also different definitions of a Minimum Viable Product. For example, Eric Ries and Steve Blank (2011) refer to the first official product increment as a Minimal Marketable Product (MMP). According to Ries, however, there may already be other MVPs before this, which are not released, but are "only" tested as prototypes in user tests, etc.

Fig. 1.3 The PDCA cycle. (*Source*: Based on Deming 1982)

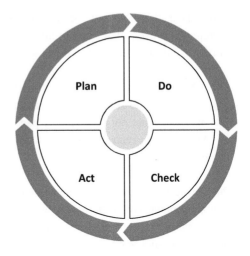

This approach corresponds to the validated learning from the **PDCA cycle,** which dates back to the work of Walter Sheward and William Deming from the 1930s. This is a concept for continuous improvement of products or processes in organizations. The cycle consists of four steps: planning (Plan), execution (Do), checking (Check), and deriving measures (Act), see Fig. 1.3.[3] In the planning phase, goals and measures are defined, which are implemented in the execution phase. In the checking phase, the results are analyzed and evaluated, after which necessary adjustments or improvements are made in the last step and the cycle starts anew (Deming 1982, on the PDCA cycle, see also in detail Chap. 17 by Jan Köster and Florian Meyer).

▶ "Your minimum viable product is comprised of the least amount of functionality necessary to solve a problem sufficiently such that your customer will engage with your product and even pay for it, if that's your revenue model." (Cooper and Vlaskovits 2013, p. 173)
"If you are not embarrassed by the first version of your product, you've launched too late." (Reid Hoffman 2017)

Generally there is a person in the product organization who focuses on the market success of the product. Their job title is usually Product Manager or Product Owner.[4]

The **product manager** determines the features of the product, specifies them, and ensures that the developers implement the product as best as possible. They are not only

---

[3] In their book "The Lean Startup", Eric Ries and Steve Blank (2011) condensed the four-phase PDCA cycle into a three-phase Build-Measure-Learn cycle, which is widely used in the startup scene today.

[4] Actually, the Product Owner role only exists in Scrum, but the title is also used in product organizations that no longer (or never did) work according to Scrum.

1 Introduction to Digital Product Management

responsible for new product development, but rather have the task of successfully managing the product throughout its entire lifecycle. Thus they have a holistic view from the perspectives of economics, technology, and above all market or user needs on their (digital) product, see Fig. 1.4. To be successful in this focal position, the product manager regularly exchanges information with the other stakeholders of the product to understand their wishes or requirements (Cagan 2018; Neuberger 2014).

To develop a product in a targeted manner, the product manager should establish a vision for the product. In the **product vision**, the core value of the future product is described by roughly outlining the central product features and formulating a motivating goal pursued with the development of the product (for the product vision, see in detail Chap. 2 by Inken Petersen).

In order for the product to receive the necessary resources and positive attention within the company, it is of enormous importance that the product vision is supported by the entire company. To achieve this, the product team should develop the product vision in close coordination with the other stakeholders. In addition to other formats, the **Product Vision Board** is a good vehicle that can be used to visualize the product vision and thus transport it into the company (Fig. 1.5).

On the Product Vision Board, the basic idea is formulated in a concise sentence as a vision statement. In addition, the target group that the product is intended to address is specified, and their wishes and needs that are to be addressed with the product are outlined. In the "Product" section, around three or five most important characteristics of the product to be developed are then written down, that satisfy the needs of the target group better than other possibly already existing solutions on the market. Finally, the revenue model for the company is listed (Pichler 2014).

True to the saying of the legendary ice hockey player Wayne Gretzky "I skate to where the puck is going to be, not where it has been", the product vision sets the

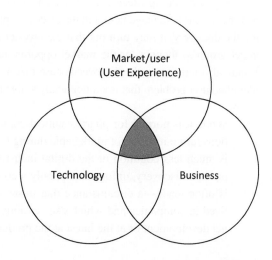

Fig. 1.4 The responsibility spectrum of a product manager. (*Source*: Based on Eriksson 2011)

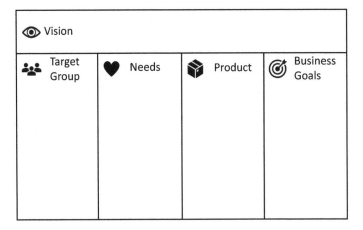

Fig. 1.5 Product Vision Board. (*Source*: Adapted from Pichler 2014)

direction and as part of the **product strategy**, it must be determined how the product organization should get there. The product strategy therefore sets the concrete goals and the path to them (for more on product strategy, see Chap. 3 by Christian Becker).

In an agile, user-centered product development, both the goals and the derived path to them initially only represent **hypotheses** ("bets"). It must therefore be checked whether there are really users in a sufficiently large number who want the planned product, so that an economic success can be expected for the company. In order to reduce uncertainties in product development as quickly as possible, the basic assumptions about the so-called **Product-Market-Fit** must be validated early on. These relate to the actual needs of the target group, the economic assumptions but also the technical feasibility of the development (Cagan 2016).

Especially for larger, fundamental new product developments, a separate **discovery phase** is initiated before the actual product development (for more on product discovery, see Chap. 6 by Philip Steen and Alexander Hipp). In practice, the challenge often lies in making it clear to management that the discovery phase is open-ended. This means that during the discovery, it may turn out that the product idea is not as brilliant in the eyes of the target group as thought, or the market opportunities are smaller than originally assumed. It may also turn out in the discovery phase that no technical solution can be found for the identified user problem that is economically viable for the company (Cagan 2007).

> While it is normal for pharmaceutical companies that a large part of drug innovations turn out to be not marketable during the discovery phase, this way of thinking is much less common in the digital industry. There, instead of a real, open-ended product discovery, unfortunately, only a concretization of the original product idea is often made—a circumstance that raises the question of how honestly agility is lived in companies and which can certainly backfire in the further course of product development or at the latest at the product launch (Gibbert 2013).

1 Introduction to Digital Product Management

In the discovery phase, the product team has numerous methods and tools at its disposal, which can be used and possibly adapted depending on the question. Ideally, a user experience expert helps with the selection and application of the right tools (see Chap. 18 by Inken Petersen for a detailed discussion of the role of UX teams in digital product development).

▶ **User Experience (UX)** refers to the user experience of a (digital) application by a user, i.e., his experiences before, during, and after the interaction. The **usability** (user-friendliness), especially the graphical operability of an application (**User Interface, UI**), is part of UX. UX also includes the relationships and processes between product, company, customer communication, etc. To ensure a good user experience, UX experts intensively analyze user needs beforehand, for which they have a whole range of methods available (see Jacobsen and Meyer 2019 and Ulrich et al. 2016 for a detailed discussion of User Experience and UX methods).

It is popular for product teams to orient themselves on the design thinking process. In **Design Thinking** (Kelley 2001), the initial focus is on understanding the problem space, i.e., determining whether the suspected yet unaddressed or inadequately addressed customer need truly exists. Besides desk research, it is important for the product team to engage with people from the target group. Ideally, there is the opportunity to observe people in their normal life reality to understand their routines and usage of existing solutions. In addition, qualitative user interviews help to understand the reasons and motives behind the observed actions. The overarching goal is to gain a deeper understanding and, if possible, even genuine empathy for the target group (Grots and Pratschke 2009).

To make the knowledge from the user analysis accessible to the entire product team and thus build an unified understanding, it is important to document the findings, often in the form of visualizations.

A popular visualization method is the creation of **Customer Journey Maps** (also called User Journey Maps). They serve to illustrate and thus understand in detail the individual phases that a user goes through in a task, problem-solving, etc., see Fig. 1.6. In product development, attempts are made to derive from this where (touchpoint) and in what form a new product could possibly offer added value to the users (see Kempe 2022 and Nielsen Norman Group 2016 in detail).[5]

The analyzed users are often condensed into so-called **personas** (also: personae). Personas are representative, realistically described prototypes of the target group. Personas are visualized as profiles including name and photo to illustrate the target group and help

---

[5]Another popular application of Customer Journeys is (online) marketing. Unlike in product development, the focus in marketing is on visualizing the touchpoints that a user has with an existing product of a company. From this, it is then derived in particular at which touchpoint the user needs which content to motivate him to make a purchase decision (see Kempe 2022).

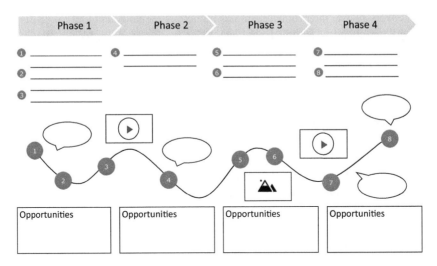

Fig. 1.6 Customer Journey Map. (*Source*: Based on Nielsen Norman Group 2016)

the team to make the target group for which it is developing the product "tangible" (Revella 2015and Cooper 1999).

After the problem space has been truly grasped by all team members, the design thinking process involves developing suitable product solutions. In the first step, many different ideas are developed to span the solution space as wide as possible. In addition to classic brainstorming, many other creativity techniques can be used for inspiration.

Subsequently, the most promising ideas are selected by the team and made "experiential" in the form of **prototypes** to validate them with the target group (see Chap. 7 by Anna Wicher for detailed validation instructions). Prototypes should be quick to implement and cheap to develop and can be worked out in different levels of detail: from simple drawings (scribbles), scenarios built with Lego bricks, to wireframes, mockups or interactive click-dummies (Grots and Pratschke 2009).

▶ **Wireframes** are layouts that are already much more detailed and provided with realistic proportions to each other compared to initial simple and often hand-drawn **scribbles**. However, colors, fonts, and effects are still missing. In **mockups**, these design elements are additionally considered, so they already resemble a finished product. **Click dummies** as the last level of detail are even interactive, although they usually focus on a few detail pages and do not yet simulate the full product scope (Jacobsen and Meyer 2019; Gläser 2014).

The created prototypes are evaluated by (target) users in **user-tests**. They should not only help to validate the conceived solution ideas, but also serve as idea generators to understand why something (does not) works. For this purpose, primarily qualitative survey

1 Introduction to Digital Product Management

methods, such as the thinking-aloud approach and eye or mouse tracking procedures, are used to obtain detailed assessments from the users.

In the **Thinking-Aloud approach**, test users are encouraged to verbalize their thoughts while using the prototype. This is intended to trace which aspects the user may not understand properly, and where he sees strengths or weaknesses in the presented solution. In **eyetracking**, the test subjects are shown the digital prototypes in the form of mockups or click dummies on a screen in a test lab, which they can ideally test, and it is recorded where a user looks or how he behaves on the presented test pages. A similar procedure is **mousetracking,** in which the movements of the cursor or touch gestures are recorded, making online-based testing possible (Jacobsen and Meyer 2019).

Depending on user feedback, the prototypes are further developed, varied or even discarded until a potentially marketable product has been found.

Important

Based on the Design Thinking approach, Google Ventures developed the **Design Sprint**. This is a five-day structured process that focuses on a clearly defined challenge or a specific question. During the Design Sprint, a multidisciplinary team works intensively together for a week to quickly develop, test, and refine ideas. The method is particularly useful for manageable questions where quick decisions and quick results are required (Jake Knapp et al. 2016).

A **Continuous Discovery** goes even further, in which, instead of isolated discovery phases, smaller reviews of product assumptions (hypotheses) are carried out with users regularly, often weekly (Torres 2021).

If a specific product approach has proven promising in the discovery phase, the product manager must bring the product to be developed onto the product roadmap. The **Product roadmap** defines the milestones and goals that a product team typically wants to achieve in the next 12 to 18 months. It describes the essential product features or versions to be created. The use of a product roadmap is very helpful in communication with stakeholders; especially to align company goals and product goals with top management and at the same time to coordinate the investment decisions and associated resource allocations necessary for product development (see Product Roadmaps in detail in Chap. 5 by Dominik Busching and Lutz Göcke as well as Pichler 2014).

> ▶ More and more companies are relying on **Objectives and Key Results (OKR),** to use their company activities in a targeted manner. The framework consists of a system of goals (Objectives) and associated performance indicators (Key Results). By using the OKR approach in conjunction with a product roadmap, companies can ensure that the entire company is working on the focal issues. The product roadmap helps to better plan the individual steps of the development process and OKRs ensures that the developed functions and features correspond to the strategic goals of the company. See the use of the OKR framework in product organizations in detail in Chap. 4 by Cansel Sörgens.

To really "get all stakeholders on board", the product manager should develop and coordinate the product roadmap in dialogue. Only in this way he receives individual commitment[6] and a real organizational alignment necessary for a successful development. **Alignment** means that a team or an organization has a shared understanding of the relevance of a topic and a uniform picture of the planned development result ("Bring everybody on the same page", New Work SE n.d.). Only if this is actually given the product team can develop its product independently. To establish this "autonomy through alignment", for example, the canvas **Auftragsklärung** (www.auftragsklaerung.com) has been developed at XING (New Work SE) and spread in the product community (see this in detail in Chap. 15 by Arne Kittler).

▶ "[A]utonomy is not something you claim—it's something you can only earn through successful alignment with stakeholders, peers and within your team. We believe that good alignment should be a collaborative effort during which

- the tricky questions about an upcoming initiative are discussed early
- the underlying thinking of an initiative is sharpened for clarity of intent
- the results are made transparent to get everyone 'on the same page'".
- (New Work SE n.d.)

1.3   Digital Product Development According to Scrum

The actual development of digital products takes place in the **product delivery** (see in detail Chap. 8 by Tim Adler). For this purpose, various agile frameworks have been developed. The most popular is Scrum, which was used by almost 90% of companies in 2022 (Digital.ai 2022).

Scrum, which originates from rugby, was first used in 1986 by Takeuchi and Nonaka (1986) as a metaphor for a closely cooperating team of software developers. By analyzing successful companies in the USA and Japan at that time, they found six basic principles that underlie successful product development. These include, in particular, outcome rather than output objectives, working in self-organized teams with an agile approach to product development, including early and regular market checks.

As an independent agile framework, Scrum was then developed by Jeff Sutherland and Ken Schwaber, both of whom are also among the original signatories of the Agile Manifesto, in the early 1990s and first presented at the OOPSLA conference in Austin

---

[6] In order to actually realize a product, each individual must be committed to make his respective contribution to achieving the goal (Drath et al. 2008; Conner 2012).

1 Introduction to Digital Product Management

(Texas) in 1995. Originally, Scrum was designed for the development of complex digital products. However, the application of Scrum is no longer limited to digital product development, but is increasingly used in many other areas of companies (Schwaber and Sutherland 2020).

▶ "**Scrum** is a lightweight framework that helps people, teams, and organizations generate value through adaptive solutions for complex problems. [...] Various processes, techniques and methods can be employed within the framework." (Schwaber and Sutherland 2020, p. 3)

The three pillars of Scrum are transparency, inspection, and adaptation. Transparency applies to the Scrum team and the stakeholders and refers to both the planned approach and the decisions taken. The progress of the (incremental) development towards a valuable product should be regularly reviewed and immediately adapted when new insights are gained (Schwaber and Sutherland 2020).

In order to be successful, a Scrum team needs autonomy and the trust of the organization to work self-organized and outcome responsible. At the same time, the Scrum team must also commit to the values of commitment, focus, openness, respect, and courage. The Scrum team must therefore commit to its goals and want to develop a valuable product through a focused pursuit of the goals. In a respectful interaction, the Scrum team should have the openness and courage to work on difficult problems and make eventually bold decisions independently (Schwaber and Sutherland 2020).

Within a Scrum team, which should consist of a maximum of ten members, there are three defined responsibilities: the Product Owner, the Scrum Master, and ideally interdisciplinary mixed developers (Schwaber and Sutherland 2020).[7]

In Scrum, the product manager characterized in Sect. 1.2 is referred to as the **Product Owner**. He is responsible for maximizing the value of the product by ensuring that the developers are working on the right tasks and that the product provides added value for the customers or stakeholders (Schwaber and Sutherland 2020; Neuberger 2014).

For his demanding task, the Product Owner is assisted by a Scrum Master, who as a "servant leader" supports the entire Scrum team in optimizing its collaboration, and helps outside the team to understand how the Scrum team works to protect it from disruptive influences. Specifically, the Scrum Master organizes and moderates most of the Scrum meetings, coaches the team to improve its interaction, and ensures that obstacles that hinder the Scrum team are removed as much as possible (Petersen 2017; Jungwirth 2016); see also Chap. 17 by Jan Köster and Florian Meyer.

---

[7] Until the 2017 version, the Scrum Guide spoke of roles instead of responsibilities, which included a developer TEAM in addition to the Product Owner and the Scrum Master (Schwaber and Sutherland 2017). To address occasional conflicts between Product Owner and developers in practice and to clarify that everyone within the Scrum team is equally responsible for the success of their product, there is no longer talk of a sub-team, but only of responsibilities.

To ensure a smooth product delivery, one of the main tasks of the Product Owner is to maintain the **Product Backlog** in addition to developing and communicating the product goal (Schwaber and Sutherland 2020). This contains all tasks that the developers need to work on to further develop the product.

The Product Backlog thus basically corresponds to the requirements document from traditional product development, but shows significant differences in handling: Unlike the requirements document, the Product Backlog is a "living" object that the Product Owner continuously adapts during the entire delivery phase when new insights are gained. New requirements are added as additional entries to the Product Backlog and existing entries are adjusted in content, reprioritized or even deleted, among other things, based on user feedback, feedback from the developers, etc. (Pichler 2014).

How individual entries in the Product Backlog should look is not specified in the Scrum Framework. However, in practice, the User-Story format is often used. A **User Story** consists of three parts: a concise designation, a brief description of the requirement, and one or more acceptance criteria. The description is not technical, but formulated from the user's perspective and is intended to make clear to the developers what outcome is to be achieved with the development of the User Story. Acceptance criteria explain relevant details for implementation and represent requirements that must be met in product development in order for the User Story to have been successfully implemented (Cohn 2004).

▶ The schematic basic structure of a User Story for new product features is: *"As a [user], I want to [action], in order to [goal]"*, for example: *"As a user, I want to be able to reload the feed to see which new content has been published in the meantime."*

▶ If, for example, product errors ("bugs") need to be fixed, it is usually not useful to formulate the backlog entries as a User Story: *"As a user, I want the app not to crash on iOS so that I can use it normally."*

A good User Story should meet the INVEST criteria. **INVEST** is an acronym and stands for: Independent (the User Story is as independent as possible from other User Stories), Negotiable (adjustments can still be made to it until it is fully developed), Valuable (the User Story has value for the user), Estimable (the development effort can be estimated), Small (the User Story can be implemented within a sprint) and Testable (the fulfillment of the acceptance criteria can be objectively verified) (Epping 2011; Wake 2003).

Example of a User Story

- **Designation:** CSV Export
- **Description:** "As a banking app user, I want to be able to download the transaction data as a CSV file in order to create evaluations in Excel, for example."

- **Acceptance Criteria:**
  - The user can download the data for each account.
  - All values are included in the CSV file.
  - The user can output the data for different reporting periods.
  - (Herwarth von Bittenfeld 2010) ◄

The order of the entries in the Product Backlog corresponds to their priority. The most important entries are at the top, are described in detail, and are implemented first by the developers. Less important entries, on the other hand, are often not yet detailed, but stand as "placeholders" at the end of the Product Backlog.

The **prioritization of User Stories** regularly poses a major challenge. Central criteria are the business value, any existing content dependencies, the deliverability, the degree of uncertainty, and of course the estimated effort in implementing a User Story.

In principle, User Stories that are highly prioritized and thus implemented promptly should have a high **business value** or **impact** (great benefit for the users, high economic success for the company). The greater the **uncertainty** with a User Story, the riskier the successful development of the product. Risky entries in the Product Backlog should therefore be prioritized high and tackled early to quickly remove the uncertainty from the development (Fail-fast principle). This goes hand in hand with the fact that software should be delivered as early and regularly as possible in order to receive market feedback and in this way also take the risk out of product development. Finally, **content dependencies** between User Stories are important in prioritization. Themes, as larger topic areas, are split into several User Stories, with User Stories that others build on, of course, having to be prioritized in implementation (Gibbert 2014a; Pichler 2014).

Numerous models are available for the concrete prioritization of product backlog entries, providing a structured and transparent decision-making process. This includes, for example, the **Kano model** (Kano et al. 1984), shown in Fig. 1.7, which is based on

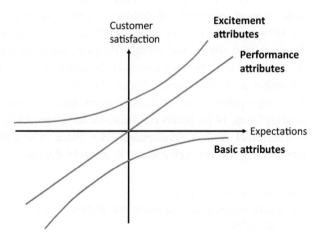

Fig. 1.7 The Kano model. (*Source*: Adapted from Nielsen Norman Group 2016)

the Two-Tactor theory of Frederick Herzberg (Herzberg et al. 1959). In its basic form, the model divides product backlog entries into basic, performance, and excitement attributes, thus focusing on their market relevance. Basic attribute do not significantly improve a product, but their absence would lead to dissatisfaction (for example, seat belts in a car). Performance attributes increase user satisfaction more or less linearly (e.g., the fuel consumption of a car), and excitement attributes are those that are supposed to trigger a "wow effect" from a user perspective or represent a real differentiation from the competitors (e.g., the self-driving function in a car) (Wille 2016).

The **MuSCoW model** goes in a similar direction, according to which backlog entries are classified as "absolutely mandatory" (Must have), "preferred" (Should have), "optional" (Could have), and "should not" (Won't have) (Wille 2016).

In an **Impact-Effort Matrix**, the expected market value of a product requirement is compared to the effort associated with its development. For backlog entries that promise a high impact and are associated with little effort, prioritization is comparatively easy (as is the case with so-called "Money Pits", which promise only a small added value for a lot of effort). Prioritizing requirements that promise a great added value but are also associated with a high (time) effort ("Big Bets") is more difficult. In the latter case, the **Rocks, Pebble & Sand model** helps, according to which Scrum teams block a fundamental part of their working time for topics that make a real difference ("Big Rocks") (e.g., 70%), allocate another part to topics that offer a certain added value and advance the product, but also consciously plan a small time share for topics that should or must be done "just like that", such as updating an SSL certificate or bug fixes (Wille 2016).

However, prioritizing product backlog entries is not just about the order in which product ideas should be implemented, but also about consciously deciding **whether they should be implemented at all**: Does the benefit—preferably expected from reliable market indications from the product discovery—justify the efforts associated with development (Gibbert 2014b; Wille 2016)?

The decision is usually not made by the Product Owner alone, but in cooperation with his most important stakeholders. For his "standing", it is important that the Product Owner is perceived as an active person. This means that he proactively presents, discusses, and aligns "his" product backlog, rather than passively waiting for others to dictate the product backlog entries or the order of entries to him. The resulting (lateral) leadership gives the Product Owner the necessary standing in the company to avoid becoming a pawn of micropolitical interests (see the topic of leadership and alignment in detail in Chap. 14 by Tobias Freudenreich and Chap. 15 by Arne Kittler).

The actual product development takes place in so-called Sprints. **Sprints** are fixed intervals that last between one and four weeks depending on the company.[8] They are the

---

[8] Originally, sprints were designed to last 30 days. Nowadays, most companies develop in one or two-week sprints.

1 Introduction to Digital Product Management

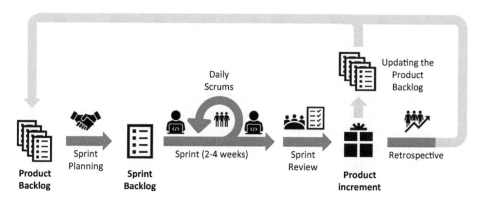

Fig. 1.8 Scrum process overview. (*Source*: Own illustration)

heart of agile product development according to Scrum. The goal is to develop a new/improved stepping stone towards the product goal within a sprint. This is called a **product increment** includes all entries from the Product Backlog that have been fully completed during a Sprint.

Sprints follow a fixed sequence with several ceremonies (meetings) and artifacts (documents), as shown in Fig. 1.8.

Before each sprint, a **Sprint Planning Meeting** takes place, where it is determined which entries from the Product Backlog will be implemented in the upcoming Sprint. In the Sprint Planning Meeting, the Product Owner shows the developers how the value/benefit of the product should be increased in the upcoming Sprint, and then explains the individual User Stories from the Product Backlog that he has prioritized highest for achieving the Sprint goal (Schwaber and Sutherland 2020). The prerequisite is that the User Stories are really considered "actionable" by everyone **(Definition of Ready)**.

A story is "ready" when all the information necessary for development is available, and the story is well enough explicated that it can be implemented within a Sprint.[9] If a User Story is associated with too many uncertainties for the developers the Product Owner creates a separate entry in the Product Backlog for the exploration of the development and prioritizes it accordingly.

▶ If it is unclear how a product requirement should be implemented, a so-called **Spike** is often set. As part of the Spike, alternative (technical) solutions are developed and tested via prototypes. The goal of the Spike is not to develop a fully elaborated, final product solution, but merely to obtain a "proof of concept", i.e. a proof of concept.

---

[9] Exceptionally, a User Story can also be pulled into the upcoming Sprint even though it is not yet factually actionable, e.g. because access data is missing, but has been assured. In such a case, a Product Owner can ask the developers to include the User Story in the Sprint anyway and flag it with a note.

Following the presentation of the User Stories, the developers discuss among themselves how the individual stories should be implemented and which development-related **tasks** are required for implementation. The Product Owner and developers also "agree" on the acceptance criteria by which it will be decided at the end of the sprint whether the implementation of a User Story was successful. Non-functional requirements for the product to be developed, such as performance specifications, are formulated as **constraints**.

In addition to the specific acceptance criteria for each User Story, a Scrum team should also agree on a basic **Definition of Done** (DoD) for Sprint Backlog entries. This is to ensure a common understanding of when a developed feature is ready for release. A DoD includes, for example:

- The code has been deployed and tested by another team member.
- New features have been approved by a designer.
- The code has been documented.

In the last part of the Sprint Planning Meeting, the developers estimate the effort (**sizing**) of each User Story. The effort is usually estimated in **Story Points**, which represent relative estimates in the form of a non-linear sequence of numbers: usually 0, 1, 2, 3, 5, 8, 13, 20, 40.[10] If developers conduct an effort estimation for the first time, the group agrees on a medium-sized reference story at the beginning and gives it, for example, the Story Point value 3. All other stories are subsequently evaluated in relation to the reference story.

A common method for determining Story Points is **Planning Poker.** Each developer receives a stack of cards with the different Story Point values noted on them (for a remote Sprint Planning, the Planning Poker can also be done digitally using apps like Miro.). If the implementation effort for a User Story is to be determined, each developer first estimates the effort for himself and draws a corresponding poker card. Once everyone has made their individual estimate, the Scrum Master asks the developers to reveal the cards. If the estimates differ, the developers with the most different values are asked to explain their estimate. A new round of Planning Poker is then played until a consensus has been found among the developers (Pichler 2014). The aim is not to force an agreement, but to engage in a substantive exchange about the implementation of a User Story through the differing estimates, which leads to more clarity and security for everyone.

---

[10]The basis of the Story Point estimate is the so-called Fibonacci sequence, in which each number is obtained by adding its two previous numbers. It was slightly modified by Cohn (2005) and introduced for effort estimation in digital product development. In an alternative, less precise effort estimation, T-shirt sizes (scale XS, S, M, L, XL, XXL) are determined for the individual User Stories (Wiegand 2015).

1 Introduction to Digital Product Management

Once the developers have estimated all high-priority entries of the Product Backlog, they set the overarching **Sprint Goal** together with the Product Owner and commit themselves to how many entries they will develop in the upcoming Sprint. From the number of promised User Stories weighted with the respective Story Points, the predicted **velocity** of the Scrum team for the next sprint can be determined(Schwaber and Sutherland 2020; Domin 2019).

▶ The Product Owner determines the order in which the entries are implemented by prioritizing the Product Backlog. On the basis of their effort estimates the developers commit themselves on how many entries they will realize within the next Sprint.

The entries committed by the developers for the next sprint are broken down into their derived tasks and transferred as **tickets** into the Sprint Backlog, and the actual Sprint can begin. The **Sprint Backlog** in its simplest form consists of three columns, see Fig. 1.9. However, additional columns are sometimes added for separate development steps, such as testing or deployment.

At the beginning of the Sprint, all tickets to be processed are in the first column "To Do". When the developers start working on a task, they move the corresponding ticket to the second column "Doing" (also referred to as "(Work) In Progress"). Once a task is fully processed, the ticket is moved to the last column "Done". The goal is that by the end of the Sprint, all tasks from the Sprint Backlog are completed and thus the tickets are moved to the "Done" column.

Various apps, such as Jira, Trello or Github Projects, are available for creating and maintaining the Sprint Backlog. However, it is—or was until the Corona pandemic—quite common to also have a physical **Sprint Backlog Board** hanging in the team space

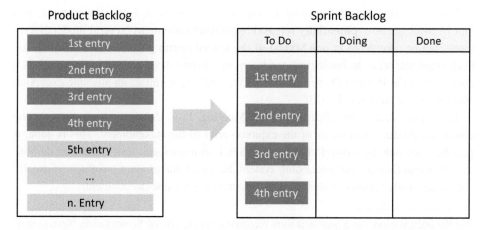

Fig. 1.9 Relationship between Product Backlog and Sprint Backlog. (*Source*: Own illustration)

of the Scrum team, with the individual tasks written on Post-its hanging in the respective columns. The Sprint Backlog Board thus provides on a high level transparency about the Sprint progress and promotes internal team communication. In addition, a burn-down(-up)-chart is often maintained, which visualizes the Story Points already implemented in the course of the Sprint.

As a self-organized team, the developers meet daily at the same time for the **Daily Scrum** in front of the Sprint Backlog Board to give each other an update on the completed and upcoming tasks as well as any impediments that may have arised. The Daily Scrum is usually moderated by the Scrum Master as a stand-up meeting, following a fixed structure and should last a maximum of 15 minutes. The Daily Scrum is solely about everyone in the Scrum team having a shared level of information about the Sprint progress. Detailed discussions are not intended in the Daily Scrum.

▶   The developers give their update in the Daily Scrum in a standardized way by usually answering the following three questions:

1. What did I do yesterday to help the team achieve the Sprint goal?
2. What will I do today to help the team achieve the Sprint goal?
3. Do I see an obstacle that prevents me or the team from achieving the Sprint goal?
4. (Schwaber and Sutherland 2017)[11].

During the Sprint, no changes are made that would endanger the respective Sprint goal. The developers should be able to fully focus on implementing the Product Backlog entries agreed upon in the Sprint Planning Meeting. The Scrum Master takes care of possible impediments, i.e. problems or disturbances that keep the developers from their work, and thus relieves the developers.

At the end of a Sprint, all tasks of the entries made should have been implemented and successfully checked for possible programming errors in a test environment, and thus be available as a **potentially releasable product increment** (several product increments can be completed in one Sprint). If the agreed Sprint goal becomes obsolete due to changed market or technological conditions or a higher-level change in the company's goal, (only!) the Product Owner can cancel the ongoing sprint as an absolute exception (Schwaber and Sutherland 2020).

Each sprint ends with a **Sprint Review Meeting.** In it, the Scrum team presents the completed product increments of the expired sprint to the stakeholders. This is done, if possible, not only by PowerPoint slides or click dummies etc., but should be demonstrated in real time on the functioning system. However, the product increment is usually not yet generally released at this point, but is running on a test environment.

---

[11] In the 2020 version, the 3 questions were removed from the official Scrum Guide. Nevertheless, they still serve as a structuring of the Daily Scrum in many companies.

The Sprint Review is designed as a working meeting in which it is jointly determined whether the Scrum team is on the right development path, or to identify any necessary adjustments for the product early on. With the Sprint Review, Scrum thus anchors a format that takes place regularly at short intervals, in which all stakeholders have the opportunity to inform themselves about the current product development status and give feedback to the Scrum team.

▶ The regular presentation and joint discussion of the product increments serves, among other things, to involve the relevant stakeholders and thus build trust in the work of the Scrum team. This usually leads to a greater freedom for the Scrum team in implementing its tasks and receiving more outcome than output goals. The close involvement of the stakeholders thus represents a superior alternative to a detailed product requirements document originating from traditional project management, especially since these only suggest a false sense of security in complex environments.

The formal task of the Product Owner at the end of a Sprint is to check whether the User Stories have been implemented by the developers according to the agreed Definition-of-Done criteria and whether the committed Sprint goal has been achieved. If this is not the case, the User Stories are to be rejected and return as incomplete entries to the Product Backlog. If the Product Increment has been accepted by the Product Owner and there are no other objections, it is made available for publication following the Sprint Review Meeting.

At the end of a Sprint a comparison between the planned Sprint Velocity and the actual one achieved is also conducted. The aim is not to become faster and faster in development, but rather to achieve long-term consistency and predictability. The current Sprint ends with the Sprint Review Meeting and the next one starts immediately (Pichler 2014).

At the end of the Sprint, a team-internal **Retrospective** is also conducted. Here, the Scrum Team reflects on the last Sprint and assesses which procedural or interpersonal aspects of the collaboration were good and which should be improved. The Scrum Master invites to the retrospective and is an equal member in the meeting, as he had a significant part in the organizational process of the Sprint.

▶ In the Scrum framework, the role (responsibility) of the Scrum Master is firmly established in a Scrum Team. In product organizations that do not work according to Scrum, this person is often also referred to as an **Agile Coach**. The activities of an Agile Coach and a Scrum Master are quite comparable. However, unlike Scrum Masters, Agile Coaches are typically not part of the actual product team, but coach it "from the outside" (even if they are employed in the same company). Since Scrum Masters often also work in several Scrum Teams, this difference blurs in practice, which is why many see both roles as synonymous.

At the end of the Retrospective, concrete improvements for a more effective and satisfying way of collaboration should be agreed upon, the implementation of which will be checked in the next Sprint in the following Retrospective in the form of a self-review (Schwaber and Sutherland 2020).

1.4 Digital Product Development with Kanban

In addition to Scrum, there are numerous other frameworks in practice for developing digital products in an agile way. In the German-speaking world, **Kanban** is particularly popular, its application in digital product development goes back to Anderson (2010) (Petereit 2017; Leopold and Kaltenecker 2013).

Kanban was originally developed by Taiichi Ohno, an employee at Toyota in the 50s and 60s of the last millennium, with the aim of creating a steady "flow" in car production and reducing the existing stock of individual parts. Against the background of the Kaizen philosophy[12], which loosely translated means "change for the better", Kanban and some other methods created the Toyota Production System, from which Lean Manufacturing emerged in the 1980s (Dickmann 2007).

With Kanban, Toyota solved the problem that in the production of a car, too many production parts were lying around at some stages, while none were available at others, thus taking too much time to produce a variant of equipment or even completely stopping the work. The solution was to provide each (intermediate) storage with a signal card (Japanese: Kanban), with which an employee goes to the main storage when the intermediate storage has dropped to a previously determined number of parts.[13] The replenishment is thus "requested" from the respective demand site, which is characteristic for Kanban as the **Pull Principle** (Dickmann 2007).

In digital product development, **Kanban and Scrum have some similarities**. A major difference, however, is that there are no Sprints in Kanban. The development is rather a continuous "flow". In addition, Kanban conceptually focuses on the organization within the IT development team, which is why a Product Owner is not initially provided for. However, in the practical application of Kanban today, a Product Owner, also referred to as a **Service Request Manager** in Kanban, is usually in charge. The development team is often also supported by a **Service Delivery Manager.** This corresponds to the Scrum Master, as he is supposed to promote the team's collaboration, organize meetings, and document and visualize the development process. Unlike in Scrum, however, according to Anderson, these two roles do not necessarily have to be newly introduced, but the tasks can also be performed by existing persons (Anderson 2016a).

---

[12] The Kaizen principle is also described in German as "Continuous Improvement Process", see Fleig (2019) for a detailed discussion.

[13] Even today, Kanban, albeit now with RFID codes and barcode scanners, is used in many production processes, see Dickmann (2007) for a detailed discussion.

In Kanban, the focus is also on self-organized, continuously improving cooperation. Thus, organizational **rules** are agreed on within the team. This includes, in particular, a rule of how many tasks can be processed simultaneously **(Work in Progress, WiP).** Maximum quantities are defined that must not be exceeded in order to be able to focus sufficiently on the individual tasks ("Stop starting and start finishing!" Roock 2012). If the maximum number of tasks that the development team is currently working on is reached, a new task can only be started when another one has been completed. The developers therefore pick up their respective new tasks as soon as they have free capacities. This is the implementation of the pull principle from the production process of physical goods (Epping 2011).

The tasks are organized on a **Kanban Board.** This can either be a physical board where the tasks are written and moved with Post-its, or software programs such as Trello, Jira or Kanban-specific programs like Leankit or Kanbanize are used in companies. In the electronic case, the board is often made visible to everyone in meetings using a projector. In any case, it is important that the tasks and processes are **visualized** and thus become transparent for all stakeholders (Millweber 2018).

Analogous to Scrum, the Kanban Board is divided into three columns in the simplest case: "To Do", "(Work) In Progress" and "Delivered" or "Done". However, additional columns are often used by further dividing the WiP column into "Design", "Development" and "Testing". The tasks in the "To Do" column are usually prioritized so that the software developers cannot completely freely decide which task they should tackle next from the "To Do" column.

The **prioritization** of individual tasks is done, among other things, through the description of the service type and their respective service class. The **Service Type** specifies what kind of task it is. This is usually differentiated into "(New) Feature" (new product feature), "Bug" (error), and "Change" (adjustment). Feature tasks are usually formulated as User Stories, as with Scrum.

The individual Service Types can be visualized on the Kanban Board in separate rows (so-called Swimlanes). If necessary, a WiP limit can be agreed upon for each individual Swimlane (Leopold and Kaltenecker 2013).

Service Classes describe how promptly something must be processed or what costs would result from a delayed delivery (Cost of Delay). Usually, the distinction is made between "Standard", "Urgent Processing", "Fixed Delivery Date" and "Indeterminate Costs".

The majority of tasks should be classified as "Standard". Here, the processing rule is usually the FiFo principle (First in, First out). Tasks marked as "urgent to process" should be tackled immediately because they would otherwise lead to high costs. However, this should be an absolute exception, in which the WiP limit may even be exceeded, as work that has already begun may have to be put on hold. Tasks that need to be completed by a fixed date do not justify exceeding the WiP limit. To ensure this, the effort of this task class is estimated.[14] Once the effort is clarified, the processing can start early enough to ensure the required delivery date. Tasks with indeterminated costs are represented as "placeholders" in the backlog. These are tasks that need to be done "sometime", e.g., performing a software upgrade. They are only processed if no task with a higher service class has to be pulled or if they become "acute" and thereby receive one of the other service classifications.

In addition to the Service Types and Service Classes, content dependencies of the individual tasks also play a role in prioritization. Tasks on which other tasks depend on must of course be developed with priority (Leopold and Kaltenecker 2013).

To provide more transparency to its stakeholders, the development team in Kanban often communicates basic **Service Level Agreements,** i.e., expected throughput times of a task ticket, which are based on previous experience. Service Level Agreements can be specified for the individual Service Types and Service Classes and their respective effort sizes, e.g.:

- Tickets of the service class "Standard" with the T-shirt size M are completed 80% of the time within 2 weeks.
- Tickets of the service type "Bug" with the size S are completed 90% of the time within 5 working days.
- (Leopold and Kaltenecker 2013).

If a problem arises during the processing of a task that cannot be immediately solved, the ticket receives a "blocker" note on the Kanban Board and is put on hold. Thus, the task does not count towards the current number of tasks in progress. If a solution to the problem is found subsequently, the ticket moves back to the "To Do" column and can be pulled by a developer again (Millweber 2018).

Due to the pull principle, the **Definition of Done** is of focal importance in Kanban. It must be fundamentally defined when a design is finished, when the programming code is final, and when a test is completed.

The Definition of Done should be defined for each individual column, including possible sub-columns, on the Kanban board, so it is clear when a task can be moved from one column to the next. For this purpose, it may be useful to divide each column into "In Progress" and "Done" to avoid misunderstandings about whether a task is already finished and ready to be moved to the next column. New tasks can be "pulled" by a developer when they are in the Done column, see Fig. 1.10.

---

[14] Analoge to Scrum, the effort estimation is usually done in the form of story points or T-shirt sizes, see Sect. 1.3.

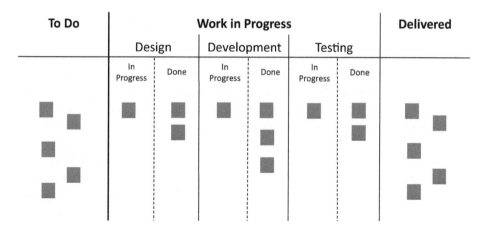

Fig. 1.10 Kanban board with a "In Progress" and "Done" breakdown. (*Source*: Own illustration)

To have a smooth workflow in Kanban, a close coordination is required, e.g., in the daily stand-up meeting, which is alsopart of Kanban, or ad hoc as needed. In addition, the Replenishment Meeting, the Release Meeting, and team Retrospectives have proven to be regular meeting formats (Leopold and Kaltenecker 2013).

The **Replenishment Meeting** regularly takes place, often every one to two weeks. Here, the product team and the stakeholders discuss which tasks are next in line for development. It is important that everyone understands the context on which prioritization is made (transparency). If a team develops products for several stakeholders, the coordination process in the Replenishment Meeting can be quite complex. Therefore, it should be time-limited and above all well moderated (Singh 2017).

In the **Release Meeting**, as in the Review Meeting in Scrum, the completed tasks are presented to the stakeholders. Unlike Scrum, however, there is no fixed interval for this. Nevertheless, a certain regularity builds trust with the stakeholders.

The **Team Retrospective**, like in Scrum, serves the purpose of the product team regularly reviewing its previous collaboration and looking for approaches for improvement.

The regular, step-by-step improvement from the Kaizen principle is a characteristic of Kanban. Unlike Scrum, when introducing Kanban, the entire existing system of previous digital product development does not have to be turned upside down, but changes can be implemented evolutionarily. Kanban is specifically designed to build on any existing method of digital product development. This often leads to less resistance within product teams or from stakeholders towards Kanban. Thus, in Kanban, it is not necessary to change or abolish existing job profiles, but the team can decide along the way which changes and possibly new roles are helpful for them (Anderson 2010, 2016a; Leopold and Kaltenecker 2013).

1.5 Other Agile Methods in Digital Product Management

Scrum, as the dominant agile development framework in digital product management, has a relatively fixed and comprehensive set of responsibilities and organizational rules. Companies that decide to introduce Scrum often face the challenge of fundamentally restructuring their previous product development. Many organizations fail at this. Even more often, however, one hears the sentence in practice: "We work with Scrum, but…".

A study conducted by the Scrum Alliance in 2017 among more than 2000 members revealed that in 78% of companies, Scrum was used in combination with other methods. And even central meetings, such as the Sprint Planning Meeting or the Daily Scrum, were consistently conducted in only 86% or 87% of companies that use Scrum (Scrum Alliance 2018). The different softenings and deviations of Scrum were once collectively referred to by Ken Schwaber as **"Scrum-But"**, where he and his co-founder Jeff Sutherland also speak of **"Scrum-And"** to optimally adapt the basic framework of Scrum to the respective organizational conditions (Schwaber 2012).

Companies for which a strict application of Scrum no longer seems suitable often orient themselves towards Kanban (Anderson 2016b; Ammons 2015). For digital product development, this means that different forms and mixtures of Scrum and Kanban implementations are lived in companies. The phrase **Scrumban** (Scrum-ban, Ladas 2008), originally conceived as a description for these mixed forms, has now developed into an independent framework for agile digital product development. Scrumban is also used, especially when implementing an agile way of working based on Scrum outside of product development (Reddy 2015).

> ▶ "Scrumban is not about using just a few elements of both Scrum and Kanban to create a software development process. Rather, it emphasizes applying Kanban systems within a Scrum context, and layering the Kanban framework alongside Scrum as a vehicle for evolutionary change." (Reddy 2015)

Scrumban adopted from Scrum that the team largely organizes itself and development occurs in short iterations. However, there is no fixed requirement for how large the team must be or what roles must exist within the team. The visualization of tasks is also central to Scrumban and is carried out similarly to Scrum and Kanban via a board divided into columns. The maximum number of tasks that can be in active processing at the same time is limited as in Kanban (WiP-Limit). The implementation planning of new tasks in Scrumban is done on demand, as soon as the number of tasks in the "To Do" column falls below a certain limit **(On demand planning).** Priorities are assigned for the individual tasks. The developers use these as a rule when they "pull" the next task for processing from the "To Do" column (Pull principle from Kanban). Shortly before the end of each iteration, there is a **Feature Freeze** in Scrumban. This means that from that point on, no further tasks are started, but only the existing ones are completed. If it is foreseeable that not all started tasks can be completed by the end of the iteration, the Product Owner/Project Manager can decide to focus only on the higher prioritized tasks and stop the development of the others **(Triage).** With the exception of a Daily Standup, meetings in Scrumban only take place on request. Thus, review and retrospective meetings are not necessarily provided in Scrumban (Reddy 2015; Ladas 2009).

Scrum, but also Kanban and other agile methods, reach their limits when they are to be used in large companies or projects with a multitude of organizational units that need to be coordinated. In order not to have to revert to traditional project management methods, the agile methods are further developed by different people and organizations to make them "scalable". For Scrum, for example, the **Nexus** framework was developed by Ken Schwaber (2015) and **Large-Scale Scrum (LeSS)** by Craig Larman and Bas Vodde (2017). The main focus here is on how the collaboration of several Scrum teams can be coordinated in order to deliver a coordinated product increment in each sprint. A fundamental meeting format to implement this coordination is a cross-team Daily Scrum, also known as **Scrum of Scrums** (Sutherland 2001).

In addition to the further developments and hybrid forms of Scrum and Kanban outlined here, there are countless other agile frameworks or methods, such as Extreme Programming (XP), Rational Unified Process (RUP), Agile Unified Process (AUP), Behavior-driven Development (BDD), Design-driven Development (DDD), Feature-driven Development (FDD) etc., which are used in digital product development. They often differ only marginally from each other and are often also proprietary developments of (consulting) companies, primarily driven by a sales motive. Providing a conclusive overview here seems hopeless and always only a snapshot. Companies that need to choose a (new) agile framework will find valuable advice on choosing the "right" agile framework in Chap. 21 by Stefan Roock.

Regardless of the specific agile framework used, an agile mindset is essential for a successful digital product management. This means that while product managers must have a good understanding of their product and target group, they should also maintain the attitude of always viewing product ideas as hypotheses ("bets") whose benefits only become apparent through appropriate market feedback.

References

Ammons, G. 2015. Ditching Scrum for Kanban—The best decision we've made as a team. https://medium.com/cto-school/ditching-scrum-for-kanban-the-best-decision-we-ve-made-as-a-team-cd1167014a6f#.s5v843snj.

Anderson, D. J. 2010. *Kanban. Successful evolutionary change for your technology business.* Washington: Blue Hole Press.

Anderson, D. J. 2016a. Emerging roles in Kanban. https://djaa.com/emerging-roles-in-kanban.

Anderson, D. J. 2016b. Are scrum & scaled agile damaging morale at your firm? https://djaa.com/are-scrum-scaled-agile-damaging-morale-at-your-firm.

Beck, K. 2000. *Extreme programming explained. Embrace change.* Boston: Addison.

Beck, K., M. Beedle, A. van Bennekum, A. Cockburn, W. Cunningham, M. Fowler, J. Grenning, J. Highsmith, A. Hunt, R. Jeffries, J. Kern, B. Marick, R. C. Martin, S. Mellor, K. Schwaber, J. Sutherland, and D. Thomas. 2001. Manifesto for agile software development. www.agilemanifesto.org.

Cagan, M. 2007. Product discovery. https://svpg.com/product-discovery.

Cagan, M. 2016. Planning product discovery. https://svpg.com/planning-product-discovery.

Cagan, M. 2018. *Inspired.* 2nd ed. New Jersey: Hoboken.

Cascio, J. 2020. Facing the age of Chaos. https://medium.com/@cascio/facing-the-age-of-chaos-b00687b1f51d.

Cooper, A. 1999. *The inmates are running the asylum. Why high-tech product drive us crazy and how to restore the sanity.* Indianapolis: Macmillan.

Cooper, B., and P. Vlaskovits. 2013. *The lean entrepreneur.* Hoboken: Wiley.

Cohn, M. 2004. *User stories applied: For agile software development.* Boston: Addison.

Cohn, M. 2005. *Agile estimation and planning.* Stoughton: Prentice Hall.

Connor, D. 2012. Understanding, commitment, and alignment. www.connerpartners.com/frameworks-and-processes/understanding-commitment-and-alignment.

Deming, W. E. 1982. *Out of the crisis.* Cambridge.

Dickmann, P., Hrsg. 2007. *Schlanker Materialfluss mit Lean Production, Kanban und Innovationen.* Heidelberg: Springer.

Digital.ai. 2022. State of Agile report. 16th ed. https://digital.ai/resource-center/analyst-reports/state-of-agile-report.

Domin, A. 2019. Scrum: Was versteht man unter dem Velocity-Faktor? https://t3n.de/news/scrum-velocity-faktor-1138393.

Drath, W. H., C. D. McClaudey, C. J. Palus, and E. V. Velsor. 2008. Direction, alignment, commitment: Toward a more integrative ontology of leadership. *The Leadership Quarterly* 19(6):635–653.

Epping, T. 2011. *Kanban für die Softwareentwicklung.* Heidelberg: Springer.

Eriksson, M. 2011. What, exactly, is a product manager? www.mindtheproduct.com/what-exactly-is-a-product-manager.

Fleig, J. 2019. Kaizen als Prinzip und was es bedeutet. www.business-wissen.de/hb/kaizen-als-prinzip-und-was-es-bedeutet.

Gibbert, R. 2013. Product Discovery—Aber bitte richtig. www.produktbezogen.de/product-discovery-aber-bitte-richtig.

Gibbert, R. 2014a. Das MVP—Problemlösung mit minimalem Feature-Umfang. www.produktbezogen.de/das-mvp-problemloesung-mit-minimalem-feature-umfang.

Gibbert, R. 2014b. First things first—Priorisierung von Ideen + Anforderungen. https://www.produktbezogen.de/first-things-first-priorisierung-von-ideen-anforderungen/.

Gilb, T. 1988. *Principles of software engineering management.* Harlow: Addison.

Gläser, T. 2014. Prototyping UX: Mit Wireframes und Prototypes zum optimalen Interface. https://t3n.de/magazin/wireframes-prototypes-optimalen-interface-prototyping-ux-233367.

Grots, A., and M. Pratschke. 2009. Design Thinking. Kreativität als Methode. *Marketing Review St. Gallen* 26(2):18–23.

Herwarth von Bittenfeld, P. 2010. User Stories: Anforderungen aus Nutzersicht dokumentieren. https://blog.seibert-media.net/blog/2010/11/29/user-stories-anforderungen-aus-nutzersicht-dokumentieren.

Herzberg, F., B. Mausner, and B. B. Snyderman. 1959. *The motivation to work.* New York.

1 Introduction to Digital Product Management

29

Hoffmann, R. 2017. https://twitter.com/reidhoffman/status/847142924240379904?lang=de

Jacobsen, J., and L. Meyer. 2019. *Praxishandbuch Usability und UX*. 2nd ed. Bonn: Rheinwerk Computing.

Jeffries, R. 2001. Essential XP: Card, conversation, confirmation. https://ronjeffries.com/xprog/articles/expcardconversationconfirmation.

Jungwirth, K. 2016. Scrum: So finden Sie einen exzellenten Scrum Master. www.inloox.de/unternehmen/blog/artikel/scrum-so-finden-sie-einen-exzellenten-scrum-master.

Kano, N., F. Seraku, F. Takahashi, and S. Tsuji. 1984. Attractive quality and must-be quality. *Journal of the Japanese Society for Quality Control* 14(2):14–156.

Kelley, T. 2001. *The art of innovation. Lessons in creativity from IDEO, America's leading design firm*. New York: Doubleday.

Kempe, M. 2022. Customer Journey in a Nutshell—Eine methodische Einführung. In *Integriertes Online- und Offline-Channel-Marketing*, Editor Kristin Butzer-Strothmann, 79–110. Wiesbaden.

Knapp, J., J. Zeratsky, and B. Kowitz. 2016. *Sprint: How to solve big problems and test new ideas in just five days*. New York.

Krasadakis, G. 2019. The minimum viable product explained. What an MVP really is and how you can benefit from it. https://medium.com/agileactors/the-minimum-viable-product-explained-8f1187ca7cec.

Ladas, C. 2008. Scrum-ban. https://leansoftwareengineering.com/ksse/scrum-ban.

Ladas, C. 2009. *Scrumban and other essays on kanban systems for lean software development*. Seattle: Modus Cooperandi Press.

Larman, C., and B. Vodde. 2017. *Large-scale scrum: More with less*. Boston: Addison.

Laudon, K. C., J. P. Laudin, and D. Schoder 2016. *Wirtschaftsinformatik*. 3rd ed. Hallbergmoos: Pearson.

Leopold, K., and S. Kaltenecker. 2013. *Kanban in der IT. Eine Kultur der kontinuierlichen Verbesserung schaffen*. 2nd ed. München: Hanser.

Mack, O., A. Khare, A. Krämer, and T. Burgartz, Editor 2015. *Managing in a VUCA world*. Wiesbaden: Springer.

Millweber, F. 2018. *Kanban für Anfänger. Grundlegendes über den Einsatz von Kanban in der Industrie und der Softwareentwicklung*. Hannover.

Neuberger, D. 2014. Die Aufgabe des Produktmanagers. www.produktbezogen.de/die-aufgabe-eines-produktmanagers.

Neuberger, D. 2018. Produkt vs. Projekt. www.produktbezogen.de/podcast-01-produkt-vs-projekt.

New Work SE. o. J. Auftragsklärung. A framework for collaborative alignment. https://auftragsklaerung.com.

Nielsen Norman Group (NN/g). 2016. When and how to create customer journey maps. https://www.nngroup.com/articles/customer-journey-mapping.

Petereit, D. 2017. Kanban versus Scrum—Was sind die Unterschiede? https://t3n.de/news/kanban-scrum-unterschiede-834533.

Petersen, M. 2017. Was macht eigentlich ein Scrum-Master? https://t3n.de/news/scrum-master-aufgaben-ausbildung-gehalt-800972.

Pichler, R. 2014. *Agiles Produktmanagement mit Scrum. Erfolgreich als Product Owner arbeiten*. 2nd ed. Heidelberg: dpunkt.

Reddy, A. 2015. *The scrumban [R]Evolution: Getting the most out of agile, scrum, and lean kanban*. New York: Addison.

Revella, A. 2015. *Buyer personas*. New Jersey: Hoboken.

Ries, E., and S. Blank. 2011. *The lean startup: How today's entrepreneuers use continuous innovation to create radically successful businesses*. New York: Crown Business.

Roock, A. 2012. *Stop starting, start finishing!* Seattle: Lean-Kanban University.

Schwaber, K. 2012. Scrum but replaced by scrum and. https://kenschwaber.wordpress.com/2012/04/05/scrum-but-replaced-by-scrum-and.

Schwaber, K. 2015. What is scaling scrum? https://kenschwaber.wordpress.com/2015/06/03/what-is-scaling-scrum.

Schwaber, K., and J. Sutherland. 2020. Der Scrum Guide. Der gültige Leitfaden für Scrum: Die Spielregeln. https://scrumguides.org/docs/scrumguide/v2020/2020-Scrum-Guide-German.pdf.

Schwaber, K., and J. Sutherland. 2017. Der Scrum Guide. Der gültige Leitfaden für Scrum: Die Spielregeln. www.scrumguides.org/docs/scrumguide/v2017/2017-Scrum-Guide-German.pdf.

Scrum Alliance. Editor 2018. 2017–18 state of scrum report. https://info.scrumalliance.org/State-of-Scrum-2017-18.html.

Singh, M. 2017. 7 Factors for running an effective Kanban replenishment meeting. www.digite.com/blog/kanban-replenishment-meeting.

Snowden, D. J. 2000. The social ecology of knowledge management. Cynefin: A sense of time and place. In *Knowledge horizons: The present and the promise of knowledge management,* Hrsg. C. Despres and D. Chauvel, 237–265. Oxford: Routledge.

Sutherland, J. 2001. Agile can scale: Inventing and reinventing SCRUM in five companies. *IT Journal* 14(12):5–11.

Takeuchi, H., and I. Nonaka. 1986. The new new product development game. *Harvard Business Review* 64(01):137–146.

Torres, T. 2021. Continuous Discovery Habits, Bend.

Ulrich, B., S. Wagner, A. Schütt, C. Grünewald, and H. Obendorf. 2016. *Experiments handbook. An overview of how and when to validate hypotheses. And with whom. For a better working product lifecycle.* Norderstedt: BoD–Books on Demand.

Wake, B. 2003. INVEST in good stories, and SMART tasks. https://xp123.com/articles/invest-in-good-stories-and-smart-tasks.

Wiegand, S. 2015. Story-points. https://agilmanagen.de/story-points.

Wille, S. 2016. Sag mal… wie priorisierst du eigentlich? 10 Techniken für klare Entscheidungen. https://www.produktbezogen.de/sag-mal-wie-priorisierst-du-eigentlich-7-techniken-fuer-klare-entscheidungen/.

Sascha Hoffmann is a professor of Online Management and Business Administration at the Fresenius University of Applied Sciences in Hamburg. He teaches subjects such as Digital Product Management, E-Commerce, and Online Marketing. Previously, he held leading positions in Business Development and Product Management for companies such as XING and blau Mobilfunk. More at www.hoffmann-sascha.de.

Contact: moin@hoffmann-sascha.de

User-Centered Product Visions

Developing and Successfully Implementing in a Team

2

Inken Petersen

Abstract

A good product vision can significantly influence the success or failure of a product. It puts customer benefit at the center and provides a long-term and inspiring guiding principle. However, product visions are often not lived collectively, are too generic, or are only about business figures. Then the hoped-for effect does not occur. In this article, you will see why you need a vision, how best to integrate it, which tools you can use, and how you can, among other things, come to a truly shared and customer-centered vision with a team workshop.

2.1 What is a Product Vision?

Successful products can only be developed with a corresponding long-term vision in mind. Without a viable vision, the drive often lacks and product development does not gain momentum. But what exactly is a product vision?

Product vision: A product vision is an inspiring and long-term guiding principle for a product. The vision formulates a clear target image for the product. The direction in which the product should develop is made clear in this usually compact formulation. It's not just about economic goals. A good vision describes why the product exists and what added value it can offer its users and the world.

I. Petersen (✉)
Hamburg, Germany
e-mail: contact@inkenpetersen.com

© The Author(s), under exclusive license to Springer Fachmedien Wiesbaden GmbH, part of Springer Nature 2024
S. Hoffmann (ed.), *Digital Product Management*,
https://doi.org/10.1007/978-3-658-44276-7_2

An important question in the product vision is the time horizon, i.e., how far the vision should look into the future. This time horizon varies depending on the industry, product life cycle, and type of product. For digital products, the product vision is usually defined for a period of 2 to 5 years. For hardware, a vision can also cover a period of 5 to 10 years, as hardware products usually have a longer product life cycle.

However, the product vision is usually just the beginning. For successful product development, the vision must be supplemented with goals and a strategy. This creates a viable foundation that helps to make the right decisions and move forward quickly.

The so-called VMOST model offers a good framework that can be used well for integrating vision, mission, goals, strategy, and actions into everyday life (Sondhi 1999). It also makes the mission of the vision clear. The VMOST model consists of 3 different levels:

(1) Vision and Mission

The vision describes the long-term target image and where the product should develop in the future. The mission describes the purpose of the product and why the product should exist. Vision and mission are often used together and the vision is derived from the mission. The added value for the user naturally plays an important role here, as it is usually the reason for the existence of the product.

> **Example**
>
> Google's mission, for example, is "to organize the world's information and make it universally accessible and useful." Google's vision is "to provide access to the world's information in one click". ◄

(2) Objectives

Based on the vision and mission, the goals for the next quarters can be defined. Here, economic aspects usually come into focus. In a typical product organization with several product teams, the vision, mission, and goals are often formulated across the board. At the lower levels, each product team can then define a strategy and the appropriate measures to achieve the goals.

> **Example**
>
> An example of a goal for an online shop could be "reaching 50,000 new buyers". ◄

(3) Strategy & Tactics

At this level, the goals are concretized in plans and measures. The product manager considers here, involving the product team, how the goals for the next quarter can be achieved. This step is very important, as it links the overarching vision and strategy with the work in the teams. However, this step is often missed in the development of visions, which is why the vision never really comes into play.

> **Example**
>
> An example of a specific strategy could be addressing a new customer segment. The derived measures are then specific functions that the product needs to be attractive to this new customer segment. ◄

It is advisable to schedule regular appointments to coordinate the goals, strategy, and measures. The overarching product manager (i.e., the "Head of Product") should use these sessions with the team to trace back the goals to the overarching vision and mission and actively involve it.

2.2 Why a Product Vision is Needed

Successful product development is always the result of successful teamwork, as various professional competencies need to work well together. A shared vision is essential for a team to work well and efficiently (Google n.d.). However, this only works if the vision is well integrated. A meaningful interlocking of the various organizational levels in the company is important here: a vision conceived in top management without involving the product teams is, in my experience, usually not accepted and not used. However, for good teamwork, a jointly supported and lived vision is very important.

The following four arguments for using a product vision in product development should convince any doubter, especially since the effort to create a product vision is manageable in relation to its benefits.

(1) Clear Direction
To work well and efficiently, a product team needs a common goal. A good vision is a shared vision that gives the team a clear direction. The team can always check whether it is on the right track based on the vision.

(2) Faster Decisions
Decisions have to be made constantly in product development. A clear vision helps in decision-making and also in prioritizing ideas for implementation. And it allows you to feel good about it.

(3) Higher Motivation
Without a shared vision, the team often lacks the drive to make an effort, as there is no overarching reason for it. A good vision for a meaningful product is therefore a great motivation for product teams.

(4) Better Communication

For good teamwork, functioning communication is extremely important. A shared vision can make an important contribution here, as common goals also improve communication among each other.

In summary, a shared product vision is not only important for strategy and planning, but is also essential for a well-functioning team.

2.3 How to Recognize a Good Product Vision

A good product vision is first and foremost recognized by the fact that the vision is known and used in the company and in the individual teams. To achieve this, the so-called SHIELD criteria are helpful as a guideline (Gibbert 2013). These criteria are particularly important when initially creating a vision.

S for "Simple"

The product vision must be easy to understand. A clear and precise formulation in a language commonly used in the company is absolutely important.

H for "Huge"

The product vision should formulate a large and challenging goal. Ambitious and good goals are an important motivation.

I for "Important"

The goal or vision should be important, i.e., address a real need. This is usually the need of the target group, i.e., a problem that is solved for them with the product.

E for "Engaging"

The vision should be inspiring and engage and captivate all participants. This is not always easy with short and compact texts. Here, good internal marketing and communication of the vision are very important.

L for "Long Term"

A vision should be long-term oriented and not just thought of in the short term.

D for "Distributed"

The vision should be known and thus shared by all participants.

2.4 Tools for Creating a Good Product Vision

There are four known tools for creating product visions: the Vision Statement, the Vision Board, the Vision Template, and the Visiontype. Each of these tools has advantages and disadvantages in my experience, which I will briefly introduce in the following.

2.4.1 The Vision Statement

The Vision Statement is certainly the best known and most frequently used tool for product visions. It is mostly used to formulate company visions, but it is also excellent for product visions. The Vision Statement is a very crisp and compact format, which has certainly contributed to its popularity. You can really get to the point with the vision here. This compactness is one of the main advantages of this tool. You can remember the Vision Statement well and the compact format practically forces you to be brief.

Example

A successful Vision Statement is that of Wikipedia: "Imagine a world in which every single human being can freely share in the sum of all knowledge." (Wikimedia Foundation n.d.). ◀

A major disadvantage of the Vision Statement is the open format, which provides little structure. It can quickly happen that a Vision Statement becomes very arbitrary, too long, or too complicated. The SHIELD criteria can help here. However, if you can handle the open format well, in my opinion, it is an optimal tool.

2.4.2 The Product Vision Board

The Product Vision Board by Roman Pichler (Pichler 2011) is a well-structured tool in the canvas format for creating product visions, see Fig. 2.1. It is particularly suitable for the development of new products, the opening up of new market segments, and major changes to existing products.

The board is quite easy to use and provides a practical overview of the product vision and also the product strategy. It consists of five areas:

- Vision: What is the overarching goal? Why should this product exist?
- Target group: Who is the target group and what can the product do for them?
- Needs: What does the target group need and what problems do they have to solve?

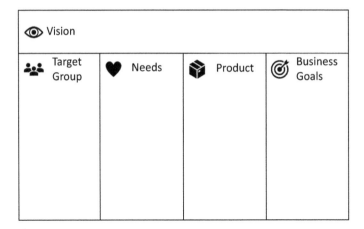

Fig. 2.1 Product Vision Board. (*Source*: Adapted from Pichler 2011)

- Product: What are the main characteristics and features of the product? What are the 3 to 5 most important features that the product needs as a USP (Unique Selling Proposition)?
- Business goals: How can the product contribute to economic success and what should be achieved with it?

The Product Vision Board is a format from agile product development and its filling therefore follows a lean and iterative approach. On the board, you can focus well on the essential core of the product. Since you cannot know at the beginning whether you are correct with your assumptions, the board should be checked and possibly revised during the course of product development.

A significant advantage of the board, in my opinion, is the structured and clear canvas format, which covers the core questions in product development. Also, the approach as an iterative tool, which may and should be checked and changed, fits the challenges of today's product development: markets and users are complex and change quickly, so product visions should also demand room for change.

A disadvantage, in my experience, is that the board as such is not very inspiring and is only moderately suitable for communicating the product vision. However, if you combine the Product Vision Board, for example, with a Vision Statement or a Visiontype, this can work very well.

2.4.3 The Product Vision Template

The Product Vision Template by Geoffrey Moore offers a very compact and lean way to formulate a vision in one sentence (Moore 2014), see Fig. 2.2. The template is also

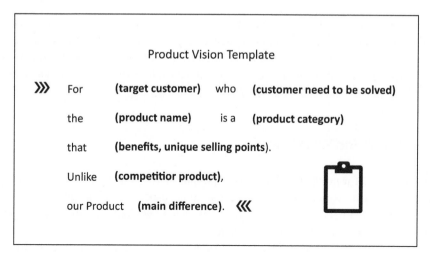

Fig. 2.2 Product Vision Template. (*Source*: Adapted from Moore 2014)

known as an Elevator Pitch, as you should be able to convey the vision of the product to a potential investor within an elevator ride. In the start-up scene, the Product Vision Template is probably the best-known tool for product visions.

With this template, you can bring the essential added value of the product to the point very well. The sentence format is structured and gives detailed instructions on what to fill in. In addition, the sentence format helps a lot to be brief.

Since the individual parts of the sentence come across like a list of facts, the Product Vision Template is not very inspiring. It is a template that is well suited for selling a product to potential partners and investors and less for inspiring and motivating the team.

2.4.4 The Visiontype

A Visiontype is a visual representation of the product vision using a prototype. With the Visiontype, the desired future of the product can be clearly and well represented. The Visiontype is still a relatively unknown tool in this country. The term was coined by product management expert Marty Cagan (2008).

A Visiontype can have different formats: from video to an interactive click dummy. The Visiontype is usually presented from the user's perspective, so in the video, for example, it is shown how the user interacts with the future product. It is important with the Visiontype that it should represent a future but still realistically conceivable version of the product. This distinguishes it from design fiction, which as a tool deliberately deals with the invention of a new fictional future (Roselló 2017). Both tools come from the UX or design area.

The main advantage of the Visiontype is the very inspiring format, which can really captivate and excite teams. With no other tool can product visions be conveyed so tangibly and understandably. A disadvantage of the Visiontype is that often a lot is built into the Visiontype and therefore, compared to e.g. the Product Vision Statement, the crisp compactness is missing. In addition, the creation of product visions with Visiontypes easily gets out of hand. Therefore, you should rather start with a Product Vision Board, for example, and create the Visiontype in a second step.

2.5 The Vision Workshop

For the success of a product vision, it is important that it is a shared vision. A product vision created in an ivory tower will have a hard time, especially in an agile environment. I am a big fan of collaborative vision workshops, where we look into the future together and work out a meaningful product orientation.

Creating a good vision is not trivial and therefore it is important to include different opinions and perspectives. Therefore, everyone who can contribute to the product vision should participate in the workshop.

2.5.1 The Right Preparation

For a successful workshop, good preparation is very important. Otherwise, you run the risk of getting lost in endless discussions about the process during the workshop. In my experience, you should plan at least two to three weeks lead time for the preparation of the vision workshop. In order for the workshop to be successful, the right foundations must be created in advance.

(1) Understand the context
In the first step, all available information, such as market data, studies on user needs, data on the use of the current product, trend studies, etc., should be collected. This is important to get a first overview. Of course, this is mostly a retrospective view, but it is important for a look into the future.

(2) Understand the customer, his problems and needs
Good product visions are always user-centered and focus on the added value for the later user or society. For this, it is important to better understand the user and his problems. Nothing is as inspiring as immersing yourself in the user's world. The Jobs-to-be-done framework is suitable as a tool for this.

The basic idea of the Jobs-to-be-Done framework is that users need or buy a product whenever they have a task to solve (Christensen et al. 2016). With this understanding of the core tasks of users, you can very well start creating the product vision. The Jobs-to-be-done analysis should definitely be carried out with a statistically relevant number of users in an interview format.

(3) Plan the workshop

Then it's time to plan the workshop. For the workshop to run smoothly, the choice of tool for developing the product vision is particularly important. All four tools presented here are generally well suited for a vision workshop. For the Product Vision Board, the Vision Template and the Vision Statement, you can work great with large posters that you hang on the wall as a work surface for the participants. Of course, all of this should be prepared. In addition, the choice of a suitable room is important. The room should ideally offer a creative and inspiring environment. After all, it's hard to imagine a big product vision in a narrow and poorly lit conference room.

2.5.2 The Workshop

Now it's time to formulate the vision! Everyone who likes to think visionary, has ideas or brings special technical expertise should participate in the workshop. For the workshop to run smoothly and a good product vision to be developed, four points should be considered in my experience:

(1) Having a good workshop moderator

In a vision workshop, many different opinions and ideas about the possible future direction come together. To ensure that everyone leaves the workshop with a common direction, it is absolutely important to have a workshop moderator. The moderator should have experience with creative team processes in product development.

(2) Working visibly on the walls

In creative and collaborative team workshops, it is very much about presenting and discussing the work results with each other. Only with this confrontation can a common result be achieved in the end. For this purpose, large working walls are used, as already known from design thinking, on which the results are visibly hung up and jointly refined until everyone is satisfied with the first version of the product vision.

(3) Thinking about the user-centered starting point

One should always start the workshop with a view to the user and his needs. For this purpose, the results of the jobs-to-be-done analysis and the hopefully already existing personas can be briefly presented. It is important to design the introduction in such a way that the participants can build empathy for the user. Without empathy, it is difficult to really think creatively about the future from the user's perspective (Hall 2019). It is perfect if everyone has already participated in the user interviews for the jobs-to-be-done analysis before the vision workshop. Alternatively, videos of the user interviews can be shown at the beginning of the workshop.

(4) Not forgetting the technical and business perspective
A good product vision focuses on the user, but also does not forget the economic and technical perspective. Only from the combination of these three perspectives do truly sustainably successful products emerge, which is also visually well represented in the Venn diagram from design thinking (Brown 2019), see Fig. 2.3.

In the workshop, the financial aspects and technological possibilities should not be lost. Of course, a lot can change in a look into the next 2 to 5 years—but since the product vision is not a design fiction, one should always stay within the realm of the probable. The triad of perspectives helps with this.

2.5.3 After the Workshop

After the workshop, the vision is usually not finished. The results of the teamwork from the workshop usually need to be fine-tuned and concretized. There is usually not enough time for this in the workshop and it is also good to take another look at the results with some distance. The communication and the first integration of the vision into everyday life must not be forgotten after the workshop. Only if you think about the following 3 points, the vision can be used successfully.

(1) The concretization of the vision
The concretization or sharpening of the vision is absolutely important. Especially too generic statements like "better product" or "best product" should be critically questioned.

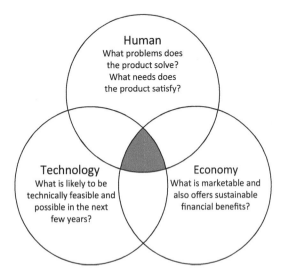

Fig. 2.3 Venn diagram of a good product vision. (*Source*: Based on Brown 2019)

If a vision type has been developed, it must be designed and produced. For the vision statement, the vision template and the vision board, however, a textual revision is usually sufficient.

(2) The communication of the vision
Now it's about sharing the final result with everyone else. It doesn't hurt to make a small event out of this. After all, it's about the future direction, which can be presented well in an inspiring setting. In addition to the initial presentation of the vision, the vision should be hung on the walls in the office or integrated on the company website. This way, the vision remains present and can have a good effect.

(3) The follow-up and use of the vision
This step is the most complicated. Integrating the vision into daily work requires discipline. Here, the product managers are asked, who should integrate the vision into regular strategy sessions and in the OKR processes. Because the vision only remains present and is used if it is continuously integrated into the processes of product development. Regularly asking how new product ideas relate to the vision is also a good way to do this.

2.6 How to Recognize that the Product Vision is Working

But how do you recognize after the workshop and if you have considered all points, whether the product vision is working well? Here are a few tips at the end of this article.

Well-functioning product visions are, on the one hand, naturally recognizable by successful products that inspire users and employees. Because only with a strong vision can product companies really be sustainably successful. Global product companies like Google or Facebook all started with a good product vision and used their strong vision to build strong products and brands. The following four points can be used to determine whether the product vision is really working:

(1) The teams are bursting with motivation and energy
Companies and teams with a functioning vision are characterized by strong motivation and energy that is generally noticeable. A common alignment and working on relevant problems are an important driving force for many and often more important than financial aspects.

(2) The teams refer to the vision themselves
Not only do the managers mention the vision in presentations and meetings, but everyone on the team refers to the vision. The vision has thus become an important reference point for product development and is included in everyday decisions and idea finding.

(3) The vision is a fixed point in an otherwise dynamic environment
A vision is rarely changed, unless it was really completely wrong. Thus, it becomes a fixed reference point for the teams, which helps to orient themselves and to question their current actions. The strategy and measures to achieve the vision are always in motion and are regularly compared and adjusted with the vision.

(4) The user plays a big role
Good visions always address the added value they want to create in the world. Therefore, they usually focus on the user or society, as purely financial goals can never have such an effect. This user focus from the vision is then also noticeable in the teams. The teams naturally always question the effect of their work on the user and thus in the long term also on the vision.

2.7 A Brief Outlook at the End

In the future, the topic of product vision will certainly gain even more relevance in product development. The current economic developments towards sustainability and gentler growth make working with a product vision even more important. Because the product vision promotes a long-term orientation and focus on generating real added value like no other tool in product development. Both are topics that are now not only important for employees, but also for later customers when buying a product.

References

Brown, T. 2019. *Change by design, revised and updated*. New York: Harper Business.
Cagan, M. 2008. *Inspired: How to create products customers love*. San Francisco: Wiley.
Christensen, C. M., H. R. Hall, K. Dillon, and D. S. Duncan. 2016. *Competing against luck: The story of innovation and customer choice*. New York: Harper Business.
Gibbert, R. 2013. Produktvision oder die Sehnsucht nach dem weiten, endlosen Meer. www.produktbezogen.de/produktvision-oder-die-sehnsucht-nach-dem-weiten-endlosen-meer.
Google. o. J. Learn about Google's manager research. https://rework.withgoogle.com/guides/managers-identify-what-makes-a-great-manager/steps/learn-about-googles-manager-research.
Hall, C. 2019. The power of empathy in product development. https://phys.org/news/2019-05-power-empathy-product.html.
Moore, G. 2014. *Crossing the Chasm*. 3rd ed. New York: Harper Business.
Pichler, R. 2011. The product vision board. www.romanpichler.com/blog/the-product-vision-board.
Roselló, E. 2017. https://lab.cccb.org/en/design-fiction-prototyping-desirable-futures.
Sondhi, R. K. 1999. *Total strategy*. Nottingham: Airworthy Publications International.
Wikimedia Foundation. o. J. About. https://wikimediafoundation.org/about/vision.

Inken Petersen has held many different roles within and outside of UX teams throughout her career as a UX designer, Information Architect, UX Lead, and Product Owner. Her passion is products and services with outstanding user experience. As a freelance UX consultant, she coaches her clients on UX strategy, UX management, Product Discovery, and Continuous Product Discovery. For new products and larger relaunches, she creates design visions with vision prototypes and builds new and efficient design systems. She is a co-founder of the Product & UX community blog produktbezogen.de.

Contact: contact@inkenpetersen.com

Product Strategy—The Foundation of Product Management

3

Christian Becker

Abstract

A key task of digital product management involves making decisions in a complex environment with nearly infinite options. The commitment to a product strategy is perhaps the most fundamental decision that a product organization must make. Surprisingly, many companies operate without a product strategy—partly out of fear of committing to something, partly out of uncertainty about how to build a product strategy in the first place. This chapter describes why a product strategy is necessary and how it can be defined.

3.1 Introduction

Many concepts from digital product management are controversially discussed. However, the purpose and function of a product strategy are largely undisputed.

At the same time, there is probably hardly any comparable construct where claim and reality diverge so far in practice: A large part of digital product organizations does not have a product strategy at all, and the vast majority only defines fragments that do not really deserve the label "strategy".

The practical problems of a product strategy already start with the term itself. There is a frighteningly large number of different definitions of "strategy", which leads to a correspondingly large number of more or less explicit opinions and assumptions coexisting in

---

C. Becker (✉)
leanproductable GmbH, Berlin, Germany
e-mail: christian@productable.de

© The Author(s), under exclusive license to Springer Fachmedien Wiesbaden GmbH, part of Springer Nature 2024
S. Hoffmann (ed.), *Digital Product Management*,
https://doi.org/10.1007/978-3-658-44276-7_3

45

product organizations about what exactly a product strategy should be. Added to this is a considerable amount of method confusion, which prevents a clear view of the structure and content of a product strategy. Strategy blurs between frameworks such as (product) vision, mission, objectives and key results, value proposition and business model canvas, or is vanishes between different principles of agile work. Finding a way out of the blur is difficult because the necessary time is often lacking in the daily operational hamster wheel to deal with the topic of product strategy deeply enough.

All these factors together form a perfect breeding ground for "product strategy" to become something intangible. Often discussed, rarely defined, but still somehow there. Because: not having a strategy is also not an option.

This chapter presents *one* possible structure for defining and implementing a product strategy in practice. As always in digital product management, there are different ways and preferences to achieve the goal. Depending on the individual context of a company and its product organization, the approach described here may need to be adapted. Much more important than the actual format is ultimately the active substantive engagement with the topic and a conscious decision within the product organization for a direction.

3.2 What is Product Strategy?

The question of what exactly a "product strategy" is can quickly end in a longer philosophical discussion. Depending on the context from which the multifaceted topic is viewed, very different aspects are important, which are reflected in different definitions and all have their justification.[1]

From the perspective of product *management,* which fundamentally includes all essential levers of a product organization that decide success or failure, a decision-oriented definition is suggested, as proposed by Alfred D. Chandler (1962):

> "The determination of the basic long-term goals and objectives of [a product organization], and the adoption of courses of action and the allocation of resources for carrying out these goals."

Following Alfred D. Chandler, product strategy thus essentially involves the determination of "basic, long-term goals and objectives" for the product organization and the derivation of a path in the form of actions ("courses of actions") and the necessary resources ("allocation of resources") to achieve them. Product strategy thus defines far more than functions or features.

---

[1] A comprehensive overview of various definitions can be found in Mainardes et al. (2014).

3.3 The Importance of Product Strategy

Every product manager aims to ensure that the product solves a problem important to the customer (Desirability), that it is technically feasible for the company (Feasibility), and that the company's financial goals can be achieved with the product (Viability) (Maurya 2019).

Technological risks are increasingly losing their terror, as digital products are technically almost limitless today. Even complex functions are often already available as standard components—often even for free and as open source.

With technology becoming increasingly available and powerful and digitalization becoming increasingly deeply rooted in target groups, more and more fragmented customer problems can be solved without major hurdles. As a direct consequence, competitive pressure for digital products is increasing. Digital product management is therefore faced with a growing mountain of options and demands in the area of desirability, which can lead to decision paralysis.

The second major challenge for product organizations remains viability: With increasing competitive pressure and often existing digital network effects, which lead to an extreme concentration on very few winners, financial possibilities and thus resources cannot keep pace with the options, so that an ever-growing gap is emerging, see Fig. 3.1.

In this environment, it is more than ever a key competitive factor for digital product organizations to learn faster than the competition which options bring success—and which do not. However, learning always costs a lot of time, even with lean, agile methods. That's why even (or especially) the very large digital companies focus on a few strategically important areas.

Those who act without a clearly defined combination of goal and path easily lose themselves in the numerous, seemingly attractive options, quickly do arbitrary things and thus reduce the so important learning speed to almost zero.

At its core, product strategy is thus a very essential necessary condition to create focus and direction in an organization and to enable it to make fast, efficient decisions and use scarce resources in a targeted manner.

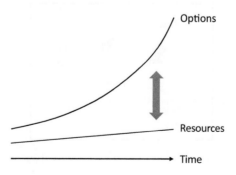

Fig. 3.1 The options-resources gap. (*Source*: Own illustration)

3.4 The Elements of Product Strategy

Even though the product strategy in the true sense is the established **goal** and the **path** to it, of course, no product strategy is conceivable without an analysis of the **starting point**. Anyone who does not know where the current position is will have great difficulty in setting a goal and a path and maintaining course along the way.

Since the goal lies in an (uncertain) future, it also makes sense to consider other relevant internal and external **future factors** in the process of creating the product strategy, which describe (assumed) important framework conditions for the product organization and thus have an influence on which goal or path is best chosen.

Given almost infinite options with simultaneously limited resources, an efficient strategy finding finally needs as a last element strong guardrails or a **product playing field**, to limit the solution space from the outset and to keep the complexity manageable, see Fig. 3.2.

Since the product playing field naturally has a massive influence on the content design of the product strategy, it will be presented in more detail first, before the other four elements (starting point, future factors, goal, and path) are described in more detail.

3.4.1 The Product Playing Field

The product playing field is of fundamental importance for every product organization, as it defines the basic positioning of the entire company—especially in comparison to the competition—for a long time. Because of the scope, many companies in practice shy away from defining a product vision in order to gain more room for maneuver and flexibility. But every good product needs a clear focus, and a product playing field is a necessary condition for this.

The basis for defining the product playing field is the vision and mission of the *entire company*, which ideally already exist. While the vision describes a relatively rough tar-

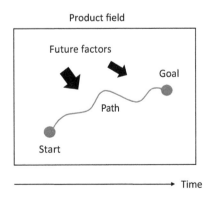

Fig. 3.2 Elements of the product strategy. (*Source*: Own illustration)

3 Product Strategy—The Foundation of Product Management

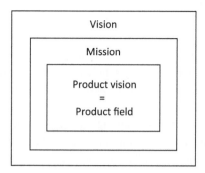

Fig. 3.3 The product vision as a product playing field. (*Source*: Own illustration)

get state for customers, the company or other stakeholders, the mission defines the basic path to get there.

For the fictitious company VetService GmbH, which is active in the field of animal health, the vision could be "Healthy pets and satisfied veterinarians" and the corresponding mission "Digitization of all processes at the vet's office".

Both vision and mission are by definition vague, allow almost infinite options for action and are therefore unsuitable as a product playing field for a product strategy. To define the product playing field, the construct of the product vision has therefore developed in practice, which hierarchically subordinates and derives from the vision and mission, see Fig. 3.3.

To formulate a sufficiently narrow product playing field via a product vision, there are various formats (see chapter "User-Centered Product Vision" by Inken Petersen). No matter which variant is chosen in the end, for the product strategy the question is whether the scope of action is clearly defined enough to enable as effective decisions as possible on the content of the elements of the product strategy and not to get caught in endless and recurring discussion loops that only cost unnecessary energy and distract from the actual necessary work.

In the following a relatively simple structured question to formulate the product vision is used:

For which target group(s) and in which context do we solve which problems with which priority in order to achieve which goals for the target group(s)?

Example VetService GmbH

For the product of VetService GmbH, a product vision based on the vision and mission described above could look like this:

- **Variant A:**
  Our VetService product enables veterinarians to handle all necessary tasks in the veterinary practice highly efficiently. In this way, we enable veterinarians to maximize their time for the treatment and care of their patients.
- **Variant B:**

Our VetService product enables medium-sized veterinary practices for all types of animals with branches of 4 to 8 doctors in the EU and the USA to handle all tasks from appointment scheduling, medical treatment, billing and payment to the purchase of necessary materials highly efficiently. In this way, we enable veterinarians to maximize their time for the treatment and care of their patients.

Both variants of the product vision are deliberately defined differently to show the possible range in formulating a product playing field as a basis for the product strategy. How concrete or vague a product vision is always depends on the given framework conditions of the respective product organization. In variant B, the product organization of VetService GmbH either needs a significantly narrower playing field to limit possible options from the outset and enable efficient decision-making processes for the product strategy—or the boundary conditions, such as the regions in which the product should be available, are already centrally predetermined by fundamental decisions at a higher company level of VetService GmbH and are no longer up for discussion. ◄

In addition to a qualitative description, suitable long-term key performance indicators (KPIs) for measuring success are essential further components of the product vision. They concretize the qualitative content and simplify the evaluation and analysis of the starting point and the definition of the goal.

Unfortunately, KPIs are often criminally neglected in practice when it comes to the product vision, because they are sometimes very difficult to define. For example, there can be intense discussion about how best to measure the "highly efficient handling of tasks" aimed at in the product vision from the customer's perspective. But precisely because the discussion about the "right" KPIs can be strenuous, it is an elementary prerequisite for cleanly defining the playing field for the product organization and, building on this, the entire product strategy.

3.4.2 The Starting Point

The starting point as an element of product strategy includes all essential numbers, data, facts, but of course also assumptions, which are necessary for the analysis and evaluation of the current situation of the product organization. According to the definition of product strategy used here, which is derived from product management, in addition to the product itself, other levers must also be considered that are necessary to build the product.

Anyone who has taken enough time in advance to cleanly define the product playing field with the help of a product vision and the associated KPIs (and of course to measure these) should find it easy to describe the essential data at the starting point of the product. In addition, possible content gaps in the product vision quickly become clear, for exam-

3 Product Strategy—The Foundation of Product Management 51

ple if a region (EU or USA) has not yet been addressed. Added to this are metrics that result from the underlying mechanics of the business model (e.g., conversions or usage rate) and finally directly or indirectly assignable financial key figures. Qualitative feedback on the product can also be valuable for describing the starting point of the scope.

The analysis of the starting point—of course always in comparison to the relevant competition—is an effective gauge for clarity and focus within the product organization. If the data points mentioned for the product strategy are not quickly and transparently available, it is always worth investing the time to build the necessary structures before taking further steps. If the foundation is not solid, the product strategy will inevitably be shaky and the actual goal will be missed.

Established products and those that are new to the market face opposite challenges when analyzing the starting point: A longer history brings the advantage of having more and differentiated data available, but carries the risk of losing sight of the essentials due to the abundance of information. Young products, on the other hand, are inevitably more focused, but may not have enough measurement points to work data-driven at all.

The other elements of product management are often forgotten in the context of the starting point analysis, because all eyes quickly turn to the product. However, the people working in the product organization, their skills, the available budget and last but not least the associated processes in operationalization are the prerequisite for being able to build products—and these can only be changed very long term. A realistic assessment of these starting point factors is therefore a very essential and necessary condition for the definition of effective product strategies.

3.4.3 The Future Factors

Certain or assumed future events can have a major influence on decisions about the goal and the path of the product strategy. Depending on the product and industry, the analysis of these future factors can include very different aspects. Typical factors are changes in competition, such as the reorientation of existing or the market entry of additional competitors, the development of the target market (for VetService GmbH, for example, the number of pets), general macroeconomic developments, legal requirements (e.g., regulations on who can offer veterinary services) or even—increasingly rare—technological leaps.

Since future factors are naturally predominantly uncertain, it makes sense to develop different scenarios by combining the relevant factors in their manifestations and backing them with rough probability values. To keep complexity within limits and focus on the essentials, it often helps to look back at the development of your own product organization and the factors that have really made a difference in the past. Alternatively, experience values from developments of other companies that have been in a similar starting position can provide important insights.

3.4.4 The Goal

The goal of the product strategy stands for itself, but is never conceivable without the context of the hierarchically superior goals and the strategy of the overall company. Depending on the focus of the overall strategy, (partial) goals of the product strategy may already be explicitly given. As a rule, however, the overall strategic goals need to be broken down further to the possible levers of the product organization.

Since the problem described in the introduction of a missing strategy is not exclusively found in digital product management, but is at least as common in the overall company strategy in practice, the challenge often arises to define the goal of the product strategy without an overarching strategic framework. In doubt, the goal of the product strategy thus arises *before* those of the overall company strategy, but should of course not be decided without a more intensive discussion with the company management.

Goals for the product strategy always require a clear temporal reference and can basically be defined across all fields of action of product management: product and resources as well as the associated processes in operationalization.

The goal of the product strategy influences the entire product organization in the long term and determines where a large part of future time and energy will be invested. Therefore, the claim must be to work out a sustainable competitive advantage with the achievement of the goal: "The essence of strategy is to perform activities differently than rivals do." (Porter 1996). The difference can be achieved through the content orientation of the goal (the what) and/or the defined target level (how much of the what).

To make the goal tangible and to better work out the assumed logic for the desired competitive advantage, it is advantageous to formulate the goal as if-then sentences: "If we have achieved goal A by time B, then we have the competitive advantage C, because …".

Example VetService GmbH

Depending on the complexity of the conditions, the amount of potential goals and content orientations can vary greatly. For VetService GmbH, for example, the following relevant goal scenarios could arise:

- If the number of our customers in France, Italy and Spain has increased by 50% in the next 12 months, then we have a sustainable size advantage in the strongest growth markets in Europe compared to our main competitor, which allows us to invest faster and more in further horizontal and vertical coverage of the veterinary process and thus further expand our lead in the product.
- If we have realized the technical prerequisites for a localization of the core veterinary processes in the next 6 months, then we have created the necessary condition for the internationalization planned in the overall company strategy into other European countries.

3 Product Strategy—The Foundation of Product Management 53

- If we have reduced the average time requirement for the sub-process "invoicing" for our veterinarians by 75% in the next 9 months, then we have increased satisfaction by 25% in a very important area for our customers in the long term and achieved a significant advantage over our main competitor.
- If we have managed to halve the duration of a learning cycle (from the definition of the experiment based on the current critical assumptions through the implementation to the evaluation and derivation of the recommendation for action) on average from 4 to 2 weeks in the next 8 months, then we will be able to work out a permanent advantage in customer satisfaction compared to our main competitor.
- If we have implemented an interface to our strategic partner A in the next 6 months, then we will significantly simplify the accounting process for our veterinarians and at the same time increase the costs for a switch to another product so much that the customer lifetime value increases by 50% in the long term. ◀

In doubt, it can cause problems to really formulate measurable causalities and goals, as strategic goals are naturally long-term and different measures can blur in their effect over time. All the more reason to invest sufficient time, as only through a really intensive discussion can the necessary clarity about the possible leverage of different options in the product organization arise.

Frequently encountered vague buzzwords in practice ("world-class UX"), KPIs without a clear problem statement and effect relationship ("increase in the net promoter score by 30%"), bare financial goals ("30 million EUR turnover 2030") or concrete orders for individual features ("build a native mobile app for veterinarians") are unsuitable as strategic goals because they are arbitrary and do not generate a clear direction. Sooner or later, poor strategic goals will become visible and noticeable through pieced-together product increments.

Good strategic goals, on the other hand, have a reference to the product vision and on the basis of the analysis of the starting point a qualitative direction, a clearly formulated cause-effect relationship and are measurable. At the same time, they leave enough freedom for the product organization to be able to go different ways to the goal.

Given limited possibilities and often several possible goals, an evaluation, prioritization and selection of goals is necessary. Which and how many goals it will be in concrete terms depends essentially on what the conditions of the product organization allow, without losing focus. In doubt, focusing on one goal is always better than losing oneself in too many goals at the same time.

3.4.5 The Path

Path and goal are necessarily closely linked in product strategy. Often a sharp distinction seems difficult or the path seems to be predetermined by the goal. However, there is great value in the conscious separation of goal (the what) and path (the how), as upon closer inspection almost every goal can be achieved in different ways. With limited capacities, it is important to choose the most efficient path to maximize the overall learning speed of the product organization. If path and goal are treated as one element from the outset, there is a great risk of thinking in too narrow terms and overlooking the most efficient path.

The goal, reformulated as a challenge, can serve as a basis for generating ideas for the how. Since many goals are not solely in the hands of the product organization, adjacent functions such as sales, marketing, and development usually need to be considered.

Example VetService GmbH

For the exemplary goals of VetService GmbH, the questions could look as follows:

- How can we (together with sales and marketing) manage to increase the number of our customers in France, Italy, and Spain by 50% in the next 12 months?
- How can we (together with development) manage to create the technical prerequisites for localizing veterinary core processes in the next 6 months?
- How can we (together with development) manage to reduce the average time requirement for the "billing" sub-process for our veterinarians by 75% in the next 9 months?
- How can we manage to halve the duration of a learning cycle (from the definition of the experiment based on the current critical assumptions through implementation to evaluation and derivation of the recommendation for action) from an average of 4 weeks to 2 weeks in the next 8 months?
- How can we (together with development) manage to implement an interface to our strategic partner A in the next 6 months? ◀

The result of the idea generation is often a bet. Therefore, whether the chosen path actually leads to the goal needs to be continuously checked during operationalization.

3.5 The Formation Process of the Product Strategy

The theoretical ideal of the formation process of a product strategy would probably look like this: first, the starting point and then the relevant future factors are analyzed in order to then define the goal and finally determine the best way to achieve it, see Fig. 3.4.

Such a linear formation process of the product strategy assumes that all necessary information is available from the start and each step can be cleanly completed before the next, which is practically impossible. On the one hand, there are far too many potentially relevant data to be fully and validly captured, and future factors need to be taken into account, which are inherently uncertain or can change. On the other hand, the process does not take place on a green field, but always in a given context and a resulting bias. In

3 Product Strategy—The Foundation of Product Management

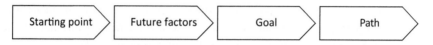

Fig. 3.4 Linear formation process of the product strategy. (*Source*: Own illustration)

particular, there will rarely be a lack of existing ideas about the specific what (goal) and how (path) of the product strategy.

In this environment, the risk is extremely high that the collection of information and discussion beforehand—even if only subconsciously—will be steered in such a way that the existing opinions on the path and goal are merely confirmed and better strategies are overlooked. The logically and objectively appearing linear process thus supports and legitimizes a suboptimal result from the outset.

An alternative to the linear process is a consciously heuristic one, in which the closely interlinked and mutually influencing elements of the product strategy can be considered in no fixed order and as often as desired. This allows a variety of different perspectives to be taken and alternative scenarios to be developed before far-reaching decisions on the product strategy are made.

Of course, a heuristic approach does not guarantee that the best goal and the best path will be found, but at least the probability is much higher.

The complex and uncertain strategy process should therefore not only have the *option* to iterate over all essential elements . The exploration of different options must be a regular and integral part of the entire process, as shown in the model in Fig. 3.5.

The basic idea behind the exploratory formation process of the product strategy is that there is a neutral point outside the content analysis and discussion of the four elements, where it is consciously decided, depending on the context, which element will be considered next—and this for as long and in as fast cycles as possible until a decision on the product strategy is made.

Example VetService GmbH

Here are three examples of an exploratory formation process of the product strategy for the fictitious VetService GmbH:

Fig. 3.5 Exploratory formation process of the product strategy. (*Source*: Own illustration)

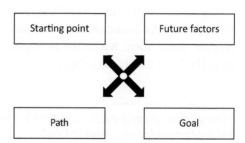

- There is a very attractive option for a strategic partnership with another company (potential path), but where are we really right now (starting point) and would the result of the strategic partnership be a worthwhile strategic goal?
- From the overarching corporate strategy, the goal of internationalization is set. The path is at least relatively clear in terms of scope. But what does the starting point for resources and operationalization look like, and what influence do these have on the path?
- The regulation for veterinarians will be deregulated in more European countries in the next 12 months (future factor). What worthwhile strategic goals result from this, and is our product organization set up appropriately for this (starting point)? ◄

When is an exploratory formation process of a product strategy finished? And which of the developed strategic options is the best? Every strategic decision is and remains a business gut decision based on assumptions. It will never be cleanly provable that a longer process or a different strategic decision would have led to better results, because multiple options cannot be tested against each other in the same temporal and content context.

A natural reaction to dealing with uncertainty is to establish comparability through risk assessments or probabilities of success, but even this can only be a pseudo-objectification in the strategic context, which refers to the future. Another possibility is to consider alternative strategies from the outset. But such alternative plans in the back of the mind also carry the risk that then no strategic direction is pursued with the necessary energy and the strategy becomes blurred. It seems more sensible to carry out a regular evaluation as part of the operationalization after the definition of a product strategy and to change the strategy if necessary.

▶ The definition of a product strategy is a conscious decision-making process and requires courage. Nothing is worse for a product organization than strategic uncertainty.

3.6 The Operationalization of the Product Strategy

The best product strategy is worthless without its implementation. The problem is that implementing a strategy is significantly more difficult than defining it: "Strategy is a commodity, execution is an art."[2] The operationalization of the product strategy is therefore of particular importance, and an understanding of its hurdles is essential for any product organization. According to Stephen Bungay (2010), there are two: the "Alignment Gap" and the "Effects Gap".

---

[2] This quote is generally attributed to Peter F. Drucker—even though it is not printed in his books and no other reliable source can be found.

3.6.1 The Alignment Gap

The Alignment Gap describes the difference between what the product organization is supposed to do according to the strategy and what is actually implemented. ("The difference between what we want people to do and what they actually do."). There are many possible reasons why the planned path is not executed in an organization: unclear and ambiguous communication of the strategy between sender and receiver, too many parallel projects or unexpected events that cause the focus to be lost, personal opinions, contexts and plans in the implementation teams or simply interpersonal problems.

Product organizations that follow a structured process in defining the product strategy and involve key people in the organization can reduce the Alignment Gap from the outset. However, experience in practice shows that over time, understanding and perception of product strategies often diverge even in relatively small organizations and can only be brought back together by further conscious measures during implementation. This is even more true in deliberately loosely coupled organizations, where largely autonomous teams work independently—but of course still have to follow the given strategic line in order not to end up in chaos.

As a central means of alignment, Bungay (2010) suggests the principle of "Briefing and Backbriefing", in which all relevant stakeholders present, repeat and reflect the derivation and contents of the strategy from their specific context at regular intervals, in order to prevent possible misunderstandings through intensive and very regular communication. An essential basis for briefing and backbriefing is a cleanly documented derivation of the strategy. The format of the "mission clarification" can also be very helpful, in which all essential elements and arguments from the process of strategy development can be centrally summarized and tracked (compare chapter XY Alignment by Arne Kittler).

3.6.2 The Effects Gap

The Effects Gap describes the difference between what is expected as a causal result of actions and what actually happens in reality. ("The difference between what we expect our actions to achieve and what they actually achieve.")

Like the Alignment Gap, the Effects Gap is a fundamental, empirical truth that cannot be argued away. No matter how good the implementation is, the plan will not survive contact with reality. Therefore, the Effects Gap must also be considered as a fixed framework condition in the operationalization of a product strategy, with the Gap occurring at two levels, as neither the path may lead to the desired goal, nor the goal may lead to the desired strategic competitive advantage.

Fortunately, the answer to the Effects Gap is already embedded in the agile product management approach. Those who divide the big picture into as small increments as possible based on a continuously maintained and prioritized list of critical assumptions and continuously test hypotheses-driven will recognize deviations early on and be able to counteract—depending on the impact, either via a new path to the goal, or, if the framework conditions have changed too much, by completely reorienting the goal.

References

Bungay, S. 2010. *The art of action: How leaders close the gaps between plans, actions and results.* Boston: Nicholas Brealey Publishing.

Chandler, A. D. 1962. *Strategy and structure: Chapters in the history of the American industrial enterprise.* Cambridge: MIT Press.

Mainardes, E. W., J. J. Ferreira, and M. L. Raposo. 2014. Strategy and strategic management concepts: Are they recognizes by management students? *Ekonomika a Management* 17(1):43–61.

Maurya, A. 2019. Lean startup, or business model design, or design thinking? Is the wrong question. https://medium.com/lean-stack/lean-startup-or-business-model-design-or-design-thinking-is-the-wrong-question-f84216fad869 . Access: 2. Jan. 2023.

Porter, M. E. 1996. What is strategy? *Harvard Business Review* 74(6):61–78.

Christian Becker supports companies in quickly and predictably moving from the initial idea to the validated digital product and business model. The focus is on product strategy, user research, conception, and testing—as a coach, embedded in teams, or in interim positions. Before he founded his own company in 2013, he led the product management, UX, and content team at mobile.de.

Contact: christian@productable.de

Implementing and Validating Product Strategy with Objectives and Key Results (OKR)

A Framework for Navigating in Complex Worlds

Cansel Sörgens

Abstract

Objectives and Key Results (OKR) as a framework promises more focus, transparency, and above all alignment within an organization. Over the past ten years, the popularity of OKR has skyrocketed, and its use in digital product management has become indispensable. This is because Objectives and Key Results enable a customer-centric mindset by focusing product development on the impact and resonance with the target audience, rather than just on implementation speed. Moreover, when used correctly, OKR promotes the continuous development and implementation of strategy as part of the daily work of all participants in an organization. This chapter illuminates the principles of action and describes what the application of the OKR framework looks like in the practice of a product organization.

4.1 What are Objectives and Key Results about?

Objectives and Key Results is a framework that helps organizations implement a vision and strategy by collaboratively aligning all participants' capacities on prioritized topics and measurable results, working on them in short iterations to validate solution ideas as quickly as possible, and learning from this to continuously improve their approach to strategic issues.

C. Sörgens (✉)
Köln, Germany
e-mail: okrs@cansel-soergens.com

© The Author(s), under exclusive license to Springer Fachmedien Wiesbaden GmbH, part of Springer Nature 2024
S. Hoffmann (ed.), *Digital Product Management*,
https://doi.org/10.1007/978-3-658-44276-7_4

Objectives and Key Results (OKR) provide guidance to navigate complexity by making abstract topics tangible and checking through measurable results whether the chosen path is still the right one.

> "We start our journey to our dreams by wanting, but we arrive by focusing, planning and learning." (Wodtke 2016, p. 102)

OKR consists of two elements that should be considered as a set and should not be separated: While an Objective provides the content direction, the Key Results specify the path to it.

▶ **Objective** is a qualitative description of a desired and time-bound goal that contributes to the implementation of a vision or strategy.

▶ **Key Results** are quantitative descriptions that make the achievement of the Objective measurable.

Objective: Users can use the product across platforms

- Key Result 1: Usage on mobile devices has increased by 50%.
- Key Result 2: Daily Active Users (DAU) have increased by 30%.
- Key Result 3: Users on mobile devices are 50% more active. ◀

Objective: With the new website, we generate attention for the topic "Diversity in Companies"

- Key Result 1: 30% of visitors return within 5 days.
- Key Result 2: 10% of visitors contact us for more information.
- Key Result 3: The campaign hashtag was mentioned 5000 times. ◀

The origin of OKR dates back to the 1950s. Peter Drucker's (1954) method "Management by Objectives" (short MbO) was in use in several companies, including Intel. When Intel was struggling with economic problems in the 1970s, Andy Grove, then CEO of Intel, decided to adapt the existing management system to increase his company's adaptability.

Annual goals became quarterly goals to define a clear direction and focus with short-term Objectives that always fit the current circumstances. In addition, Grove supplemented the Objectives with concrete, measurable Key Results to make achieved progress tangible. This adapted form of MbO is considered the origin of OKR.

John Doerr, then an Intel employee, later an investor in Silicon Valley, introduced the OKR framework to Google founders Larry Page and Sergey Brin in 1999, and since then Google has been working with OKR.

In 2013, Rick Klau, then YouTube product manager, published a video (Klau 2013) in which he explained how Google works with OKR. Since then, countless renowned companies worldwide have adopted the OKR framework. Not only large companies, like Amazon, Spotify, Netflix, Slack, Daimler, Bosch, Telekom, are using OKR today, but also many start-ups as well as small and medium-sized companies worldwide.

Through its use in different corporate contexts and thanks to the expertise of some influential people in the field of product management worldwide, OKR continues to evolve, so that Andy Grove's original idea of output management (Grove 2015) has been significantly modified today, namely towards "Outcomes" (see Sect. 4.3.3).

When it comes to the advantages of the OKR framework, the following are usually mentioned.

- **Focus:** The exchange around OKR creates clarity about what is most important in the current situation and what is not. Questions like "Why", "Why now" challenge the participants to discuss the reasons and decide together what they should work on next.
- **Alignment:** Linking day-to-day work with company success creates organization-wide cohesion and meaningful work.
- **Commitment:** OKR promotes structures to enable "Aligned Autonomy", which increases the intrinsic motivation and commitment of employees.
- **Trackability:** Measurable results continuously check whether the selected initiatives or measures are helpful or need to be reconsidered.
- **Stretch:** Ambitious goals push limits and create a space for experimentation where creative and innovative ideas can emerge.

4.2 What Problems does the OKR Framework Solve?

Most of the management concepts currently in use solve problems of "yesterday", when efficient mass production was the biggest challenge in transitioning from small local markets to larger markets. However, since the liberalization and globalization of markets in the last decades of the 20th century, and especially since the internet connects the world with a click, distances no longer matter. Local markets have become a global village. This phenomenon has greatly changed the way we think, consume, and communicate. However, the way we work has often not yet been adapted to modern times.

In many companies, weeks or even months are spent working on AOPs (Annual Operating Planning), roadmaps or project plans for the next one to three years. Such detailed planning of prefabricated solutions suggests that the right solutions are already known, and the internal and external factors that influence implementation and results are under control. And although it is found year after year that these plans are valid at best for three to six months, these practices are repeated every year. Why? Because it gives a (pseudo-) sense of security and control.

Is there a way to have a sense of security and control without meticulously pre-planning everything? Yes, there is. However, the volatility, uncertainty, complexity, and ambiguity (VUCA) of our time must be recognized and it must be accepted that it is not possible to know or predict all solutions and answers in advance. Working with hypotheses, as is common in science, should become the new norm for all organizations.

In complex contexts, as Dave Snowden (2020) describes in the Cynefin framework, the relationship between cause and effect is not known in advance and can only be analyzed in retrospect. The higher the uncertainty, the higher the risks of "backing the wrong horse". For this reason, it is economically advisable to keep the implementation effort as low as possible in complex environments until the added value of the idea is validated. Since the knowledge of experts alone is not sufficient for complex problems, work must be done in short iterations with "safe to fail" experiments (probe). Hypotheses can then be validated (sense) to derive the next steps from what has been learned (respond).

The "probe-sense-respond" approach is at the core of the OKR framework and can therefore be the lifeline for complex challenges. Working in short OKR cycles (three to four months) through experimenting (probe), measuring (sense), and reflecting (respond) promotes a way of working with hypotheses instead of prefabricated solutions and enables an adaptive implementation of the strategy.

4.3 How are Objectives and Key Results Defined?

An OKR set consists of an Objective with two to three Key Results per Objective. Both elements provide different information that complements each other. Therefore, Objectives and Key Results should not be considered separately, but only together do they create a complete goal description.

OKR sets are ideally defined every three to four months. To create a focus, the number of OKR sets should be limited. Following the motto "start less—finish more", it is advisable to define a maximum of three OKR sets ($3\times$ Objectives and two to three Key Results per Objective), as only completed solutions can generate added value.

Before the definition of Objectives and Key Results is explained, it must first be understood at which work level, for whom and for what purpose OKR sets provide valuable information. OKR sets are used as a link between (product) vision and (product) strategy and their implementation. As visualized in Fig. 4.1, a (product) vision and (product) strategy are therefore prerequisites for effective OKRs, just as the OKR sets are the prerequisite for the definition of initiatives or an action plan.

▶   Transparency is an indispensable principle when working with OKR. To establish a vertical (top-down—bottom-up) and horizontal (cross-team and cross-departmental) alignment between vision, strategy, and implementation, all information (vision, strategy, OKR sets, initiatives) must be freely and unrestrictedly accessible to all.

4 Implementing and Validating Product Strategy with Objectives ...

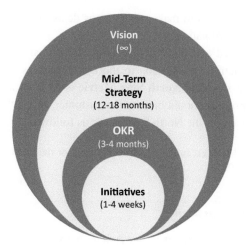

Fig. 4.1 OKR as part of the whole picture (*Source*: Own illustration)

4.3.1 Mid-term Strategic Goal

The (product) vision is indeed indispensable information, but it is usually quite abstract, leaving a lot of room for interpretation and possibly leading teams to work in different directions. To ensure that all forces are channeled in the same direction or that the short-term OKR sets (three to four months) from different teams move in the same direction, a tangible strategic goal for a predictable future (12 to 18 months) is needed to establish strategic alignment and focus.

In practice, it has often been shown that the usual business KPI dashboards or visionary evergreen statements are not sufficient for strategic alignment. The mid-term strategic goal should rather answer two central questions posed by Roger L. Martin (2013, pp. 14–15) in his "Playing to Win" framework: "Where to play" and "How to win".

The mid-term goal should therefore be a synthesis of continuous market observations, analyses, and customer contact, and describe a hypothesis of how customer needs or problems and market trends could provide competitive advantages.

Richard Rummelt (2011) describes a good strategy as follows:

> "The core content of a strategy is a diagnosis of the situation at hand, the creation or identification of a guiding policy for dealing with the critical difficulties, and a set of coherent actions." (Rummelt 2011, p. 78)

Accordingly, the mid-term goal should provide direction and focus without specifying exactly what to do, while at the same time excluding what not to do. The strategic clarity later helps the participants to make autonomous decisions in the OKR process, thus reducing the need for coordination.

This customer-centered and qualitative medium-term goal can be made measurable through quantitative metrics. In addition to the usual business KPIs, such as revenues and market shares, the so-called **North Star Metric** is an ideal addition that represents the core value that a product should offer to the customer. In the "North Star Playbook", John Cutler (2022) describes the North Star Metric as follows:

> "… is the North Star Metric, a single critical rate, count, or ratio that represents your product strategy." (Cutler 2022)

Examples of the North Star Metric

- Netflix: Number of subscribers who watch more than X hours of content per month
- Airbnb: Booked nights
- Spotify: Time a user spends listening ◄

4.3.2 Objective

An objective is derived from the mid-term strategic goal and is a qualitative description of a desired target state. The objectives provide orientation and are activating.

As shown in Fig. 4.2, an objective describes a concrete change that delivers added value for a specific target group and becomes visibly tangible at the end of an OKR

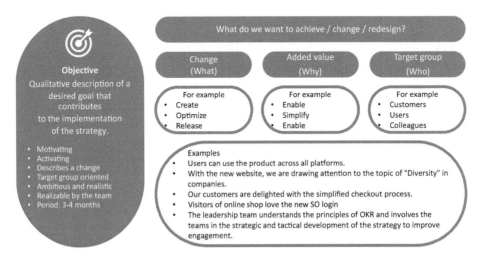

Fig. 4.2 How are objectives defined? (*Source*: Own illustration)

4 Implementing and Validating Product Strategy with Objectives …

cycle. The objective is defined by the (product) team itself, which can also work on it and implement it independently within the next three to four months.

The following questions can help identify the most relevant objectives:

- "Why is this important/more important?"
- "Why is it important now?"
- "Does the idea contribute to the (product) vision and (product) strategy?"
- "If work is being done on the one to three objectives, what other topics would have to be stopped or delayed?"

These questions not only help to limit the number of OKR sets, but also promote valuable exchange about situational perception.

It is recommended to define ambitious objectives so that the participants challenge their limits and also try out unconventional ideas, so that creative and innovative solution ideas can emerge. Whether an objective is ambitious enough should be the decision of the (product) team alone.

▶ Objective is not a new term for a project, but in the OKR context, it describes the added value that is to be created for a specific target group.

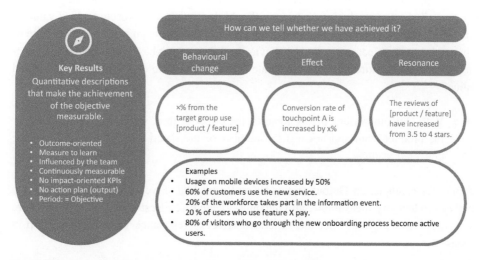

Fig. 4.3 How are Key Results defined? (*Source*: Own illustration)

4.3.3 Key Results

Key Results are quantitative descriptions that make progress towards achieving the Objective measurable. Each Key Result covers a different perspective of the Objective, thus establishing a balance between different aspects.

As shown in Fig. 4.3, a Key Result should typically answer the following question:

"How can we measurably observe whether or to what extent the Objective is being achieved?"

The following five criteria help in defining good Key Results.

1. Output vs. Outcome

Although originally Key Results were the measurable steps to achieve the Objective, an outcome-oriented mindset is now becoming established. According to this, a Key Result should not measure productivity or performance, but the effectiveness of measures. Two terms have now become established in this context to clarify the difference between output and outcome:

1. **Output:** The product, the delivered or produced
2. **Outcome:** The effect, resonance or behavioral change

Joshua Seiden (2019) describes an Outcome in his book "Outcomes over Output" as follows:

"Outcome is a change in human behaviour that drives business results." (Seiden 2019, p. 12)

The delivered or produced is indeed a concrete result, but the use of the products (Output) is not always guaranteed. Therefore, it is problematic to control the Output solely by prescribing to a product team what it should do. Rather, the expected added value or the effect of the Output should be the focus. So, if a product team is asked to generate or change a certain effect or a certain behavior in the customer base, this enables the product team to work more freely on adequate solutions that also deliver this desired added value.

▶ With Outcome-oriented Key Results, the effect of their work is more in focus for the product team and not just the number or the speed of implementation of the delivered features.

While, for example, an Output-oriented Key Result like "Five blog posts written" only makes productivity measurable, an Outcome-oriented Key Result like "Blog posts were shared 100 times" would put the generated effect or resonance with the readership in focus.

2. Measure to Learn

It should be avoided that the metrics in Key Results become an end in themselves. That is, achieving a metric should not be the goal, but what should be important is what these metrics signal about the impact of the work.

> "When a measure becomes a target, it ceases to be a good measure." (Goodhart's law Wikipedia n.d.)

Goodhart's Law describes: When a metric becomes a goal, it loses its effectiveness as a metric, because then the actual impact is not in the foreground, but achieving the goal at all costs (Wikipedia n.d.).

The Key Results should rather help to navigate in complex contexts, to gain certainty despite uncertainty, by validating the metrics work hypotheses and indicating what kind of work works well and what resonates with the respective target group. A Key Result that is not achieved can thus be just as valuable as one that is achieved if new insights about products, customers or environment were gained.

3. Influenced by the Product Team

In order for a product team to measure, reflect on and adjust the impact of its work – which is the core idea of working with OKR to navigate in complex contexts – the teams should be able to influence their Key Results themselves. Because if a solution or hypothesis has been worked on for weeks or even months, but the team cannot immediately see the results, the team does not know whether and to what extent its work has a positive or negative impact on the result. This means that the team has no opportunity to learn because it cannot reflect on cause and effect. Moreover, there is probably nothing more frustrating than when the impact of one's own work cannot be seen or measured.

4. Continuous Measurability

If Key Results are used for learning, the impact of the work should be measured promptly so that it can be validated what works well or poorly or what more or less should be done or when possibly the right time to pivot (shift in product strategy/orientation) is. If a product team works on ideas for three to four months, the outcome of which it can only see at the end of an OKR cycle or even later, this means that the team has

Tab. 4.1 Comparison between Lead- & Lag-Measures. (Based on Covey et al. 2016, pp. 55–73)

	Lead-Measures	Lag-Measures
Time	Predict whether and to what extent a goal will be achieved	Show whether a goal has been achieved
Predictability	Drive progress and increase the likelihood of achieving a goal	Demonstrate the success of past performances
Influenceable	Are directly influenced by the team	Are influenced by various factors
Actionability	Are dynamically adaptable	Can no longer be influenced

used its capacities for something for three to four months without knowing whether it has really generated added value.

To counteract this, the concept of **Lead & Lag Measures** (see Tab. 4.1) from the book "The 4 Disciplines of Execution" by authors Sean Covey, Chris McChesney, Jim Huling, and Andreas Maron (Covey et al. 2016, pp. 55–73) helps.

Lead Measures, which are continuously measured and can increase the likelihood or predictability of achieving the desired goals, help to make data-driven decisions in a timely manner. For this reason, Lead Measures should be used when defining OKR sets to enable fast and continuous learning.

5. No Impact-oriented Business KPIs

The concept of "Lead & Lag Measures" also helps to understand that financial business goals (Business KPIs) such as EBITDA, revenues, market shares, etc. are not well suited as Key Results because they a) measure the results of past performances at the time of measurement and b) are too abstract and outside the sphere of influence of a product team.

Joshua Seiden (2019) explains in his book "Outcomes over Output" this type of business goals with the term **Impact** and emphasizes that the outcomes should be selected in such a way that they positively influence the (Business) Impact as much as possible.

> **Example: Relationship between Output, Outcome and Impact**
>
> Publishing five blog posts per month (Output) may help increase the number of website visits by 20% (Outcome), thereby potentially increasing the number of customer inquiries and revenues (Impact) by 10%. ◀

4.4 The OKR Cycle

Defining good OKR sets alone is not enough, as they also need to be implemented. To work on OKR sets and discuss progress, appropriate routines must be agreed upon.

The OKR cycle presented in Fig. 4.4 serves as a guide to enable regular conversation between the (product) teams and leadership, and can be adapted depending on the context and environment.

4.4.1 Workshop for OKR Definition

After the management or leadership has defined the (product) vision and the medium-term strategic (product) goal for the next 12 to 18 months, the product teams can define their OKR sets at the beginning of an OKR cycle (duration three to four months).

4 Implementing and Validating Product Strategy with Objectives …

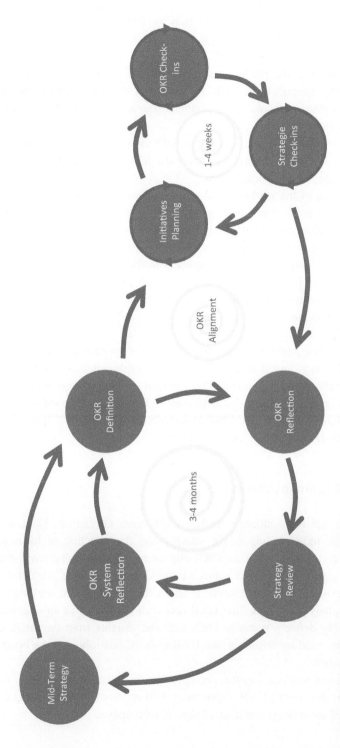

Fig. 4.4 OKR Cycle (three to four months) (*Source:* Own illustration)

The central question of the OKR definition workshop is: "What do we, as a team, want to achieve in the next OKR cycle to make a results-oriented and visible contribution to the medium-term strategic goal?"

Good preparation in the product teams is essential for productive OKR definition workshops. Ideally, product teams collect information about problems or needs of their target group and illustrate these using customer journeys, touchpoint descriptions, etc. for all team members.

In the OKR definition workshop, which usually lasts three to four hours, team members can exchange their observations and analyses, discuss possible strategies and tactics, and decide what they should focus on next.

At the beginning of the workshop, all possible ideas should be collected uncensored (divergence), which are then grouped and categorized in active exchange to clarify similar ideas or tendencies (convergence). Through joint discussion, the product team selects the one to three most important objectives and then defines the corresponding key results.

The active participation of all team members in this workshop is very important, as the perspectives of each individual person bring a valuable contribution to the discussion and the exchange about the achieved "impact" often serves as an eye-opener, in contrast to the usual roadmap meetings.

> Good facilitation and moderation play a big role in the course of all workshops and should therefore not be underestimated. For this reason, all "events" in the OKR cycle should be accompanied by a person who ensures good facilitation and moderation and also helps with their OKR expertise. Depending on the organization, this role is called OKR Master, OKR Champion, OKR Ambassador, OKR Shepard or OKR Agent (see Sect. 4.7.3).

4.4.2 OKR Alignment Workshop

The goals of the OKR alignment workshop are diverse: On the one hand, it serves to build a common understanding of the strategy and the selection of focus topics for the next OKR cycle. In addition, an OKR alignment helps in scaled environments, for example when several sub-product teams are working on the same product, to identify dependencies, synergies or duplications. If teams find that they are working on similar strategic topics, they could link their OKR sets with each other in an alignment workshop and possibly define a common OKR set. The insights from the OKR alignment workshop can be used to streamline the OKR system, possibly also the organizational structures as a whole.

Ideally, all teams working together on a product, including infrastructure, marketing, sales, etc., participate in this OKR alignment workshop. Because establishing a common understanding of the strategy and tactics helps all participants.

Formats such as an Open Space or Marketplace work wonderfully for OKR alignment workshops: First, each team briefly and concisely presents its OKR sets to all participants. Meanwhile, the listeners take notes (dependencies, synergies, duplications) on everything they want to discuss later in this regard. Afterwards, rooms can be opened for breakout sessions in which the team representatives can visit each other to give/take feedback, exchange solution ideas, how the identified dependencies could be solved, or how they could support each other in implementing their OKR sets.

After these breakout sessions, everyone comes back together, all teams present their most important findings and share which adjustments they will make to their OKR sets.

The duration of an OKR alignment workshop varies greatly depending on the number of teams and participants. With five to ten teams, the workshop can last two to four hours, while with ten to 20 teams it can also last a whole day and with over 20 teams it can last two days.

After the OKR alignment workshop, the teams should tackle the agreements made with the other teams in the next one to two weeks, make necessary adjustments and finalize the OKR sets so that the next OKR cycle can officially start.

4.4.3 Initiative Planning

Initiatives are measures, experiments or solution ideas that can be implemented within one to four weeks to get quick feedback on their impact on the target group. The results of implemented initiatives should contribute to the key results of the OKR sets.

To counteract the phenomenon of "set and forget", initiative planning is a central event in which each team plans the measures and activities for the actual implementation of its OKR sets.

How exactly this appointment is structured depends on the team context. It is important that this appointment becomes part of the team's daily work routine. If team meetings are already taking place, they can be expanded to include the point "initiative planning".

Experience has shown that the initial initiative planning, i.e. the first meeting after the definition of new OKR sets, takes about two hours. Afterwards, the team should meet regularly (e.g. every two weeks) so that the initiatives can be continuously adjusted or new ones defined depending on interim results. The tasks for implementing the initiatives must be clearly distributed within the team so that everyone knows at all times what is currently being worked on.

> ▶ If the product team works with Scrum, there is the possibility to link both frameworks. To do this, the Scrum team can formulate its product goals as OKR and align the product backlog according to its OKR sets. The initiatives (epics, user stories, features, etc.) that were defined in the sprint plannings for the realization of the OKR sets are then implemented in the sprints.

4.4.4 OKR Check-ins

The central question in an OKR check-in is: "What progress do we recognize through the implemented initiatives in the Key Results and what does this say about our next steps?"

In OKR check-ins, the product team and possibly their managers come together to discuss the effectiveness of the initiatives.

This appointment takes place regularly (at least every two weeks), like the initiative planning, and should be kept as short as possible (maximum 30 minutes). For the appointment to run effectively, it must be well structured and needs good moderation. The following three questions can provide a good structure:

1. Progress: What progress have we made so far?
Product teams should enter the current status of the Key Results before the appointment in the tool agreed upon by the team (Excel, Miro, Jira, Wiki etc.) so that the changes can be viewed directly during the appointment and the content exchange can start immediately. Here, each team can record a kind of "degree of fulfillment" for itself. For example:

- <30%: We are not making progress.
- 30–70%: We are making good progress, but need to step up the pace.
- 70%: Things are going very well.

2. Confidence: How confident are we that we will achieve our OKR sets?
Perhaps the numbers do not tell us the whole truth. Because a Key Result, where no progress is yet visible, does not automatically mean that the team is not working on it. It may take two to four weeks longer until the effect can be observed measurably. Similarly, good progress can be misleading if, for example, an unforeseen obstacle occurs that will negatively affect all further activities. For these cases, the question of "confidence" is a good addition for effective exchange.

Here too, for example, three levels can be defined as follows:

1. We can do it.
2. We might be able to do it if…
3. We can't do it because…

3. Reflection: What have we learned so far?
An OKR check-in should also serve for reflection by exchanging the most important insights. Useful questions include:

4 Implementing and Validating Product Strategy with Objectives ... 73

- Which hypotheses have been validated so far?
- What worked particularly well?
- What did not work?
- What is slowing us down?

Subsequently, new measures, initiatives, to-dos etc. can be recorded and addressed.

▶ If a product team works with Scrum, the Sprint Review offers a good opportunity to integrate the OKR check-ins. After all, the goal of a Sprint Review is to "discuss the progress towards the product goal." (Schwaber and Sutherland 2020, p. 10)

4.4.5 Strategy Check-ins

In larger product organizations, it is recommended to regularly (at least every four weeks) conduct strategy check-ins. These are similar to OKR check-ins. The main difference is the circle of participants. The product team representatives (possibly the product managers) and the managers (e.g. the CPO) come together to discuss the current progress, insights and obstacles that have arisen in the pursuit of the OKR sets. In addition, the impact of the OKR sets on the business impact is reviewed. The goal is to identify possible problems, opportunities or trends early on and to incorporate them into the strategy as well as to consider necessary course corrections if necessary.

4.4.6 OKR Reflection

At the end of an OKR cycle, each team reflects on its results and working methods. The principle of **Inspect & Adapt**is the focus of this meeting. The entire team involved in the implementation of the OKR sets participates in this meeting.

The OKR reflection is divided into two parts.

Part 1: Review (approx. two hours)
The goal of the review is for the team to discuss whether and to what extent it has achieved its OKR sets and what it has learned from them. The focus is on the content.

In the OKR check-ins, the progress of the Key Results was regularly discussed, but what does this now say about achieving the Objectives? A mistake often made at this point is the assumption that achieving an Objective can be mathematically calculated by the average of the achieved Key Results. However, the relationships in a complex world are not linear. For this reason, each team should take time in the OKR review to evaluate whether and to what extent it has achieved the Objectives. If the team believes that the Objective has not been or not fully achieved, the team should discuss the following options:

- Change it: We need to continue working on it, but the Objective needs to be adjusted.
- Drop it: The Objective was not achieved and is no longer relevant.
- Keep it: We absolutely need to continue working to achieve the Objective.

> With the "Keep it" option, one should be particularly attentive, as there is a high risk that the Objective has been described as an "Evergreen" and is therefore carried over from one OKR cycle to the next. In such cases, it makes sense to create focus and specify what change should be visible in three to four months.

The OKR review not only serves to assess the achievement of the OKR sets, but also to make explicit what has been learned. The following questions enable the product team to have a qualitative exchange:

- Which hypotheses were validated or not validated?
- To what extent have we contributed to the implementation of the product strategy?
- What have we learned about customer behavior?
- What new insights about the market have we gained?
- What of this is important for the further development of the product strategy?

If a North Star Metric was recorded in the strategy (see Sect. 4.3.1), it is now time at the latest to check the impact of the OKR sets on this metric.

Part 2: Retrospective (approx. two hours)
Working with OKR is a change for everyone, and especially in the first OKR cycles, the product teams realize that they need to adjust their working methods. The OKR retrospective opens the space to reflect on what is going well, what is not, and what needs to be adjusted so that the product team can work together better and more effectively in the future, which in turn would have a positive effect on the quality of the OKR sets.

While the review is about achieving the OKR sets, the retrospective takes a close look at the collaboration of the product team. The central question is: "How do we want to design our collaboration in the future (better)?"

In addition, valuable insights can be gained in the retrospectives with individual product teams, which provide information for optimizing the entire OKR process.

The following questions can structure the retrospectives (Derby and Larsen 2018, pp. 3–4):

- Collect data: What happened?

- Gain insights: Why did it happen?
- Decide on measures: What do we do?

▶ If the product team already conducts regular retrospectives, it is recommended to supplement the scheduled retrospective with an OKR retrospective at the end of each OKR cycle.

4.4.7 Strategy Review

Based on the insights gathered during an OKR cycle, the product strategy can be reviewed, validated, and updated if necessary. This allows the organization to continuously adapt to current market events, enabling true business agility.

Similar to strategy check-ins, product team representatives and executives meet at the end of each OKR cycle during the strategy review to discuss insights from the respective OKR reviews of the product teams.

In this meeting, the North Star Metric and company KPIs (Business Impact) are also reviewed to draw conclusions. The conversation can be structured with the following questions:

- What are the key insights regarding customer behavior (problems, needs, trends)?
- What significant market changes (disruptions, competition, economy, politics, society) have we observed that could affect us?
- To what extent do these changes play a role in our product strategy?
- What could give us competitive advantages?

The strategic insights and decisions from the strategy review serve as an important basis for the upcoming OKR definition workshops to start the next OKR cycle.

4.4.8 OKR System Reflection

Working with OKR changes the communication and structures within a team, between teams, and thus throughout the entire organization. There are new questions, such as about impact orientation, strategy development becomes part of everyday professional life, teams collaborate in a different way, the work of the teams is structured differently, thinking shifts from planning the prefabricated solution to validating hypotheses, and much more. All of this drives a culture change in the company. This is a highly complex matter that should be continuously reviewed, validated, and adjusted.

This is exactly the goal of an OKR system reflection. In the middle or at the latest at the end of each OKR cycle, those responsible for the OKR introduction (e.g., the OKR integration team—see Sect. 4.5) should come together and discuss the insights from the respective OKR retrospectives of the teams to derive possible changes for the next cycles from them.

The goal is to find out to what extent the OKR framework helps to establish alignment and focus, and how working with OKR can be taken to the next level, so that it is increasingly internalized and institutionalized.

The following questions serve as a guide to structure the meeting:

- What is going well?
- Where do we need to adjust?
- Are we missing certain checkpoints or communication paths?
- Where can we streamline?
- Are new OKR topics or teams being added?
- How can we make working with OKR visible or tangible throughout the organization?

For the review and validation of whether and to what extent working with the OKR framework helps, it is necessary to have clarity about which problems are to be solved with an OKR introduction. It is advisable to deal with this question at the beginning of an OKR introduction.

4.5 OKR Introduction

The idea of OKR seems simple, but the implementation is definitely more complex than it appears. Each introduction is different because each organization is different and has different needs. For this reason, there is no "one-size-fits-all" solution. Nevertheless, the following provides some guidance on which phases are typical in an introduction and what to look out for.

▶ Since working with the OKR framework drives a complex culture change, the principle of "Probe-Sense-Respond" applies to the OKR introduction—as with all other complex challenges. According to this, it is advisable to introduce the OKR framework not for an entire company at the start, but incrementally, so that the potential (and very likely) start problems do not appear throughout the entire organization, but OKR can be tested and learned in a small environment.

The beginning of an OKR implementation is critical for later success and should therefore be carefully planned. The following four points help to structure the first steps well:

1. **Create clarity about the reasons for an OKR implementation**
   Firstly, before any OKR implementation, the question should be asked why the framework should be introduced or which problems should be solved with it. Here, as for all complex challenges, it is recommended to define the medium-term strategic goal of the OKR implementation and then to define OKR sets every three to four months, implement them, regularly review, validate and possibly adjust them.
2. **Formation of an OKR integration team**
   Ideally, an interdisciplinary OKR integration team is formed, which will deal with the introduction and further development of the OKR framework in a company in the long term. Members from the People & Culture team, organizational development, management, and product teams could be part of this team, so they can view the (further) development from different perspectives and regularly meet for OKR system reflection.
3. **Find a good starting point**
   Since the first OKR cycles are primarily about learning how to work with OKR, it is advisable to find teams, areas or topics that are well suited for working with OKR at the beginning. The following factors help in the selection:
   - **As broad and deep as possible:** Find a topic that requires vertical (different organizational levels) and horizontal (adjacent teams or areas) alignment, so that the new type of collaboration can be tested as effectively as possible.
   - **Not too complex, but also not too simple:** Find topics that are complex, so that working with OKR makes sense, but at the same time is not influenced by too many unknown factors. The topics should not be too simple either. After all, it should be made tangible how the OKR framework can help.
   - **Create visible impact:** The selected topics should be interesting for all employees, so that indirect curiosity and interest for OKR can be generated and the results can be experienced by everyone.
4. **Start with volunteers**
   There are so-called early adopters in every organization, i.e. people or teams who like to try out new frameworks, tools, etc. first and enjoy shaping changes. For the beginning of the OKR implementation, it is recommended to start with these people or teams in order to learn together how the OKR framework can work best in the respective organizational context. They can become ambassadors of change in the further course of the OKR implementation.

The first OKR cycles
The necessary effort to get the OKR framework rolling in a company is high at the beginning and the advantages are not immediately apparent. As shown in Fig. 4.5, it usually takes at least three to four OKR cycles until the "OKR language" and logic are learned and internalized. Once this phase is over, the phase of institutionalization begins,

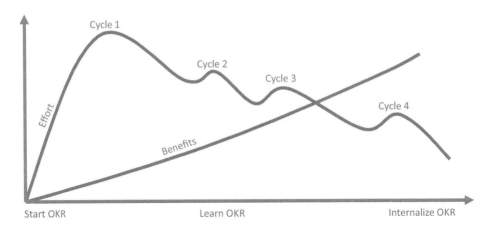

Fig. 4.5 Effort and benefits of an OKR implementation (*Source*: Own illustration)

which usually lasts another three to four cycles until OKR can no longer be imagined without in the everyday life of an organization.

▷ It is recommended to work with experienced external OKR coaches at the beginning of an OKR implementation, who can not only present certificates, but have actually accompanied several OKR implementations in different company contexts and pursue a holistic approach to organizational development. The wealth of experience of people with OKR expertise saves the participants a lot of time and trouble by helping them avoid the typical pitfalls.

Building internal OKR knowledge
The more areas and teams that adapt the OKR framework, the more support is needed. Since the use of external OKR coaches cannot be sustainably scaled, it makes sense to start building internal knowledge early enough.

To do this, external OKR experts can train internal OKR agents and accompany them through coach-the-coach programs for a certain time until a certain level of maturity is reached, so that the internal OKR agents can eventually take over the accompaniment of the OKR process completely on their own. In addition, a long-term cooperation with external OKR coaches can enable continuous supervision of the internal OKR agents and sustainable knowledge building.

4.6 OKR Architecture

OKR architecture refers to the organizational levels and team structures. These are very diverse and should be taken into account when introducing OKR. The reasons for an OKR implementation, the challenges to be solved, and the current structures of the organization play a major role in defining the OKR architecture.

One of the most common mistakes in OKR implementations is that the existing organizational chart is adopted one-to-one in defining the OKR structure. This means that every team depicted in the organizational chart is expected to define OKR sets. However, since most organizational charts do not represent the actual communication paths for value creation, the usual dependencies between the teams will continue to exist in the new OKR process. If teams cannot implement their OKR sets without input or support from other teams, this not only increases the coordination effort, but also the frustration of the team members, as they spend more time coordinating than realizing their OKR sets. The promised effect of effective work falls by the wayside.

The introduction of OKR offers the opportunity to consider the actual collaboration between teams and areas and to found the "OKR teams" as the teams actually create value together. An OKR architecture should enable dynamic collaboration in networks.

4.6.1 Dynamic Networks Instead of Strict Cascading

Although the understanding has prevailed for decades that the OKR sets must cascade from top to bottom to establish alignment, this approach repeatedly proves to be impractical. A cascading OKR architecture has the following disadvantages:

1. In a cascading OKR architecture, where the lower organizational level must adopt the OKR from the level above, there is too little leeway for those involved. This type of cascading OKR architecture restricts any creativity and autonomy.
2. The OKR change at one point triggers a chain reaction, so that all associated OKR sets must also be adjusted.
3. The teams have to wait until all higher levels have defined their OKR sets, which slows down the entire coordination process.
4. The larger the organization, the greater the effort until everyone has defined their OKR sets and coordinated with other teams and areas. This causes a lot of time to be spent in OKR workshops and coordination meetings, which is certainly not in the spirit of an OKR introduction.

Thanks to influential OKR experts, such as Christina Wodtke (2021) and Jeff Gothelf (2021), OKRs are now formed differently. Because actually, the introduction of OKR should establish a connection between the vision, strategy, and implementation so that

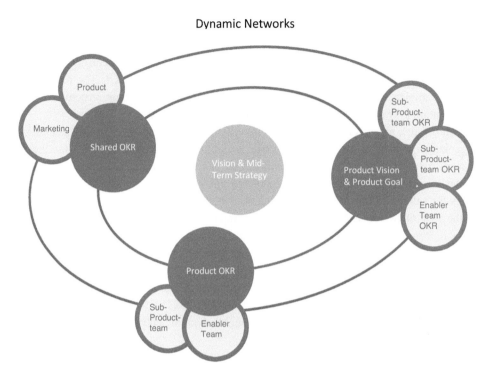

Fig. 4.6 OKR Architecture (*Source*: Own illustration)

those involved can make decisions as self-organized as possible in their professional everyday life. However, a cascading OKR architecture is not the solution for this. Rather, a tangible and directional strategic goal is needed around which the teams can organize themselves (see Sect. 4.3.1). The OKR architecture can be built like a "solar system" through the vision and the mid-term strategic goal.

As shown in Fig. 4.6, the sun represents the mid-term strategic goal and the OKR teams are the planets. Due to the gravitational pull of the sun, the planets remain bound to it; however, each planet also rotates around itself and has its own rhythm. In addition, some planets also have their own satellites that orbit them.

4.6.2 Types of OKR Teams

Since organizations are very diverse, this should also reflect their OKR architecture. The following explains two types of OKR teams that are often seen in product organizations.

Product-OKR
In a product-oriented organization, it makes sense to first define the product vision and the mid-term strategic product goal. After that, the OKR sets can be defined. There are

two possibilities for this, which can be selected depending on the context and size of the organization.

1. The first possibility is that the team representatives, who can contribute to the development and implementation of the product strategy with their insights, insights and experiences, define OKR sets for the main product every three to four months. After that, the sub-product teams (teams working together on a product) and enabler teams (teams working on central services, such as IT infrastructure) plan their activities, initiatives, measures etc. based on these product OKR sets.
2. The second possibility is that the sub-product teams each define their own OKR sets, which are linked to the product vision and the strategic product goal. This variant only works well if the sub-product teams can work as autonomously and independently as possible.

Ultimately, opportunities should always be sought that enable lean structures and effective collaboration. The decision is up to the product teams themselves, as they know their work context best and can assess which variant is better suited for them.

Shared-OKR

Areas such as marketing can work independently on their own OKR sets (e.g. conclude new marketing partnerships), but the strategy for launching a new product must be developed and implemented in collaboration with the product teams. For such cases, it is recommended that the areas jointly define so-called Shared-OKR sets. Afterwards, each team derives its respective tasks from it accordingly.

In this case, one team may be responsible for a specific Key Result alone. In other cases, two teams are jointly responsible for a Key Result, or no team is solely responsible for a Key Result, but each team defines its initiatives to show how they will contribute to achieving the Shared-OKR.

The teams or the representatives of the respective teams should meet regularly (at least every two weeks) for OKR check-ins to synchronize and discuss the next steps. This may initially sound like additional meetings. However, this is not the case, as the teams would have met anyway to synchronize. Through OKR, however, the impact of the work of all teams together will be more in focus and a sense of unity will be created or strengthened by the common goals, so that a true culture of collaboration can emerge.

4.7 Roles in the OKR Process

Working with OKR requires the support of people in different roles. Only the interaction of all ensures effective OKR. The following outlines the central roles and their tasks in the OKR process.

4.7.1 Executives

Without the conviction of executives, an OKR introduction will quickly reach its limits, because strategic alignment needs a leadership that paints a picture of the future that inspires participation. Through a clear strategy and common goals, executives enable autonomy, so that teams can work self-organized within the given context.

Executives have several opportunities in the OKR process to make communication with their employees more effective. For example, they can bring the teams closer to the background and context for the selected strategy in OKR definition workshops and involve the teams more in the strategy development process. In addition, executives can, for example, become aware of possible obstacles early on in OKR or strategy check-ins and support the teams in removing them as quickly as possible. Furthermore, they can discuss the professional and personal development path of individual team members in regular feedback talks and see which individual skills would be beneficial for the realization of the (product) strategy and OKR.

Ultimately, the way executives contribute to the OKR process plays a major role not only in the success of the process, but also in the sustainable establishment and further development of a product.

4.7.2 Team Members

Working with OKR can promote structures in which strategy development and implementation is no longer understood as the task of top management alone, but critical engagement with the strategy becomes part of the daily work of all participants.

A clear strategy and continuous exchange during the OKR cycles give everyone a "structured flexibility". Teams can design their professional everyday life more self-organized in the given context, make informed decisions about what they work on and when, in order to contribute to the strategic goal and the OKR sets. They see and are seen as they contribute to the bigger picture, and experience the effectiveness of cross-departmental collaborative work.

Structured flexibility needs committed teams that take responsibility for their decisions and work. Effective OKR needs team members who identify and implement solution ideas for the needs of their target group with their expertise. This means, on the one hand, that the teams must know their target group well and be in regular contact with them, and on the other hand, that they regularly check whether and to what extent the solutions they have chosen influence the (product) strategy and business impact.

Through working with OKR, team members become active designers of product or company success, which may require an expansion of their skills to think and work more customer-centric, strategic, and economically.

4.7.3 Internal OKR Agents

Effective work with OKR requires both OKR expertise and well-structured and moderated workshops and meetings. OKR Agents can support teams with their OKR knowledge and create a collaborative and trustful environment with good facilitation and moderation skills.

As described in Sect. 4.5, external OKR Coaches can train interested employees to become OKR Agents and accompany them for a while, so that they can later take over and continue the OKR process independently.

OKR Agents support teams during the OKR cycle in their OKR workshops and meetings and ensure that the "new" rituals and ways of thinking become a habit. However, they are not responsible for the content quality of the defined OKR sets, but accompany the teams with questions and advice to raise knowledge and help the teams to formulate their ideas as good OKR sets. OKR Agents should therefore not support their own team, as they must maintain a neutral attitude in moderation.

▶ Agile Coaches, Scrum Masters or Team Coaches are very suitable for the role of the OKR Agent due to their skills, if they supplement their knowledge with OKR expertise.

The internal OKR Agents could form a Community of Practice to strengthen each other, develop common ideas and work out how the use of OKR can be made even more effective.

4.8 Principles of OKR

Although many decision-makers are quickly convinced by the advantages of OKR listed in Sect. 4.1, the necessary framework conditions and principles are often not taken into account. To experience the benefits of OKR, the usual patterns and beliefs must be questioned, which requires a genuine willingness to change.

The following describes three principles of operation that are indispensable for successful work with OKR.

4.8.1 Finding the right balance between Top-down and Bottom-up

While leadership communicates an inspiring (product) vision and an activating and directional (product) strategy and provides a clear mid-term goal for orientation, the teams develop corresponding tactics and solution ideas and decide for themselves what they implement when and how.

However, if goals are only defined top-down, the motivation of the employees will suffer, because people identify primarily with things they have set for themselves. On the other hand, if goals are only defined bottom-up, there is a great risk that the individual teams will not take into account the "big picture", but only optimize locally.

There is no universal formula for the right balance between top-down and bottom-up. Instead, it is created through a participatory OKR process in which managers and teams collaborate across departments at a strategic and tactical level and continuously exchange information.

4.8.2 Do not link OKR with Performance Management

If ambitious goals, creativity, and innovation are to be promoted through work with OKR, an environment of psychological safety is needed where people do not have to fear sharing their ideas and taking risks, even if they could fail. Therefore, a culture is required in which mistakes are understood as part of the development process.

However, if teams are judged or evaluated based on the OKR results, if OKR is used for employee evaluations, monetary incentives, etc., people will only define OKR sets that they can certainly achieve. This means that the comfort zone will not be left or a transition to the learning zone, where innovative ideas can arise in the first place, will not take place.

For this reason, OKR should by no means be linked with performance management or similar systems. Instead, a culture of continuous and frequent feedback should be established, replacing the annual or semi-annual, often one-sided employee discussions. Instead of filling out standardized forms, the participants can discuss in 1:1 conversations how the employees can engage more effectively and how the managers can support them.

4.8.3 Do not use OKR for Everyone and Everything

Some teams tend to formulate everything they do as OKR. This phenomenon can be observed when working with OKR has been communicated as the most important thing in an organization. So if it is suggested that those who have no or few OKR are not working on anything important, OKR will be used inflationarily for everything.

To counteract this, two types of work must be distinguished:

- Business as Usual (short BAU): The work for stability today (Keep the lights on)
- Strategic changes: The work for competitiveness tomorrow (Turn the lights on)

Both types of work are equally important, but require different approaches. Even if the intention is understandable that everyone in an organization should use the same framework to have a uniform approach, it is time to accept the complex reality of the 21st century, according to which there is not the one right answer (methods, frameworks, tools, etc.) for all kinds of problems. Here, ambidexterity is required.

For problems where the relationship between cause and effect is already known (complicated problem situations), the prior knowledge of the experts is sufficient to implement suitable solutions without having to experiment. Therefore, if teams have to write OKR for topics such as monthly payroll or regular security updates, the participants rightly feel like they are in an "OKR theater".

On the other hand, until the introduction of OKR, teams are hardly confronted with visualizing, prioritizing, and making their BAU transparent and measurable. But introducing OKR just to remedy this deficiency is not treating the cause, but the symptom, and should therefore be avoided. There are numerous other frameworks and tools suitable for handling recurring tasks or implementing known solutions, while OKR is suitable for validating hypotheses and learning in a complex environment.

4.9   Final Thoughts

As it is often said, "All models are wrong, but some are useful." If a framework is blindly copied without engaging with it, rarely anything good comes out of it. To avoid a "cargo cult", the approach must be considered and designed differently in each individual context. No OKR introduction is comparable to another.

When introducing OKR, but also other frameworks, it is important to first ask the question "Why?" All participants must be clear about what the framework is supposed to help with or which problems are to be solved by OKR, how the success of an OKR introduction becomes visible, and at which behavior the participants should be alarmed.

If only one aspect could be taken from the entire OKR framework, it would be the focus on outcomes. Because this means not working harder, but smarter, by not focusing on the quantity of produced outputs, but on the outcome generated with as little investment as possible.

References

Covey, S., C. McChesney, J. Huling, and A. Maron. 2016. *The 4 disciplines of execution*. Simon & Schuster.
Cutler, J. 2022. North star playbook. https://amplitude.com/north-star .
Derby, E., and D. Larsen. 2018. *Agile Retrospektiven: Übungen und Praktiken, die die Motivation und Produktivität von Teams deutlich steigern*. O'Reilly Media.
Drucker, P. 1954. *The practice of management*. Harper Business.
Gothelf, J. 2021. OKRs at scale. https://jeffgothelf.com/blog/okrs-at-scale/ .
Grove, A. 2015. *High output management*. Vintage.

Klau, R. 2013. How Google sets goals: OKRs/startup lab workshop. https://www.youtube.com/watch?v=mJB83EZtAjc .

Martin, R. L. 2013. *Playing to win*. Harvard Business Review Press.

Rummelt, R. 2011. *Good strategy, bad strategy*. Profile Books.

Schwaber, K., and J. Sutherland. 2020. Der Scrum Guide. https://scrumguides.org/docs/scrum-guide/v2020/2020-Scrum-Guide-German.pdf .

Seiden, J. 2019. *Outcomes over output*. Sense & Respond Press.

Snowden, D. 2020. The cynefin framework. https://thecynefin.co/about-us/about-cynefin-framework/ .

Wikipedia. o. J. Goodharts Gesetz: https://en.wikipedia.org/wiki/Goodhart's_law .

Wodtke, C. 2016. *Radical focus*. Cucina Media.

Wodtke, C. 2021. *Radical focus*. 2nd ed. Cucina Media.

Cansel Sörgens has been working in product organizations since 2008, which rapidly scaled from 100 to 1000 employees, where she led strategic, cross-departmental projects as a product and portfolio manager and was responsible for (Agile) organizational development. Since 2016, she has implemented OKR in B2B, B2C, and B2B2C organizations of all sizes from different industries. She shares her long-standing and practical OKR expertise as a speaker and founder of international events such as OKR Lean Coffee, OKR Open Space, Reshaping the Future of OKRs.

Contact: https://cansel-soergens.com I okrs@cansel-soergens.com

Product Roadmaps

5

Opportunities and Risks of a Classic in the Product Management Toolkit

Dominik Busching and Lutz Göcke

Abstract

Product managers use a variety of tools in their daily work to drive the development of digital products. A much-discussed artifact is the product roadmap. As roadmaps, in addition to some advantages, also bring a number of risks, they have recently been increasingly criticized in modern product management in the agile development context. This article shows that, when used correctly, product roadmaps are a very effective tool in the toolkit of product managers. Since the aim of this chapter is less a theoretical treatise than a tangible illustration of the benefits and risks of roadmaps in practice, the fictitious and tongue-in-cheek Internet of Things (IoT) company "DigiDog" will accompany us through the chapter. This illustrative case study is based on the authors' experiences in the context of developing IoT products (Smart Home, Automotive, Mobility).

5.1 Classification of Product Roadmaps

Product roadmaps can be understood as artifacts of product strategies. They represent a bridge from the product strategy to concrete product tactical artifacts (release plan, product backlog, etc.) and decisions (Pichler 2016). Fig. 5.1 illustrates this relationship.

D. Busching
tado°, München, Germany
e-mail: dominik.busching@tado.com

L. Göcke (✉)
Nordhausen University of Applied Sciences, Nordhausen, Germany
e-mail: lutz.goecke@hs-nordhausen.de

© The Author(s), under exclusive license to Springer Fachmedien Wiesbaden GmbH, part of Springer Nature 2024
S. Hoffmann (ed.), *Digital Product Management*,
https://doi.org/10.1007/978-3-658-44276-7_5

Fig. 5.1 Delineation of Product Strategy and Product Roadmaps. (Adapted from Pichler 2016; Lombardo et al. 2017; Bassino 2021)

Product roadmaps provide orientation for future product development and the involved stakeholders. Therefore, product roadmaps represent a strategic plan and a tool for alignment and communication (Pichler 2016; Lombardo et al. 2017). In this context, various contents of future product development, e.g. goals or features, are defined on a timeline.

The central benefit of product roadmaps is seen in improved alignment between different participants in product development (see also detailed Chap. 15 by Arne Kittler): **Within a product team**, product roadmaps contribute to all team members having a clear understanding of the necessary steps in product development. This gives team members orientation. This can contribute to better planning of the team's competencies and budgets. Teams can recognize earlier when specific competencies (e.g., data scientists) are needed in the team.

Increased clarity about resource needs is also beneficial for **vertical alignment** with a company's management. For the individual team, this can, for example, facilitate access to specific competencies. Roadmaps can also be useful for strategic planning in the sense of product planning at the portfolio level. And last but not least, roadmaps are often required to determine or justify the need for financing vis-à-vis investors.

And also in **horizontal alignment** with other stakeholders, product roadmaps can be useful. They can support the planning of communication activities. Furthermore, roadmaps can be helpful in training sales and service staff in a timely manner. They can also be useful for integration planning with other software or hardware systems. It is crucial to emphasize that alignment is not a one-way street from a product manager towards the team, management, or other stakeholders, but the product roadmap can be a good basis for generating feedback and input for additional iteration of the product.

5.2 Types of Product Roadmaps

For strategic planning of product development and alignment with various stakeholders, different types of roadmaps can be used. In a systematic literature review, Münch et al. (2020) identify four types of roadmaps: Feature-Based Roadmaps, Goal-Oriented Roadmaps, Outcome-Driven Roadmaps, and Theme-Based Roadmaps. These types differ according to the focused content of the roadmap and the respective ordering criteria of the individual roadmaps.

5.2.1 The "Classic": The Feature-Based Roadmap

Deriving concrete implementation plans with essential milestones from a desired target state corresponds to the classic understanding of strategic planning and has a military origin. In the context of digital product development, such an approach resembles a **Feature-Based Roadmap** (sometimes also briefly called "Feature Roadmap").

In the Feature-Based Roadmap, future development is defined based on a concrete specification of product functions or features (see also Fig. 5.2). Individual features thus receive a concrete temporal assignment (Pichler 2022). Fig. 5.2 illustrates this functionality.

As we will explain in Sect. 5.4, especially Feature-Based Roadmaps carry some risks. For example, the agility and learning of teams are restricted by the specification of concrete features. At the same time, challenges arise for teams in stakeholder management.

5.2.2 Thinking from the End: Goal-Oriented and Outcome-Driven Roadmaps

In addition to planning focused purely on output (i.e., realized features), alternatives have been increasingly developed in recent years. Pichler (2016) suggests, with a **Goal-Oriented Roadmap**, to integrate the underlying goals of individual development steps into the roadmap in addition to features. This gives the features a direction and a justification, which can be helpful for a common alignment. Pichler (2016) aligns the goals with the Pirate Metrics:

Pirate Metrics
Pirate Metrics represent a common categorization of metrics, which was developed by Dave McClure (founder of "500 Startups"). Pirate Metrics got their name from their acronym AARRR. The Pirate Metrics are based on a customer lifecycle model (Croll and Yoskovitz 2013):

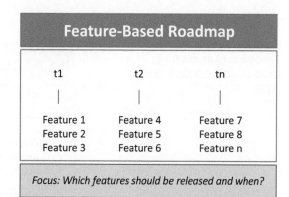

Fig 5.2 Feature-Based Roadmap. (Adapted from Pichler 2016, 2022; Münch et al. 2020)

- **Acquisition**—Example: What percentage of ad viewers visit the website?
- **Activation**—Example: What percentage of website visitors register?
- **Retention**—Example: What percentage of users use the app daily?
- **Referral**—Example: What percentage of users recommend the product 7 days after starting to use it?
- **Revenue**—Example: What percentage of registered users purchase the subscription?

Outcome-Driven Roadmaps represent another alternative to Feature-Based Roadmaps. The basic idea here is that not specific outputs, i.e., product features, but outcomes in terms of Customer Value or Business Value are planned. From an Outcome-Driven Roadmap, it is therefore not clear when which feature will be realized, but which customer problem or business value is to be solved or achieved at which time (see Fig. 5.3).

t1 = 2nd Quarter 2023

- Outcome I: Increase the conversion rate from 5% to 7%
- Outcome II: Solve the problem of people with impaired vision not being able to use our product.
- Outcome III: Reduction of the dropout rate in the checkout process (20% → 17%) ◄

The introduction of Goal-Oriented Roadmaps **and** Outcome-Driven Roadmaps creates a small language confusion (Pichler 2022), as goals (Goals) are always also designed to achieve the targeted results (Outcomes) when these goals are achieved. Thus, desired Outcomes are always also Goals. Nevertheless, the focus of the Outcome-Driven Roadmap more strongly acknowledges the customer perspective and is therefore more compatible with other current developments in digital product management. This focus creates a high complementarity of the Outcome-Driven Roadmap to the Opportunity-Solution-Tree (see Chap. 6 by Philip Steen and Alexander Hipp) and the development of OKRs (see Chap. 4 by Cansel Sörgens). In addition, by contrasting Output vs. Outcome, the difference to Feature-Based Roadmaps is more clearly highlighted than with a Goal-Oriented Roadmap. For this reason, we will continue to talk about Outcome-Driven Roadmaps.

Fig. 5.3 Outcome-Driven Roadmaps. (Adapted from Lombardo 2017; Münch et al. 2020)

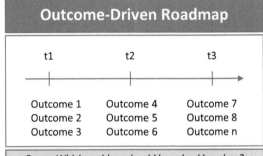

Fig. 5.4 Theme-Based Roadmap. (Adapted from Lombardo 2017; Münch et al. 2020)

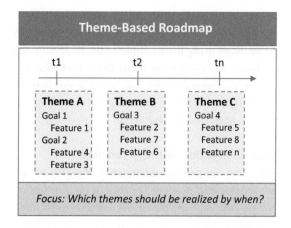

5.2.3 Packed in Boxes: Theme-Based Roadmaps

In **Theme-Based Roadmaps**, the targeted outputs are categorized into themes and the themes to be achieved are assigned to a specific time period. The themes can be defined from different perspectives, e.g., the customer benefits they aim to achieve, feature groups, or a business goal. The crucial point with Theme-Based Roadmaps is that the themes are understood by all members of the organization (Lombardo et al. 2017). The following example and Fig. 5.4 illustrate the function of a Theme-Based Roadmap.

---

t1 = 2nd Quarter 2023

- Theme A: Accessibility for users with impaired vision
  - Outcome II: Solution to the problem of people with impaired vision not being able to use our product
    Feature 1: Manual adjustment of font sizes
    Feature 2: Increase in color contrast ◄

The charm of Theme-Based Roadmaps is that themes can have a pulling power when the underlying goals and features are aligned with an understandable theme.

5.3 The Benefits of Product Roadmaps

As you can see, there is not "the one" Product Roadmap, but different companies use very different variants. Despite numerous risks and pitfalls, which will be discussed later, Product Roadmaps are a widely used and popular tool in product management. In digital product management, Goal-Oriented and Outcome-Driven Roadmaps have established themselves in recent years. As will become clear in the further course of the chapter, their decisive practical advantage for product managers lies in the focus on customer value. At the same time, the greatest risks arise from the typical characteristics of Feature-Based Roadmaps. The practical benefits of Product Roadmaps will be illustrated in more detail using the example of the fictional company "DigiDog".

DigiDog develops and sells Internet-of-Things (IoT) products—namely dog bowls that can be connected to the internet. The modern dog of today eats from a DigiDog bowl, which offers numerous advantages for dog and owner. With many millions of dogs worldwide, a billion-dollar business.

Operationalizing Strategy Tangibly

Why does the product manager of DigiDog maintain a Product Roadmap? DigiDog has a sophisticated product strategy in the form of a multi-page text document. It describes which customer problems the company considers essential and how DigiDog intends to address them with its products in the coming years. This gives the strategy a clear direction. For example, it explains that singles in urban areas are increasingly getting small dogs that are alone and hungry at home during the day and that DigiDog wants to develop a solution for their specific needs. Derived from this, the product manager of DigiDog defines in her roadmap that the company will introduce its own (smaller) product variant in the second quarter of next year and how solutions for the most important customer problems will be gradually delivered via software updates. For example, the problem of dog owners wanting to know when their dog had its last meal when they come home is on the agenda for the third quarter. This breaks down the big strategic idea into manageable parts that can be implemented and delivered incrementally.

Planning through Transparency

For the other departments, the additional level of detail in the Product Roadmap compared to the strategy is very helpful. The sales team now knows that it needs to find new sales partners for the product by the end of the year. The marketing team can start developing a campaign and corresponding marketing assets in good time. And the supply chain team can coordinate with the Vietnamese contract manufacturer to set up new production lines and purchase critical components at favorable prices in good time. Thanks to the transparency provided by the roadmap, other stakeholders become capable of planning and taking action.

Better Communication Thanks to Visualization

In theory, the product manager of DigiDog could also inform her colleagues about planned product launches by email or publish them in a table. However, the intuitively understandable visualization on a timeline makes it easier to see the product launch in the context of other planned product innovations. For example, the marketing manager immediately notices that the planned market launch coincides closely with another, long-awaited innovation by customers. He then decides to design a joint campaign instead of two independent ones. The supply chain manager realizes when looking at the timeline that the peak of production would fall exactly into the Christmas season and planned factory holidays. She then plans additional shifts in the pre-Christmas period to be able to meet all expected delivery obligations in time.

Opportunity for Feedback and Input

The roadmap makes it clear that the introduction of the new product is still several months away. This gives various stakeholders in the company the opportunity to incorporate their experience and expertise into the development. For example, an employee in DigiDog's customer support notices that a customer problem frequently mentioned in support tickets is only supposed to be solved months after the product launch via a software upgrade. He shares his experiences with the product manager and substantiates his assessment with corresponding figures. Subsequent analyses by the product team confirm the hint, whereupon the product manager reprioritizes and updates the roadmap.

Product Evangelism

Among the employees of all departments at DigiDog, there are many enthusiastic dog fans who strongly identify with the company's mission. The product manager knows that the success of her product ultimately also depends on how much the colleagues from other departments will put themselves into it. After all, the new bowl not only needs to be developed, but also produced, advertised, distributed, and represented in customer support. Therefore, the product manager regularly invests time to not only inform her colleagues about upcoming changes, but also to inspire them for it. The product roadmap is an important tool for her in this regard. Long before the development of the product begins, it already expresses that DigiDog plans to address a certain customer problem. The product manager makes the roadmap available centrally in the company and ensures that eventually everyone in the company knows it. She regularly shows the roadmap in meetings and presentations to graphically support her explanations, and she repeatedly refers to it in her internal communication. Because what is already a well-thought-out and sensible plan for her as a product manager is still abstract and diffuse for many of her colleagues. The roadmap helps her to transport the "storyline" behind the product strategy. The more often her colleagues see the planned product on the timeline, the more it imprints on them. This not only gradually turns it from a diffuse intention to a concrete reality in the minds of the DigiDog employees, but it even creates real anticipation. Many employees are filled with pride and confidence that their company has recognized the most important problems in the market and has planned solutions for them. But not only employees, but also the owners and investors of DigiDog are pleased to see that the relevant challenges have been recognized in product management and that they have put their money on the right horse.

Expectation Management and Focus

A strategy allows for focus by not only outlining which opportunities one wants to seize, but also making it easier to say "no" to all other opportunities. This focus is also expressed on the product roadmap. So it also becomes clear what DigiDog does not intend to develop for the time being.

Some customer needs are therefore explicitly not addressed, even though they are considered important by various stakeholders in the company. This allows these stakeholders, on the one hand, to seek dialogue with the product manager to understand her strategic considerations and possibly influence them. On the other hand, it also allows them to possibly put their own expectations aside and focus on the actual plans.

5.4 The Risks of Product Roadmaps

The benefits of product roadmaps are countered by some risks in product management. These risks are explained in more detail below. We distinguish between risks for stakeholder management and risks for product development. At this point, it is important to note that the risks can occur with all types of roadmaps. However, the risks are particularly pronounced with the feature-based roadmap, while outcome-driven roadmaps reduce a number of the risks through their focus on results.

5.4.1 Risks for Stakeholder Management

Some of the risks lie in communication with stakeholders outside the product team responsible for development. These risks can lead not only to a loss of trust, but also to financial costs.

Illusion of Predictability and Disappointed Expectations
A significant risk of roadmaps is that they create the deceptive appearance of reliable predictability of the future, especially in the typical representation on a timeline.

In modern digital product management with ever faster innovation cycles, it has been recognized in recent years that developments in the future often occur differently and more dynamically than expected (Bennet and Lemoine 2014). On the one hand, the external context of a company changes, for example when competitors release new products or technical innovations open up new opportunities and risks. On the other hand, the internal context of the company also changes, for example when the product team better understands customer needs, central assumptions prove to be wrong (Lichtenthaler 2020; Göcke and Weninger 2021) or the solution of a technical challenge turns out to be unexpectedly difficult or easy (Silva et al. 2020). Decision-makers can easily fall prey to the illusion of perfect predictability in uncertain contexts (Zhang and Cueto 2017). However, companies that manage to respond quickly to such changes in uncertain environments are more successful than those that rigidly stick to their outdated plans.

For this reason, agility has established itself as a central concept in software development in recent years (Rigby et al. 2016). If a company wants to remain flexible in a dynamic environment, a product roadmap can only be a snapshot at a certain point in time. The roadmap takes into account the internal and external context at this moment as best as possible, but continues to evolve with the changing context. While the roadmap is logically a living document for product managers, whose strength lies precisely in its constant updating, other stakeholders in the company (e.g., controlling) often assume more stability and bindingness.

Problems arise when stakeholders in the company make irreversible and cost-related decisions based on a supposedly long-term stable roadmap. For example, if the marketing manager of DigiDog commissions a large billboard campaign for the market launch of the new product and the market start or scope of functions changes at short notice, this is not only annoying, but also expensive. The product manager is then accused of not being able to "plan sensibly", even though she did not want her roadmap to be understood as a binding plan. The risk of an illusion of predictability and disappointed expectations is therefore particularly pronounced in feature-based roadmaps.

Misunderstandings due to Different Interpretations

Product roadmaps can only be a useful tool in stakeholder management if all stakeholders interpret the elements on the roadmap identically. This is particularly likely to fail with feature-based roadmaps, where not the customer problem to be addressed is outlined, but the supposed solution is anticipated before it has even been validated and developed. In the worst case, this solution—the feature—is even given a catchy name instead of just describing it qualitatively. This opens up a wide space for interpretations, into which all stakeholders can project what they personally consider important (Weick 1995; Weeth et al. 2020). In addition to the feature-based roadmap, this risk can also arise with outcome-driven roadmaps or theme-based roadmaps if the outcome is not concretely formulated or a too vague theme has been defined.

When the marketing manager of DigiDog discovers the feature "DigiPlay" on the roadmap, he is pleased that the dog bowls will soon be playing Spotify songs, which he has long been demanding as a "killer feature". A saleswoman, on the other hand, enthusiastically tells the buyer of a large pet supply chain that he will soon be able to order DigiDog bowls in a robust version for playful puppies from her. Meanwhile, the product manager of DigiDog wonders why no one in the company is starting to prepare for the introduction of the new product category of internet-connected dog toys, even though she has come up with a catchy working title with DigiPlay.

5.4.2 Risks for Product Development

In addition to communicative risks towards other stakeholders in the company, roadmaps also offer a number of psychological pitfalls for the product teams themselves. Product managers with the ambition to develop the best possible product for their customers should be aware of these so that they and their teams do not stumble over them. The risks occur primarily with feature-based roadmaps.

Analysis Paralysis

Ideally, only things for which there is a data-based value hypothesis should be on a road-map, so that the subjective opinions of individuals do not determine which products are ultimately built. As elsewhere in product management, balance and pragmatism are important in practice during analysis, so that an excessive demand for accuracy does not lead to paralysis and ultimately no forward-looking planning in the team.

Fixations

Product managers aim to develop products that create great value for the company. However, at the time of planning a roadmap, it is often not yet clear which elements will generate particularly high value, for example because customer needs have not yet been sufficiently well analyzed and understood. The planning of a roadmap can easily lead to so-called fixations in the minds of team members. Fixations limit cognitive operations and can thus influence the effectiveness of problem-solving processes (Smith 2003).

Fixations occur subconsciously and can refer to both concrete ideas for realization and generic solution approaches (Jansson and Smith 1991; Smith 2003). If fixations occur when creating a roadmap, they can limit a team at a later point in time in the search for the best solution. This can lead to the team or stakeholders no longer being open to other solution approaches or unconsciously preferring the solution approach in the roadmap.

Learning Trap

For product managers, another risk can arise from the development of a roadmap: Due to concrete ideas of the product at the time of planning, teams or individual team members can easily fall victim to a confirmation bias. Here, new information is identified, selected, interpreted, and processed based on previous assumptions and ideas.

This means that as humans we seek or interpret information in line with our previous opinion. At the same time, a lot of energy is used to defend the previous assumptions and ideas against the new results (Beck 2014). Therefore, a detailed design of the roadmap can lead to a learning trap, which restricts openness to new results.

Escalation of Commitment and Premature Commitment

Especially in very uncertain environments, innovators run the risk of falling into a "Sunk Cost Fallacy" or an "Escalation of Commitment" (Furr and Ahlstrom 2011; Zhang and Cueto 2017): When product teams invest resources (e.g., time, energy, money) in a specific solution approach, costs are incurred. These make it difficult for decision-makers to abandon the chosen path, even if it is not optimal when viewed objectively. The creation of the roadmap can result in high wasted costs (so-called Sunk Costs), which can, for example, make a pivot (change of product orientation) more difficult.

Linked with the illusion of predictability, many temporal and financial resources flow into alignment processes between stakeholders. This investment in the alignment processes represents not only sunk costs for a single team, but for several involved actors. A premature commitment can therefore further increase the risk of wrong decisions due to sunk costs.

Delivery Pressure at the Expense of Customer Value and Team Health
Not only for other departments, but also for the own product team, the public commitment to a roadmap can have unintended consequences. Once the scope of a new feature or the solution to a customer problem is defined and anchored on the roadmap with a possibly arbitrary release date, pressure builds up in the product team to meet this deadline.

What in the positive case ensures a healthy focus on the result can in the worst case lead to the team delivering an immature product or completely exhausting itself to meet an arbitrary deadline. Product managers are themselves part of this product team and could theoretically intervene in time. However, for them in particular, a deviation from their public and widely known plan in the company can feel like failure. Changes to the plan must be explained and justified to colleagues and superiors who may ask uncomfortable questions and exert pressure.

5.5 Success Factors for Product Roadmaps

Product roadmaps can therefore be an extremely useful tool in stakeholder management if you manage to avoid some typical risks. What are the key success factors in their creation and practical use?

5.5.1 Problem Focus Instead of Solution Focus

It is generally wise advice to think in solutions rather than problems. However, in product management in general and in product roadmaps in particular, it is usually the other way around. Especially for product managers, whose job it is to develop solutions for problems, it is tempting to prematurely commit to seemingly obvious solutions and place them as features on the roadmap.

As already explained in Sect. 5.4, this can be psychologically problematic in various ways. However, if instead only the problem to be addressed is found on the roadmap (see Sect. 5.2.2 on Outcome-Driven Roadmaps), not only are false expectations avoided, but the product team also approaches the solution finding process more unbiased and creatively.

The DigiDog product manager also adheres to this design principle of roadmaps to protect her team from the learning trap. Under the "illuminated dog bowl", everyone at DigiDog can imagine more than under the problem "dogs can't find their bowl in the dark". It also costs her some discussions with the DigiDog CEO not to commit to this solution early on, which he personally considers absolutely without alternative. But when her product team starts analyzing the problem in the future, it may unexpectedly find a more effective and simpler solution. Do dogs perhaps respond more positively to sounds than to lighting? Or does the team ultimately find that the supposed problem does not exist at all because dogs simply smell their food in the dark?

5.5.2 Short Review and Update Cycles

As already discussed, plan changes in a dynamic environment are inevitable. The sooner changed circumstances are reflected on the roadmap, the sooner others in the company can react to the new plan.

Although such reviews and updates often occur ad hoc in practice, it is helpful to establish a standard process to always guarantee a minimum level of roadmap currency.

Once a week, the DigiDog product manager checks whether the elements on the product roadmap that are closest in time are still up to date, and makes minor adjustments in consultation with her team if necessary. Once a month, she subjects her roadmap to a detailed review together with colleagues from other departments, during which the medium-term elements are also checked. Has sales heard of an impending innovation from the competition, which is why DigiDog should bring forward a planned market launch? Does the planned marketing campaign and therefore also the feature announced there have to be postponed? Once every six months, the product manager finally checks together with DigiDog management whether the long-term elements of the product roadmap are still consistent with the company and product strategy.

5.5.3 Avoiding Pseudo-Accuracy and Artificial Deadlines

The impression of supposedly perfect plannability is reinforced when even elements far in the future on the roadmap are provided with exact release dates. Since such precise planning not only presupposes that the solution is already known and its implementation is planned through, but also that the context does not change on the way there and the team does not gain new insights, the risk is high that such milestones often have to be postponed.

It is a truism in project and product management that you cannot fix all three variables duration, scope (or quality) and cost. So if you commit to the release date, you logically have to remain flexible in terms of scope or quality or cost. Since resources are usually scarce and costs are therefore fixed and quality should not be planned to be compromised in a customer-centric product development, it generally makes the most sense to deliver a good product a little later if necessary. Exceptions, of course, confirm the rule.

Since the DigiDog product manager wants to reduce time corrections first and secondly does not want to signal to her product team that adherence to deadlines takes precedence over quality, she does not work with arbitrary estimates of release dates far in the future on her roadmap, but with a realistic temporal blur. Elements that are more than three months in the future, she represents on a quarterly basis. For example, the new product line for small dogs is noted for the second quarter of next year, not for May 3rd. Elements that are more than a year in the future, on the other hand, she represents on a semi-annual basis, thus making it clear that her team will tackle the problem "dogs can't find their bowl in the dark" sometime in the second half of the year after next.

Even more consistent are categories like "Now/Next/Later" (Lombardo et al. 2017), which do not make any calendar classification, but only show a basic temporal order.

But even one of the most prominent critics of roadmaps, Marty Cagan, admits in his book INSPIRED that in exceptional cases a commitment to a fixed date is necessary to run a company. He suggests that in such cases the product team should make a "High Integrity Commitment" to a date. However, only after the relevant problem or desired goal has been clearly defined and the team has had the opportunity for thorough product discovery; i.e., they could validate a solution to the problem with customers (Cagan 2017).

How well the future can be planned and how necessary precise planning is ultimately also depends on the industry and the respective product. As explained in Sect. 5.6, the requirements in the hardware sector, for example, differ significantly from the development of a software product.

5.5.4 Not less, but better Communication

Roadmaps can tempt product managers to communicate less directly. Finally, there is no need to constantly explain the planned product innovations to all colleagues, but one can conveniently refer to a centrally available document that everyone can keep an eye on independently, and anyone can simply get in touch if they have questions.

However, this is also a dangerous pitfall at the same time. Product roadmaps as an artifact are usually not 100% self-explanatory. Even if they describe customer problems instead of listing features, there is room for interpretation and the derivation from the overarching product strategy is not obvious to everyone. Even a good roadmap therefore needs explanation and contextual classification to be effective as a tool in product management. Therefore, it should not replace direct/personal communication, but support it. This is exactly what the product roadmap is a helpful tool for (see also Chap. 16 by Petra Wille).

Whenever the DigiDog product manager talks about current and future plans, she shows the product roadmap to graphically place the product plans in a larger context. When she explains the product strategy to colleagues over and over again, she uses the roadmap to clarify temporal and content dependencies. Which customer problem needs to be solved first and what follows after that? How do smaller building blocks fit together into a larger strategic initiative? Sometimes she feels like a stuck record, repeating the same story over and over again. In fact, the product manager talks about the roadmap so often that her colleagues in sales and marketing already have her voice in their ears when they look at the roadmap alone. But only through frequent repetition does the roadmap bring the product strategy to life in the minds of the employees and imprint itself as a narrative. Through repeated explanation, the customer problems remain permanently in their consciousness. Only through frequent exchange and discussion about the roadmap does the DigiDog product manager also elicit useful feedback from the reticent supply chain manager. And only through this repeated confrontation of other important stakeholders with the roadmap does it anchor itself in the collective consciousness of the company as a living document, the regular updates of which are no longer surprising, but a matter of course.

5.5.5 From Product Strategy and Vision to Roadmap

A good product roadmap translates a product strategy into a granular, iterative plan to achieve a long-term product vision. As already explained, it is more appropriate to depict relevant customer problems on roadmaps instead of their presumed solutions in the form of features.

But how does a product manager decide which customer problems land on the roadmap and which do not? The starting point is product strategy and vision. There, it should not only be described which overarching value is to be created for customers in the long term, but also which essential customer problems need to be solved on the way there (see also Chap. 3 by Christian Becker).

The product vision of DigiDog can be summarized as follows: "The dog is a completely independent pet." The main problems that need to be solved to achieve this ambitious vision, according to DigiDog's product strategy, are:

- *"The dog cannot provide itself with food."*
- *"The dog cannot play alone."*
- *"The dog cannot go for a walk independently."*
- *"The dog cannot provide medical care for itself in an emergency."*

These customer problems can form the first large thematic blocks on the roadmap as "Epics".

5.5.6 Prioritizing Data-driven and Coordinating with Stakeholders

Ideally, the product strategy already allows for a prioritization that enables the major topics to be arranged in a logical order. A core task in product management is to objectify such prioritization through data. In principle, customer value (Value), usability (Usability), economic viability (Business Viability), and feasibility (Feasibility) must always be weighed and substantiated by hard data as much as possible.

5 Product Roadmaps 101

These factors cannot be evaluated by the product manager alone. The input of various stakeholders is important for a as objective as possible picture and a realistic plan, which is why coordination with other departments is important from the beginning.

From many interviews with dog owners, numerous observations in the field, and initial experiments, the product manager of DigiDog has developed a strong hypothesis that self-supply of food would create the greatest value, including corresponding willingness to pay, for dog owners. Therefore, she sets this main topic as a prioritized epic on the roadmap. Through her field research, she has also gained a deeper understanding of the problem and can further break it down and arrange it in order of relevance: dog food spoils at room temperature in the bowl after two days; a dog needs culinary variety, etc. In her research, she also identified various problems that sound interesting at first glance, but are not strategically relevant on second glance: dogs dirty the floor around their bowl; dogs like to play with their bowl, etc. She therefore does not transfer these customer problems to the roadmap, but notes them in her product backlog. With a preliminary version of her roadmap, the DigiDog product manager makes a first round of coordination with the most important stakeholders: Does her prioritization match the market view of sales? Are the first solution ideas that she has generated together with her product team within the rough time frame that management envisions? Are all necessary development resources available? Little by little, a clearer plan crystallizes. The short-term elements on the roadmap are given more attention in terms of initial dedicated product discovery work, as these customer problems are the first to demand solutions from product development.

5.5.7 Different Representations for Different Target Groups

Since a roadmap must meet different information needs of different target groups throughout the company, it may be advisable to choose different forms of presentation. The top management is mainly interested in whether the product adequately supports the strategic goals of the company. Sales is mainly interested in release dates and the expected added value for customers. And the product team, consisting of developers and designers, primarily needs more transparency about any imminent deadlines and dependencies. Variants with different temporal or content detail levels and an adapted visual representation, for example of dependencies and risks, can meet these needs.

5.6 Product Roadmaps for Hardware or IoT Products

Products in the "Internet of Things" (IoT) area are physical objects or devices that are connected to the internet to exchange data with other objects or systems and thereby create a certain added value for the customer that would not be possible physically alone. Examples are networked industrial machines, vehicles, light bulbs, "smart speakers", or thermostats, all of which can be remotely controlled, read out, or updated via the internet for different purposes. Due to the ever-decreasing costs of sensors, actuators, and connectivity, IoT products have gained significant importance in recent years (Porter and Heppelmann 2014).

IoT products thus combine hardware and software components to create value for customers. From the user's perspective, the separation between hardware and software should generally blur and a holistic perception as "one product" or "integrated solution" be achieved. This claim poses a major challenge to product development, as the development of software and hardware has very different requirements and degrees of freedom.

5.6.1 Hardware versus Software Development

Much modern literature on product management refers explicitly or implicitly to the development of software and services or "Software as a Service" (SaaS). In recent years, agile principles and the concept of "Continuous Discovery and Continuous Delivery" (CI/CD) have become established there.

Recently, these principles from the software world are also increasingly being adapted for the area of hardware development. A prominent example is the aerospace company SpaceX, which successfully applies the agile principle of rapid prototyping to the development of large carrier rockets at considerable capital expenditure. Methods such as 3D printing also allow hypotheses to be validated relatively quickly and cheaply not only on the digital drawing board, but with physical prototypes. Nevertheless, agile principles encounter limits in the development of physical hardware compared to software.

A modern software product is never "finished" and is usually perceived by customers as a living product (for example smartphone apps, PC or console games, office applications). Both small bug fixes and security updates as well as major upgrades can easily be made after the initial "delivery" of the product. In hardware development, however, there is at least a "point of no return" when the physical device goes into series production. For this, tools such as injection molds must be manufactured, machines purchased, production lines and test stations set up, and supplier parts purchased in relevant quantities. Produced devices must be stored, packaged, and transported to retailers and end customers. All of this is complex and expensive. Once the series production of a complex physical product has started, subsequent changes to the product are therefore usually associated with considerable costs. Therefore, long-term and reliable planning has a much higher importance in the hardware area.

5.6.2 Requirements for Hardware Roadmaps

The special planning requirements also affect the roadmaps of hardware products. To provide the benefits discussed above, hardware roadmaps require a longer planning horizon. The need for stability and commitment, even for elements further in the future, is higher than for software, as other stakeholders also need to plan further in advance (for example, ordering components).

Hardware roadmaps are naturally more feature-based than outcome-driven: If, for example, the DigiDog roadmap still only describes the customer problem "owner does not know when the dog last ate" six months in the future, the supply chain team does not know whether it needs to plan the production of a new dog bowl or whether ultimately only a software update should be applied to existing products.

While in the software sector the discovery-delivery cycles can be designed so high-frequency that they practically occur continuously and in parallel, production-based restrictions in the hardware sector require longer iterations between discovery and delivery. Because unlike in the software sector, physical improvements to the device generally cannot be delivered in small increments, but rather accumulate over time to culminate in a new product version.

A prominent example is Apple's iPhone with its annual update cycles. This "Big Bang" logic is also reflected on the hardware roadmap, where in relation to new physical devices, you will find larger, but less frequent releases instead of frequent smaller increments.

However, even in the area of automated mass production, there are now innovative methods that increasingly allow small changes to a product to be phased into ongoing production flexibly and without long retooling times or downtimes. For example, the design of the production lines in Tesla's "Gigafactories" is already optimized for constant changes. As a result, Tesla manages to implement approximately 20 changes per production line per week (Viguié and Justice 2020).

It will be exciting to observe how these new degrees of freedom will change the planning and development of hardware including roadmaps and benefit from the experiences in the software sector.

5.6.3 Roadmaps for IoT Products

Now, in the IoT sector, a particular challenge is that IoT products are hybrids of hardware and software components. First, software (firmware) runs on IoT devices and they are also connected to the internet by definition. And second, many IoT devices can be controlled by applications from a smartphone or PC. This opens up the opportunity to deliver additional "digital added value for the customer" even after the physical devices have been delivered, through firmware updates and improved applications. Here, many principles of agile software development can be applied and this can be reflected accordingly on the roadmap.

The roadmap of an IoT product is therefore also a hybrid. It represents physical hardware components with longer viewing periods, higher stability requirements and less frequent release cycles, and contains software components with shorter viewing periods, more frequent updates and many smaller increments for delivery to customers.

If the end result is to be a product in which software and hardware components interlock seamlessly to create a great user experience "from a single source", then these two "worlds" must closely coordinate in product development and must not operate in silos. Reconciling these different requirements and mutual dependencies between hardware and software is a major and exciting challenge for product managers in the IoT environment.

This coordination is a core task of product managers and a properly used roadmap is a powerful tool in this regard. At the same time, the importance of a long-term product strategy increases, because a roadmap does not define the strategy, but derives from it, makes it transparent and supports its implementation. If there is no product strategy with, for example, a three-year outlook into the future, no meaningful hardware roadmap can be developed for this period and dependencies on firmware and application software can be managed in a timely manner.

5.7   Conclusion

In recent years, the development of product roadmaps has often been critically viewed, particularly in practice-oriented literature. Not a few see the roadmap as a tool that "through the back door" transforms agile processes into a waterfall process. This criticism mainly refers to feature-based roadmaps, where specific functional scopes are planned for a certain point in time. Accordingly, the risks are high when roadmaps are used thoughtlessly and without appropriate classification.

Therefore, alternatives have been increasingly (further) developed in recent years, which put the outcomes in terms of customer value and business value in the foreground. In addition, there are many situations (e.g., financing rounds at start-ups) and environments that benefit greatly from roadmapping or where the development of a roadmap is even of great importance for the success of the project.

The development of IoT products is one of these. The multi-layered structure of IoT products—consisting of software and hardware components—often requires "High Integrity Commitments" in order to develop the hardware correctly and to be able to procure the right parts at the right time.

For product managers to benefit primarily from the development of roadmaps, they should consider important success factors in the development and management of roadmaps. A strong problem focus, short review and update cycles, but also avoiding pseudo-accuracies in the development of roadmaps can contribute to reducing the risks of product roadmaps. Through data-driven prioritization and target group-appropriate presentation forms, product roadmaps are powerful tools to achieve better communication and better alignment with stakeholders.

References

Bassino, N. 2021. *Product direction. How to build successful products at scale*. Happy Self Publishing.
Beck, H. 2014. *Behavioral economics*. Wiesbaden: Springer Gabler.

Bennett, N., and G. J. Lemoine. 2014. What a difference a word makes: Understanding threats to performance in a VUCA world. *Business Horizons* 57(3):311–317.

Cagan, M. 2017. *Inspired: How to create tech products customers love.* Wiley.

Croll, A., and B. Yoskovitz. 2013. *Lean analytics: Use data to build a startup faster.* O'Reilly.

Furr, N., and P. Ahlstrom. 2011. *Nail it then scale it: The entrepreneur's guide to creating and managing breakthrough innovation.* NISI Institute.

Göcke, L., and R. Weninger. 2021. Business model development and validation in digital entrepreneurship. *Digital Entrepreneurship* 71.

Jansson, D. G., and S. M. Smith. 1991. Design fixation. *Design Studies* 12(1):3–11.

Lichtenthaler, U. 2020. Agile innovation: The complementarity of design thinking and lean startup. *International Journal of Service Science, Management, Engineering, and Technology (IJSSMET)* 11(1):157–167.

Lombardo, C. T., B. McCarthy, E. Ryan, and M. Connors. 2017. *Product roadmaps relaunched: How to set direction while embracing uncertainty.* O'Reilly Media, Inc.

Münch, J., S. Trieflinger, E. Bogazköy, P. Eißler, B. Roling, and J. Schneider. 2020. Product roadmap formats for an uncertain future: A grey literature review. In *2020 46th Euromicro conference on software engineering and advanced applications (SEAA)*, 284–291. IEEE.

Pichler, R. 2016. *Strategize: Product strategy and product roadmap practices for the digital age.* Bd. 2. Pichler Consulting.

Pichler, R. 2022. *Strategize: Product strategy and product roadmap practices for the digital age.* Bd. 2. Pichler Consulting.

Porter, M. E., and J. E. Heppelmann. 2014. How smart, connected products are transforming competition. *Harvard Business Review* 92(11):64–88.

Rigby, D. K., J. Sutherland, and T. Hirotaka. 2016. Embracing agile: How to master the process that's transforming management. *Harvard Business Review* (50):40–48.

Silva, D. S., A. Ghezzi, R. B. de Aguiar, M. N. Cortimiglia, and C. S. ten Caten. 2020. Lean startup, agile methodologies and customer development for business model innovation: A systematic review and research agenda. *International Journal of Entrepreneurial Behavior & Research.*

Smith, S. M. 2003. The constraining effects of initial ideas. In *Group creativity: Innovation through collaboration*, Hrsg. P. B. Paulus and B. A. Nijstad, 15–31. Oxford University Press.

Viguié, A., and J. Justice. 2020. Tesla Agile Success. https://en.abi-agile.com/tesla-agile-success/.

Weick, K. E. 1995. *Der Prozess des Organisierens.* 8th ed. Suhrkamp.

Weeth, A., J. K. Prigge, and C. Homburg. 2020. The role of departmental thought worlds in shaping escalation of commitment in new product development projects. *Journal of Product Innovation Management* 37(1):48–73.

Zhang, S. X., and J. Cueto. 2017. The study of bias in entrepreneurship. *Entrepreneurship Theory and Practice* 41(3):419–454.

Dominik Busching is the Head of Product Management at tado°, a leading European "Smart Thermostat" provider based in Munich. The product range of tado° extends from connected hardware, smartphone apps, and paid subscriptions to innovative energy contracts. As a trained psychologist, Dominik Busching places particular emphasis on product development oriented towards customer needs. Prior to his role at tado°, he worked as a business consultant for European energy suppliers, focusing on strategy and product issues, most recently as a manager for Deloitte.
Contact: dominik.busching@tado.com

Lutz Göcke is a Professor of Digital Management at Nordhausen University of Applied Sciences. He is the initiator and head of the Digital Product Management (B.A.) degree program as well as the University Incubator for Entrepreneurship (HIKE) at Nordhausen University of Applied Sciences. He teaches and researches on digital innovations, business model innovations, and corporate entrepreneurship. Before his appointment at Nordhausen University, Lutz Göcke worked for several years as a digital product manager at Volkswagen AG.
Contact: lutz.goecke@hs-nordhausen.de

Product Discovery

Understanding Problems and Developing Promising Solutions

6

Philip Steen and Alexander Hipp

Abstract

The article describes how important Product Discovery is in order to work on the right product solutions in digital product management that generate real added value for customers. To this end, the basic goals and principles, such as outcome orientation, user centricity, and the iterative approach in an interdisciplinary team, of a Product Discovery are explained. Following this, the differences between a project-based and a continuous Discovery are presented, before individual Discovery frameworks and tools are introduced. The article concludes with some practical tips for implementing a Product Discovery.

6.1 Goals of Product Discovery

"Product discovery is a process to define a product that is valuable, useful, and feasible."
– Marty Cagan, Silicon Valley Product Group

Product Discovery involves all activities of a product team related to the decision of which products, ideas, and features should be implemented. Product Delivery is the way

---

P. Steen (✉)
Norderstedt, Deutschland
e-mail: mail@philipsteen.de

A. Hipp
Beyond, London, England
e-mail: al3xhipp@gmail.com

© The Author(s), under exclusive license to Springer Fachmedien Wiesbaden GmbH, part of Springer Nature 2024
S. Hoffmann (ed.), *Digital Product Management*,
https://doi.org/10.1007/978-3-658-44276-7_6

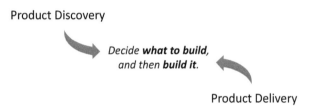

Fig. 6.1 Relationship between Product Discovery and Product Delivery. (*Source*: Adapted from Torres 2016a)

these ideas are actually implemented to generate value for the customer (Torres 2017). While Delivery is about implementing ideas correctly, Discovery, as illustrated in Fig. 6.1, is about implementing the right ideas.

To decide which ideas should be implemented next in a product, there are various methods. In the agile environment, the evaluation and prioritization of ideas using a **backlog** has become established in recent years. Here, all ideas and requirements are collected in a list. This list is then put into a prioritized order by the product manager, often together with other stakeholders, and implemented in this order. However, this approach assumes that all requirements are clear and that there is sufficient knowledge about the customers' requirements. Some critical risks in product development are usually not addressed or only addressed after successful delivery with this approach (see Cagan 2018):

- Benefit (Value Risk): Will the customer use the product and is he willing to pay for it?
- Usability (Usability Risk): Does the customer understand how to use it?
- Feasibility (Feasibility Risk): Is implementation technically possible?
- Economic viability (Business Viability Risk): Is the product profitable?

Without the use of Product Discovery, one would only find out how customers interact with a product or product increment and whether it is actually accepted in the market after its completion and marketing. This is the most expensive way to find out the value of an idea.

In contrast to traditional requirements engineering, where requirements are (exclusively) obtained and prioritized from clients, Discovery focuses on user needs and maximizing customer value. It is not about a detailed examination of technical feasibility, but about gaining a deep understanding of the customers. Without researching the needs of the users and validating assumptions about the target group before implementation, product teams run the risk of developing products and features that are ultimately not used by the customer. Correcting this retrospectively in further iterations would cost a lot of time and money and tie up valuable (development) resources.

These risks can be reduced by regularly using Product Discovery. Instead of testing product increments with customers only after completion, the basic assumptions behind a product or feature should be validated with customers during Product Discovery. This involves checking whether a real customer problem is being solved, whether the solution is usable by the customer, and whether it is technically feasible. Thus, ideas are improved early in the process through real customer feedback, the market is already analyzed, and the business opportunity is validated. This helps to identify the ideas with the highest potential before product development. This can reduce uncertainty in the product development process and the duration of the feedback cycle.

As a rule, there is always more ideas in a product team than there is capacity for implementation. Upon closer inspection, however, it is usually found that not all ideas are as promising as they initially appear. People in general, and product managers in particular, are good at finding solutions and directly solving an identified problem. However, when solving problems, people often rely on their own experiences or personal needs and values. This pattern works well for solving everyday life problems. However, when creating digital products, it is usually not about solving personal problems, but the problems of users, who usually have different personalities, life circumstances, and abilities.

Before a solution can be developed in the form of a product or feature, the actual customer problem and – even more importantly – the people for whom the problem is to be solved should be sufficiently researched and understood. To do this, it is essential at the beginning of a Product Discovery to seek personal conversation with people from the target group in order to build a relationship with them. This is one of the great opportunities of Product Discovery: to identify the most important user problems early on and to see whether implementation makes sense at the current time. This means that there is additional effort before the actual implementation; however, this can save valuable time in the Delivery phase and avoid wrong paths. In the **Product Delivery,** it is then ultimately about integrating the Discovery results sensibly into the product.

The ratio of Discovery to Delivery often falls in favor of the Delivery phase in most companies. On the one hand this is due, to the unequal distribution of developers to user researchers, designers, and product managers. On the other hand, many teams, once they identified a potential solution through a successful Discovery, quickly fall into a "Delivery mode".

Product teams should therefore regularly answer the following questions critically
- Are we still solving the most important customer problem and at the same time creating the highest counter value for our company?
- Do we fully understood the problem to be solved?
- What did we learn last week, and could this new insight bring about a change of direction?

To validate ideas before implementation, the previously mentioned backlog can be divided into two separate areas. Based on the product strategy and the roadmap, all ideas first come into a **Discovery Backlog** (often also called idea backlog). The ideas from this backlog are then validated through a discovery and their priority is determined.

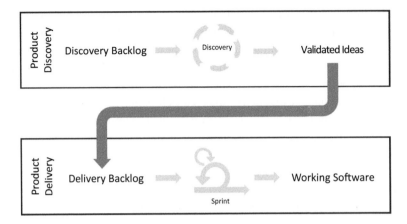

Fig. 6.2 Process in Dual Track Agile. (*Source*: Own illustration)

As a result of the discovery phase, a validated **Delivery Backlog,** is created, which only contains user stories for which the critical risks in terms of usability, feasibility, and viability have already been assessed.

This separation between delivery and discovery is often referred to as **Dual Track Agile** and is shown in Fig. 6.2.

6.2 Basic principles of a Product Discovery

The specific design of a Discovery depends on various factors. Depending on the company, product, team composition, and current question, product teams have different methods and procedures available. Nevertheless, there are some basic philosophies or principles that apply to every discovery and are briefly presented below.

6.2.1 Outcome Orientation

While the delivery phase is about implementing already validated ideas as efficiently as possible, the goal of Product Discovery is to find out which ideas have real customer benefit. It's not about implementing as many functions as possible, but rather finding out exactly those ideas that have actual added value for the customer and are therefore worth implementing.

It is important to focus on the outcome rather than the output. While output refers to the produced results, i.e., the finished product features, **Outcome** describes the changes in customer behavior that are achieved through the implemented features.

6.2.2 User Centricity and Problem Focus

In Product Discovery, the focus is always on the user. Instead of taking an internal, product-focused or sales-driven perspective and defining solutions from a company perspective, the customer is at the center.

The starting point for a Product Discovery can be a product idea, a change in the market, or an identified customer problem. Regardless of the starting point of the discovery, the first step is to understand the customer problem as comprehensively as possible. Instead of generating solutions and specifying a concrete implementation for an idea, the discovery is more about initially validating an idea by understanding the problem in detail. Customers should be directly involved in the discovery, as this can question and identify their needs, problems, wishes, concerns, goals, and motivations. Only when a deep understanding of the problem and the associated reasons and behaviors has been gained, meaningful solution approaches can be developed. Instead of committing to a solution path too early, the problem should be thoroughly understood from different perspectives within the team. This leads to a more comprehensive understanding, diverse solution ideas, and ultimately better products that are used more intensively.

6.2.3 Iterative and Experimental Approach

A fundamental assumption in conducting Product Discovery is that many initial ideas are wrong and products or features will not work. The difficult task is to find out which ideas will not work and which assumptions turn out to be wrong.

Simply asking customers is usually not enough, as they can often describe their problems well, but rarely know a (good) solution to the problem. To find out what really works, it is often better to let customers try out a product idea and observe their behavior and reactions.

There are often multiple alternative ways to solve a customer problem. Therefore, to find out how good or bad an idea is, potential solutions must be tested iteratively. Depending on the type of product, this can be done through different methods. Instead of delivering finished features, prototypes can be used and validated "on the customer". Based on user feedback, it is then decided which ideas should be pursued and which ideas should be discarded. This approach allows ideas to be validated with relatively little effort and only the most promising ideas to be actually implemented.

Openness to Outcomes
Product Discovery is not about finding out how to best implement a feature, but rather about finding out what should be implemented at all. For this reason, the process of discovery must be open to outcomes.

The following results can come out of a Product Discovery:

- More Discovery: The result of a discovery could be that not enough information was collected. In this case, further iterations are needed to understand individual problem areas more deeply, identify the most important customer problems, and develop suitable solution approaches.
- Discard Idea: Another result can be that an idea should not be pursued further. Reasons for this can be, among others, that no real customer problem is being solved or that no usable or technically feasible solution for the customer problem can be found with reasonable effort.
- Implement Idea: If a relevant customer problem is identified and a suitable solution is found that is viable, usable, and implementable, it should be implemented in the delivery phase.
- Pivot: If it is found in the discovery that the original idea cannot be implemented or that the customer problem is actually a different one, the direction or focus should be changed. In this case, the original idea is discarded in order to pursue a different, more promising idea instead.

6.2.4 Interdisciplinarity

While the composition of a product team in Product Delivery is usually fixed, the composition of the people involved in a discovery often varies from discovery to discovery. The composition depends, among other things, on the topic, the available time, and the available people.

At first glance, it may seem sensible to use the development team only in Product Delivery to maximize implementation speed and thus generate customer value more quickly. However, in recent years, the idea has gained ground that, in addition to the product manager and a user experience designer, software developers should also participate in Product Discovery.

The reason is that technology is a central driver of a product's functionality and today's software products cannot be created without a deep technical understanding.

Depending on the topic and company structure, additional stakeholders e.g. from marketing, sales, customer support, legal or finance can be useful participants in a Product Discovery to enable true cross-functional collaboration.

The advantage here is that problems and potential solutions can be viewed from different perspectives, expertise from various areas can be included, and all participants can learn about the problems to be solved directly from the user and generate solution approaches with their own expertise.

6.3 Manifestations of a Product Discovery

While the goals and basic principles of a product discovery are independent of the product, product team, and company, the specific design of a product discovery and its interaction with product delivery can vary. This chapter will illustrate the difference between a continuous and a project-based discovery and explain in which cases which variant should be preferred.

6.3.1 Project-based Discovery

A project-based discovery describes a project-like, limited period prior to implementation of a new product or idea, in which the customer problem is to be understood more deeply and a solution is to be defined. Especially in a product development that is organized in a waterfall-like manner, a discovery phase is practically always organized in a project-like manner. Often, a project-based discovery is carried out by agencies or external contractors.

Many methods of project-based discovery, such as the Design Sprint (see Sect. 6.4.1), work according to a similar principle and mostly take place isolated and outside of product delivery. Putting a product team into a complete discovery mode for a certain period of time to conduct intensive user interviews and usability tests can be particularly useful in the following situations:

- at the start of a time-limited project (e.g., agency work);
- to gain deeper clarity on a specific problem area;
- when many stakeholders need to be involved who either have different levels of knowledge or are geographically separated;
- when conducting hackathons.[1]

Since this requires interrupting the actual work rhythm of the product team this type of discovery is difficult to integrate into the regular agile development process.

Another problem with project-based discovery is that user feedback can usually only be obtained for already finished solutions in the form of products or prototypes. This mainly tests whether the developed solution is usable for the customer, instead of integrating the users from the start in finding the solution, to ensure from the beginning that the right problem is solved or the right product is built.

---

[1]A hackathon is an event where software and hardware are developed as part of an organized event. The goal of a hackathon is to produce useful, creative, or entertaining products or find solutions to given problems within the duration of the event.

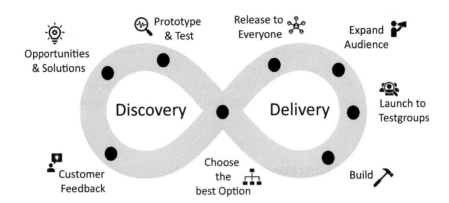

Fig. 6.3 Schematic process of a continuous discovery. (*Source*: Based on Boduch and Wylie 2019)

In all scenarios that focus on the continuous improvement of a product, new product ideas should therefore be validated through the use of continuous discovery.

6.3.2 Continuous Discovery

One of the biggest changes to develop software in a contemporary way is to switch from a project-based to a continuous discovery (Torres 2016a).

In continuous product discovery, the focus is on a product team working together with users to define a problem and then develop a solution. The most important factor here is the frequency with which the product team refers back to user feedback. The goal of this regular interaction is to iteratively find out users' reactions to planned features or existing products and to directly incorporate the insights gained into product development. In continuous discovery, customer contact becomes a fixed part of a product team's weekly routine, analogous to sprint planning or retrospectives in product delivery. An exemplary process of a continuous discovery is shown in Fig. 6.3.

6.4 Frameworks for Structuring a Product Discovery

In addition to the goals, principles, and manifestations, this chapter will present three frameworks for a product discovery to illustrate concrete procedural models. First, the Design Sprint for project-based discovery will be described, and then the Product Kata and the Opportunity Solution Tree for continuous product discovery will be presented.

6.4.1 Design Sprint

Especially for teams that are new to the topic of Product Discovery, the multitude of possible methods can make entry into discovery difficult. Google Ventures has developed a project-based framework called Design Sprint, which is a fixed sequence of methods that allows complex problems to be understood as completely as possible within a week, solutions to be developed, and these to be tested with customers (Knapp et al. 2016).

A Design Sprint is designed for a working week and provides specific goals, methods, and checklists for each day. Suggestions are made for the required team size, team composition, and time allocation of tasks. The process of a Design Sprint is as follows:

Monday
The first day of the sprint is used for goal definition. Here it is determined which users should be considered and which section of the user experience should be examined more closely. Questions that should be answered in the sprint are recorded and graphically represented. To obtain as detailed a goal definition as possible, expert interviews are conducted.

Tuesday
On the second day, initial solution ideas are developed. First, existing ideas are researched and presented. Then, the entire team develops new/alternative solution ideas and visualizes them in the form of sketch-like drawings.

Wednesday
Ideally, by the start of day three, the team already has a stack of potential solution approaches. Since not all ideas can be tested, Wednesday morning is about evaluating each approach and filtering out the ideas that best contribute to the goal defined on Monday. These ideas are then transferred into a sequence plan in the afternoon, which presents the individual steps of the solution in more detail and at the same time forms the basis for creating a prototype.

Thursday
On the fourth day, the sequence plan from the previous day is transformed into a prototype. This is intended to answer the most important questions regarding the goal set on the first day in user interviews. The prototype should look as realistic as possible for the customer and have a sufficient level of detail to enable valid customer feedback.

Friday
On the last day of the Design Sprint, the created prototype is tested with real users. It has often been found that five interviews are sufficient to validate a solution idea (Nielsen and Landauer 1993): The test persons are guided through the prototype by an

interviewer, while the rest of the team watches via video chat in a separate room and takes notes. At the end of the day, it is then jointly evaluated which ideas will be pursued further and which adjustments may be necessary.

6.4.2 Product Kata

The Product Kata is based on the Toyota Kata, a framework for continuous improvement. As with a kata in martial arts, a process is repeatedly executed to optimally learn the technique. The goal of the Toyota Kata is to achieve improvement in the company by focusing on rapid learning. The Toyota Kata describes a procedural model for analyzing problems and solving them with the help of small experiments (Blum 2016; Rother 2009).

Melissa Perri (2015) has transferred the principles of the Toyota Katas to the development of software products and described with the Product Kata a framework that uses short, user-centered iterations to discover solutions for existing customer problems. The Product Kata helps product teams, through a constant repetition of the discovery process, not to think directly in solutions, but first to gain a sufficient understanding of the users and their environment and problems, in order to then move in small steps towards a suitable problem solution. Fig. 6.4 shows how an iteration of the framework runs exemplarily.

In the first step of the Product Kata, the **current situation** in the company, the company vision, and the company goal are explored. Based on this, a product goal in the form of a product KPI or a desired target state is defined. An exemplary target state could be to reduce the number of support calls to zero through a self-service area in the product.

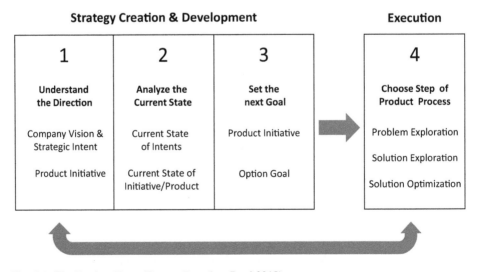

Fig. 6.4 The Product Kata. (*Source*: Based on Perri 2018)

6 Product Discovery 117

In the second step, the **status quo** is analyzed in relation to the set goal. This involves analyzing the current customer behavior and working out the biggest problems and obstacles to achieving the set goal. Instead of now directly implementing one or more solutions, the Product Kata is about first clarifying open questions regarding customer behavior. The basic idea is that every open question is an obstacle to achieving the target state. For the example of customer service, the calls per day and the reasons for the calls should be examined more closely.

In the third phase of the Product Kata, a **first subgoal** is then defined, which should contribute to achieving the overall goal. This is worked out using the following questions:

- What is working well so far?
- What is bad?
- What needs to be improved to achieve the goal?

An exemplary subgoal could be to reduce the calls per day by 10%. If no current data is available, data acquisition for a better understanding of the situation could also be a first subgoal.

In the fourth step, individual **experiments to achieve the subgoal** are then defined and carried out. The experiments are about comparing the expected customer behavior with the actual customer behavior.

For example, if it is found in the second step that customers often call with a certain question, a newsletter with content to answer exactly this question could be sent as an experiment. Afterwards, it is measured whether and how the call behavior changes after the newsletter.

The results from the experiments then represent the initial state for the next iteration of the Product Kata. This process is repeated as often as necessary until the goal initially defined in the first step has been achieved.

6.4.3 Opportunity Solution Tree

The Opportunity Solution Tree is a method for continuous product discovery, used to visually represent a plan to achieve a desired state. The method serves to make implicit assumptions explicit and helps product teams to move away from a pure solution or implementation focus. An Opportunity Solution Tree consists of the following four areas:

- a desired outcome,
- opportunities on how this outcome can be achieved,
- concrete implementation ideas for each opportunity, and
- experiments to validate the ideas themselves or their assumptions.

To create an Opportunity Solution Tree, a desired outcome is first clearly defined. This can be expressed in the form of an increase or decrease in a target metric. The objective of an OKR definition, for example, is a suitable format for this.[2] In the case of a social media platform, a desired outcome could be, for example, to increase user engagement.

Subsequently, all opportunities that contribute to the desired outcome are recorded. Opportunities can be customer needs or unresolved customer problems and desires. If there is no knowledge about this, assumptions can initially be made, which are later validated through user research. In the case of the social media platform, an opportunity could be to make better use of existing content on the platform. Another opportunity could be to encourage users to create more new content.

In the third step, solution approaches or implementation ideas are recorded for each opportunity. Only the ideas that can be assigned to an opportunity are considered. If an idea cannot be assigned to an opportunity, it is not pursued further. Exemplary ideas for the opportunity to make better use of existing content on the social media platform could be features like a like button, a personalized news feed, or notifications for users.

In the last step, experiments are defined for each idea. The experiments should not test the idea itself in the form of a product increment, but the central assumptions behind a solution idea. Exemplary methods for these experiments can be: a concierge test, Wizard-of-OZ tests, Smoke Screens, or Fake-Door tests.[3]

When you connect outcomes, opportunities, ideas, and experiments, you get the Opportunity Solution Tree (Fig. 6.5), which gave the method its name:

Since the Opportunity Solution Tree does not directly think in solutions, but considers opportunities and solutions simultaneously, it is well suited to structure continuous discovery. Furthermore, the method is well suited to retrospectively integrate discovery into an already established delivery process, as discovery results can be assigned to each backlog with this method. By linking the ideas in the backlog with qualitative and quantitative data, the desired outcome behind the ideas becomes clear.

6.5 Product Discovery Toolbox

In addition to the frameworks for project-related and continuous discovery presented in the previous chapter, there are a multitude of individual discovery methods to learn more about users, a product idea, the competition, or your own company. The common goal of these methods is to reduce various risks, such as economic viability, usability, the benefit

---

[2] Objectives & Key Results (short: OKR) is a procedural model to define and track goals and their outcomes. For the OKR concept, see Chap. 4 "Implementing and validating product strategy with Objectives and Key Results (OKR)" by Cansel Sörgens.

[3] For detailed information on the individual methods, see Jacobsen and Meyer (2019).

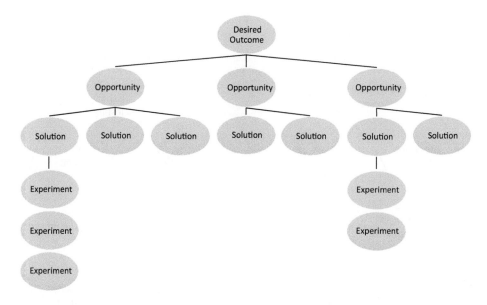

Fig. 6.5 Opportunity Solution Tree. (*Source*: Based on Torres 2016b)

or the feasibility of a product idea. Due to the large number of available methods, the selection can be difficult for beginners in the topic of product discovery.

The selection of a specific method should always start with a clear problem description. The topic and the objective, what to find out in discovery, should be recorded. Possible subject areas of a product discovery are:

- Users: Questions about users, e.g. about behavior, problems and needs
- Product: Questions about your own product, e.g. about usability
- Competition: Questions from an external company perspective, e.g. positioning against the competition
- Organization: Questions from an internal company perspective, e.g. strengths and weaknesses

Based on the subject area, various methods are available. An overview of useful methods divided by areas is shown in Fig. 6.6.

Detailed information on the methods and their specific applications can be found in Erika Hall (2013), Bella Martin and Bruce Hanington (2012) or on the website www.designkit.org/methods.htmlfrom Ideo.org (2020).

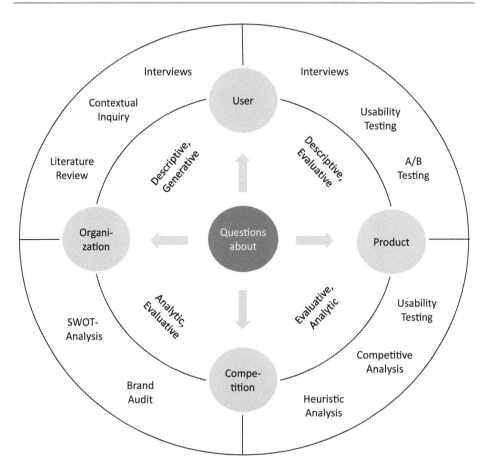

Fig. 6.6 Overview of product discovery methods. (*Source*: Adapted from Hall 2013)

6.6 Practical Tips for Implementing a Product Discovery in the Company

Since product teams always face the challenge of having to achieve results in both discovery and delivery at the same time, the first section critically examines the developments in the two areas and the spread of product discovery in companies. Finally, it describes the challenges that arise when introducing continuous product discovery and how these can be addressed.

6.6.1 Consequences of a Focus on Product Delivery

Significant progress has been made in the professionalization of product delivery in recent years. There have also been such developments in product discovery, but so far they have not become a fixed part of the daily work in many product teams. While, for example, the daily standup has become part of practically all product teams in product delivery, methods from design thinking or the regular conduct of user interviews have not yet been widely adopted.

Although the advantages of a user-centered discovery, which is based on a consistent validation of one's own assumptions by interviewing real users, are known to many companies and in principle also find broad approval, there are still many companies that do not carry out an explicit product discovery.

There are several reasons for this: On the one hand, the recruitment of users and the conduct of interviews are cost-intensive and time-consuming. On the other hand, the insights from user interviews are often not communicated well enough within the company, but remain isolated in individual departments or teams, which diminishes the acceptance of the user interviews. In addition, many teams believe they know their users and their needs well enough and therefore assume that they can predict their behavior in response to product changes.

The assumption of already knowing user needs often also strongly manifests itself in the way a product discovery is conducted: Product teams that assume they know what the customer needs tend to "discover" for a longer period of time in order to then fill their product backlog for several weeks of "delivery" with the result. This results in teams committing themselves at the beginning of a quarter, usually in the form of a detailed roadmap, to develop certain features that have been defined in the discovery and to complete them by a certain point in time.

However, creating a detailed roadmap is based on the false assumption that features can be completed exactly according to plan and directly solve a specific customer problem 100%. Too many teams describe product discovery as a linear process. However, reality shows that a good discovery is anything but linear. Marty Cagan (2012) aptly describes the process as "messy". Therefore, one must be able to react to new insights from analytical data, user interviews, or changes in the market. Therefore, it makes more sense for most teams to continuously identify, validate, and describe new product improvements.

6.6.2 Potential Pitfalls in Implementing Product Discovery

In addition to the challenges already described in Product Discovery, the introduction of continuous Product Discovery often presents additional challenges for product teams.

6.6.2.1 External Control of Product Teams

A typical conflict in the development of digital products lies in the degree of self-determination of the product team. To successfully integrate continuous discovery into the product development process, product teams should be empowered to make decisions independently. Instead of having to work through a product roadmap with predefined features, the team should be responsible from start to finish for validating product features and the path to achieving the goals.

However, this responsibility can only work if the product team has been assembled as a true cross-functional team. For this, the product team needs access to experts from various company areas (e.g., law, customer support, sales, marketing, finance) to independently identify problems and find suitable solutions. Many companies struggle with this. In operational reality, many product teams cannot really act independently and still find it difficult, especially in the area of business evaluation of products, to make decisions independently (Cagan 2019). As soon as the economic decisions of a product lie with a stakeholder outside the product team who determines the roadmap, the team cannot make independent decisions about what should be implemented next. As a result, Product Discovery cannot be properly implemented.

One solution to increase the degree of self-determination of product teams may be to make transparent agreements with stakeholders about decision-making spaces early on. In this way, all participants know which decisions can be made independently within the team and from when stakeholders need to be involved.

6.6.2.2 Output Instead of Outcome

While Product Delivery eventually delivers features and thus the work results become visible, a Product Discovery as a process with unclear results and possibly even an indefinite duration is often difficult for executives to grasp. A feared loss of authority therefore often prevents them from giving the teams the necessary autonomy. Thus, traditional leadership methods of authoritarian management meet modern working methods with self-organized teams. In order to exercise control over the process and make it seemingly predictable, a Product Discovery is then, for example, given a fixed period. This takes away the necessary scope of action from product managers and focuses the product team's attention solely on Product Delivery.

In this case, a practical solution may be to set clear quarterly goals together with the management level, which are formulated in the form of key figures and metrics and not in the form of specific features. This gives product teams the necessary scope of action to implement the right features, hopefully leading to more successful products.

6.6.2.3 No Regular Exchange with the User

Since the recruitment process for user interviews is often complex and expensive and the preparations for an interview usually involve a fairly high amount of time, many companies and teams lose the urge to regularly interact with the target group after some time.

However, this can be significantly simplified by automated or so-called ad-hoc recruitments. Instead of conducting complex personal user interviews, users can be surveyed directly while using a product via smartphone notifications (push notifications), online questionnaires, or even a chat. For B2B products, sales or customer support can also be used to recruit users with a certain usage behavior for a personal interview. It is definitely important to regularly interact with real users so that Product Discovery leads to effective products.

References

Boduch, E., and J. Wylie. 2019. Continous discovery in product-led companies. www.slideshare.net/jfalk415/continuous-discovery-in-productled-companies.

Blum, C. 2016. Die Toyota KATA – Kampfsport oder echtes Erfolgsrezept? www.management-circle.de/blog/die-toyota-kata-kampfsport-oder-echtes-erfolgsrezept.

Cagan, M. 2012. Dual-track agile. https://svpg.com/dual-track-agile.

Cagan, M. 2018. *Inspired – How to create tech products customers love*. 2nd ed. New Jersey: Wiley.

Cagan, M. 2019. Product vs. feature teams. https://svpg.com/product-vs-feature-teams.

Hall, E. 2013. *Just enough research*. New York: A Book Apart.

Ideo.org. Hrsg. 2020. The field guide to human-centered design. www.designkit.org.

Jacobsen, J., and L. Meyer. 2019. *Praxisbuch Usability und UX*. 2nd ed. Bonn: Rheinwerk.

Knapp, J., J. Zeratsky, and B. Kowitz. 2016. *Sprint – Solve big problems and test new ideas in just five days*. New York: Simon & Schuster.

Martin, B., and B. Hanington. 2012. *Universal methods of design*. Essex County: Rockport Publishers.

Nielsen, J., and T. Landauer. 1993. A Mathematical model of the finding of usability problems. In Proceedings of ACM Interchi'93 Conference, Amsterdam.

Perri, M. 2015. The product Kata. https://melissaperri.com/blog/2015/07/22/the-product-kata.

Perri, M. 2018. *Escaping the build trap: How effective product management creates real value*. Sebastopol: O'Reilly Media.

Rother, M. 2009. *Toyota Kata: Managing people for improvement, adaptiveness and superior results*. New York: McGraw-Hill.

Torres, T. 2016a. The rise of modern product discovery. www.producttalk.org/2016/03/rise-modern-product-discovery.

Torres, T. 2016b. Why this opportunity solution tree is changing the way product teams work. www.producttalk.org/2016/08/opportunity-solution-tree.

Torres, T. 2017. The evolution of modern product discovery. www.producttalk.org/2017/02/evolution-product-discovery.

Philip Steen supports small and medium-sized enterprises in digitization and the development of digital products. He initially worked as a product manager and later as a freelancer for companies including Fielmann AG, AIDA Cruises, and Costa Cruises in Asia. In this role, he drove the establishment of new product teams and was responsible for mobile apps and web applications in e-commerce. He completed his master's degree in Business Informatics/IT Management at the Nordakademie in Hamburg.
Contact: mail@philipsteen.de

Alexander Hipp is a Co-Founder of Beyond. Previously, he was active as a Product Lead at the Neobank N26 in Barcelona. There, he worked on the bank's subscription products and card provisioning. Before that, he was part of XING, where he collaborated with the Mobile App Team and Data Engineering. In addition, he is a co-founder of the product management book recommendation platform "PM Library" and has completed a Master's in Communication and Media Management in Karlsruhe and London.
Contact: al3xhipp@gmail.com

Validation of Product Ideas in the Market

7

Experiences, Inspirations and How to Know if Money Can Be Made with Them

Anna Wicher

Abstract

This chapter describes what validation processes can look like and which tools are useful for this purpose. The author shares helpful experiences from practice and leads from the initial conditions of validation to the importance of research work, demonstrating how relevant such preliminary work is in practice for a project. Furthermore, prototyping with elements to be clarified, such as goal definition, UX and UI, and the question of adequate technology, are introduced and subsequently testing is illuminated. Finally, it is shown how successful project ideas can be continued.

7.1 Why Validation?

"One morning, I was standing in the shower and had a great product idea. All I needed afterwards was a little bit of money to implement this idea and make an incredible amount of money."

This is how the development of a new product often begins. Whether as a startup founder who is then looking for an investor, or as an idea generator in a larger corporation who pitches the idea to management, gets an investment for implementation, and begins implementation. The theoretical process of developing a new idea is basically quite simple: Someone has an idea, money is invested, and a new, great product comes onto the market.

A. Wicher (✉)
MissionMe, Hamburg, Deutschland
e-mail: awi@missionme.de

© The Author(s), under exclusive license to Springer Fachmedien Wiesbaden GmbH, part of Springer Nature 2024
S. Hoffmann (ed.), *Digital Product Management*,
https://doi.org/10.1007/978-3-658-44276-7_7

But what is often forgotten—especially in corporate startup projects? All that should happen on the way from the idea to the market-ready, investment-worthy product in a user-centered development: The view of the market and the answering of a few very important questions: What problem of real users out there does the idea actually solve? And is the idea the right solution for this problem? How many people have this problem? How do they solve the problem so far? And most importantly: Are they willing to spend money on the new solution to their problem? If you implement the original idea for a new product in isolation from the outside world—without checking (aka validating) along the way whether you are solving a real user problem—then you skip the often diverse improvements or changes in direction (pivots) that are necessary in most cases to actually make a product from an idea that triggers the necessary willingness to pay in the market to build a functioning business on it.

In reality, the process of developing a new idea is much more chaotic. During the development and validation in the market, you learn a lot about the market and target group, which usually changes the idea and the resulting business model several times.

For ideas that arise in a corporate environment, such changes to the original idea often depend on long decision-making processes. A lot of money has often already been spent on implementing the first idea. Due to limited innovation budgets, only a few ideas can be tested at the same time, and there is a lot of pressure on those who were able to secure an investment. Therefore, and due to the high initial costs, it is very difficult to change the first idea, or even to decide to declare a project as failed and to end it.

How can this be solved? The investment decision for a new product must be separated from the validation by preceding the validation with a small budget. Only with valid market figures and a business plan that includes a view of the market and the answering of a few important questions is the actual investment decision then made. This also works by promoting a culture that sees an innovation project as successful if it has been successfully tested and a data-based decision can be made on this basis as to whether the idea is worth investing in or not. Of course, this requires time, resources and know-how for such preliminary validation—but investing in it saves, in my experience, on the one hand innovation funds, on the other hand, teams can learn a lot about markets, users and mechanisms through such test-driven work, which also determine the success of other products and thus promote better products in the long term.

7.1.1 What Will This Be About?

What such a validation process can look like and which tools and working methods can be helpful in this process, I describe in this chapter—much of it comes from the areas of agile development, design thinking and lean startup. However, what I describe is by no means pure doctrine or the only right way, but is based on the experiences I have made in the course of working on many different projects. My focus is mainly on the *what* to do and *why*, less detailed on the *how*. In each phase there are tools that are recommended and can be helpful. It's not just about the right tool, but above all about the right selection. It doesn't help much to throw 10 tools at a problem; it's more important to recognize which tool can really help in which situation to advance a product idea. Therefore, this contribution cannot be a guide for every validation project, but can at most provide inspirations in which direction one could go with one's own project.

Now to the point: Basically, the validation of new product ideas can be divided into three phases, which will be discussed in the following:

a) Research
b) Prototyping (MVP development)
c) Testing & Evaluation

Especially at the end of the first phase, it is important to take a step back and evaluate whether it makes sense to continue the project in the planned form or whether it is already foreseeable that the business success of the idea is very unlikely. The second and third phases are rather artificially separated, as they merge into each other and depend on each other; one should not or will not take place without the other.

7.1.2 How Long Does Such a Validation Usually Take?

To be honest, it's a bit of crystal ball gazing, as the answer depends on what the MVP (Minimum Viable Product, more on this in the next section) looks like in the end. If one is serious about separating the validation from the implementation and investment decision, the validation project should not take longer than 3–5 months, see Fig. 7.1.

Anything beyond that usually requires larger investments, so it can hardly be called pre-validation, but rather the incubation of a startup idea. This can also be justified, but should always be an active decision. It is worth questioning whether an initial validation could not be faster and thus cheaper.

A major time factor in validations within a corporation is usually coordination with other areas in the corporation. In my experience, it is therefore often helpful for the first validation to take a path that is as independent as possible and influenced by few other areas.

Fig. 7.1 Project phases of a validation project. (*Source*: Own illustration)

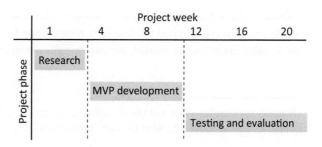

7.1.3 What Kind of Team Do I Need for Validation?

The required expertise or skills vary greatly in the three phases that the project goes through. If the required skills are not available, the Project Lead should ensure that he plans and brings on board this expertise in good time: Usually, especially in the first phase, you only need a Project Lead and someone who asks him/her the "right questions" along the project, i.e., a sparring partner who helps to check thoughts and juggle ideas. Everything else results from the project and especially from the MVP to be tested.

The Project Lead is, in my view, essentially the Product Manager; his or her tasks in the approach to market validation explained here are often project management tasks; hence I speak of the Project Lead. Basically, however, all tasks of the Project Lead are best filled with a Product Manager, especially when it comes to validating an innovation idea from an existing product team.

In the first phase, prior experience in the field of User Research or Design Thinking is helpful. In the second step, when it comes to implementing the MVP, the required expertise depends on the type and form of the MVP. If a technical MVP is being tested—which is the focus here, as it is probably the most interesting case for product managers—a small product team is usually needed: product expertise of the Project Lead, a designer who takes care of the **UI** and **UX**[1], i.e., the appearance and functionality of the product, and developers to implement it. Depending on the type of product, additional content expertise may be needed. In the testing phase, marketing expertise, know-how for data evaluation, and finally business administration knowledge to set up a good business plan are particularly important.

7.2 Research—Where do We Start?

With a product idea in mind, you usually already have a lot of knowledge that led you to this idea. The most important and often most difficult step to really validate a new product idea is to put the product idea aside and work out the underlying user needs for the research (the "market research")—to check their actual existence. The research serves to find the real problem behind a product idea, to understand how relevant this problem really is and how or if it is already being solved on the market by other existing products or workarounds.

Once we have done that and spoken to users who have this problem, and at the end of the day find that our original product idea might really be a good solution for a problem that actually exists on the market, we can bring it out again and develop it. However, if

---

[1] UI stands for User Interface and usually refers to the design, UX stands for User Experience and refers to the functionality, i.e., what the user "experiences".

we have the idea in our heads all the time, it will distort our research results, as we are not really trying to find or understand a problem, but are simply trying to find evidence that our product idea is good and someone likes it.

The most important step of a validation project is not the implementation of the prototype, but the preparatory research, which serves as the basis for the MVP definition with the test plan, as well as the look at the numbers at the end, which are relevant for the calculation of the business plan.

7.2.1 Hypotheses—What are We Assuming So Far?

To initially get an overview of the assumptions that are important for the success of the product and what we already know, we formulate hypotheses. Making a list of existing assumptions and potential knowledge in the form of hypotheses to prove or disprove helps to question all the information we may already have. Where do we already bring validated knowledge and where are we merely making an assumption? What are our assumptions based on? Do we need to check them or is the existing data basis sufficient? And finally: Are the assumptions important for the success of the idea at all? This will be illustrated using a specific example.

Example

We are successful in the market with a print magazine on the topic of "mindfulness". The idea arises that one could also look at what can be done digitally on the topic of mindfulness.

What do we already know from the existing print business and what can we only assume? Here is an excerpt of what the first hypotheses on this topic might look like, which structure and guide the user research:

- There is a target group for the topic of mindfulness that is interested in using a digital product on the topic of mindfulness.
- The market is large enough to be successful in it: According to a study, the meditation and mindfulness business field is almost 1 billion US dollars.
- There are still gaps in the existing market; problems of the target group have not yet been exhaustively solved.
- With our knowledge and our existing resources in the field of mindfulness, we have an advantage over other players in the market. ◄

For each hypothesis that forms the basis for the success of the business model, it is necessary to define what the verifiable **Key Performance Indicator (KPI)** is; i.e., the number with which the correctness of the hypothesis can be measured. It must also be recorded what the test should look like **(Testcase),** with which the KPI can be measured—if this is possible at the beginning of the research phase. And finally, it must be agreed upon what value the KPI must have (at least/at most) in order to classify the test as successful **(Breaking Point).**

Hypotheses that we formulate in this phase can change significantly during the research phase; new ones can be added and previous ones can become obsolete. It is even very likely that we will have to redo the work on the hypotheses after the research phase. We then create new testing hypotheses for the MVP that we have defined by then and want to implement, as we may have learned so much new by then that our original hypotheses are no longer sufficient or helpful. Nevertheless, it is important to do the work on KPIs, test cases, and breaking points once at the beginning. It helps to constantly question oneself: What did I initially think success meant, and what did I assume? Otherwise, one easily adjusts reality and success based on later results. For example, results for success are then sufficient, where one might have said at the beginning of the project: If we do not achieve this value, it cannot work. This may be legitimate, as one may have gained new insights that change the business model; these insights are then reflected once again by checking the original hypotheses, which usually leads to better decisions.

The aim of formulating hypotheses is therefore to check and structure the existing knowledge, to separate assumptions from facts, and to outline a first scope for the project based on the hypotheses.

7.2.2 Market Analysis and Target Group Definition—What are Our Initial Assumptions Based On?

To make an initial basic potential analysis for the market and the topic, it is important to take a closer look at the relevant market. This quickly gives a better feel for the context of an idea. The market research should answer the following questions:

- Which players are already on the market; what does the potential competition look like?
- What do current solutions of these players on the market look like?
- Which target groups are they addressing?
- How large are these target groups according to initial estimates?
- How can these target groups be reached?
- Which problems of these target groups are already being solved with existing products and which are not?
- How high is the willingness to pay among the target groups for solutions to these problems?

Answering these initial research questions is often possible through a simple desk research within a few days or 1–2 weeks. If it is already apparent here that the market

7 Validation of Product Ideas in the Market

is too small, all existing problems are already being solved to the fullest satisfaction of the target group, there is no willingness to pay, or the target group is not reachable at all, one should reconsider the orientation of the validation project or end it after the research phase.

The goal is to be able to make an assessment of the market potential at the end of this first part of the research and to know who to talk to in the next part of the research, where to find the target group and how to reach it.

7.2.3 Qualitative Research—What does the target group say?

It is difficult to put one's own prior knowledge and assumptions about a topic in the background, especially when one is part of the target group. Qualitative research is the best way to get closer to the real target group, to get to know the real underlying problems and to work user-centered when developing new product ideas. In my experience, the most fruitful are 1:1 interviews lasting 30 to 60 minutes with an open research guide along the **User Journey**[2].

The most important tool here is the creation of an open research guide, which provides orientation in the interview along the hypotheses to be clarified, and above all allows the interviews to be evaluated comparatively in the end.

Valuable insights (**Customer Insights**) can be gained from the interviews by evaluating the results of each individual interview and breaking them down to the essentials. The interviews often reveal recurring statements that help to better understand the problem under investigation or the solutions used so far. The information is often only implicitly mentioned by the interviewees. This means that some prior experience in conducting and evaluating interviews should be present in the team.

What we want to know in detail from the target group should result from the hypotheses previously set up, as well as the results of the market research. The following areas are always central to the query in the interviews or should already appear as assumptions in the hypotheses:

- Attitudes, experiences and needs around the project topic
- Behavior along the existing User Journey around the problem area

So if, for example, in the case of the mindfulness application, one tries to understand the User Journey of a person who gets her moments of mindfulness through yoga classes after work, there could be hints hidden in her stories about her everyday life about what she might still be missing or which problem is not yet solved for her.

---

[2] The User Journey is about understanding a user's previous problem/solution path. It is important to understand each step in detail in order to derive clues for a meaningful product solution.

The result of a comprehensive evaluation of the individual user interviews is often the creation of **Personas.** This means dividing the users into groups according to their characteristics and describing the "typical" user(s). Such personas can help to improve the design of the MVP for its target group and to make the target group more tangible for the product team.

In search of a rule of thumb for how many users one should talk to, I have found that seven people are usually sufficient per group of people with mostly matching characteristics (sub-target group that can be represented as a persona) to work out the most important insights. More interviews often only bring repetitions of content that is already known. However, sub-target groups can often only be defined more precisely during the first interviews—accordingly, one should be flexible to possibly adapt the number of interviews.

It may be that at the beginning of the qualitative research, ideas can already be developed from the results of the first market research as to which direction a product idea could go. If you want to discuss these first ideas with the users at the end of the user interviews, it can be helpful to work them out in a short design sprint into **paper prototypes** or similarly quickly producible Minimum Viable Products (MVPs)—this way, even in this early phase, first insights into actual ideas can be gained quickly and easily.

Other helpful tools in this phase of evaluation, in addition to "persona development" and the "User Journey", include creating a "problem statement" or working out "jobs to be done" as well as the "pains and gains" (for example, using the templates from the Value Proposition Canvas). All tools serve to better understand the target group and to make their needs and problems to be solved tangible for the development of the MVP. Descriptions of these tools and how to use them can be found, for example, in the Strategyzer books "Value Proposition Design" (Osterwalder et al. 2015), "Business Model Generation" (Osterwalder and Pigneur 2010) and "Testing Business Ideas" (Bland and Osterwalder 2020).

7.2.4 Quantitative Validation—How Many Are There?

With the personas developed from the qualitative interviews in hand, it is now necessary to find out how large the target group is in the market. We want to know, on the one hand, whether the personas developed through the interviews exist in this form in the market at all and, on the other hand, how large this target group is. The quantitative validation of the qualitative results helps to generalize gained insights to a certain degree and above all to get a feel for how much economic potential the target group really brings with it.

When setting up a quantitative survey, various aspects are particularly important to consider: Can I play out my survey via a market research panel that is representative for the target group I am looking for? Can I achieve a sample size in the time available to me that is sufficient to be representative for the target group? Can I condense the questions I have so that the survey is not distorted by a too high dropout rate among the participants? Can I view my personas distinctly enough from each other? Should I play out the survey myself, or use a panel provider or service provider for quantitative research: Do I get all the necessary information to draw conclusions about the overall market (For example: How many users could not participate in the survey due to possible filter questions at the beginning—to address only the target group I am looking for)?

One should deal intensively with these questions to prevent the quantitative analysis from producing just another nice statistic, of which one does not exactly know what it really brings, but offers real added value and produces valid findings. In addition, after the qualitative research, it is always worth asking whether a quantification of the results really helps, or whether the results can change the further course of the project. For some projects, quantification is not necessary or helpful.

7.2.5 MVP Definition and Resource Requirements—What Do We Need for Testing?

So far, there has been no explicit part that describes how a new product idea actually emerges from the research. This is somewhat due to the fact that there is not really a fixed point in time where this makes the most sense. Ideas for products that potentially solve discovered problems can emerge from any part of the research phase. For example, perhaps there was an idea at the very beginning of the project that we initially put aside, and we found out during the interviews that this idea actually solves existing problems and there may be a willingness to pay for this solution.

Basically, it's always about putting so much effort into customer-centric idea development that in the end you can "prove" that an idea you had or that may have newly emerged, not only looks like a good idea in your own eyes, but the market or real users also find the idea exciting and there are indications of a willingness to pay.

The desired result of the research phase is to get a clear idea of what the later product could look like, what its USP (Unique Selling Proposition, i.e., the unique selling point) is, and whether and why people would spend money on it.

The question of the business model **(Business Case)** can be very well represented using the **Business Model Canvas** (found in the book "Business Model Generation" by Osterwalder and Pigneur (2010)—but there are also numerous templates online), as you can quickly see here which are the relevant influencing factors for a functioning business model, see Fig. 7.2.

This knowledge, in turn, is enormously important for the next step: We define as detailed as possible which KPIs we need to measure the success of the product idea. Once we have done this, we can determine what the MVP for the product idea must contain at least so that we can measure these KPIs exactly.

In detail, this means that we certainly have many features in mind during the development of the product idea that make it a great product. However, the MVP usually comes

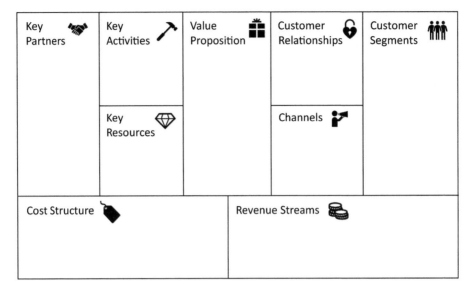

Fig. 7.2 Business Model Canvas. (*Source*: Adapted from Osterwalder and Pigneur 2010)

with a much smaller set of features (**Feature-Set**), because this already allows the relevant questions to be answered that are asked in the validation in order to calculate a business case at the end. When designing the MVP, it must always be weighed up what is really essential to be able to test sensibly and how much effort is behind it. The motto should always be to really only build the minimally necessary functional scope. So, one should not be tempted to build the "perfect product" if the basic question could perhaps be determined with just five features.

When deciding how much time and money to invest in creating the MVP, it is always necessary to weigh up several aspects at the end of the day:

- The strategic aspect:
  – What is the most sustainable way to finance innovation projects in the future? (Or, put another way: How is the failure of a project most likely to be forgiven and am I allowed to test the next idea?)
- The operational aspect:
  – How is an MVP in development best turned into the final "real" product in the event of project success?

Basically, the same question and the same dilemma lie behind both aspects. If I set up the MVP as a real MVP (cheap and quickly implemented in development, but probably with many technical debts, i.e., not scalable or sustainably set up in technology), I will be able to do the tests for little money and implement many projects with a small innovation budget. For all projects that are successful, however, this usually means that the technical implementation has to be redone to continue the product—which then costs time and money afterwards. So is it better to set up projects cheaply and quickly and rebuild the one that is successful after the test phase? Or would the rebuilding potentially take so long that I would have missed a market opportunity that is crucial for the success of the product?

Asking these questions and trying to answer them as best as possible with all those involved often leads to better decisions. In any case, it leads to more informed decisions. Once it has been determined how much time and money should and can be invested for the MVP, the feature set can be derived from this and the research results, and the MVP definition is established.

From the MVP definition, it finally becomes clear which team is needed for the next phase: If it's about a landing page that only explains the product, probably a designer and a developer are enough. But if we want to sell a largely finished product in the MVP, we certainly need more resources: If the mindfulness example is about audio-guided meditations that are to be offered, we need at least a mindfulness and meditation expert, a charismatic speaker, and an audio conceptor for the content. Having all the necessary resources quickly available is often crucial here and should not be underestimated in terms of effort.

7.2.6 Design vs. Technology—Where is the Focus in Creating an MVP?

In my experience, product design is often more important in innovation projects than a "clean", sustainable engineering (programming of the software). For the calculation of the business model, I of course need a good idea of what a scalable setup with a good technical setup costs in the end. However, this can usually also be estimated quite well on the basis of a technically less detailed MVP. The appearance, or functionality, that the test persons see, however, must be good, as test results otherwise do not allow any statements about the product for which the MVP was built. In my experience, one can always orient oneself well by the saying *"pretty on the outside, ugly on the inside"*. This way, good test results can be achieved without the technical effort blowing the budget. In addition, during the testing phase, you really focus on building only what you need for the test and spend less time thinking about how to build the tech setup sustainably and prepare for scaling. These are immensely important steps, but often still superfluous for an MVP. In addition, during the testing phase, you learn a lot about what works and what doesn't in product development for this product. As a result, the product that you build anew with all this knowledge will be set up much better than you would have done the first time.

7.3 Prototyping—What are We Building Now?

We now have a good idea of what the product is that we want to test. We have also defined what the MVP should look like, which we now want to implement. Prototyping can take very different forms and dimensions. From simple low-fidelity prototypes (e.g., paper prototypes, wireframes, simple landing pages), which we may have already used in the research phase, to detailed variants, such as click dummy mockups or MVPs, in which only a complex technical part is simulated, to programmed products with frontend and backend.

Examples of Low-Fidelity Prototypes

Paper Prototype
Paper prototypes are drawn versions (sketches) of the product. These are made by hand on paper. The goal of this simple technique is to quickly and easily reflect initial ideas and product considerations on the user. In user testing, a "facilitator" is needed, i.e., someone who simulates the interactive elements (such as turning to a new sheet of paper where a "click" occurs or speaking announcements).

Wireframe
Wireframes are a kind of blueprint for a product and show, usually in black and white and without design, the structure of a product. The goal of wireframes is usually to show functionalities and UX. Wireframes are rarely suitable for testing on inexperienced users, as they often do not "look nice" and most users get stuck on the (lacking) design instead of evaluating the functionality.

Simple Landing Page
Simple landing pages or pre-order pages are single websites that allow preliminary statements about a product that does not yet exist. Unlike the first two low-fidelity prototypes, it is quite easy to do not only qualitative but also quantitative tests here. Usually, the landing pages show a preview of a product and allow interaction to test interest and willingness to pay, for example by entering an email address if you want to be informed at the start of the product, a pre-order can be made or even a fake purchase process can be started. ◄

Examples of High-Fidelity Prototypes

Click Dummy Mockup
A mockup is the finished designed product, but it consists only of designs that have not yet been technically implemented. Unlike the wireframe, the product now "looks nice". With the help of tools like proto.io, such mockups can be assembled into click dummies, so that it is visually and in terms of interaction possibilities (clicks) indis-

tinguishable from the actual product. It is a replica of the finished product. Functions, content and design can be tested with users before any technical effort has been made in frontend development.

MVP with Simulated Technology

Such MVPs are also referred to as Wizard of Oz MVPs. Unlike the mockup and click dummy, the frontend is usually already programmed here, but not the functionality in the backend. Logics and processes that will later run automatically are manually simulated here.

MVP with Programmed Technology

Programmed prototypes are most similar to the finished product that is to be tested. They contain the core features defined in the test plan that are needed for the validation of the product and are programmed in terms of UX and UI, as well as functionality, backend and tracking. ◀

How far we have to go, meaning with which type of prototype we can test, depends on the test plan. The result of this phase is a prototype that can be tested on the market, with which we can answer all questions that must be answered for the calculation of the business plan.

7.3.1 Test Plan & Feature Definition—What Do We Want to Know and What Do We Need For It?

We now have a good idea of the product we want to test. However, for the feature definition of the MVP, it is primarily decisive which KPIs we need in the end to calculate a business case and to be able to assess whether the product for which we are building an MVP promises success. This means that before we really start prototyping, we should set up a test plan. Only from this does our feature set emerge. The focus here is not on what would be cool for the product from a user's point of view or even our point of view—but what is needed for the tests. It always helps me to explicitly distinguish between the product we want to test and the MVP we use for the test.

What does a test plan include? Basically, we have already looked at this in general when it came to formulating hypotheses. It is now time to bring these hypotheses back to the fore and refine them for the product idea that has emerged.

To maintain a better overview, it often makes sense to divide the hypotheses into areas along the user journey that leads to our product.

To explain this using an example: We have a digital product idea that we want to sell to consumers. We want to sell paid content and offer it as a subscription model (like Netflix or Spotify, for example). With such a business model, the following questions become particularly important for testing:

A) Customer acquisition & Target Group: How do which users come to us and what does it cost us?
B) Positioning & Branding: In what context does the product work for the users and is it used?
C) Content, USP & Value: For which content and in what form are users willing to pay?
D) Monetization & Payment: How do users pay? What is important to them in this regard? What does the business model look like and how expensive can the product be?
E) Activity, Retention & Customer Development: Do users stay for a long time? What are the reasons for this and what do we have to do for it?

For each area, we have either already formed hypotheses from the research phase or we are now developing them based on user research and with a view to the product idea. It is often helpful to write down the user statements and the insights generated from them, on which the hypotheses are based, in order to bring the user research back to mind. For each hypothesis, it is then necessary to determine three things in the next step:

1. KPIs: Which KPIs do we need to measure in order to confirm or refute this hypothesis?
2. Test scenario: What does the test scenario look like with which we get these numbers?
3. Breaking Point: What values must the KPIs at least assume so that we can consider the test successful and the hypothesis confirmed/refuted or our business case pays off?

The following example explains what a hypothesis could look like in two areas (I have chosen area A and D as examples) if Netflix were the product idea to be tested.[3] As a rule, unlike in the example, you do not have just one hypothesis per area, but a multitude.

> **Customer Acquisition & Target Group—How do different users come to us and what does it cost us?**

Hypothesis 1: Users are more likely to be distracted while reading emails and drawn into audiovisual stories than when passing by a billboard.

1. KPIs: Click rates (calculated from views and clicks), Cost per Click (CPC), Watch-Time
2. Test scenario: Display ads on various email providers. Book billboard advertising with discount code for tracking and install a camera at the billboard to evaluate the number of views.

---

[3] Disclaimer: The numbers in the example described here are not based on any research or business plan calculations (as should be the case in a project that has just come out of the research phase), but were chosen arbitrarily for illustration.

7 Validation of Product Ideas in the Market

3. Breaking Point: General success of the measures: Click rates from view to use from 15% are considered a success. CPC max. 3 €, Watch Time >5 min. Differences between the two measures are to be evaluated with a significance test.

What required features for the MVP result from this?
Different ad formats for display and billboard advertising, landing page with a few contents that can be unlocked with a discount code, tracking of traffic costs, views, clicks and user behavior on the landing page.

Monetization & Payment—How do users pay? What is important to them? What does the business model look like and how expensive can the product be?
Hypothesis 1: The purchase conversion is better when various payment methods are available.

1. KPI: Purchase conversion (calculated from traffic on the landing page and number of purchase completions).
2. Test scenario: Checkout page with various payment options in A/B test compared to a checkout page that only includes the most common and easiest payment method for the user or the cheapest for us. A preliminary test may be necessary using the checkout page that provides various options to find out which payment method is preferred by users.
3. Breaking Point: General success is seen with a purchase conversion of more than 3%. Differences in the A/B test are to be evaluated with a significance test.

What required features for the MVP result from this?
Checkout process on the landing page with a selection of various payment options (it may be sufficient to simulate the payment option, i.e., not to connect real payment providers), A/B testing capabilities and tracking of all values needed to calculate the purchase conversion. ◄

Often, after creating the ideal test plan and a resulting feature list, it is necessary to determine the order of the scenarios to be tested and, above all, to define the impact of failure of individual scenarios. To work cost-effectively, it may be worthwhile—if possible—to test one area first and not to implement all defined features at once. For example, if you find that you cannot find a working way to make users aware of the product, you should first find a promising solution for traffic acquisition before building features that can check the purchase conversion.

In any case, the most important feature in every MVP is the corresponding KPI tracking. No feature for the user is of any use if the related KPIs cannot be tracked. Therefore, it is important to always list tracking of all required KPIs as a feature of the MVP and to include it in the backlog for technical implementation from the start. Otherwise, it will be forgotten, not taken into account in the cost and time estimate, and will trip you up just before you want to start the tests.

7.3.2 UX and UI—What Should the MVP Look Like?

With the completed feature list in hand, we should next consider what the UX and UI of the MVP will look like. This is the basis for being able to say more precisely what and how long we need for the development of the MVP. That means, we need a design. The project lead should work closely with the designer and provide all previous insights. This means that the briefing for the designer should include what the product idea is and how it came about. This means that everything that has been learned so far in research must be clearly prepared and shared. On the other hand, it must be made very clear what is planned for the MVP as opposed to the final product and why. This means that the test plan and the resulting feature list should be reviewed with the designer so that he or she is as informed as the product management itself: Where should the project lead and what is the goal of validation?

It is recommended to really explicitly separate the development of UX and UI from the final programming, as you can already go into testing with first click dummies based on the designs (for example using tools like proto.io) without having development costs.

Example

This can be illustrated with an example: Innovation projects can also be implemented in the form of research & development projects. Unlike a product innovation project, this means that there is actually no user problem for which we have ideas on how to solve it. Rather, there is a new technology that seems promising to us and that we would like to try out and test for its potential as a basis for new business models. Concrete example: Chatbot technology has just emerged on the market and a publisher is wondering if this is a channel that could become relevant for digital content. For such projects with new technologies, it is particularly worthwhile to rely on incomplete interim solutions for the first tests, which may even only simulate what exciting features the new technology brings with it.

In the mentioned example, the test scenario looked as follows: For a use case that is to be validated in the first test, a first draft for the conversational design (design in which a conversation flow between user and product is designed instead of visual components) and the UX is made. Subsequently, team members sit behind computers and chat for a week and simulate the chatbot using a decision tree based on the conversational design and pre-made responses. So that the "bot" can respond quickly enough, it is necessary in the test phase that a team member can always respond without delay; toilet breaks are therefore made alternately. In this way, countless insights could be generated with little technical effort within a week, which massively influenced the subsequent technical implementation of the chatbot. Based on user behavior, the conversational design could be quickly iterated and improved. It became clear that some features were not needed at all. Others were missing, which had a major impact on the activity rate of the users. In addition, initial ideas could be generated on how to make money with the chatbot. These ideas could then be tested in the subsequent, technically implemented prototype. ◀

7.3.3 Development—How and with Which Technology Will the MVP Be Implemented?

UX and UI requirements, considerations for tracking but also available developer resources should be the basis for the selection of the technology with which the prototype is implemented. I will not go into detail on the *how* of the technical implementation and delivery of the product here, as there are other contributions to this in this book (Developing really good products efficiently, Tim Adler). In essence, the delivery of an MVP does not differ from the delivery of any other product. Possibly the scope of an MVP is somewhat smaller and there should be less focus on pre-planning for scaling in order to keep the effort and thus the costs low. In addition, as explained in detail above, it is not the pure user or business need that determines the feature set, but primarily the test plan, and which KPIs can be tested with which features.

7.3.4 Team—Who is Building This?

Implementing an innovation project with a team that otherwise works on products that are already live presents a different challenge than assembling the majority of the team virtually from scratch, and it only comes together to this extent for the development of this prototype. Both have their advantages and disadvantages and bring different challenges. In the setting in which I have accompanied many innovation projects, there was only a very small permanent team for the technical implementation.

For us, it has proven beneficial to definitely have UX and UI firmly in the team, as they are actually needed in every project and often new tasks in this area arise very quickly, which want to be implemented. Especially since UX and UI have such a fundamental influence on user behavior, conversion rates and thus the chance of success of the product, there should always be a strong focus on this.

Depending on the scope and technical requirements, the rest of the team is then to be assembled. If you add team members who are permanently employed in the company and have other tasks besides the innovation project, it is extremely important to fight for them to be fully available for the project during the period in which the MVP is to be implemented, and to be completely withdrawn from their actual tasks. Otherwise, you quickly get into situations where priorities are not clear and you veer off schedule.

In many cases, it therefore makes sense to fill gaps in the team with freelancers. Firstly, you are more flexible in the choice of technology and have the freedom to work with the tech setup that seems most suitable for the intended prototype. Secondly, this allows resources to be built up for a very limited period of time and the assembly of a permanent team, which produces fixed costs, can take place at a later point in time when the idea has already been validated.

Of course, it is necessary to weigh up here as well: If you want to further develop the MVP into the final product after successful completion of the validation project, this is best done with the same team that implemented the MVP. However, if the team is no longer available in this form or if it is too expensive for long-term operation of the product due to the freelancer salaries, it is essential to have a team that can handle the tech setup just as well as the validation team. It is best to think about this not only when the validation project is completed, because then it may be too late. You should anticipate the continuation early on and plan for it.

I admit that I am contradicting myself a bit here: On the one hand, the project organization should be kept lean so that the testing does not become too expensive, and on the other hand, planning should be done in advance so that continuation can also be achieved efficiently. I believe there is no perfect solution here—the important thing is just to think about it and have an idea of how it could work, so that you are not surprised by the question at the end.

7.3.5 Time Estimate—How Long will It Take?

With a time estimate, a cost estimate usually also arises. It is obvious that duration and costs completely depend on the defined and desired feature set. Simply calculated: Number of working days that are expected to be needed per team member, times daily rates of a team member times number of team members.

As a small rule of thumb, it can be said: If the development will take longer than 3–4 weeks, it is no longer an MVP. If no testing has been done yet, you should look for an alternative "low-fidelity prototype" with which you can subject the hypotheses you have set up to initial tests more quickly and cheaply.

With high-fidelity prototypes, this can then possibly be different and the development can also take two months. At that point, however, you should already have gathered some insights that speak for the success of the idea. Then it is more worthwhile to put a little more effort into the sustainability, i.e. the reusability after the validation, of the prototype. Building such a prototype should therefore already be a very conscious and informed decision.

Example

Let's assume that the following insights could be generated in the first research and with low-fidelity prototypes:

- There is a willingness to pay for digital audio content if the user feels that they own these meditations after purchase to use them over and over again.

7 Validation of Product Ideas in the Market

- A subscription model for digital audio content appears to be the most promising business model.
- Digital content that is not provided as a download is best sold via an app; as a user develops more of a sense of ownership with apps that he downloads to his device than with content on the web with login and user area.
- IOS users show a greater willingness to pay for digital content and other in-app purchases. ◀

From the insights of the example, it follows quite clearly that it makes sense to first develop an app for the IOS Appstore from Apple. However, since Apple does not allow beta versions with unfinished content in the Appstore, you are forced here to develop a prototype that comes very close to the actual product. Implementing this in three to four weeks is then rather unrealistic and you have to plan more development time and thus also a higher budget for the prototype.

7.4 Testing—How Do We Get the Numbers?

Of course, many steps of the previous phases are already part of testing. If I show a paper prototype in a qualitative interview, that's testing. If I present a product idea at the end of a quantitative questionnaire and offer users the opportunity to enter their email address if they want to be informed about the product launch, that's also testing. If I make a design mockup, walk around the streets with a click dummy, and hand it to people to find out how they handle it, that's also testing. At every step that has brought me to the point where I hold a test plan and a market-ready MVP in my hands, testing should have been done. This chapter is therefore particularly about testing digital, programmed prototypes that are brought to the market for validation like a new, "finished" product.

7.4.1 Launch & Marketing Plan—Who will test the MVP?

The research focused on who the target audience for the MVP is, and found out how to reach this target group for conversations. This knowledge is now needed again to bring the prototype to the market and to generate traffic in a quantity that can provide the necessary test numbers. At this point, it is usually advisable to not only focus on the target group, but to broaden the approach in order to have the opportunity to test the hypothesis of which target group is interested in this product in the market.

At its core, all known online marketing methods are suitable for acquiring traffic to a website or into an app, or for delivering the MVP via existing digital channels, such as a note on your own website. This allows the necessary KPIs to be tracked.

When creating the launch and marketing plan, it is important for testing to look at the chosen channels in advance, make a forecast of how much traffic is expected from them, and calculate whether this can be sufficient to achieve significant results. This way, you know in advance how much budget is likely to be needed and how much time it will take to generate enough visitor or conversion numbers. If the estimates do not fit, the test plan can be adjusted if necessary to ensure that meaningful test results will be shown within the time and budget frame.

7.4.2 Pivot—Everything New Again?

The first two weeks of testing are completed, the results are in, and we find that everything turned out quite differently than we thought. What then? Throw away the project and start over? Adjust and try again? Process what has been learned and end the project? All valid options that need to be weighed depending on the result.

If the results after the first round of testing do not match what we assumed in the hypotheses, this is usually the point at which a project takes longer than planned. Because the planning of research, prototyping, and testing, in my experience, never actually includes a plan for a major pivot (a change in the idea, business model, target group, or similar). However, this happens in eight out of ten cases. So you should try to calculate with it—but at least make stakeholders aware at the beginning of the project that this could happen and what it could mean for the time and thus the budget of a project.

If this case occurs in the project reality, the most important thing is not to make uninformed decisions driven by an idea or product love, but to look at the numbers and identify in which direction it makes sense to continue.

If the results provide indications that suggest that adjusting the product is promising, you basically start again with the test plan. The test plan is adjusted, any newly needed features are defined, the team for it is brought to the start to implement the whole thing, and test phase two is started.

Another case that often occurs in the test phase is that we do not solve the intended problem with the tested product, but find another problem along the way that is worth solving. As a result, a new idea could emerge that could then go into a research phase.

However, if you achieve results that make it clear that the problem, for example, is not serious enough for a solution to trigger a willingness to pay in the target group, or if you discover external factors in the testing that change the numbers so much that the business model will not be profitable, you should not hesitate to end the project. In this case, it is important to openly share what has been learned with stakeholders and other interested parties in order to learn from it for the future.

If you lead two out of ten projects to success, that is a good rate from my experience, especially since it is generally assumed in the startup scene that nine out of ten startups fail.

7.4.3 KPIs & Business Plan—Are We Making Money Now?

And now we dig out the knowledge from our last statistics lecture or bring in someone who is familiar with data evaluation, synthesis, and interpretation. Essentially, the last task is to enter all collected data into the test plan, calculate results from it, and check which hypotheses have been confirmed or refuted. This shows where we have reached the breaking points and if not, to consider why that was the case. Were there assumptions at the beginning of the project that were not confirmed?

This also makes it clear once again why so much value should be placed on a good test plan and a derivation of the MVP features from the test plan and the required KPIs: If I only realize at this point in the project that I am missing a number for a calculation because I did not track it, the project may not come to a proper conclusion in the worst case.

How can this be prevented? I like to perform the calculation, which I will actually only do at the end of the project, already at the beginning when I create my test plan. On what basis? With the numbers I have in the breaking point list. These are my assumptions of what a good value should look like. And if I set up my business plan with these numbers, it hopefully shows that money can be made with this project. This also has the advantage that I base my breaking point assumptions not only on market values from research, but also on my own business needs. Possibly, a purchase rate of two percent "out there" is something that is rated as good or average, but it is not enough for my business case, because I actually need at least three percent for the calculation to work out. Realizing this at the beginning also has the advantage that you quickly get a feel for where the project needs to perform significantly better than others on the market and where you have more leeway.

7.5 And What Happens Next?

We have now tested all of this on the green field: It went great, the business plan is in place and shows profits from the first year. And now?

Especially in the corporate environment, this question should not be asked only now. Corporate innovation often struggles with the fact that new ideas cannot keep up with the agility and adaptability of "real" startup teams, as it ultimately depends on a corporation that brings with it decision-making processes that make quick and user-centered responses to the market difficult. An innovation project that has emerged and been successful on the green field can then fail in its continuation for exactly these reasons if they were not considered beforehand.

Part of the result and recommendation for such projects should therefore always be an assessment of what kind of setup the project can have long-term success with. If the success lies, for example, in the fact that the project can use certain resources or expertise in an existing department of the corporation and thus has a great market advantage, this department should not only find out about it at the end of the project. Ideally, such results should be anticipated before the start of the project and the relevant department should be involved in the project in order to develop an "ownership" (sense of belonging or responsibility) and to obtain a commitment from them before the start of the project to continue the project in case of success. The challenge, however, is to maintain the necessary flexibility and openness to results for the product that is yet to be evaluated, despite having already obtained a commitment.

The project team should therefore have the opportunity until the end to give their own recommendation for continuation, independent of the wants and needs of other stakeholders.

References

Bland, D., and A. Osterwalder. 2020. *Testing business ideas: A field guide for rapid experimentation.* New Jersey.

Osterwalder, A., and Y. Pigneur. 2010. *Business model generation: A handbook for visionaries, game changers, and challengers.* New Jersey.

Osterwalder, A., Y. Pigneur, G. Bernarda, A. Smith, and T. Papadakos. 2015. *Value proposition design. How to create products and services customers want.* New Jersey.

Anna Wicher is Head of Product at a corporate startup in Hamburg, which originally started as a project in the Greenhouse Innovation Lab, the former think tank of the publisher Gruner + Jahr and the RTL media group. As part of this project, she has been working as a product manager since the beginning of 2019 and previously validated innovation projects in the market for two years as Project Lead in the Greenhouse Innovation Lab.This contribution aims to document the experiences she has been able to gather while leading various innovation projects and others she has accompanied. It is intended to provide inspiration on how to validate new ideas quickly and efficiently in the market.

Contact: awi@missionme.de

Product Delivery

8

Developing Really Good Products Efficiently

Tim Adler

Abstract

From the product idea or the new digital business model to the successful launch, as a product manager, one must manage the actual product development or "Product Delivery". Agile project management methods such as SCRUM are widely well established for this. However, they also leave some important questions unanswered: How much does the new product cost and how long will the development take? When are we even ready to start product development? Why do my programmers always leave so punctually? This article provides answers to these questions and recommends how product development can be pragmatically organized.

8.1 Let's Get Started

Ideas for a new product are deceptive: Sometimes they seem so catchy and clear that one does not understand why the implementation should be a problem at all. Therefore, it is not uncommon for the implementation of a product idea to be thought of as "an expensive purchase": You pay a large amount of money and in the end you get a new fitness app, a pet supply website, or a new cryptocurrency. The ingenious simplicity of many apps and the large range of digital products reinforce the impression that the path from the finished concept to the finished product cannot be that far.

T. Adler (✉)
Hamburg, Deutschland
e-mail: mail@tim-adler.de

© The Author(s), under exclusive license to Springer Fachmedien Wiesbaden GmbH, part of Springer Nature 2024
S. Hoffmann (ed.), *Digital Product Management*,
https://doi.org/10.1007/978-3-658-44276-7_8

By "implementation" we mean the section of product development in which the product actually comes into being. This is usually easy to recognize by the fact that somewhere, someone is producing program code—regularly, every day, and sometimes without daylight.

If you already have some experience with product implementation, you may find the perception of product development as a "purchase" irritating. You may then have the feeling that even smaller projects are more like an expedition into somewhat uncertain areas. Sometimes the analogy of building a house is also appropriate, because the statics of a house should still hold when the gable is put on.

All these are reasons why strange situations in product implementation keep cropping up: from the effort estimation, for which there is hardly more than a spoken sentence as a basis, to such tight constraints that there is only a "it-has-to-be-like-this". Wherever you look, there is then only: "This must be finished by the end of the month.", "This absolutely must have the Apple Health connection and push notifications for the launch." and "Oh yes, this must not cost more than 10,000 €."

The tools described in the following will help you deal with such situations. With these tools, you can organize the development of a designer fashion marketplace in a race with a competitor, as well as analyze whether the launch date of an app is realistic in three to four weeks after returning from two months of parental leave. At least I have actually used them successfully in both of the situations mentioned.

The working methods and tools I describe here are strongly oriented towards the well-known process framework SCRUM for agile projects. However, there will be neither a detailed description of all the tools and meetings contained in SCRUM, nor will the working method described please the "SCRUM dogmatist"—I'm pretty sure of that.[1]

Rather, I would like to give product managers, who are facing the challenge of implementing a product for the first time, a roadmap to get started. But also to readers who have already implemented one or the other project with SCRUM and may then wonder why with SCRUM the answers to some important questions can only be given with difficulty at the beginning of a project: "What will this cost?" or "How long will it take?"

My goal here is to describe my interpretation of agile methods: As I have established them in many successful projects together with the team and painfully missed in aborted projects. I try to fill the gaps that SCRUM leaves unanswered in daily "business" and would like to share my assessment of which components of agile methods are indispensable and how certain tools become really useful in practice with small adjustments.

---

[1] For a detailed presentation of SCRUM see Chap. 1 by Sascha Hoffmann.

8.2 What You Need Before You Start

8.2.1 MVP vs. MLP

For once, let's assume at this point that it is already clear what product is to be built. The ups and downs of user research and prototyping are long behind us. Testing, verification, and even a brand have already been developed for the new product. Hopefully, a few features have also been cut and the scope has been condensed to define a product that gives a first round picture for the user. I like to call it MVP ("Minimum Viable Product") at this point. But since this term is also often used for prototypes during user research, we can also use MLP ("Minimal Launchable Product"). This also conveys the nice message that, when time and money are tight, there is often still a product that can be launched with fewer features than defined in the MVP, without embarrassing oneself.

So there is a very concrete idea of what your new product should be able to do, even if it is not yet comprehensively documented for implementation.

8.2.2 Documenting Features

First and foremost, it's best to write a rather boring text document about your new product. "Oh, a specification sheet?" you might ask now, and surely a reading agile evangelist will throw his hands up in horror.

But believe me: If you write such a document more as an outline or mind map, it will be very useful for all the following steps. Especially as a briefing for the design and the pressing questions of "How long will it actually take?" and "What will it cost?"

Optimal for the level of detail aimed for here are "outlining tools", such as Omni-Outliner or Dynalist. These tools are made to create a kind of mind map of thoughts on a topic (in this case your new product). However, they use a form of presentation that already looks like a document and does not have the usual network form of a mind map.

Try to describe the new product roughly, but with as many aspects as possible. Also think about which things need to happen in the "frontend" (i.e., directly usable for the user) and which in the "backend" (e.g., interfaces to other systems). At the latest when it comes to necessary infrastructure topics (setting up the project, configuring servers), you should have a developer you trust look over the list again.

If we are really developing an MLP here and not the next SAP competitor, then I would say that this document should not be longer than five to eight pages. Otherwise, you have become too entangled in details at this stage, see Fig. 8.1.

8.2.3 First, Make It "Pretty"—Preparing the Design

You should now brief a designer with this exact document and start with the UI/UX design—even though the agile methodology usually allows for this to be developed

> **▼ App Intro**
> - Swipe through the three intro screens
> - Last swipe opens the registration page "Get
> - started now" switches to registration "Log in"
> - switches to login
>
> **▼ Login / Registration**
> - Login with existing user/password
> - **▼** Facebook login
>   - If a user is not yet registered, they will NOT be created automatically when they log in to Facebook
> - Data protection information and terms and conditions are linked and open in a new
> - window Switch between login/registration via text link
> - Registration via e-mail/password
> - Registration via Facebook
>
> **▼ Onboarding (after registration)**
> - Thank you message
> - Short intro video
> - Transition to the first mind profile
>
> **▼ Pricing**
> - Monthly subscription / annual subscription trigger corresponding purchases via AppStore/PlayStore as a subscription
> - One-off payment triggers a corresponding individual InApp-Purchase
> - The user is then activated in the backend
> - Restore purchases works accordingly
> - AGB are linked in a separate window
> - A thank you screen appears after purchase

Fig. 8.1 Product description at the beginning of a Product Delivery. (*Source*: Own illustration)

during the course of the project. I believe it's good to have developed a color scheme, typography, and the basic navigation options of a new product in advance. In any case, it is most efficient to quickly go through iterations of the design with a small team (perhaps even just you as the product manager and a designer) and also collect a "Go!" from your stakeholders. Especially when there is only a tight budget (in time or cost), such an approach makes sense because it prevents unnecessary delays in implementation later on. Above all, it also avoids the implementation of features in a suboptimal form that were never intended to be that way, thus avoiding double work.

A design should definitely include the following aspects of the later product:

- Click-flow (see Fig. 8.2),
- States of the screens for "Loading", "Normal" and "Error",
- Typography classes.

8 Product Delivery

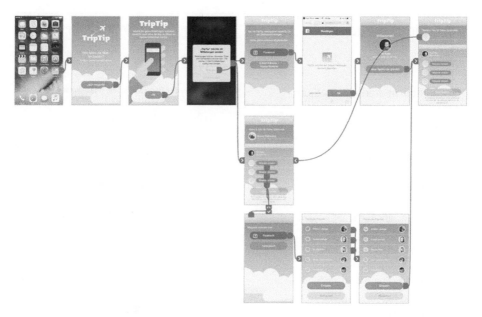

Fig. 8.2 User Interface design with click-flow. (*Source*: Own illustration)

To make access easier for programmers later on, it's good to ensure that the design is implemented in a tool that allows screenshots to be connected via click paths (e.g., "Sketch"). In the end, the whole thing should also be made available online (the two tools mentioned above, for example, come with this feature). This has the advantage that you can quickly link to individual screens from emails and tickets and there is only one "leading source" for the design. Otherwise, no one can keep track of the many files that claim to be "_Final_v2_finally" in different forms.

For another real efficiency boost in implementation, have the typography and colors standardized in the design. This means that all fonts (size, typeface) are standardized to form "classes" of fonts.

Why? You should avoid having a few words in 17 px as well as a headline in 18 px. Instead, you should strive to achieve standardization in the design that will have to happen in programming anyway. This supports the effort to write "clean" program codes and avoid repetitions or unnecessary details. Any typography not intended as a class (even just 1 px larger text) must otherwise be individually mapped by the programmers, see Fig. 8.3.

Don't forget to think through the basic states of each screen:

- "Loading": this is always when the screen does not yet have all the data and the user should wait a bit.

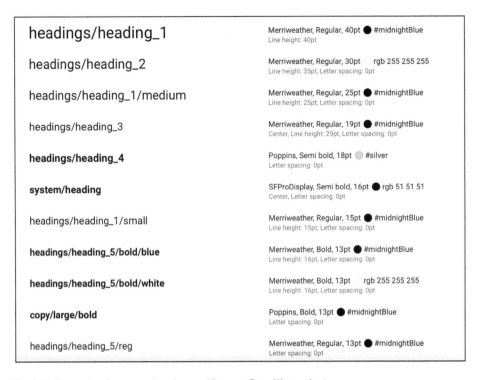

Fig. 8.3 Example of typography classes. (*Source*: Own illustration)

- "Error": you may not believe it, but it happens more often than you hope: Something has gone wrong and you have to tell the user.
- "Normal": what you actually want to do on the screen.

A developer will have to map all these states later anyway. Therefore, it is better if they are thought out in the design, rather than leaving them to chance.

And finally, as a product manager, a well-prepared click-flow, i.e., the planned sequence when "clicking through" by a user, also helps you to see all parts of the product to be implemented again and to realize the extent of the upcoming task.

8.3 Knowing in Advance What It Will Cost

8.3.1 Classic Project Management FTW

It's time to work with a tool that Ötzi used to plan his clay oven: the Gantt chart. This beast, which pretends to be precise, plans resources to 50% and chronically no longer corresponds to reality, is incredibly good for one thing: time estimates.

8 Product Delivery

SCRUM only offers us a good way to make preliminary time and cost estimates: team-based estimates based on large (and therefore also "epic") feature blocks. Usually, one tries to estimate sizes that correspond to T-shirt sizes (S, M, L, XL). However, since there is hardly any experience behind the estimates at this point in product implementation, this method has the major disadvantage that it is difficult to translate into time and money. Most of the time, however, stakeholders want to know in advance what product development will cost. Therefore, we resort to the extreme: we plan a "waterfall".

A waterfall project plan is an alternative name for Gantt charts, which are very far from "agile" in their nature (besides "project committees" and "requirements specification" of course). Nevertheless, we will now use it to plan our sprints, and surprisingly come to a relatively good estimate of time and cost of our implementation project.

8.3.2   An Idea of Team Size

One size that can often be determined relatively easily is the composition of the product team that should be available for implementation. Even if the team size changes, this can at least be anticipated with some certainty.

The idea with "waterfall planning" is now very simple: one tries to estimate how many topics one can handle per sprint based on the team size. At this point, we assume a sprint length of two weeks (more on this in the next section). A few simple rules of thumb for the estimate:

- A designer can often support one to two developers quite well in their work.
- A developer can deal with one to two different topics per sprint.
- If you are developing a product with a clear frontend/backend distinction (e.g., an app with backend connection via an API), you often need a frontend developer and a backend developer for the one to two different topics per sprint.
- In a team of up to three people, you as a product manager can still take over the Quality Assurance (QA)/testing of new features. For larger teams, you should leave this to a separate team member specifically responsible for QA, otherwise you will not be able to give feedback to the team quickly enough.

These are very concrete and admittedly quite general rules of thumb and there are good reasons why they might not fit perfectly in individual projects. However, they have often proven to be a good basis for time and cost estimates in my projects.

8.3.3   Time and Cost Estimation

We now use the rough rules of thumb and place the topics from our feature documentation on a timeline. Start planning with a "setup sprint". There is always

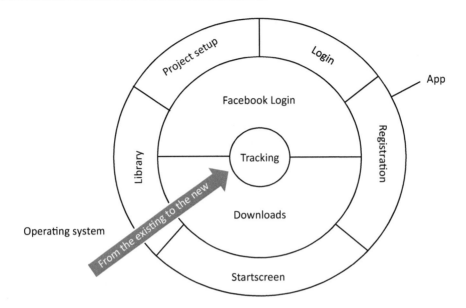

Fig. 8.4 Diagram of feature priority. (*Source*: Own illustration)

a lot to prepare—especially when there is a significant difference between frontend and backend (e.g., the repository for source code and its connection to a build server/CI, accounts in third-party tools like Google/Amazon, etc.).

Then, you set one to two topics per sprint from the feature documentation that should be worked on. Ideally, you work your way from the outside in (i.e., from the part where your product connects to existing things or, for example, starts with the login) towards the more specific features that already build on other new parts of the new product. This view results in a good order for the sprints (see Fig. 8.4).

If you have planned more than four to five sprints: Also plan a "post-launch sprint". Even if you don't know exactly what might happen there, there will certainly be errors to fix due to the complexity of the product.

In the end, you should have a nice list of sprints that build on each other, each lasting two weeks, and thus already provide a first time estimate for your product (see Fig. 8.5).

Since you have already assumed a team composition, you can now relatively easily convert the time estimate into project costs.

▶ **Project costs = Number of team members * average daily rate * number of days per sprint * number of sprints**

An important tip for cost estimation: Always communicate very clearly that you are paying for sprints and you cannot "buy" the product. A "product price" communicates the wrong security that it is very clear how complex the product will be. We have estimated

8 Product Delivery

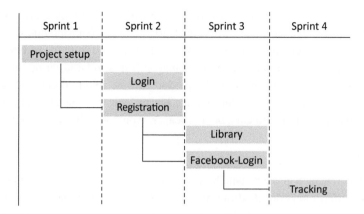

Fig. 8.5 Waterfall planning for sprints. (*Source*: Own illustration)

this—but still, there will be shifts in topics and team composition that can also mean one sprint more or less.

8.3.4 What to Do If It's Too Expensive or Too Slow?

At this point, there is now the unlikely but possible case that everything you have so far as an estimate fits completely into the existing budget and exactly to the hoped-for timing. Maybe you even have money and time left over for a lunch snack. It is more likely that this is not the case and you are one or two small cars away from the target budget and a couple of seasons away from the target date. Unfortunately, there are only two options: Either you enlarge the team with more developers and thus create more topics per sprint. Or you let things be.

Expanding the team is of course only an option if you have no time left, but still have money. However, a team cannot become infinitely large, because at some point the team members will get in each other's way:

- Due to the larger number of team members, there may suddenly be a greater need to exchange information about the internal functioning of the product, as everyone is developing it and must use it at the same time.
- Frontend developers are waiting for progress in the backend and cannot complete their work.
- Some problems simply cannot be distributed among several heads, e.g. creating a database structure or setting up the project.

For a product team in implementation, I would recommend a maximum of six people in the peak phase. However, the potential to parallelize will be harder to find at the beginning of the project than in the middle. More teams are of course always possible, but they should then also be able to work on clearly definable (sub-)products.

The more likely scenario is that you have reached the end in terms of both time and budget. Then unfortunately only one thing remains: If it is to be faster or cheaper, compromises must be made. This means: The product will be able to do less at launch than previously planned. There is no other choice but to look for a feature set that already meets the most urgent requirements, but is cheaper. Would you like an example?

Example

In an app relaunch project, which was supposed to replace a pure iOS app with a multi-platform version (Android and iOS), it was urgently necessary to be faster on all platforms than a complete feature set would have allowed. We decided at the time to launch the Android version in a minimal beta version and upgrade the "old" iOS version so that it could cope with the necessary changes in the backend. We only released the new iOS version later. This reduced the complexity and was also a more controllable launch scenario. ◄

At this point, do not be deterred from thinking radically about the necessity of features again. A common fallacy is that you could get to the result faster and cheaper by putting pressure on the working hours of employees. This is based on the false assumption that time and cost have nothing to do with each other. This becomes clear when you think not of permanent employees, but of freelancers: Here, every overtime hour is paid extra and the project may be faster, but not cheaper.

A much more important reason against the "pressure method" is, however, that the necessary pressure can hardly be maintained over a period of several months. But this would often be necessary to be consistently faster. In addition, pressure is completely counterproductive to the necessary way of working during development: Concentration and the freedom to try out alternative solutions are essential. This concentration can often only be maintained for a regular working day—after that, a break is needed.

Experienced developers are aware of this and it often manifests itself in a stringent handling of their own working hours. But one should generally be aware: It is called "sprint", but the way of working in product implementation is more like a "marathon" with a very formalized, recurring process.

8.4 Setting Up the Toolbox

8.4.1 Even More Preparation, Seriously?

You're getting impatient, aren't you? It could start slowly, right? It's a bit annoying that I'm starting the fourth section and not a single feature has been implemented, right?

8 Product Delivery 157

For that, I promise you something: What's coming now is essential for efficient implementation. If you don't prepare it, it will happen "just like that" during implementation and you had no chance to influence it. Therefore: It's worth it. And: These are really the last preparations that need to be done before something is finally developed.

8.4.2 Choosing a Name

The new product must bear a name. A really good name. One that is loved equally by marketing, management, and the customer. However, such a name often takes time to find. Sometimes you have to go round in circles for a long time before it is final—or it changes again at the last minute.

Nevertheless, you need an internal name right from the start, one that stays forever. The customer and management will never see it. Marketing probably will—if it ever writes tickets. This name will be used for everything: from the repository for the source code to the configuration of accounts with third-party providers (you don't want to code the payment system yourself, do you?), which are needed for the product. Therefore, choose a simple name and don't think about it for too long. Above all, do not give in to the temptation to choose a supposedly funny name. But also don't take the name idea that is currently being considered for the product—if you are not yet sure that it will stay.

Example

If it's going to be a real estate app, then you'd better call everything "real_estate_app" instead of "immotep" (after the Egyptian pharaoh). The name is right when even a developer who comes on board in three years can easily distinguish the "real_estate_ app" from the "homeowner_app". ◀

The final product name can still be inserted "just before launch" so that the user will never see the "internal" name.

8.4.3 Preparing the Backlog

The two most important tools that a product manager has for implementation are setting "priority" and the most detailed possible description of requirements. This does not necessarily mean that you have to use a lot of prose to describe something; rather, thinking through as many scenarios and special cases as possible for a requirement in advance is a key factor for efficient implementation. The priority, in turn, determines the order in which requirements are processed.

You may now be wondering what this has to do with the backlog? Well, to define priority transparently and consistently, you need the backlog or later the sprint board as a tool. The backlog contains everything that is not currently being worked on. You have to distinguish and prioritize requirements from each other. This also means, among other things, that a basic law should apply during implementation: "No ticket, no work."

In particular, changes to requirements that appear in the middle of the process are forgotten if they are not documented. Requirements that are not prioritized against others cause confusion when selecting the next to-do during implementation.

Which tool you use to compile the backlog is comparatively irrelevant. However, as always, expect the convenience of the users of your backlog and therefore choose a tool that is as close as possible to the actual code. I have had good experiences with Trello so far and would now also recommend Github Projects as an alternative, which with its column display and direct integration into the Github issue tracker is simply unbeatably closely interlinked. If you like—and it's already there—feel free to use Jira. However, I usually find its complexity much too high for the purpose it is supposed to serve. But if you don't have to have the difficult discussion "We already have something for that" with your admin, then use it.

For the backlog, you now need to transfer your feature breakdown into tickets. SCRUM recommends using a user story format, where you describe your requirements in the form: "As a (user type) I want to (function description) to achieve (purpose)." In addition, you should provide acceptance criteria for a user story, without the implementation of which a ticket is not considered completed.

This is definitely a good format and you can stick to it. However, variations often occur during implementation and the classic user story does not fit requirements such as "bug fixing" or purely technical requirements. If you formulate them as a user story, then absurdities like: "As a registered user, I want the changing of my email address to work properly" or "As a developer, I want us to adhere to coding guidelines" happen.

Therefore, I would rather point out the points that you should not forget in any case: Always describe the "use case" or the desired scenario to be implemented in your tickets/user stories, and think through the special cases in particular in the acceptance criteria. Note the acceptance criteria as a checklist that can be ticked off as much as possible during development.

What often happens is that the technological implementation or the solution path is described in the tickets. But you should not invest your time in this in any case, even if you are rightly proud of your technological understanding. Because this kind of ticket description collapses immediately if exceptions are discovered along the way that require a completely different approach. Then your ticket is suddenly worthless. This happens more often than you think, and then until the requirement is implemented, the ticket is often only used as a "reminder" and unfortunately no longer describes anything in detail.

Detailed, but not technical, requirements are one of the main tools for implementation. Therefore, the following may sound a bit silly. But believe me, this happens much faster than you think when you are short of time: Avoid using the words "all" or "every" in your tickets/stories. This leaves obvious gaps in the feature definition or causes questions from your developers. In the worst case, at this point, simply "do what you think" is done and then of course only in the rarest cases exactly what you want comes out. Rather, describe (even if only in keywords) the scenarios or states that you have in mind when you say "all".

Choosing a good "granularity level" for writing your stories is certainly not entirely straightforward. After all, you ultimately have to decide how to convert your feature breakdown into tickets. As a rule, I would recommend initially making a ticket out of every point in a breakdown that is not a heading or clearly a detailed description. Often, it fits to simply use the penultimate level. However, it doesn't matter too much if you don't get it "right" from the start, as the following SCRUM process will ensure that the tickets are broken down to the "right" level of detail. Together with the team, you will anyway review each ticket, evaluate it, and if necessary, split it up.

So try to prepare a broad thematic area with the tickets and especially tickets for almost the entire duration of the project. Not to really have every single ticket already, but rather to constantly have visibility over "what else needs to be done".

For structuring the backlog, you should limit yourself to a few types of categories:

- "Upcoming Sprints": Tickets that you have already selected for a next sprint. Normally, it is useful to know what will take place in the next two sprints.
- "Business Purpose": Structure all other tickets according to the purpose they serve. For example, "Marketing Optimization" for tracking features or "More Efficient Customer Support" for backend improvements.
- "Bugs": There will always be some.
- "Product Areas": Like "User Profile", "Registration" or "Library".

For the last point, I would only use the (sub-) categorization as long as the basic functionality of your new product is not yet fully established or until you implement a larger new feature. Once the basic functionality is in place, you can discipline yourself more easily to always keep the immediate benefit in mind by structuring the backlog according to "business purpose". In addition, the argument for implementing individual features for your stakeholders is then immediately obvious.

A good and usefully structured product backlog could therefore look approximately like shown in Fig. 8.6.

8.4.4 Setting up a Sprint Board

Your most important work tool in the daily work of product implementation consists of the sprint board, which we will look at next. This board contains everything that is currently being worked on. That is, you populate this board together with the team in a planning meeting and within the sprint everything is (hopefully) processed and nothing (hopefully) is added.

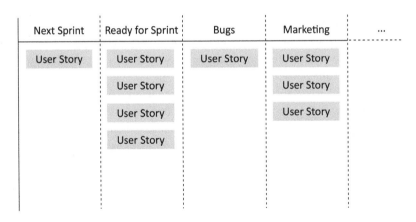

Fig. 8.6 Structure of a product backlog according to business purpose. (*Source*: Own illustration)

The sprint board is best to have the following columns, which you can regularly look at together with the team:

- "To-dos": At the beginning of the sprint, all tickets are in this column. Here, the team members can find "new" work during the sprint. If you are worried that not everything planned will be accomplished in this sprint: Also assign a priority here.
- "Doing": When someone starts working on a ticket, the ticket moves to this column. Make sure that there are no dead files here during the sprint. It often happens that too many topics accumulate per person and in reality not everything is being worked on that is in this column.
- "Code Review": After completing a ticket, there should definitely be an intermediate step for a code quality check, which your developers perform mutually. You should only omit this column if there is actually only one developer at all or only one backend and frontend developer—i.e., people who can hardly give each other feedback on the code.
- "QA" (Quality Assurance): When the code review is completed, a ticket moves to the QA column. When a ticket moves to the QA column, it should be the responsibility of the developers to ensure that the implementation of the ticket can actually be tested, i.e., that it is either available on a test system or you can install and try out a version of your product on a test device.
- "Ready for Deploy": If the testing was successful, tickets move to this column. It signals that the change or the feature can go to the live system. This, in turn, should be the responsibility of the developers. If your new feature possibly still needs to go into a review, e.g., at an AppStore, then this column is also a good place to let the ticket wait.
- "Done"/"Live": Here are all tickets that are really finally completed and accessible to the user.

8 Product Delivery 161

Since you will be looking at this board in your daily work again and again with the team, it makes sense that it can either be shown very clearly and simply on a projector or TV large and visible to all, or directly physically somewhere. Personally, I have not been able to identify any real advantages of physical boards over virtual ones, provided that you actually meet "in real life" for the daily. The virtual version of the board has the advantage that there is "infinitely" much space on the tickets and designs and concepts can be easily linked. Therefore, I recommend a virtual board to you.

8.5 Running a Marathon

8.5.1 Choosing Sprint Length

At the beginning of the implementation and setting up of the associated meetings, you finally determine the sprint length. In the previous parts, we had already assumed a sprint with a length of two weeks and I would advise you to simply keep it that way. It can occasionally make sense to let a sprint run for longer than two weeks. However, these reasons are usually found in special circumstances, such as vacations, absences of team members, or the Christmas season. But as a goal, keep the two weeks in mind, because often with longer periods, "disorder" or too much "on top stuff" creeps into the sprint board and then it makes sense to find a stopping point.

You should be particularly skeptical of shorter sprints. I have already experienced product teams several times where there were one-week sprints. In my experience, they occur when stakeholders either expect short-term results or are skeptical of the team and want to control it more closely. However, I have never seen it become faster, better, or more transparent as a result.

What I have experienced positively, on the other hand, is that a launch was made in the middle of the sprint. So I would strongly recommend resisting the temptation to switch to shorter sprints under pressure and instead introduce additional "launch days".

At its core, this definition of sprint length is also about finding a rhythm or the "pace" in which there is a balanced mix of overhead/planning time and working time. In the end, the individual sprints have to merge into a marathon that achieves a certain goal in a certain time.

8.5.2 Meetings, Meetings, Meetings … are the Sprint

A particularly important task in product implementation is conducting "good" meetings with a clear purpose and (often short) follow-ups that result from these meetings. The frequency and purpose of the meetings are defined by their place in the sprint.

All the meetings described in the following are pretty much exactly what a SCRUM manual imagines them to be. Therefore, I only briefly mention the purpose of the meetings here and try to focus more on what to pay attention to in practice to keep the meetings really efficient and useful.

Basically, the meetings are sorted, as shown in Fig. 8.7, as follows: At the beginning of a sprint there is a sprint planning, in which the to-dos of the next sprint are compiled. Every day of a sprint, "dailies" are conducted and at the end there is a "review" with all stakeholders.

8.5.2.1 Sprint Planning

At the beginning of a sprint, the entire team comes together to compile a selection of tickets/user stories that should be implemented in the next sprint. Schedule a 1.5 to 2 hour meeting for this sprint planning. Attempts to get it done in an hour are usually doomed to fail—at least if you allow enough time for discussions. Part of this meeting is also the estimation of the selected tickets.

Try to schedule the sprint planning for a day that is neither the beginning nor the end of the week. This way, you won't regularly fall into a team's beginning or end of the week slump. Wednesday is usually a good day for a sprint start.

At its core, it is your responsibility to be so prepared for this meeting that you can present the team with a selection of prioritized tickets that you would like to have implemented in the next sprint. If questions arise during your presentation of the tickets, especially about the intended scope of the tickets, then clarify them.

It can happen that the opinion emerges that a ticket needs to be split or merged with other tickets. In my experience, it is good to do this directly in the sprint planning—even if you then occasionally have highly paid people watching you word process. But this way, the meaning of the ticket is always clear to everyone and the wrong thing is not accidentally implemented later in development—that would then be really expensive.

8.5.2.1.1 Estimation

Once the team round has provided sufficient clarity about what the ticket describes, you move on to the estimation. The estimation is intended to give the ticket a magnitude, but it is not a highly accurate prediction that someone has to stake their life on. Nevertheless, you will be able to use the sum of the estimates both for an assessment of whether the

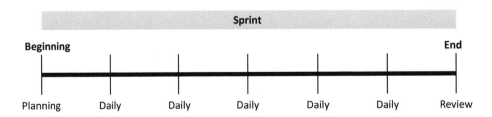

Fig. 8.7 Meetings during a sprint. (*Source*: Own illustration)

sprint is "too full" or possibly even "still has room", and for recording the actual performance (sum of the completed stories).

In order not to create the impression of an exact estimate in the team, we like to use the question of complexity as an estimate size for a ticket. That's why there is no time as a possible estimate size, but a selection of numbers (1, 3, 5 and 8). At this point, you should always choose an estimate size that is easy to add up. This does not work well with T-shirt sizes (see above). You will see why later. It is actually important that you limit the selection options for the estimate sizes, otherwise endless discussions can easily arise about whether this is "more of a 1 or a 2".

By the way, the estimation is easiest to achieve with SCRUM poker cards. This means that you distribute a card set with the possible estimate sizes to the team and each team member holds up his size as an estimate. If there are stark differences, you should discuss the understanding of the ticket with the team again.

You don't know what to do with these numbers? What are they supposed to mean and which one should you choose? Take comfort, many in the team who are supposed to estimate with these numbers feel the same way. Therefore, it makes sense to choose a reference story at the beginning that everyone in the team understands well and has an idea of the work involved. You then simply give this story a first number that you think is appropriate. I have always tried with my teams to take something from the midfield and not to start directly with an 8. As soon as several people in the team can work with the numbers, new team members will quickly get an idea of what the numbers mean.

But you can also estimate with "time", everyone can imagine something under that. However, you should also limit the selection options here and, for example, only offer 30 min, 2 h, 4 h, 1 D and 3 D. This means: If something is likely to take longer than 2 h, it automatically takes 4 h. Understanding this concept is not easy later on—similar to the numbers.

Estimating with time as a measure has a few more peculiarities:

- If you and your team are wrong in estimating tickets (and you will be), it will seem strange to you if you can only complete a ticket estimated at 2 h after 3 D. However, you should resist the impulse to change the estimate afterwards in any case. After all, you want to learn to estimate better in the end, which automatically means that you can and will be wrong. This way, you will only get a better estimate with these numbers if you do not change them afterwards. Because you want to estimate how much can be achieved in a sprint—including your own error in estimating, which you will probably still make in the future.
- You can easily show a sum of complexity degree estimates to your stakeholders without triggering major justifications. E.g. "We have managed tickets of the order of 65 points in the last 3 sprints". If you do this with time estimates, e.g. "We have managed tickets of the order of 7 D 6 h 30 min in the last 3 sprints", you will look into puzzled faces and next you will get the question what happened in all the "free time".

8.5.2.1.2 Unfinished Tickets

There will only be one sprint that you start with an empty sprint board—the first one. After that, there will practically always be tickets on the board that have not yet made it to the completely finished state. We deal with these tickets according to a fairly simple principle:

If the ticket is almost finished and has even been tested, then it can be agreed that it already counts as completed.

- If there is still QA to be done, it moves to the QA status and gets the estimate that is usually needed for work in QA.
- If further implementation work needs to be done, a "remaining estimate" is made. That is, the ticket responsible describes what still needs to be done, and then the team estimates the remaining size of the ticket.

In the last case, it is not uncommon for the ticket to remain the same or even get bigger. Similarly, you might wonder if the ticket is now smaller, because suddenly points have disappeared from the current sprint that you are just closing, which will not be recorded later. Moreover, work has already been done on the ticket, but this work is not acknowledged anywhere. However, this is intentional: We consciously only want to record the tickets that were actually completed. At the end of the sprint, half-finished tickets help no one and therefore they are not counted.

8.5.2.1.3 Sprint Size and Velocity

Two important assessment and planning sizes for your sprints are the size of a sprint and the velocity. Both represent the same value, namely the sum of all estimated sizes (story points) in a sprint—once at the beginning of the sprint (= sprint size) and at the end with a focus on all completed tickets (= velocity).

You should note both values for a sprint in a list (yes, Excel is fine too) and continuously update them. This way, you gradually get a feel for the team's speed—i.e., what can be achieved per sprint. In direct comparison with the sprint size, you thus have an indicator of how much can probably be achieved per sprint, see Fig. 8.8.

By the way, it's good if you also record a third value in addition to these two values, namely the number of "on-top tickets". These are all tickets that neither you nor the team knew about at the time of sprint planning and that have been added out of urgent necessity during the sprint. Although these have no estimate, they can certainly be recorded and appreciated as a team's performance. That's why we give these tickets the size "on top" instead of an estimate.

By the way: If an on-top ticket is not completed at the end of the sprint, you should give it a proper estimate for the next sprint.

8.5.2.2 Daily Standup

This short daily meeting should take place at the same time every day and not last longer than 15 minutes. Every team member who is currently working on the project is asked

8 Product Delivery

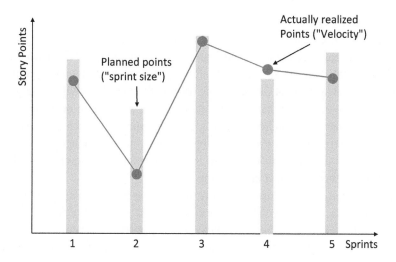

Fig. 8.8 Sprint size vs. velocity graph. (*Source*: Own illustration)

to give a brief status update on what they did the previous day and whether there are any problems. The goal is to quickly identify situations where someone is waiting for something or there is a more serious problem that needs to be decided together.

For the daily, we usually only open the sprint board for everyone to see and talk in turn about the tickets being worked on. Since it always takes place at the same time, it is usually easy for remote employees to "attend". The only important thing is that the video conferencing tool used supports screen sharing. The main screen with the sprint board and the video conferencing software should run on your computer so that you can make any necessary changes to tickets directly yourself and they are immediately visible to everyone.

The most common problem with dailies is that people get "stuck" on an implementation problem. This happens quickly when you delve deep into details and discuss solutions for problems. It needs someone in the round who quickly notices such a situation and points out that solution discussions should happen outside of the daily. This bores fewer people who have nothing to do with the problem and is more efficient and cheaper anyway.

Since the daily is a danger zone where it could be forgotten: Let me remind you of the hint "No ticket, no work" once again: Quickly things are said in the daily that either "should also be done again" or that are a detail for a ticket that has not been noticed so far. Either note these things immediately in a ticket (whether in the backlog or on an existing ticket) if they seem important, or let happen what is the fate of any unnoted thing in the sprint anyway: Forget it immediately.

Note everything that seems even remotely important to you as a ticket. And: Try to remember this rule when something important was not implemented for the first time, although "it has been said before".

8.5.2.3 Sprint Review

At the end of each sprint, there should be a "Sprint Review". This meeting is primarily intended to engage stakeholders and customer support and show them what has been achieved in the last two weeks. Schedule this approximately 45-minute meeting at the end of the sprint. Again, not at the beginning or end of the week. Tuesdays are good.

The function of informing stakeholders about the current state of development should not be underestimated. You should keep this in mind, especially when you yourself learn daily in dailies and plannings about the progress and which challenges have been mastered. The people you invite to the Sprint Review meeting, on the other hand, usually have no idea what has happened in the last two weeks.

Most of the time, stakeholders have other things to do than sit in a review for 45 minutes, but that's exactly why you should insist that they come. Otherwise, after two or three sprints at the latest, stakeholders will certainly get the feeling that there is hardly any progress. Or worse: That the really important issues (from the stakeholders' point of view) are not being worked on. It is much more work to dispel such misconceptions than to demand attendance for these meetings every two weeks.

And especially customer support quickly gets used to explaining the same thing over and over again and otherwise doesn't even notice when a long-standing problem has finally been solved.

For the team itself, a review has the nice effect that there is a goal to work towards. It also always represents a communication tool in which one's own work, which is often technically complex, must be presented as simply and visibly to the customer as possible so that it becomes understandable in a demo.

Conduct a review even if there is little to show. Even this helps to highlight and explain the problems that have arisen and why things take longer.

The process of a review is actually quite simple. You ask the question "What have we achieved in the last sprint?" and then let the team present the results of the tickets they have worked on. This does not have to happen ticket by ticket, but can also be done for large topic complexes "as a whole". However, the real product should definitely be shown and demonstrated. No PowerPoint slides—or only in rare exceptions, if, for example, a certain scenario/feature is difficult to demonstrate in real time. However, it is always better if the team takes the time to make a feature "demonstrable".

Be prepared for comments, remarks and new requirements to come up in the review, which you will need to note down and sharpen and prioritize afterwards.

At the end of the meeting, it is good if you briefly outline your plans for the next sprint as "This is what we will do". And based on this, there should be the next sprint planning the day after.

8.5.2.4 Retrospective

I briefly considered whether to heretically omit the "Retrospective" and not mention it at all. I believe that the way SCRUM wants you to use the retrospective, it definitely comes too often and therefore doesn't bring anything. Even more: I have often experienced that teams gather in retrospectives for whining sessions or drag them out forever.

In retrospectives, you are actually supposed to reflect on the past sprint and consider how things could be done better. I would recommend conducting these retrospectives every 3 months or when you notice that there are really problems in the team. Then they can really uncover problems and opportunities for improvement can arise. I don't see a retrospective as necessary after every sprint conducted.

8.5.3 Are We Still on Schedule...?

Depending on how many sprints you have planned, sooner or later you will ask yourself whether you are "still on schedule". Or to put it in the words of your stakeholders: "Will we make it by <any date>?" and five minutes later "No, seriously we have to make it by <any date>!" To answer this question, you can use two tools that you have already set up in preparation: Your sprint rough planning from Sect. 8.3 and the velocity measurement from Sect. 8.5.2.1.3.

In principle, I would advise you not to make any statement until two or three sprints have passed. "And what if I only planned that many in the first place?" you might ask now. Then you have to live with the corresponding uncertainty in this short time.

Why this period? To gain a few more data points about the actual speed of the team. It could just as well be that you start the marathon with a zero-point sprint or that you achieve more than you had planned at the beginning. Neither should worry or overly please you, because only when the average speed is measured over a longer period of time do you have the chance to really recognize how fast you are. There are constantly outliers in the velocity and they are very often unpredictable. The only constant I have experienced so far is a large speed spike in the sprint just before Christmas. So far, I have not been able to find an explanation for this. Probably one just wants to quickly get everything done in order to have virtually no work in the new year.

After this time, you will have some velocity measurements available. You will also have a feeling for whether the large topic blocks can be processed in the order and speed as you had planned them. Don't let it unsettle you if you bring topics from future sprints forward and possibly push topics further back. It should only make you thoughtful if you only push things back.

8.5.4   … And If Not, How Do We Get Back "On Plan"?

At the latest two sprints before your planned launch date, you should feel that the launch is "achievable". That is, your product has reached a maturity where you have the good feeling that you can release it to your customers. You should definitely tie this good feeling to things other than statements from your team: you should have already tried out and approved interim stages of your product. If there are still bugs or parts of the functionality do not exist at this point, that's okay as long as you can see from the velocity and sprint rough planning that you can still manage these issues.

> Unfortunately, I have often experienced situations where even at this point, people have relied solely on statements from developers or, worse still, "the nodding" of developers. Again: this alone is unfortunately not enough. You need something tangible to try out.

Do you already feel before this point that your team could handle more speed? Then there is a simple, but expensive tool for this: more employees. Unfortunately, there are few alternatives, provided your tickets are well prepared. Your team will not suddenly finish things "without reason" faster than they have in the past.

Especially on the developer side, you can often—to a certain extent—increase staff to become faster. Here too, I would advise taking two sprints to assess whether more personnel has really led to an increase in speed. The first sprint may have involved too much "onboarding" effort.

The only other option you have to become faster is simply "omission". Please do not try to negotiate with your team whether "more can be achieved": Ultimately, it is the responsibility of the entire team to get a feel for the possible speed. You are part of it.

So if it is not possible to bring more team members on board (usually there is a limit at six developers), then try to rethink the feature set for the launch. Leave out things that are not really essential. Always remember: It is quite possible and even common today to first launch new products as "beta" and then deliver afterwards.

8.6   Little Helpers in Everyday Life

After you have hopefully successfully (and by that I mean all the setbacks, additional costs and emotional meetings you have encountered along the way) brought your product to the customer, I would like to shed light on two topics that two groups of people will approach you with during the work on your product.

8.6.1   Developers Call for "Refactoring!"

The topic of "refactoring" is difficult for you as a product manager to assess because you do not work with the code every day and cannot see the problems buried there. The only thing you can perceive at all are the wishes and statements of your team, "how bad the code" looks and "that it needs to be redone".

I recommend that you listen to both the team's statements and pay attention to a phenomenon that you can observe in your product: Do problems regularly occur when implementing new features that no one would have suspected before? For example: Does the ability to change the email address suddenly break when a Facebook login is installed? By this I do not mean that adjustments had to be made at this point during the sprint because otherwise it would not have worked anymore. At this point, it is more about seeing whether the team has noticed and fixed this circumstance.

If the phenomenon of "side effects" of new features occurs more frequently and has also made it into your final product once or twice, this suggests that the team is having difficulty keeping track of the complexity of the product. At such times, it is worth investing more in "refactoring" and then keeping an eye on whether this phenomenon is reduced.

However, these side effects can also indicate that your product lacks "automated tests". I hope that this is no longer the way things are developed, but it can always happen. Therefore, you should check this question again with the team before you throw yourself into "refactoring". Investing work in "automated tests" also makes QA easier because standard cases can then simply be tested "automatically".

8.6.2 Customer Support Warns of "Bugs!"

When your new product has been launched and has reached the hands of customers, one thing is certain: there are always bugs. Whether small visual blemishes or difficult to reproduce crashes that no developer can reliably reproduce.

At the latest when these problems appear in customer support, the question will arise: How do you prioritize bugs that you encounter in the "wild"? Every bug will always seem very important if it only appears to the right people or stakeholders.

Therefore, you should try to assess bugs in a similar way to how you assess the profitability of new features for your product. However, with bugs you are not trying to estimate the potential profit for your KPI, but the number of affected users. This can hardly be guaranteed through personal contact or observation of customers or stakeholders. You need an exception and stability tracker that keeps an eye on this automatically. Possible tools for this are e.g. Bugsnag, Rollbar or Google Firebase.

These tools record all crashes and errors that the user encounters for you and your team. You can even deliberately record "errors" with these tools to, for example, record payment cancellations, which can occur regularly, but you would like to know their frequency.

The tools group errors into error types and measure their frequency and the circumstances under which they occurred to the customer. Such a breakdown helps you to better assess the actual frequency of errors. Prioritize the errors that occur more frequently here. However, keep in mind that these exception trackers are always full of messages after a period of live operation. There is simply no crash-free or error-free operation. It is not desirable and especially not efficient to try to fix every error.

8.7 That's It

I hope that with these tips and tools from practice I was able to help you as an aspiring digital product manager to bring your first products to the customer successfully and efficiently.

But I am also sure: You will encounter further phenomena that are worth writing down and sharing. I firmly believe that it is very worthwhile to always compare the agile frameworks with their practicability and implementation in real practice. This is also the actual "craft" of the product manager: to know when which tool should be used and in what form it is really "practical".

I would be happy to hear from you if you have further suggestions for such tips from practice…

Tim Adler is a freelance tech lead and coding coach. He was most recently CTO of the largest European recipe platform chefkoch.de. Previously, he worked as Managing Director of an Innovation Lab and as CTO at a Company Builder. There, he successfully helped build a large number of start-ups. As a project manager, he also accompanied major restructuring measures in the digital area of a large German publishing house and, as a product manager, brought the first edition of a large German news magazine to the iPad. He trained product managers, advised top managers, and wrote hundreds of lines of code as the lead developer of various projects.

This contribution attempts to document the experiences from the agile development projects of this time and to give recommendations on how to achieve results most efficiently.

Contact: mail@tim-adler.de

Growth

The Thing About Growth

9

Markus Andrezak

Abstract

In business, it is not enough to simply bring good and economically successful products to the market. All too often, growth figures must also increase continuously or even exponentially to achieve the promised corporate goals. The article shows that growth cannot simply be "announced", but is the result of hard, protracted work. In this process, a company needs not only the courage to allow different working methods within its organization, but also a large portion of luck.

9.1 Everyone Wants Growth

Growth! Wachstum! Everyone wants it, right?. The reason?, We don't know! Perhaps it is simply due to the stock or venture capital market, driven by the desire for rapid wealth accumulation. Growing, becoming larger, making more sales, hiring more employees—almost every company strives for this. And when a company breaks with this creed, like Patagonia, it can use it for advertising—and still continue to grow…

Already in the 70s and 80s of the last century, the report "Limits of Growth" carried out by the Club of Rome at MIT was on everyone's lips. Anyone who went to school at that time was aware that growth cannot function indefinitely. It was even clear how complex local business and global growth are interconnected. This knowledge also entered the canon of business administration and economics. But what we observe in

---

M. Andrezak (✉)
überproduct, Potsdam, Deutschland
e-mail: markus@ueberproduct.de

© The Author(s), under exclusive license to Springer Fachmedien Wiesbaden GmbH, part of Springer Nature 2024
S. Hoffmann (ed.), *Digital Product Management*,
https://doi.org/10.1007/978-3-658-44276-7_9

171

the economy, contrary to this knowledge, is an emotionally driven persistent desire for growth. Who would want to manage a company or a product that does not grow?

Since everyone wants to continue growing on a small scale, everything continues to grow globally. And if growth doesn't work out once because bubbles burst, then you have to push down the interest rates and it goes a little further. If the bubble finally bursts, the banks are saved, a few consumers are sacrificed, a growth program is launched and off we go…

In the role of a product manager, it is relatively little career-promoting to be the sensible one in every conversation with superiors or clients and to always emphasize resource conservation, to bring up the report of the Club of Rome and to insist on "Sustainable Growth". Therefore, the rest of the article will now deal with how to work towards growth specifically.

One might think that things are different in the digital world: Our goods are not tangible and the thought that we do not consume so many resources is tempting. This starts with programming languages that fill existing computer resources like perfect gas at any time—even if it's for a notebook app. The economic model of most product managers' evaluation is accordingly not to meticulously find out which feature contributes how much to sales, but much more: We have 200 developers, they are and were expensive—the main thing is that they always have plenty to do. Just like in the early days of industrialization, but with programmers.

This chapter is primarily about growth from new things and not about growth that results from the maintenance of existing things. Because the latter is always linear. We usually manage this type of growth quite well. The pain arises from unrealistic expectations regarding growth from new things. It becomes difficult when the boss or the organization orders "Hockey-Stick-Growth" or "Triple-Digit-Growth" or something similarly popular.

"The purpose of business is to create and keep a customer"—(Peter Drucker 1973).

Growth arises from the first task described in the sentence. The second part of the sentence ensures that we do not go under. A problem in growth is that companies of a certain size almost only know mechanisms that help not to lose customers. But winning customers is quite different. It feels more insecure. And you don't know exactly if it will work. The culture of keeping customers and preserving does not help much in winning customers.

"Satisfying a large group of users is a by-product of satisfying one user. Satisfying nobody is a by-product of trying to satisfy a large group of users" (Alan Cooper 2019).

This sentence describes the dialectic that makes growth so difficult for us: We want to be attractive to many customers as quickly as possible. But we have to take the detour of first serving very few customers very well and thoroughly.

The recipe we need to serve many lies in abstraction and simplification. Good products for the masses are always a compromise. A good compromise that many *somehow* like. The necessary abstraction and simplification, the *recipe,* we can only discover and learn "on foot" by repeatedly serving a few.

Or shorter and simpler: **"There is no overnight success."**—There is no shortcut.

Even Karina's Boss Wants Growth

Karina is a product manager, like all of us. Karina comes back shocked from a one-on-one meeting with her boss to her colleagues. She is part of a Scrum team. As it should be, they are co-located and share almost everything with each other. They get along well. They work well together. The colleagues smell a rat and after a grace period, which Karina urgently needed for recovery, comes the question that must come: "What happened?" Karina's email still works. So she wasn't fired. "Martin [her boss] found a great opportunity in his Excel sheet." A business analyst (Big Data, of course!) whispered to him that not everything is going as the benchmarks of other products promise in the funnel of the product part that Karina is responsible for. There must be something to do... The rest went very quickly: 23% growth in her area should be achievable in the next two quarters..!

One or the other will surely have heard the demand for Hockey-Stick-Growth, "growth above the market" or similar. Karina is supposed to "only" optimize towards the benchmark. The goal is quickly defined as an objective of an OKR.[1] Now Karina can bring the news to her team.

For the team, this is all a bit of a slap in the face: They are currently pursuing completely different goals because of a similar meeting a few months ago. Above all, they have completely different, qualitative indications of what is currently preventing customers from being more satisfied. Despite all the frustration, the team sets about crafting the missing Key Results for the Objective. There are several problems with this:

- The team doesn't even know yet what is preventing customers from converting, there is a lack of qualitative knowledge.
- The team doesn't really know what is meant by growth. And: Are they allowed to sacrifice margin for it?
- The team doesn't understand the direct connection between their product part and growth.
- Are 6 months meant seriously or just an order of magnitude, a thought incentive?

Even if the next one-on-one is just around the corner: The uncertainty is great and the hope for real clarification is vague. But the clock is ticking.

Of course, I made up Karina. But I know many Karinas in very similar situations. Maybe just two incidents from my own product life: I once worked in a company that grew by about 17% per year. In 2008, we made about 120 million EUR in sales. The motto was suddenly "210 in 2010". We had about 18 months left for that. A simple calculation made it clear that we would have to more than double our growth from the day of the "announcement" to achieve an increase in sales of more than 50%...

Any normal person would have had to know that from that day on, no stone in the company would have remained unturned in order to achieve these goals. Probably

---

[1] For the OKR concept, see Chap. 4 by Cansel Sörgens in detail.

everyone was aware of this. But: More change was probably not bearable. So, in fact, people continued to work as before, just under a different motto, a bit differently organized, a bit "more agile" and hoped. Questions about the seriousness of the numbers were always answered with "yes, that's what we mean", as were questions about the time horizon. What was sorely missed was help that went beyond issuing the motto. The cynicism was right: The goal was missed by a long shot.

The second incident: In the same company, I was later allowed to build an early iPad app. Everyone was looking at the beautiful new device. Almost everyone was somehow a stakeholder. The CEO then came up with the good-sounding requirement that I should achieve 35% mobile traffic with the release of the app. We already had 30%— and every year at Christmas, new percentages were automatically added due to newly gifted smartphones with new mobile tariffs. The nice relatives got new smartphones, data rate included. That didn't sound so bad at first. But the question was: Why 35%? Would 50% be better or worse than 35%? Actually, we didn't know that exactly. Because we didn't know how and if our mobile traffic could be monetized at all, i.e., generate sales or profit. To this day, my suspicion is that it was simply about a catchy phrase and more sounds more determined than differentiated discussions about which goals of the product make sense beyond increased advertising revenues.

The demand for growth confronts us at all levels: company, portfolio, product, subproduct, etc. In order to be able to cope better in such situations and to be able to discuss better, I now want to introduce what we know about growth, where it arises and which models exist to understand growth. In the end, I want to explain what skills are needed to be able to manage growth. I hope that product managers can then deal a little better with demands for growth, so as not to have to express an uninformed "Sure, I'll do it!" or a defiant "No, that never works", but to be able to enter into a differentiated, clarifying discussion. In my experience, this does not help in the short term with every assignment. However, repeatedly bringing up discussions about these models does help in the medium and long term to create awareness for it.

9.2 How Long Does Growth Take?

Who knows off the top of their head how long Facebook has been around? How did the growth of well-known products like the Ford Model T progress? How long does growth usually take? How much do you have to do for it? Can you simply think up growth or the idea for it? How does someone come up with the idea that great growth just works like that? And if we try it: why is it then so hard? Has there ever been sudden growth? Just like that, overnight? Why doesn't our founder seem to remember how hard, tough and creepingly slow growth was for him at the beginning?

To learn more about growth and to be able to assess expectations of growth more realistically, it helps to look at the growth of well-known products.

9.2.1 Henry Ford and the Model T

The growth curve of the Model T is quite impressive: even today's numbers from Tesla show a very similar curve. And this, even though Tesla really makes an effort, has a visionary CEO, state-of-the-art manufacturing technology, and consultants from all over the world. Just as Ford had to establish the combustion engine and the carburetor, Tesla today has to research and establish the battery-based electric drive train. Both companies are incredibly successful in what they do. Both are led by impressive personalities. And yet: The statistics of growth are to be considered in years, not in months, see Fig. 9.1. Growth does not happen in months even today. In the first year, Ford produced just 10,660 Ford Model T. In the second year, almost a doubling to 19,050 units, then far less than a doubling, at some point an incredible leap in production. From 1919, ten years after its introduction, the growth engine then stuttered and after 1927 the sunsetting, the discontinuation of the Model T took place.

Much more exciting than the actual growth curve of the product is the prehistory. Who knows that Henry Ford worked for about eight years from his 28th year of life (1891) as chief engineer for Thomas Alva Edison? In his role as chief engineer, he had the carburetor patented and built the Quadricycle (a precursor of the car). In 1899, he then founded Ford and after some twists and turns, everything culminated in the Henry Ford Company in 1903. The first Model T was thus the fruit of *18 years of preparatory work;* six of them alone in Ford's own company.

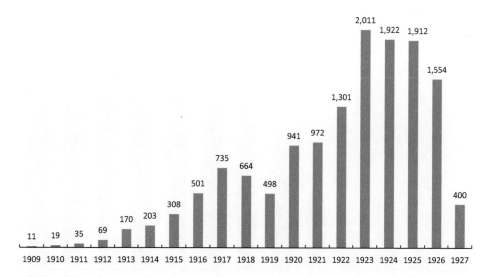

Fig. 9.1 Production numbers Ford Model T (in thousand). (*Source*: Own representation with data from the Model T Ford Club of America 2020)

9.2.2 The iPhone

Fig. 9.2 shows the sales volumes of perhaps the most successful product of all time. Here too, a comparatively modest beginning: While today, in times of stagnation of sales, after "only" 13 years about 217 million iPhones are sold per year, the first model sold "only" 1.4 million iPhones in the first year. The press could not agree whether this was a success or not. Whether the iPhone worked commercially or was just a brilliant invention. If the expectations of this success had been brought to the original team, this would have been paralyzing for the creativity behind the innovation. But above all, the initial 1.39 million sold models would probably have been booked as a failure. This is still the case with the Apple Watch today. Not big enough—although its sales figures are higher than those of Rolex.

Growth is therefore difficult to assess. And very relative: For Apple, the sale of a million units is nothing, considering the size of their customer platform. Here too, the time to real success is not measured in weeks or months, but in several years.

9.2.3 Digital "Growth Miracles"

One might get the idea that the examples from the world of hardware in a book on digital product management are misleading. So let's take a look at a digital, very successful product: Facebook!

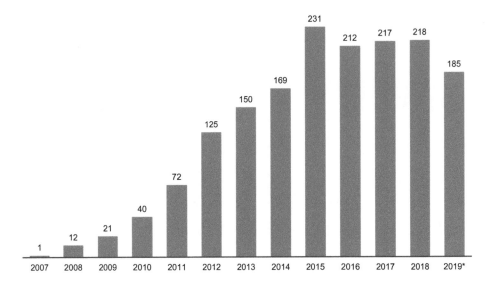

Fig. 9.2 Sales of Apple iPhones worldwide (in million). (*Source*: Statista 2020)

Facebook was founded as early as 2004. At the time of publication of this book, Facebook is therefore a recalcitrant teenager of 16 years. Until 2008, growth was still quite slow, as Fig. 9.3 shows. Remember: At that time, Studi-VZ also thought they could compete with Facebook—at least locally. The company that operated Studi-VZ then went bankrupt in 2017 with 45 million EUR in debt. That sounds like a lot of money. In fact, the unsuccessful network accumulated in all those years not even as much debt as Facebook makes in profit every day.

The explosion of Facebook came from 2008 to 2009, as Fig. 9.3 shows. This coincides noticeably with the introduction of the Like button in February 2009. So is there the "killer feature" that triggers growth on its own? Probably not. It is more likely that the foundations for the business model based on customer data and derived targeting were laid in the years before 2008 and 2009. The Like button was just another feature to increase engagement and become an "octopus". It is a symptom of a found recipe.

If you ask who knows an "overnight success", you occasionally get the answer "Flappy Birds". As long as the opposite cannot be proven, this online game may be the big exception. However, the success was also over as quickly as it came. The "inventor" quickly gave up in frustration. In the end, he committed suicide.

Another suspicion is Pokémon GO. However, Pokémon GO builds on the brand power of Pokémon and the spread of Nintendo. More weighty, however, is that the "inventor" of Pokémon GO reaped the fruits of about 20 years of work with this game. John Hanke has been working on computer games since around 1995. In 2001, he founded the company Keyhole, which built large geolocation software. He always

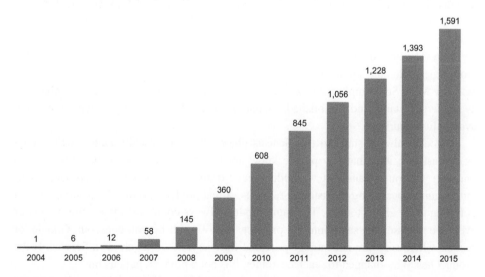

Fig. 9.3 Number of Facebook users worldwide (in millions). (*Source*: Statista 2016)

wanted to use this for entertainment. Keyhole was used for Google Maps, Street View, and Google Earth. With the help of Google, he finally founded Niantic, the company that released the precursor to Pokémon GO, "Ingress", and recruited a million players within a year after all those years of groundwork. Impressive—but not an overnight success. Pokémon GO built on the same data and has now recorded over a billion downloads with a different game mechanic. So growth needs foundations!

9.3   Growth Happens in Two Phases

Growth occurs in a surprisingly predictable way: During growth, a—becoming—product goes through different phases with very different challenges. Each of these phases requires a different way of thinking and acting as well as a different "culture". It is important to understand the different phases in order to be able to deal with the specific challenges.

▶ A small warning on the side: Both the models in this section and those in the next section prepare one intellectually for what is to come. But when the predicted phenomena occur, it hits one almost unprepared and dealing with the difficulties often remains emotionally difficult. Here it helps to look at the models again to be able to deal with the situation more relaxed: "Oh, it was clear and predictable that this would happen." Growth is usually only nice when it has already happened…

Simon Wardley (2018) has built a model for the natural growth of products and services into his visualization and thinking tool for strategy, the **Wardley Maps,** see Fig. 9.4.

The vertical axis in a Wardley Map denotes the visibility or availability of an offer. The more people have access to something, the higher the offer is arranged in the Wardley Map. The horizontal axis describes the security or maturity of an offer. The clearer, more repeatable, and predictable an offer is, the further to the right it is arranged on a Wardley Map. So, completely new things are arranged at the bottom left (invisible, not available/uncertain) and established, standardized products are at the top right (high availability/security).

A product always starts in the Genesis phase: A startup usually begins with a cool or at least nice idea that few people know about and have access to (perhaps even no one yet). Custom means that we build special designs: A guitar maker produces individual guitars according to customer requests. A real product has the characteristic that it is the same for all customers. The same product always comes off the assembly line, or everyone accesses the same internet product, such as with Immobilienscout, Google, or models where software is centrally provided for everyone: Software as a Service. If the product has to be changed for each customer, it is not a product, but custom.

When an offer becomes a commodity, it is available to all demanders in the relevant market. The standardization of the offers is now so high that the offers become largely interchangeable. Examples of commodity offers are nails or electricity from the socket.

9 Growth

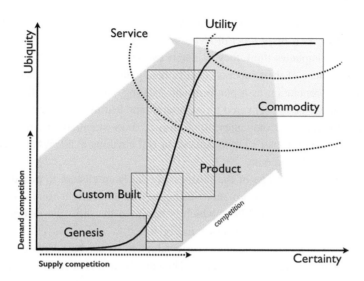

Fig. 9.4 Wardley Map. (*Source*: Wardley 2018)

"The main thing is that I have a nail." or "My electricity just comes from the socket." are typical statements about commodity offers. Accordingly, customer preferences and profit margins in the commodity sector are also only marginally present.

There are two essential growth leaps for an offer: The transition from the custom to the product phase. This is the productization of an offer. The transition is tempting because no scaling effect can occur in the custom area. To build 20 times as many individual guitars, you also need 20 times as much staff. But this guarantees the love of the customers. The transition to the product now consists of limiting the offer to five fixed guitar models. Individualization no longer takes place. Once you have built enough individual guitars, you get an idea of what a good guitar looks like for many people. With this knowledge, a scaling production line for five guitar models can be built and subsequently hardly any more staff is needed for 20 times as many customers. However, since the guitar is now a standard model, the individual customers probably stay away or are dissatisfied. This is the price that the producer pays. To further drive the product into a commodity, the guitars would then simply have to be ordered in the Far East and the own company would merely be the marketing or sales shell. The guitars will probably get even cheaper. They are only suitable as birthday gifts for children's birthdays. But the market for this is surprisingly large.

The model makes a first fallacy clear: We usually only know companies after their growth leap to the product. The preconditions of slow learning and limited growth in the custom area are forgotten. But the fact that the company and its offer became known and more visible is exactly the reason why we know them. The common notion is therefore that one can get directly to the product. But this is not possible, because one would have to guess the recipe for the product. An approach that guarantees failure.

This would be exactly the approach that Alan Cooper (2019) describes when he says: *"Satisfying nobody is a by-product of trying to satisfy a large group of users"*. Particularly successful companies think they can start everything new directly as a repeatable, good product because of their success. Unfortunately, this is a fallacy: These companies do have a certain reputation as a platform and existing sales channels. But every additional product has to be rediscovered through work and learning in the custom area. Surprisingly, the founders of companies often "forget" how strenuous the beginning was. How they sat on the customer's lap to achieve or sell anything at all. What setbacks they had to experience and overcome.

A small warning: A change of the business model from custom to product is (especially socially and in perception) more difficult than one might think. The concept **Crossing the Chasm** (Moore 1991), which is based on the diffusion theory of Everett Rogers (1962), describes the effect shown in Fig. 9.5.

With a new product, the so-called "early adopters" must be addressed first. Early adopters are generally eager for new things. They are the first chance: If you talk to them, it fuels their curiosity and makes them satisfied. They are thus an early source of qualitative information from which one can learn and understand. Only with them can you start something new. Only with their knowledge, can you really understand context, market, and requirements. As soon as the company has learned enough and turns to the large market, however, the relationship with these early customers changes: Until now, you sat with them in workshops and asked about their wishes. As soon as we had finally identified these (Eureka!), we tried to answer them directly in the product. In the transition to the product, you then ask a lot of customers. Now you have to build compromises that fit well for most customers, but are usually perfect for none. These are the generalized recipe for satisfying many customers. This opens up a dangerous chasm: Hardly anyone is as enthusiastic as before, but many find it good. Serving everyone exactly according to their needs would be the death of the product, as it would become too confusing and complicated. Only products for highly enthusiastic niches or experts may be complicated.

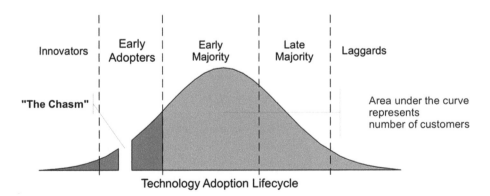

Fig. 9.5 Lifecycle of technology adoption. (*Source*: Dihen 2018)

9 Growth

Everyone knows the effect from their life and has a brand that used to be really great and listened to customers, but is now somehow "mass". Ed Hardy shirts or on a larger scale maybe Apple. Who doesn't have a "creative" acquaintance who bought Apple products 20 years ago, still does today, but has the impression that "everything was better in the past, they used to take care of us"? Despite all the grumbling and separation pain from the early adopters, Apple is still doing very well with its growth today.

So once again: There is no shortcut. We have to take the long, arduous path. Growth to success takes years, not months, and the initial sales figures are always meager in comparison to the later expected success or potential.

9.4 Growth Models

The following are some models that explain how to generate growth. Growth has a lot to do with discipline, intellect, and overriding instincts. And relatively little to do with intuition, genius, and the "right idea" in the shower or while walking. We actually know how it works. It just feels very tedious when you do it.

9.4.1 The Hockey Stick

Karina's and my boss each had a demand on us that could be graphically represented as a **hockey stick**: "Make sure to start growth so that we can grow like crazy soon". Everyone wants the hockey stick or "triple-digit growth".

In fact, the original definition of the hockey stick graph by climatologist Jerry Mahlmann has a rather sad meaning: As shown in Fig. 9.6, it shows the dramatic warming of our northern hemisphere over the last thousand years (Monastersky 2006). We would all like to do without this hockey stick, but we have worked on it for a long time.

Why a hockey stick is so popular has two reasons: The shape of the exponential curve suggests a sweet explosion to the top right: We are growing like crazy. But before the curve catapults upwards, it goes up quite leisurely. As a person in charge, the curve means that you can *promise* phenomenal growth "upwards", but you don't exactly know *when* the explosion starts. Every quarter, you just crawl in the flat area of the curve. It's like the promise of a life after death in paradise: The best is yet to come. And that every quarter. And it *could* start at any time. "Downwards", on the other hand, you can always set the big growth target and impatiently ask when the growth explosion will finally start and who has not done their job properly.

If you look closely, however, the hockey stick first points flat downwards before it goes steeply upwards. In fact, you have to imagine the hockey stick as a J-curve: The J-curve describes the macroeconomic effect that a devaluation of money, contrary to all expectations, does not immediately boost exports, but crazily shrinks exports first, which then only go upwards with a delay, as also shown in Fig. 9.7.

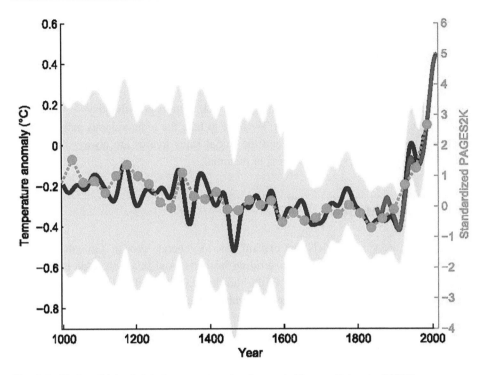

Fig. 9.6 Hockey Stick of global temperature development. (*Source*: Rahmstorf 2013)

Fig. 9.7 Reaction of the trade balance to a devaluation in the form of a J-curve. (Source: Based on Blanchard and Illing 2014)

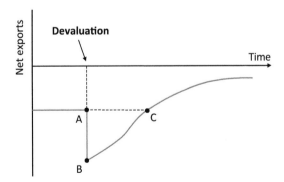

There is a simple reason for the **J-curve effect**: When something new is done in a company, employees are pulled away from the existing. But since the existing usually still works well (the company is not bankrupt), less of what works is initially produced.

We always think that everything is different in the digital world and that economic rules do not apply here. But in fact, this is not the case: Software and operation do not work because they are automated, but despite being automated. What holds everything together for the customer are indeed the people who come up with products, define, build, operate, take care of customers, or do marketing. In the digital world, it's just easier to scale.

With the J-curve, you face the following psychological problem: Before success, you are forced to go through a trough of failure and loss. Unfortunately, it is not clear at the beginning whether success will really come. It doesn't always come! And almost as bad is that it is also not clear when success will come.

Life in the trough of the J-curve is therefore very uncomfortable. Here, only intellect and discipline can help. You have to go through it. We cannot seriously answer the question of whether success is still to come, as we do not have any data from the future. So we face the halting problem according to Alan Turing (Davis 1958): We do not know whether it is better to continue or to stop.

9.4.2 The 3-Horizon Model

But what helps? What constructive approach is there to deal with growth? The **3-horizon model** was described by Baghei et al. (1999) in the classic among growth books "The Alchemy of Growth". For this, they looked at how companies manage to grow continuously over decades, even though the environment changes. They observed that consistently growing companies work towards three different time horizons at any given time.

The three horizons in Fig. 9.8actually represent S-curves. **S-curves** originally depict the diffusion of innovation: How does the spread of new ideas or technologies progress? They spread slowly at first, then faster, rapidly, eventually flatten out, and sadly, they also die off at some point (Sunsetting). The S-curve is suitable as a model for growth, as the curves of growth and the sales of innovation run similarly (Baum et al. 2013).

Actually, S-curves have more sad sections than happy ones: The beginning is hard, stagnation after growth does not feel good, and when the product dies completely, it is even more terrible. Perhaps the core of the problem with growth has already been identified here: You do not get the beautiful part of rapid growth without the other three, less pleasant parts. Cherry-picking does not work.

The growth phase in the S-curve model is also not so nicely attributed. Problems encountered here are possibly luxury problems. But that does not make them any more bearable: The market wants more than we can deliver. Quality suffers because we have not yet learned to deliver large quantities in quality or to serve many customers well. Internally, we suffer from the constant experience of scarcity: We do not get enough work resources and qualified employees are hard to find in sufficient numbers. In short: We are overwhelmed.

9.4.2.1 Horizon 1

Let's imagine a company with a business model. Then the company's turnover is well described by an S-curve (bottom left). This is the first horizon. It contains the currently

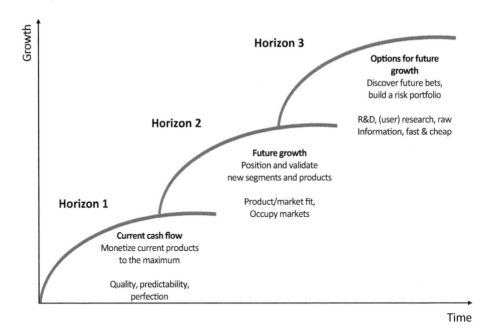

Fig. 9.8 The 3-Horizon Model. (*Source*: Adapted from Baghei et al. 1999)

existing offers. The task now is to milk these offers as much as possible. The company must increase the quality and be able to deliver more and more of the same, always cheaper. It must practice "Operational Excellence" to maximize the use of the existing offer and thus become maximally cheap, predictable, and repeatable for the customer.

Growth is also possible in Horizon 1. But in Horizon 1, growth is linear. The company and the product already exist. The market knows them; they are established. This is probably the situation in which most—even digital—product managers work. You cannot expect growth leaps from working on the existing, established product. The hockey stick does not originate here. If the demand is to grow with the market, evolutionary growth in Horizon 1 must be meant! Because anything beyond that does not work here.

New growth is only achieved in the second horizon.

9.4.2.2 Horizon 2

We know that the curve of the first horizon will eventually go down. What can we do about it? One might think that a few new features could save the company. But this is like the new features on the new iPhone or Google Pixel: It's just evolutionary growth— or further stagnation. All that is achieved with new features is to extend the first S-curve or to build in a few small bumps. As Drucker (1973) says, one can work on retaining existing customers and monetizing them more and more.

But the big growth lies in constantly generating new customers. For example, Apple was said to have managed to achieve linear customer growth over 20 years. The curve looked so frighteningly linear that one might think it was their control variable. But how do you get new customers? By solving problems of people who were not customers before. So we need to solve bigger problems that we haven't solved before. Our current offer solves a specific problem at its core. It is not enough to win new customers by continuing to work here. Work on the existing offer is there to prevent customers from migrating (and maybe get a few new ones).

So we need to come up with new products that solve problems we haven't solved before. Ideally, these are also problems that we could somehow already solve, but whose solution we have not yet offered. We must already be able to do the work at its core. If we don't solve new problems, the 3-horizon model, in which the S-curves add up, doesn't apply.

Examples of new products that solve new problems are, for example, the iPhone, which replaced the iPod, which was responsible for about 70% of Apple's revenue at the time. The iPhone could do everything the iPod could—and much more: *A widescreen iPod touch, a revolutionary mobile phone, and a groundbreaking internet communication device* (Apple 2007).

Another example of new products that solve new problems: The introduction of the Frappuccino at Starbucks also has Horizon 2 qualities: For the company, which—at least at its founding and in the USA—stands for the niche "slightly better coffee at higher prices, personal service and the third place between office and home", the introduction of the Frappuccino was something completely new. The target group were teenagers who inexplicably met at Starbucks in the afternoon to be "adult" and ordered bitter "swill". Sweeter (sometimes even still) coffee-containing drinks could really appeal to them.

Perhaps the most radical Horizon 2 product from perhaps the most radical 3-horizon CEO, Jeff Bezos, is Amazon Web Services (AWS). Who else in his company, which lives from shipping books and other things and has just undergone a huge conversion to logistics (Marketplaces), could successfully suggest selling computing power—and all under one roof.

There are two difficulties with the second horizon: The people who work on Horizon 1 will hate every Horizon 2 idea. "What's that supposed to be?", "And that's supposed to be us?" are sentences that will be said. And rightly so: Those who work on Horizon 1 protect the existing, have countless meetings and 150 emails a day and do everything to improve the existing offers. "And that's not enough?", "We need Frappuccino?", "Really?"

The Innovator's Dilemma (Christensen 1997) is so named because it is a dilemma. The second problem is that many think that new products must constantly be launched on Horizon 2. But that would be foolish and too much. Good companies release a new groundbreaking product every few years. More is not possible because we have to access resources in the company that are occupied with Horizon 1, and we would get lost. More does not bring more. It is more important to occasionally make a big bet than many small ones. It is expensive to bring a Horizon 2 product to market. It is also said: it is the attempt to establish a new standard. You don't do that all the time.

A Horizon 2 attempt is successful when the product transitions into a regular Horizon 1 operation. But how do you find a new Horizon 2 product?

9.4.2.3 Horizon 3

Horizon 3 is there to look for new products and ideas that can be placed in Horizon 2 and then developed into Horizon 1. Here, small samples are taken and experiments are conducted. The task is to acquire raw information very quickly and often—and as cheaply as possible. This is more about research and market analysis. Many smaller activities that crystallize into a picture of what you want to try next. You do this until you are certain that it is this one product that you want to bring to the world. Just like, for example, the Apple Watch or the Frappuccino. Horizon 3 work can be quite disappointing for a long time, as you are constantly looking for clues, most of which turn out to be meaningless or ineffective.

9.4.2.4 The Interplay of Horizons

The 3-Horizon Model makes it clear that one must constantly work in all three horizons. However, this is difficult, as the work looks very different in all three horizons:

- Horizon 3: Searching and exploring in a rough manner. Cheap, fast, and raw ("They're just playing around").
- Horizon 2: Project management, bringing a new product—albeit still flawed—to the market against all resistance (even from within) ("Is this supposed to be the breakthrough?").
- Horizon 1: Maximizing existing products: precision, quality, repeatability, predictability ("How boring, they always do the same thing").

The complexity in growth, therefore, lies in coordinating and coexisting all three work methods, even though they are so contradictory. Horizon 3 is dominated by qualitative impressions and data. However, Horizon 1 needs quantitative data and precision. Horizon 3 work is child's play and fantasy from the perspective of Horizon 1. Conversely, Horizon 1 is pure prevention of new things and hesitation from the perspective of Horizon 3. And Horizon 2 ultimately only steals resources for pointless new ideas that are then poorly brought to market.

The management (no one else can take responsibility for this) must enable, support, and reconcile all these work methods and areas. This works best when the management exemplifies the coexistence of cultures. It is also important to make explicit for each task in the company in which horizon it is located and what is expected: Is the work an experiment at the Horizon 3 level, where one wants to see what happens? Or is it a new feature that should work directly for millions of customers in Horizon 1?

In recent years, there has been recurring criticism of the 3-Horizon Model. For example, the time frames of 18-36 months for each horizon may be too generous. Of course, the model can also be played faster in dynamic environments. It's about the principle. Another point of criticism is that the model looks very much like a waterfall model. But in fact, it is a matter of interpretation. The horizons can just as well be (semi-)permeable. In my practice, I often see that Horizon 1 cleverly quickly incorporates and exploits insights from Horizon 3. That's how the model is actually intended.

9.5 What Do We Need to Master to Achieve Growth?

Let's finally look at what we need to be able to do to successfully shape growth: First, we need patience. We know that the time to successful growth is measured in years, not quarters, months, or even weeks—even if the rhythm of quarterly business reports suggests otherwise. Once again: There is no overnight success.

Then we need to understand that a variety of work methods are needed to generate sustainable growth. We need to understand that all good products start small and with qualitative data. If we stick with it long enough, we have earned and worked out the starting position for quantitative data and the certainty to scale up with a recipe. Guessing the recipe practically doesn't work.

We also need to understand that we initially conduct small experiments in a rough manner (Horizon 3), very rarely take a big bet (Horizon 2), and almost everyone in the company protects and improves the existing (Horizon 1).

All of this must be done explicitly and lived out. Overall, this is called: creating an ambidextrous organization. This also requires patience and time. Instructions do not help.

To be able to evaluate the best options from Horizon 3, we need a good strategic understanding to select options that fit our overall development. New options must show a strategic fit. To be able to judge this, the different company levels must be well networked and enough exchange between bottom-up and top-down must be established. That is, hierarchy levels must be permeable and interconnected. Plans cannot simply be dictated from above, but must be worked out together. A good way to stay true to oneself is, as with Amazon, to expand existing internal capabilities so well that they can eventually exist as an external offer (computing, logistics in the case of Amazon).

In the area of digital products, it should be mentioned that one of the growth engines is personalization. Personalization helps to have a standard product at its core for everyone, but that looks and feels different for everyone. Individual adaptability to the specific customer, possibly by him or herself, is therefore already built in. This ensures that the customer perceives the product as "his own", even though it is actually standard. This way, we can easily avoid the danger of extreme margin loss and indifference among customers in the digital world.

So it turns out: Growth is more difficult than thought. More difficult than Martin thought when he went to Karina. Karina won't be able to solve the problem alone.

Growth is based on the understanding of an organization. With enough models and knowledge and skills, we can learn to operate growth as something organic, natural, feasible, and manageable. Away from magic and genius towards normal work. Even if it requires a bit of patience.

References

Apple. 2007. Apple reinvents the phone with iPhone, Press release from 09.01.2007. www.apple.com/newsroom/2007/01/09Apple-Reinvents-the-Phone-with-iPhone.

Baghei, M., S. C. Coley, and H. W. White. 1999. *White, „Alchemy of growth"*. New York: Basic Books.

Baum, H.-G., A. G. Coenenberg, and T. Günther. 2013. *Strategisches Controlling*. 9th ed. Stuttgart: Schäffer-Poeschel.

Blanchard, O., and G. Illing. 2014. Makroökonomie. 6th ed. Pearson: Hallbergmoos.

Christensen, C. M. 1997. *The innovator's dilemma*. Boston: Harvard Business School Press.

Cooper, A. 2019. https://twitter.com/MrAlanCooper/status/1165088908947800064.

Davis, M. 1958. *Computability and unsolvability*. New York: McGraw-Hill.

Dihen, R. 2018. Wie sich das Buch Crossing the Chasm auf den Marketing-Erfolg auswirkt! https://diri-socialmedia.de/crossing-the-chasm.

Drucker, P. 1973. *Management: Tasks, responsibilities*. New York: Harper Business.

Model T Ford Club of America, Editor. 2020. Model T Ford production. www.mtfca.com/encyclo/fdprod.htm.

Monastersky, R. 2006. Climate science on trial. www.chronicle.com/article/Climate-Science-on-Trial/34665.

Moore, G. A. 1991. *Crossing the chasm*. New York: Harper Business Essentials.

Rahmstorf, S. 2013. Paläoklima: Die letzten 2000 Jahre. https://scilogs.spektrum.de/klimalounge/palaeoklima-die-letzten-2000-jahre-hockeyschlaeger.

Rogers, E. 1962. *Diffusion of innovations*. New York: Free Press.

Statista. 2016. Anzahl der Facebook-Nutzer und Internetnutzer weltweit in den Jahren 2004 bis 2015. https://de.statista.com/statistik/daten/studie/245101/umfrage/facebook-nutzer-vs-internet-nutzer-weltweit-zeitreihe.

Statista. 2020. Absatz von Apple iPhones weltweit in den Geschäftsjahren 2007 bis 2019. https://de.statista.com/statistik/daten/studie/203584/umfrage/absatz-von-apple-iphones-seit-dem-geschaeftsjahr-2007.

Wardley, S. 2018. Wardley maps. Topographical intelligence in business. https://medium.com/wardleymaps.

Markus Andrezak has been designing internet products since the mid-90s. Since then, he has been combining design with customer orientation and agile work. In the 2000s, he invented portfolio management with new techniques from Kanban for knowledge work. His latest works help companies to better implement strategy in highly dynamic times. He is the founder of the product and strategy consultancy überproduct in Potsdam.
Contact: markus@ueberproduct.de

Product Changes

Why Users Reject Them and What We Can Do About It

Rainer Gibbert

Abstract

As product managers and UX designers, we strive to continuously develop and constantly improve our products. However, no matter how much effort we put in, there are always users who do not appreciate our optimizations, reject them, or in the worst case, hate them so much that they trigger a public "shitstorm". There are several reasons for this, and psychology plays an important role. But there are also means and ways to confront the resistances of the users, reduce them, and in the best case, completely eliminate them.

10.1 Resistance to Change

In June 2011, the time had come: After many months of hard work, the (then) new XING with a new design and many other changes saw the light of day. This relaunch was preceded by many hours of user interviews and usability tests, several surveys, and further research. The core of the new XING was, in addition to a new visual design, a new homepage. Instead of a multitude of small, configurable containers for various information, it included a central feed, surrounded by a few (as our research had shown) relevant pieces of information.

R. Gibbert (✉)
Star Finanz GmbH, Hamburg, Germany
e-mail: rainer@produktbezogen.de

© The Author(s), under exclusive license to Springer Fachmedien Wiesbaden GmbH, part of Springer Nature 2024
S. Hoffmann (ed.), *Digital Product Management*,
https://doi.org/10.1007/978-3-658-44276-7_10

Fig. 10.1 A XING user threatens via Twitter to cancel his premium account after the XING redesign (see https://twitter.com/MadeMyDay/status/24651504153)

However, the redesign of XING led to an outcry among XING users after the release. They felt robbed of their control over the homepage content, the feed was inflexible and not relevant - and in general, the new design was rated beeing not appealing at all. Users threatened, as shown in Fig. 10.1, to cancel their XING premium membership or even to leave the network entirely.

Eight years later, March 2019: XING had meanwhile become a unicorn, had significantly increased its memberships, and the central feed on the homepage was still present (and of course further developed).

I was no longer employed at XING, but at Star Finanz and responsible for the product development of the multi-banking application StarMoney. StarMoney also had an individually configurable overview page with various small containers. These offered professional users a high degree of flexibility, but were rather difficult to understand for new users with simple requirements. So we conducted a product discovery, spoke with existing users and those who might want to become one, and developed a new concept for the StarMoney overview page. With less flexibility, but with a set of information relevant to most users. We conducted user tests and surveys, did a beta phase, collected and analyzed feedback, measured satisfaction with the new concept - which was significantly higher than with the previous overview - and finally published the new overview page.

The result: Especially long-standing customers flooded our support channels, complained about the removed flexibility and control, and threatened to migrate and cancel, as the tweet shown in Fig. 10.2 impressively demonstrates.

Fast forward to the present: The StarMoney overview page is still based on the concept developed in 2019, StarMoney is still successful in the market, and the users' minds have calmed down. However, we have further developed the overview and given users more options for configuring the displayed information.

XING or StarMoney are not the only products where users have expressed very critical views on changes. Services like Twitter (Best 2019), Snapchat (Hiebert 2018), Google (Booth 2020) and many other well-known applications and sites also regularly struggle with negative feedback from users who do not appreciate changes.

Fig. 10.2 Criticism from a Twitter user about the adjusted design (see https://twitter.com/madmanweb/status/1425660635581358082)

What do we learn from these exemplary stories?

"In fact, anytime you release a redesign, prepare for a flood of angry emails from customers. It's a law of nature that users hate change, and they'll complain every time you move anything around or otherwise reduce their ability to just do what they've always done."—Jakob Nielsen (2009)

Especially long-standing users have a resistance to change. No matter how user-centered you proceed and how much research you conduct beforehand: There will always be users who are dissatisfied, threaten to cancel (and sometimes do so) or even publicly call for a boycott. However, this discontent usually subsides over time and users get used to the changes, often even finding them better later on.

10.2 Why Changes are Rejected

The reasons for a sometimes strong rejection of changes are psychological in nature. Even if a change has been extensively tested with users and "objectively" represents an improvement over the known, users often react negatively to it. This has various reasons (Lashbrook 2020; Panagiotidi 2021; Ru 2020).

10.2.1 Users (Mostly) Don't Care About Design

In contrast to product managers and UX designers, most users spend little time analyzing or admiring a product or its design and features. They are satisfied with a product when they know the necessary functions, can find them quickly, and can use them efficiently.

> "Users don't care about design for its own sake;
> they just want to get things done and get out".—Jakob Nielsen (2009)

Changes in the product are disruptive, leading users to have to relearn how to find and operate the functions. The result is frustration.

This leads to another problem, which John Gourville, a professor at Harvard Business School, described as the "9x effect":

- Users value what they know three times higher than what they can gain through a change.
- Designers, on the other hand, value their improvements by the same factor.

"The result is a mismatch of nine to one or 9x between what innovators believe consumers want and what consumers really want," Gourville wrote in a Harvard Business Review article in 2006 (Gourville 2006).

10.2.2 Users Love Routines

Humans are creatures of habit, love security and routines. Routines simplify our lives in many areas, make decisions for us or at least make them easier, and therefore save mental energy. Users who regularly use an application or who have even become "power users" have developed a multitude of routines. These help users to achieve their goals quickly and efficiently.

However, routines also inhibit the courage and willingness to try new things and accept changes. Because changing something means changing behaviors, modifying routines, and modifying, expanding, or completely replacing what has been learned. To do this, people need to be motivated.

However, for users, it is often unclear or incomprehensible why a functional or design change was made, so the motivation to deal with the change is lacking.

10.2.3 Users Like Familiarity

Familiarity or the so-called "Familiarity Bias" is a reason why users do not like or reject changes in products. It refers to a cognitive phenomenon where people choose familiar options, even though these lead to less favorable results than available alternatives.

The "Familiarity Bias" was first described by Israeli psychologists Amos Tversky and Daniel Kahneman and is a well-documented heuristic (shortcut) of our brain that makes us prefer familiar experiences (Tversky and Kahneman 1974).

10.2.4 Users Tend Towards the Status Quo

Another psychological effect, first described by psychologists William Samuelson and Richard Zeckhauser, is the "Status Quo Bias". This leads to an excessive preference for the status quo over changes (Samuelson and Zeckhauser 1988).

In other words, people want things to stay roughly as they are, even if a change would be beneficial. Even if a redesign or other product adjustment ultimately improves the user experience or increases usability, many users (initially) prefer to stick to what they know and are used to.

10.2.5 Users Prefer What They Already Own

Another theory explaining why users reject new things is the "Endowment Effect". This was described by American economist Richard Thaler (1980) and states that people prefer what they already own because they are afraid of losing something - regardless of the benefits they could derive from the new.

A study from 1990 helps to understand how the endowment effect works. The study divided participants into three groups:

- In the first group, participants had a choice between two items: a coffee mug or a chocolate bar. The subjects chose one or the other item more or less equally.
- In the second group, all participants initially received a coffee mug, which they could later exchange for a chocolate bar if they wished.
- The third group received a chocolate bar and could later exchange it for a coffee mug.

The subjects of the last two groups largely refrained from exchanging their original items for something new, even though - as the first group showed - both items were of equal value. The researchers concluded from this experiment that people who are offered something new are more likely to choose the item they already own (Kahneman et al. 1990).

10.2.6 Users Fear Loss of Control

In addition to the previously mentioned psychological effects (which admittedly are very similar and all lead to the realization that users love routines), another problem leads to a high aversion to change: loss of control.

In many cases (as in the examples of XING and StarMoney), users cannot influence the changes or consciously decide for or against them. This often leads to a perceived loss of control and thus to high dissatisfaction. Regardless of whether a change is positive or even brings advantages: when people feel bypassed or deprived of their freedom of choice, they often reject the change.

10.3 Creating Acceptance for Change

The fact that people usually have an aversion to change does not mean, of course, that we should not change and improve our products. However, product managers and UX designers should know and understand the psychological principles presented and how and why people react to changes.

In addition, there are various approaches and strategies to create more acceptance for change and to make it easier for users to deal with changes.

10.3.1 Change Not As an End in Itself

It's logical, but still worth mentioning: changes to the product or functions should only be implemented if they

- support the product strategy,
- create new added value,
- make usability more efficient,
- improve the product for users in other ways,
- or fix errors.

Changes, especially in terms of visual design, should not be implemented for their own sake or because a designer, a product manager, or a stakeholder thinks they are better or prettier.

Therefore, my appeal: Define in advance what you want to achieve with the changes and how you want to measure whether your changes are successful. What KPIs and metrics do you want to change? By what factor should they be changed? Only if you set a benchmark will you know later whether you are successful.

10.3.2 Accompanying Changes in a User-Centered Manner

Keep your users in focus during the change process. This starts with getting to know your users and target groups and understanding their needs and ways of working. Describe the different user groups, for example, using personas (Faller 2019) and consider what effects possible changes could have on the workflows or the general user experience of the users or personas.

Conduct interviews, user tests, or surveys as early and continuously as possible to quickly identify problems and measure user satisfaction and acceptance. Use surveys or the KANO model (Pfeifer and Schmidt 2007) to determine which functions in the product are most important to users. Analyze how often functions are actually used based on tracking data and take this into account when making changes, e.g. in navigation or in individual product functions.

Particularly take into account the different needs of new vs. existing users. New users have very specific requirements for entry and onboarding, while loyal existing users or power users have established their own workflows and therefore want as few changes as possible.

10.3.3 Make Changes Testable for Users in Advance

If possible, let your users try out the changes in advance, as Microsoft does, see Fig. 10.3.

Create a beta program in which you give interested early adopters the opportunity to try out new features early and give you feedback. In StarMoney, for example, we have a

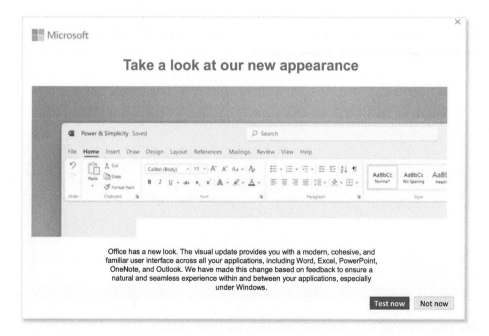

Fig. 10.3 Microsoft allows users to test a new appearance in advance

"Coming Soon" area where users can view and test new features, but can also deactivate them if necessary. We allow these users to describe their impressions, suggest improvements, and also measure satisfaction with the new features.

Build up a pool of interested test users to whom you can provide preliminary versions. Use tools like TestFlight, for example, to distribute initial versions of your apps to the test users.

If your product is web-based, you can also deliver new features to subgroups of your real users using AB testing tools and observe their behavior via tracking data, measure KPIs, and also run targeted surveys.

The feedback from users will be all the better the more realistic the use of the changed functions or new interface is. A usability test using a prototype is a good first step, but real usage data will give you more valid insights into actual behavior.

10.3.4 Let Users Choose

To give users a sense of maintaining control, allow them a transition period to choose. Offer - at least initially - the option to switch back to the old version or to try out the new version temporarily. Fig. 10.4 exemplifies how a private bank allows users to return to the old user interface. Users who wish to return are asked what their reasons are.

Even if you have to flip the switch completely at some point (because maintaining both old and new functionality doesn't make sense in the long run for cost reasons), you can in the meantime find out why users have stuck with the old version and what they might still miss in the new, revised function.

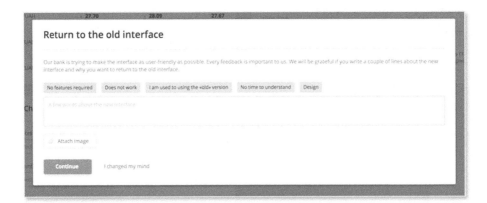

Fig. 10.4 Querying the reasons why users prefer the old user interface

10.3.5 Prefer Incremental Changes

A complete redesign is often not necessary and not advisable due to the psychological effects described earlier. If possible, instead make smaller changes more frequently that do not require too drastic changes in user behavior. Deliver the changes incrementally, where appropriate, instead of changing everything in a big-bang release.

Facebook, for example, does this regularly. There, changes are often very nuanced, so that users do not even consciously perceive them. Nevertheless, every change is tested and its effects are evaluated (Hill 2014). Because Facebook has billions of users and any negative effect costs the company a lot of money.

10.3.6 Communicate Changes and Make Them Appealing

If you have planned changes in the product that have a major impact on the user experience or the operation of functions, then communicate these early. Before users are negatively surprised by the changes, you should manage expectations and inform about what will change. Ideally, you present the changes in such an interesting way that users become curious and eagerly await them - just like Apple manages to do with new product versions and iOS updates.

Communicate the changes via a newsletter to the users, write a blog post or an article within your support area, or possibly even publish a press release about it.

If possible, explain the reasons for the changes and your approach. Show the users that you did not sit in a quiet chamber or in an ivory tower and decided to change something. Explain that you involved users in the process and evaluated the changes in advance (if this really happened). This will not calm every critic, but it shows your professional approach.

> "People need to feel reassured and supported. You need to provide assistance and to guide them through the transition phase. Be there for your users, support and explain the nature of the changes, reassure them about how to do it."—Ricardo Ortega (n. d.)

Point out the changes to users within the product, for example via a "What's new" tour, as Microsoft does within the Office products, see Fig. 10.5.

Present the changes not only in text form, but also create video tutorials in which you show step by step what exactly the changes are or how to operate the revised functions.

If you want to be completely transparent, then perhaps even publish your product roadmap in a version prepared for outsiders. This way, you can show users and interested parties early on what changes are still planned.

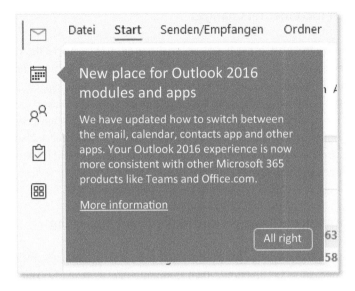

Fig. 10.5 Microsoft communicates within the products when there are changes

10.3.7 Patience and Perseverance

Once you have published the changes, don't let negative feedback or a minor "shitstorm" unsettle you - after all, you have taken all the points mentioned above into account and are well prepared. Be patient and don't become activist immediately. In most cases, the waves smooth out and the criticism subsides after a few weeks. Fig. 10.6 shows the average rating of a well-known German app after the release of a major redesign. After about two months, the users had gotten used to the changes and the app was rated positively again.

Gradually, more and more users get used to the changes and eventually even prefer them to the previous version.

> "The good news is that while people don't like changes and redesigns, they get used to it. First weeks you will meet a lot of bad reviews, the fall of the rating. But they will return to the old place and can be even better if your redesign was really good. Remember that any system can't change immediately, it needs time for it."—Vitaly Dulenko (2018).

Evaluate the feedback you receive from users through various channels and identify the key issues. Constructive and understandable criticisms that are mentioned by a relevant number of users (in relation to your entire user base) should be taken into account in the further development of your product. You should look at "strong" individual opinions, but discard them if they are not relevant to a larger user base. Simply ignore unconstructive comments, insults or even hostilities and don't let them demotivate you.

Don't just look at your users' feedback, but also evaluate their behavior after one to two weeks, a month, and beyond. Has activity increased or decreased? Is a new or

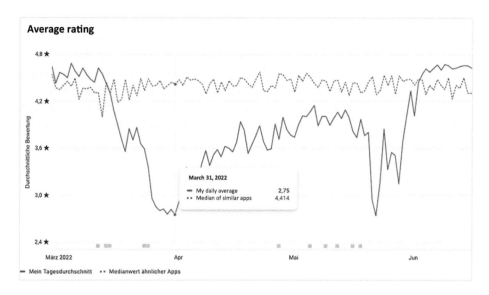

Fig. 10.6 Average rating of a well-known German app after the release of a major redesign

changed function used more or less frequently than before? How have your KPIs and metrics developed? Give users some time to get used to the changes and work with them.

Engage in active stakeholder management and help your management and colleagues understand the psychological mechanisms that are currently driving your users and how you plan to deal with them. Especially the colleagues in support, who receive the most negative comments and criticisms from dissatisfied users, should be shown a lot of understanding, offered an open ear and informed about your strategy.

Collect data and evaluate it calmly. Then decide on a solid basis whether the changes were successful or a failure. If the latter is really the case, you need to consider how to proceed. Do you want to roll everything back (with all the consequences) or can you, based on the feedback, make further changes that lead to an improvement?

> "Having users complain about a redesign doesn't necessarily mean that it's bad; if the new design actually has better usability, people will eventually grow to like it. Customer complaints are thus not a reason to avoid all redesigns; they're simply a reason to avoid changing the design purely to stay fresh."—Jakob Nielsen (2009)

10.4 Conclusion

Changes in products are important and necessary. Without further development and continuous optimization, we run the risk that our products will become outdated, no longer relevant, or competitors will offer better solutions, causing customers and users to migrate.

However, changes always require users to rethink. Routines must be abandoned, familiar things must be given up and new knowledge must be acquired. All of this requires time and cognitive effort, which often leads to changes being rejected.

But this should not hold us back from striving for better solutions. It is important to know, understand and counteract the psychological mechanisms that lead to rejection.

Therefore, changes need to be well prepared. This includes a user-centered approach, good communication, constructive handling of feedback—and last but not least, a thick skin and some patience!

References

Best 2019. https://www.mirror.co.uk/tech/hate-twitter-redesign-heres-how-18781006.

Booth 2020. https://thenextweb.com/news/thanks-hate-new-google-docs-sharing-drive-menu.

Dulenko, V. 2018. Why redesigns don't make users happy. UX Planet. https://uxplanet.org/why-redesigns-dont-make-users-happy-f1b29cc940ce.

Faller, P. 2019. Putting Personas to work in UX design: What they are and why they're important. Adobe. https://xd.adobe.com/ideas/process/user-research/putting-personas-to-work-in-ux-design/.

Gourville, J. T. 2006. Eager Sellers and Stony Buyers: Understanding the psychology of new-product adoption. *Harvard Business Review*. https://hbr.org/2006/06/eager-sellers-and-stony-buyers-understanding-the-psychology-of-new-product-adoption.

Hiebert. 2018. https://today.yougov.com/topics/technology/articles-reports/2018/05/10/consumer-sentiment-drops-snapchat-redesign.

Hill, K. 2014. Ex-Facebook data scientist: Every Facebook user is part of an experiment at some point. Forbes.com. https://www.forbes.com/sites/kashmirhill/2014/07/07/ex-facebook-data-scientist-every-facebook-user-is-part-of-an-experiment-at-some-point.

Kahneman, D., J. L. Knetsch, and R. H. Thaler. 1990. Experimental tests of the endowment effect and the Coase theorem. *Journal of Political Economy* 98(6):1325–1348. https://www.jstor.org/stable/2937761?seq=1.

Lashbrook, A. 2020. Why everyone always hates redesigns, even when they're good. OneZero. https://onezero.medium.com/why-everyone-always-hates-redesigns-even-when-theyre-good-26776604b5e9. Accessed: 17. Sept. 2022.

Menton, M. 2021.Kritik eines Twitter-Nutzers zum angepassten Design. https://twitter.com/madmanweb/status/1425660635581358082.

Nielsen, J. 2009. Fresh vs. familiar—How aggressively to redesign. nngroup.com. https://www.nngroup.com/articles/fresh-vs-familiar-aggressive-redesign/.

Ortega, R. o. J. Baby duck syndrome: Why users hate change and what you can do about it. Keepitusable. https://www.keepitusable.com/blog/baby-duck-syndrome-why-users-hate-change-and-what-you-can-do-about-it/.

Panagiotidi, M. 2021. Why do people hate redesigns? UX psychology. https://uxpsychology.substack.com/p/why-do-people-hate-redesigns.

Pfeifer, T., and R. Schmitt. 2007. *Qualitätsmanagement in der Produktentwicklung*, München: Handbuch Qualitätsmanagement. Carl Hanser Verlag, 405–432.

Ru, C. 2020. This is why users hate redesigns. The startup. https://medium.com/swlh/this-is-why-users-hate-redesigns-5e7c88c6e414.

Samuelson, W., and R. Zeckhauser. 1988. Status quo bias in decision making. *Journal of Risk and Uncertainty* 1:7–59. https://link.springer.com/article/10.1007/BF00055564.

Thaler, R. H. 1980. Toward a Positive theory of consumer choice. *Journal of Economic Behavior and Organization* 1(1):39–60.

Tversky, A., and D. Kahneman. 1974. Judgment under Uncertainty: Heuristics and Biases. *Science* 185(4157):1124–1131. http://www.jstor.org/stable/1738360.

Rainer Gibbert is a product manager with a great passion for good, customer-oriented, and economically successful products. He currently heads the product development for the StarMoney product family at Star Finanz GmbH in Hamburg - Germany's most well-known multi-banking applications. Previously, Rainer Gibbert worked, among others, at the startup REBELLE as Head of Product, at Fielmann Ventures as Senior Product Manager, and at OTTO as Product Manager in the E-Commerce Innovation Center, and led the User Insights Team at XING AG.

Contact: rainer@produktbezogen.de

A/B Testing in Digital Product Management

Optimizing Products Based on Real User Behavior

Sascha Hoffmann

Abstract

A/B tests are a standard tool in product management to validate ideas or qualitative indications from a product discovery for the optimization of digital products based on real user feedback. This article first explains the basic structure of A/B tests, before discussing the fundamentals of hypothesis formation and the statistics used in A/B tests. The article concludes with specific advice on how A/B tests can be optimally used in digital product management.

11.1 Introduction

Before the (further) development of a product, conducting a product discovery is standard in digital product management to analyze the three fundamental challenges in advance: the new product or feature should offer a relevant added value from the perspective of the target group and should be desired accordingly (desirable), it should be technically and organizationally feasible (feasable), and ultimately also generate financial returns for the company (viable) (cf. Maurya 2019 and for product discovery in detail Chap. 6 by Philip Steen and Alexander Hipp).

The content of this chapter is partly based on Hoffmann (2018).

S. Hoffmann (✉)
Professor of Online Management, Fresenius University of Applied Sciences, Hamburg, Germany
e-mail: moin@hoffmann-sascha.de

© The Author(s), under exclusive license to Springer Fachmedien Wiesbaden GmbH, part of Springer Nature 2024
S. Hoffmann (ed.), *Digital Product Management*,
https://doi.org/10.1007/978-3-658-44276-7_11

To validate the product-market fit, user tests are usually conducted in addition to the analysis of studies, qualitative user interviews, etc. For this purpose, prototypes at different stages of development are created and tested under as realistic conditions as possible. These usually do not yet contain the full range of functions, and functions are often even simulated as so-called Fake Door tests, which do not yet exist ("Click here if you are interested in XY."), in order to be able to estimate market interest in advance based on measured user behavior—for example, operationalized via the click rate (cf. Kohavi and Longbotham 2017).

In the further course of product development, if it is less about whether a product is marketable at all, but mainly about how a product can be optimized, A/B tests are typically used. Regularly obtaining valid market feedback through A/B tests thus forms an important element for the iterative improvement of digital products.

While the effect of a new physical product cannot usually be checked easily based on real usage behavior, digital products can be tested relatively easily and variants can be tried out. Digital companies therefore often make adjustments to their websites or apps and systematically test whether this results in improvements to their Key Performance Indicators (KPI), i.e., the relevant company metrics.

A simple before-and-after measurement is not sufficient, however. For example, even with increasing sales figures in an online shop, one could not be sure that the increase is really the result of a redesign carried out and not due to other unobserved factors occurred coincidentally. In order to really be able to determine the effects of changes made, they are regularly tested as **field experiments** under live conditions in digital product development or online marketing.

In an A/B test, for example, two variants of a website or app are compared with each other, with the original version (A) being tested against a modified version (B). The variation, for example, as shown in Fig. 11.1, has a different text on the call-to-action button.

To find out whether the change actually has the intended outcome on, for example, the conversion rate or surfing behavior on the website, an experiment is conducted. During a test period, visitors to the website are shown **either variant A or variant B** and their respective behavior on the website is measured. This provides market feedback based on

Fig. 11.1 A/B test of alternative call-to-action buttons

real user behavior of website visitors, which is much more reliable than it would be the case with a survey or laboratory experiment (cf. Kohavi and Longbotham 2017).

To ensure that the results of such an A/B test are really valid, it is important that it is set up correctly. For this, it is important that it is precisely specified   and the KPI to measure the difference are set befor the test is run. For this purpose, hypotheses are formulated in advance.

11.2   Basics of Hypothesis Formation

In general, hypotheses make statements about relationships between two or more factors, through which a situation is assumed to occur. In order to be able to verify the suspected causal relationships in an experiment, the hypotheses must be formulated precisely and logically correct. Normally, they are formulated as **conditional if-then sentences**: "If X is present, then Y results from it.", whereby a distinction is made between directed (e.g. "If X occurs, then Y increases.") and undirected hypotheses ("If X occurs, then Y changes.").

For statistical verification, in addition to the hypothesis to be tested (H_1), a so-called null hypothesis (H_0) is also formulated, which formulates the assumed relationship in a negated form ("There is no relationship between X and Y."). This null hypothesis is then tested at a predetermined significance level (α), where α **is the probability of error** for the null hypothesis being rejected even though it would have been correct (see Fantapié Altobelli and Hoffmann 2011).

Background
In practical application, the null hypothesis is usually not explicitly formulated, although in a statistical sense it represents the hypothesis to be refuted.

From the probability of error, it follows that an empirical hypothesis test is always associated with a certain degree of uncertainty. In addition to real reasons, such as measurement errors and a selective consideration of possible influencing factors in empirical tests, the scientific-theoretical **principle of falsification** of Critical Rationalism (Popper 1934) is the underlying reason. According to this, it is assumed that a hypothesis or theory can never be definitively proven, but is always only provisionally accepted until it is refuted by an empirical test (see Hildebrandt 2008).

In practice, a probability of error of a maximum of 10%, often even only 5%, is usually accepted (see Fantapié Altobelli and Hoffmann 2011). If the empirical verification of a hypothesis, for example, results in a probability of error of $\alpha = 0.04$, this means that the probability that the difference in a conversion rate determined in the sample occurred by chance is only 4%. So one can be 96% "sure" that the observed effect is due to the redesign of a website carried out in the experiment **(confidence level).** Statistically correct, this means that the null hypothesis could not be empirically confirmed, which is why the alternative hypothesis (the website redesign led to the higher conversion rate) is accepted.

With an $\alpha = 0.11$, the confidence level (1-α) that the difference found in the sample is not due to chance is only 89%. This is generally considered too low, which is why the null hypothesis cannot be rejected. It is therefore "not sure enough" that the website change made leads to an improved conversion rate.

11.3 Statistics in A/B Testing

During the experiment, for example, different variants of a website are shown to website visitors and it is recorded whether a so-called conversion, i.e., a purchase, occurs or not, see Fig. 11.2.

In this case, both variants of the website must be shown to a larger number of visitors in order to make statistically reliable statements about the advantages of one variant. The smaller the observed difference, the larger the required sample must be in order to make a statement about statistical significance. And finally, the display of the website variants must be **random** to prevent systematic distortion of the results (see Fantapié Altobelli and Hoffmann 2011).

If different conversion rates were determined for the compared variants after the test period, the question arises whether the difference is significant. To assess this, the results are subjected to a statistical review.

As a rule, a **Chi-square test** (χ^2 test) is carried out, in which the null hypothesis (H_0) assumes that the difference found in the sample occurred randomly and the variation made had no influence. In contrast, the "alternative hypothesis" (H_1), which is actually in focus, assumes that the change made in the experiment is responsible for the different results (conversion rates) (see Backhaus et al. 2021). For the example from Fig. 11.2,

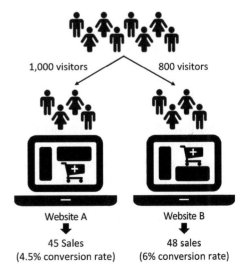

Fig. 11.2 Exemplary result of an A/B test of a website

the χ^2 test is used to check whether the higher conversion rate of 6% (48 sales from 800 visitors to website B) compared to the 4.5% for the original variant A is actually due to the changed design variation of the website.

To verify this, the observed conversion rates are compared with the theoretical ones. The null hypothesis is tested, which assumes that the conversion rates in both variants are identical. The more the actual empirical conversion rates observed in the sample deviate from this equal distribution, the less likely it is that the difference occurred randomly, and therefore the less likely it is that the null hypothesis is correct. Depending on the predetermined probability of error and taking into account the statistical degrees of freedom, it can be read whether the difference found occurred randomly or not (see Backhaus et al. 2021).

In the present case, the test statistic results in an accepted error probability of max. 5%, that the null hypothesis cannot be rejected. The change of the website from variant A to variant B has therefore not led to an increase in the conversion rate.

11.4 A/B Testing in Practice

Fortunately, in digital product management no one has to calculate the test statistics manually. There are numerous online tools for this, which usually even calculate the significance of the determined test results for free, see Fig. 11.3.

And also the actual implementation of A/B tests is often quite straightforward thanks to numerous no-code or low-code providers, such as AB Tasty, Optimizely or VWO, and requires no or only minimal programming skills, so that A/B tests can sometimes even be carried out by the product manager or UX designer themselves.

Background
A/B tests are not only used in digital product development, but are also widely used in online marketing. For example, at the beginning of advertising campaigns, differently designed display ads or

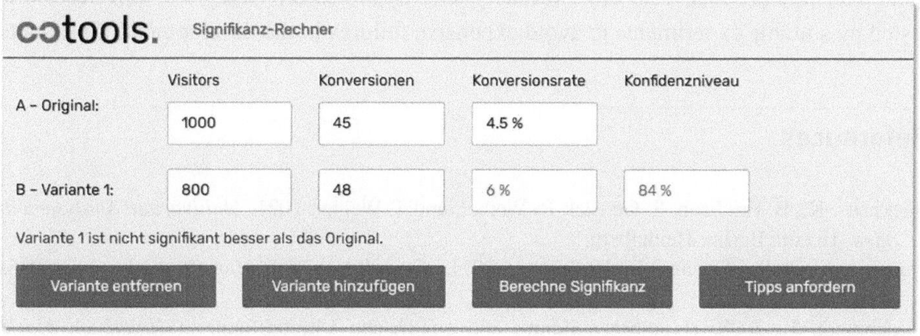

Fig. 11.3 A/B test statistics at converlytics

alternative text ads are tested in parallel to identify the "most successful" ones. Typical KPIs are the click through rate or the conversion rate (see Kreutzer 2021).

In customer retention marketing, A/B tests are conducted in the form of so-called headline tests. Before a mailing campaign, a smaller test campaign is sent to a randomly selected test group from the customer distribution list before the main mailing, in which emails with different subject lines are tested. The goal is to determine, for example, the subject line with the highest opening rate for the actual campaign (see Kreutzer 2021).

In e-commerce, A/B tests are used, for example, to investigate whether different sales promotion actions lead to different levels of sales. However, due to the **metric scaling** of sales (€), a χ^2 test is not used here, but a t-test or a variance analysis (ANOVA) is used to check whether the average amounts of the shopping carts differ significantly from each other (see in detail on the t-test and variance analysis Backhaus et al. 2021).

Of course, it is possible—and quite common in practice—to test not just one variation, but several elements at the same time in different versions. In this case, these are so-called **multivariate tests** (see Kohavi and Longbotham 2017). They work basically like A/B tests, but here very quickly a lot of test variants come together: For example, if the effect of two different call-to-action buttons (e.g. "Buy now" vs. "Add to cart"), three different texts and four different images on a website are to be tested at the same time, this results in $2 * 3 * 4 = 24$ different website variants. In addition to the effort of creating all the websites, the test also has to be carried out with a very large number of people so that each variant is played out frequently enough to make statistically reliable statements. In addition, other, sometimes significantly more complex statistical analysis methods, such as a conjoint analysis, are used. For this reason, product organizations in practice usually prefer to carry out several A/B tests one after the other (see Siroker and Koomen 2013).

It is also important to know that the possibly surprising, non-significant result of the exemplary A/B test in Sect. 11.3 is the norm in the development of digital products. Even at companies like Alphabet, Meta, Netflix etc., about 90% of the imagined optimizations turn out to be a mistake after an experimental review on the market (see Kohavi and Longbotham 2017). However, this proves even more how important A/B tests are in product management to validate internal beliefs or qualitative discovery results. Even the most plausible product ideas are ultimately only hypotheses ("bets") that still need to be tested by suitable experiments to avoid expensive failures in the development of products.

References

Backhaus, K., B. Erichson, S. Gensler, R. Weiber, and T. Weiber. 2021. *Multivariate Analysemethoden*. 16 edn. Berlin, Heidelberg.

Fantapié Altobelli, C., and S. Hoffmann. 2011. *Grundlagen der Marktforschung*. Konstanz, München.

Hildebrandt, L. 2008. Hypothesenbildung und empirische Überprüfung. In *Handbuch Marktforschung*, Eds. A. Herrmann and C. Homburg, 81–105. Wiesbaden.

Hoffmann, S. 2018. A-/B-Tests. *WiSu – Das Wirtschaftsstudium* 47(10):1125–1129.

Kohavi, R., and R. Longbotham. Online controlled experiments and A/B testing. In *Encyclopedia of machine learning and data mining*, Eds. C. Sammut and G. I. Webb, 2. edn, 907–914. New York.

Kreutzer, R. T. 2021. *Praxisorientiertes Online-Marketing*. 4. edn. Wiesbaden.

Maurya, A. 2019. *Lean startup, or business model design, or design thinking? Is the wrong question.* https://medium.com/lean-stack/lean-startup-or-business-model-design-or-design-thinking-is-the-wrong-question-f84216fad869.

Popper, K. 1934. *Logik der Forschung*. Wien.

Siroker, D., and P. Koomen. 2013. *A/B testing. The most powerful way to turn clicks into customers*. Hoboken.

Sascha Hoffmann is a Professor of Online Management and Business Administration at the Fresenius University of Applied Sciences in Hamburg. He teaches subjects such as Digital Product Mangement, E-Commerce and Online Marketing. Previously, he held leading positions in Business Development and Product Management for companies like XING and blau Mobilfunk. More at www.hoffmann-sascha.de.

Contact: moin@hoffmann-sascha.de

Product Management Understood Holistically

Tips to Help Become an Outstanding Product Manager

Patrick Roelofs

Abstract

Product managers are responsible for the (further) development of their product and are entrusted with a wide range of tasks. However, product management is always also a team sport, involving many different stakeholders and sometimes conflicting objectives. All too easily, the necessary communication and coordination between the product manager and his stakeholders can be pushed into the background, when concrete product decisions and acute problems that immediately need to be solved come to the fore. The article shows how important it is for product managers to consistently invest in relationship maintenance and proactive communication with their stakeholders in order to develop better products more efficiently in the long term.

12.1 The Tasks of the Product Manager

Product Manager: This profession, unlike many others along the digital value chain, has a multitude of contrasting facets that need to be balanced with the aim of creating a user-centered and commercially successful product. To achieve this, the job of the product manager usually involves a very clear **end-to-end responsibility**.

End-to-end in this context means, that it is the product manager who must keep an eye on the processes, measures, and constantly changing inputs in the areas relevant to

---

P. Roelofs (✉)
Aroundhome, Berlin, Germany
e-mail: hello@patrickroelofs.de

© The Author(s), under exclusive license to Springer Fachmedien Wiesbaden GmbH, part of Springer Nature 2024
S. Hoffmann (ed.), *Digital Product Management*,
https://doi.org/10.1007/978-3-658-44276-7_12

a digital product (law, technology, user experience, marketing, data, etc.). He acts as an interface between all these competencies to ensure the success of "his" digital product.

So, looking at the diverse challenges facing product managers, the question arises as to which aspects are important in order to be able to make an above-average contribution in this role in a tech company. This contribution is often expressed in two overarching result dimensions that must be fulfilled together:

12.1.1 Result Dimension 1: User Satisfaction with the Product

The methods for measuring user/customer satisfaction are diverse. Two of the most commonly used measurement methods are the Net Promoter Score and user or customer activity:

Net Promoter Score
The Net Promoter Score (NPS) is a metric that correlates business success based on a single question among customers. The question is: "How likely is it that you will recommend company/brand X to a friend or colleague?"

The possible answers range from 10 (very likely) to 0 (very unlikely). Those respondents who answer with 9 or 10 are referred to as "promoters". On the other hand, those who answer with 0 to 6 are considered "detractors". Customers who answer with 7 or 8 are considered "indifferent". To calculate the score, the percentage of detractors is subtracted from the percentage of promoters. The difference gives the Net Promoter Score, which can range between -100 and 100.

User/Customer Activity
The measurement of how many people or paying customers use a product per quarter/month/week/day usually also provides information about user satisfaction with the product. Common views of this activity metric are

- QAU (Quarterly Active User)
- MAU (Monthly Active User)
- WAU (Weekly Active User)
- DAU (Daily Active User).

For example, if 750 out of 1000 customers use a product daily (DAU), it can generally be assumed that they are satisfied with the product. Conversely, it does not necessarily mean that users who predominantly use a product "only" once a month (MAU) are dissatisfied with it. Rather, it is important to understand what kind of product a company offers: Is it a product that aims to "activate" users daily (e.g., Instagram)? Or is it a product that, based on normal interaction habits and the business model, is more aimed at monthly activation of the user (e.g., the digital customer center of an electricity provider)?

12.1.2 Result Dimension 2: Commercial Success of the Product

The product manager must, of course, also keep an eye on the most important commercial key figures. A product that is gladly used by customers (e.g., in the freely available basic version), but for which customers do not want to spend money or for which the company cannot sell revenue-generating advertising spaces to marketers, is not financially viable in the short or long term.

For example, if you develop a software product that is sold via a monthly subscription (e.g., Spotify), a product manager must closely monitor the development costs, but above all the number of sold subscriptions, the distribution of subscription durations (1, 3, 12 months), the churn rate (attrition rate of paying customers) or at least the revenues per time period (e.g., revenue/month). Of course, there are also a multitude of other key performance indicators that can provide information about commercial success.

What is important: Fulfilling only one of these two result dimensions is not sufficient in the medium and long term. The mandatory *and closely tied* relationship between these two that must be fulfilled, shows how demanding the development of a customer-friendly product offering combined with tight sales management is. This is something a good product manager must be able to ensure for his company.

The product manager is the primary responsible person and central contact for all stakeholders and senior management and is held responsible for product success in most companies—whether this is justified or not. This is also why the task of the product manager is so demanding. It often becomes apparent very early in the project whether product managers can meet the expectations of their role. This may also be the reason why the recruitment and selection process for product managers in many companies is extremely intensive and carried out over several rounds. The risk of failure should be minimized in this central role.

So, what aspects are important to be able to make an outstanding contribution as a product manager in a tech company to fulfill the two result dimensions? The most common answers given to this question in the product community and by companies refer to the **methodological and process competencies** of product managers. Examples include product discovery or design thinking methods, agile user experience testing, and knowledge of how to build backlogs in Jira.

It is often exactly these methods and processes that are discussed within the product community and taught in further training. Of course, this is a perfectly valid perspective on the role of the product manager, but it is certainly not the only or sufficiently differentiated one: Equally important, if not even more important, are the aspects that serve as the "glue" between all the methods and processes and in collaboration with many different experts and stakeholders within a company. Aspects that help the product manager achieve maximum value for himself, his team, the stakeholders, and the company. Because much more is required than just mastering good design thinking methods.

Unfortunately, it is exactly these aspects that are still discussed too little in the product community today and that are rarely found in role profiles or structured further training offers for product managers. Therefore, the following will focus on five central aspects that should help to gain a more holistic understanding of this diverse role.

12.2 The Product Manager as a Proactive Relationship Manager

Good relationships with stakeholders and, in sum, a good business network are essential for everyone in professional life. This does not refer to the often very fleeting LinkedIn or XING contacts, but to real relationships. Relationships that arise when you engage in personal exchange, meet in person if possible, and share time, experiences, and challenges. Even in times when decentralized remote work has gained importance and is indispensable in modern companies, this aspect is of particular importance.

For product managers as the interface to many areas within a company, relationship building and maintenance are once again one of the most important tools to master. Whether it's about developing a product together with other experts and successfully establishing it in the market. Or at some point along their own career to have access to good people or even to receive the one decisive call for the even more interesting next job: All this only works if product managers become aware of their role as networkers and "relationship managers".

And yet it often seems to be the case that product managers have not sufficiently understood this aspect of their role. They do not see the necessity to invest in the quite complex process of personal relationship building and maintenance. Because building good relationships takes time, requires proactivity and commitment (especially when working remotely) and sometimes also the use of financial resources (e.g., for a lunch invitation). If you add all this up, the role of a product manager as a relationship manager is a complex and sometimes unfortunately quite expensive, but in any case a value-adding contribution for themselves and the company.

The art now is to use all the available communication possibilities, such as Slack, to engage in spontaneous and proactive 1:1 communication (i.e., "just call without an appointment") with people, thus creating occasions for exchange that go beyond the written word.

But of course, direct and real on-site interactions between people should not be missing, especially for product managers. Ideally, there are days when employees meet in the office, or at least team events that contribute to building and further strengthening these so necessary relationships. Here too, the product manager can take a central role and become aware of how these digital and real interactions are designed and executed in order to then lead by example.

Because what needs to be done at the end of the day, namely developing products with a multitude of different stakeholders (often with very different views and personal goals), is still "People's Business".

Not an artificial intelligence does this work for us and takes the decisions, but it is the people. These people have to interact with each other every day in order to make the necessary decisions for the greater whole. The relationships these people have with each other have a direct influence on the resulting product quality.

A good starting point to understand how to build and maintain your own network is the book "Never eat alone" by Steve Ferazzi and Thal Raz (2005). Many aspects in the book can also be applied to the purely digital interactions between people that have increasingly dominated the working day in recent years.

In their book, the authors describe in a very vivid way and with many personal examples what each individual can do to become an outstanding networker and relationship maintainer. For example, they discuss the aspect of "generosity", which in their view is the core of every strong, healthy network. Giving something without expecting anything in return, and helping whenever others need help, in their view also reduces one's own natural barriers to contacting others. This makes it easier to ask for help in your own network (because everyone needs it from time to time), and can further strengthen social bonds.

Ferazzi and Raz show in their book with many other examples that maintaining one's own network is a continuous process that ideally follows a strategic "Relationship Action Plan". Because once you have experienced for yourself the power that can unfold in teams and among colleagues who maintain good relationships with each other and trust each other, you probably never question this central aspect of the product manager role again.

This is also product management

12.3 The Product Manager as an Outstanding Communicator

A its has already become clear in the previous section, outstanding product management requires proactive, direct, and often immediate communication with people in many respects. Truly understanding what my counterpart feels, thinks, or how they interpret my messages, only works through direct, personal contact (regardless of whether this takes place via Google Meet or in a personal meeting on site).

Frequently heard (product manager) statements like *"Of course, I communicated that very clear. I posted it in our Slack channel, now everyone knows."* however, shows how little the communicative responsibility that this role brings with it is understood in practice. Because with digital, written exchange, it is just as it has always been with the exchange via letters and emails: You would not believe how many misunderstandings can arise when tonality, body language, and resulting interpretation possibilities are missing.

Direct, proactive, and reflective communication is therefore a critical success tool for product managers. In fast, complex projects, the lack of good personal communication poses a huge risk for the product manager and the product's success. "Management by walking around and talking to people" (i.e., engaging in conversation) is therefore an essential part of the product manager's role. Because product management communication is the ability to distribute and obtain information precisely and at the right time, in the right frequency, and via the right channel.

Product managers who have understood this and consciously apply it within their organization will be more successful than product managers who let communication "just happen" or who, out of convenience and/or fear of conflict, mainly rely on purely written exchange via digital channels in their communication.

Interestingly, even today, in the rapidly changing and challenging world of work, communication is not understood as a tool to be learned. Instead, it is implicitly expected that you are already a communication expert as soon as you graduate from university and step into the role of product manager. Far too rarely are proactive trainings offered by companies that make outstanding communicators out of the acting players to better meet the diverse challenges. There are many offers that have been available on the market for years. Workshops on "Better Remote Work" (How do I manage work in decentralized organizations?), "Lateral Leadership" (How do I lead without direct authority?) or on the topic of change management (How do I achieve a change in my organization to establish a desired state?) are just a few offers that can make a valuable contribution to more professional communication for product managers. However, it is usually also the task of the product managers to actively demand these training modules from superiors and not to limit themselves to learning the next design thinking method.

This is also product management

12.4 The Product Manager as a "Decision Maker"

As a product manager, you have the important task of ensuring that decisions can be made at any time and by all stakeholders in their area of responsibility. Because only when small and large decisions are made can they also be implemented promptly.

However, it is explicitly *NOT* about the product manager making all decisions alone. It's about keeping together all the different and rapidly developing work strands with the constantly incoming information. And about enabling all those involved in product development to remain aligned with the overall goal and capable of making decisions.

The following aspects play a crucial role in this:

12.4.1 Clearly Formulated Goals

Goals are nothing more than clearly formulated expectations. It is important to convey a clear and comprehensible picture to the stakeholders of what expectations are placed on the success of the product. It is of enormous importance to provide as much relevant context as possible: why something should happen, what strategic reasons speak for it, or what explicitly should not be achieved.

Central to this is a precise description of the output to be achieved and the outcome. With these two goals, you lay the foundation for further questions and of course also for letting the stakeholders go together in the right direction:

The **output** describes the expected production result. For example, the implementation of two optimized variants of an already existing input form in an iOS app, which should be shown to users evenly distributed via A/B tests. The goal is to find out whether better registration rates can be achieved with them than with the existing input form.

The **outcome** describes the effect to be achieved on the user. For example, an increase in the conversion rate of at least +2%, i.e., +500 new customer registrations/month.

With the help of this provided information, it is much easier for the stakeholders to make comprehensible and goal-oriented decisions in the Product Discovery (see Chap. 6"Product Discovery" by Philip Steen and Alexander Hipp) and Product Delivery (see Chap. 8by Tim Adler "Product Delivery").

12.4.2 Maximum Transparency ("Connecting the Dots")

One can only react to what one sees. Therefore, it is important to ensure the necessary transparency for all stakeholders in order to be able to react adaptively to new developments/influencing factors.

On the one hand, this involves establishing the right level of overview for all stakeholders, which allows the progress in the individual teams involved and their dependencies on other teams to be depicted. On the other hand, it is important to combine this view into a higher-level "output". Central questions that need to be answered include, for example:

- Responsibilities: Are the responsibilities per stakeholder and per topic 100% clear?
- Work packages: Are all work packages and dependencies clear to all stakeholders?
- Written overview: Is there a consolidated list of work packages and dependencies as a reference? Where can I find this?

- Existing uncertainties: On which topics do more information need to be collected before a binding statement can be made about complexity/scope/dependencies/time expenditure?
- New insights: Are there new developments that we need to consider? For example, whether a work package is significantly more complex than expected and thus influences the output of another team?
- Project progress: Which work packages are currently being processed and are these on schedule?

However, the transparency thus established is only a means to an end. Its task is to encourage stakeholders to engage in regular exchange with each other. Often, this automatically results in a "need for discussion" based on the available (now very transparent) information. If this is not the case, the product manager can also help.

Because even if it may seem too cumbersome to a stakeholder according to his individual perception: A weekly one-hour meeting with the most important other stakeholders is time well invested to go through the latest developments and to remain able to take decisions as an "organization".

12.4.3 Necessary Escalations

Escalation is one of the most underestimated aspects to prevent critical delays due to unmade decisions in fast, complex projects. Unfortunately, most people see escalation as something negative. Something that should only happen in extreme emergencies, instead of seeing it as the "clarifying and quickly leading to decisions" process in a conflict.

This may be due to the fact that an escalation is often not carried out according to the right rules of the game out of ignorance by the parties involved. It is often observed that first, there is no or incorrect communication among the affected conflict parties. And second, one or more conflict parties are left out when presenting the conflict to the final decision-maker. This makes the conflict—at least for one of the conflict parties—(too) one-sided. Personal frictions are preprogrammed here.

So let's assume that in every project/every larger initiative there is a person who can make the necessary decision finally (usually the product manager or the next higher department head). Let's further assume that two teams have each developed good, but very different approaches to solving a problem and these teams insist that exactly their solution is implemented.

In order to bring about an escalation in this case that is fair and transparent for all conflicting parties, the following steps can be taken:

1. One of the two conflicting parties should personally and ideally in writing point out to the other conflicting party that an escalation seems necessary due to a lack of agreement and that this is now being "initiated".

12 Product Management Understood Holistically

2. The other conflicting party and the decision-makers are invited to a clarification meeting.
3. Before meeting the decision-makers , the problem and proposed solutions are presented in writing and coordinated in advance with the other conflicting party ("Is this correctly presented? What do you see differently?").
4. The jointly coordinated description of the conflict situation is then sent in advance to the decision-makers on behalf of both conflict parties.

If you follow these steps, an ego-free and factual discussion is possible in most cases. And even if it doesn't always seem that way: Conflicts and escalation in complex tasks with many stakeholders are completely normal and necessary. Only in this way can the right discussions be held and ultimately the right decisions be made.

This is also product management

12.5   The Product Manager as a Supplier of Answers

Since the product manager acts as an interface to all parties involved in the product development process, it is also one of his central tasks to provide answers to many relevant questions that typically arise in such processes.

After a few years as a product manager, one often finds that these are often the same questions. And yet, product managers are often not well enough prepared to provide the appropriate answers immediately, with as little effort as possible and thus little delay.

John Cutler, a product manager from California/USA, has compiled a comprehensive list of questions for this very reason, which every product manager should be able to answer at any time. The scenario used for this is based on a typical dialogue between the product manager and his superior, who asks:

> "Dear product manager, I'm speaking with our CEO in 5 minutes. You have 30 seconds to inform me: What do I need to know?"

With the following questions, which should be printed out on every product manager's desk, and the continuous self-review of these questions, one should be well prepared for most situations.

Briefing Questions for a Product Manager (John Cutler 2018)
- Do you have good news? If so, based on which data points?
- Have we learned something new since we last spoke? If so, based on which data points?
- What do we still need to learn/understand? How do we go about it?
- Has the overarching story about the product/development process changed? If so, how?
- Do you need help? Where can I untie a "knot" for you?
- What information/context do you need from me to make good product decisions?

- Have there been any new developments I should know about?
- How do you measure the success of your current mission?
- What is the one thing we should definitely be working on right now? Why now?
- How does your current work increase our revenue/reduce our costs?
- How does your current work change customer behavior? From which customers(-segments) exactly?
- What does this make possible (for us as a company)?
- Why did you choose this solution out of all the possible solutions to achieve the goal?
- What is the bet being made here? How does this compare to other bets we could have made?
- Are there any emerging risks? How do we address these risks?
- When would your current mission/project be stopped?
- Have initial work results already been shown to customers? What is the customer feedback on the current mission/project?
- What is the next important milestone?
- What is your vision for the next 6 months?
- What do Marketing, Sales, Customer Success, Data (and other stakeholders) need to know about it?
- How is team morale? What are you doing to keep it strong/improve it?
- What are you doing to give the team insight into the contribution they make to the company? What is their feedback on this?
- If old decisions made were not an issue, what would you do differently in 3, 6, 12 months?

Let's not kid ourselves: From the stakeholders and management, the product manager is the first point of contact for all these questions. The faster and more precisely they can be answered, the more trust and thus freedoms will be given to the product manager.

This is also product management

12.6 The Product Manager as a Clear-Thought-Provider

Another important contribution that a product manager must deliver within his organization is clear and structured (ideally written) formulated thoughts. Sounds simple? It is not at all.

Not only must the product manager be clear that this is a central part of his value contribution to his stakeholders, he must also become clear that he is the one who must try to include all relevant perspectives. The clearer the product manager can present his thoughts or get others to do so, the easier he will achieve good results.

And at the same time, the product manager faces the challenge that in today's agile organizations it is becoming less and less "usual" to elaborate his thoughts in structured written form. Far too rarely are complex issues examined from all relevant sides. On the contrary: For coordination and discussion purposes, manageable short presentations with—at best—a few bullet points in PowerPoint are presented. In this way, however, only the surface of complex issues is scratched. *"A detailed examination is too time-consuming and also not really agile,"* are then often raised objections (excuses?) that are brought against a structured process.

The result: Not all stakeholders have the same understanding of the planned approach, the necessary aspects of product development or the scope of the product. The later it is noticed that the expectations of the stakeholders differ greatly from each other, the greater are the resulting conflicts and the additional effort of possible corrections, since the project is already far advanced. "Oh, I had imagined it quite differently!" is then a typical, but also consequential statement.

Help in working out a detailed examination and weighing up different perspectives is now provided by quite mature frameworks, such as the **assignment clarification** (Assignment Clarification). This was developed by product managers at XING specifically for the purpose of early synchronization of expectations and structured communication among stakeholders (see also Chap. 15 by Arne Kittler "Alignment as a core competence for product managers"). The assignment clarification provides a solid guideline along relevant questions as a framework, which help to bring all stakeholders "on the same page" as early as possible in a product development process. In addition, topics can be discussed at the necessary depth of information and finally adopted bindingly. In this context, XING also often talks about the **Spice-Girls question**: *"Tell me what you want, what you really, really want."*

Some of the aspects covered in the order clarification are:

- Complications: What is the problem or trigger for this project/initiative?
- Intention: What is it that we really want to achieve with this initiative?
- Hypotheses: What must be true for our "output" to lead to the desired "outcome"?

If you work as a product manager along this framework, it will become clear to you—and hopefully to everyone else—relatively quickly how much substance your own (written) thoughts on the product development process have.

The real value, however, is not created solely by writing down the thoughts, but rather by sharing them with his stakeholders and the necessary discussions that result from it.

This is also product management

References

Cutler, J. 2018. PM tip: 30 seconds answers (to common questions). https://medium.com/@johnpcutler/pm-tip-30-seconds-answers-to-common-questions-2c8a33b6643c.

Ferazzi, S., and T. Raz. 2005. *Never eat alone*. New York: Currency Doubleday.

Patrick Roelofs is the Chief Product Officer at Aroundhome, responsible for all product-related topics of the ProSiebenSat.1 subsidiary. Previously, he worked for several years as VP Product & User Experience at Lotto24 AG, the German market leader for online lottery brokerage. At XING, he also spent over five years as Director of Product Management, responsible for both B2C monetization and various B2B products. Prior to this, he founded eparo GmbH in Hamburg, one of the leading user experience agencies in Germany.

Contact: hello@patrickroelofs.de

Product Sense

The Inestimable Value of Intuition in Product Management

Robert Schulke and Nikkel Blaase

Abstract

Product Sense describes the ability to predict effects in complex systems and to make good decisions in product development based on this. This requires a special degree of empathy for the target group as well as a holistic understanding of the product, business, and domain. In this article, we explain what Product Sense is, why it is essential for good product management, and how it can be developed. Finally, we provide practical tips for immediate application.

13.1 Introduction

Agile product development describes the process of bringing a valuable product to the appropriate target group as effectively and efficiently as possible. By testing critical hypotheses through cost-effective experiments and qualitative customer feedback, a gradual approach to the right solution is achieved. Misdevelopments can thus be detected and corrected at an early stage. The journey from a promising opportunity to a potential product and finally to a successful business model requires hundreds of decisions—and

R. Schulke
Freiburg, Germany
e-mail: me@robertschulke.de

N. Blaase (✉)
Orbit Ventures GmbH, Hamburg, Germany
e-mail: hello@designmadeforyou.com

often even complete changes of direction before a product that is equally valuable from a customer and company perspective has emerged. Every wrong decision is associated with unnecessary costs and, in the worst case, gives the competition a lead that is difficult to catch up with.

As a product manager, one is repeatedly faced with the challenge of having to make good decisions. New, still immature product ideas but also very concrete feature requirements need to be understood, classified and correctly assessed in terms of their expected impact. A good product sense—or a good feel for the product—helps in these situations to be able to evaluate the desired effect of an idea or requirement. Product sense is thus a crucial factor for better decisions in product development and helps to save costs and time. At the same time, however, a strongly pronounced product sense is no substitute for testing product ideas. The verification of ideas and hypotheses remains necessary.

According to a survey of 1000 product managers from 2020, product sense was named as the most important skill in product management after "communication" and "execution" (Rachitsky 2020). However, it is also one of those skills that are least clearly defined in product management. Therefore, we want to explain the term product sense in the following and describe how this skill can be built up.

13.2 What is Product Sense?

Product sense generally describes an intuition for good decisions in product development. However, this is not an innate ability, but something that can be learned and developed over time (Cagan 2022). A good product sense is therefore the acquired ability to design products or changes to existing products in such a way that they have the intended effect on their users or customers and at the same time generate a positive effect on one's own business.

▶ *Great product sense = generally being right about which product changes will have the intended impact. (Rachitsky 2021)*

A good product sense is essentially based on four factors (Walter 2022):

1. Empathy to be able to identify meaningful user needs.
2. Product and domain knowledge about how successful solutions can work in the market.
3. Creative problem solving to effectively meet both user needs and business needs.
4. And finally, the experiences that one collects over time in product development.

In the further course, the first two factors will be examined in more detail, as they form the basis for subsequent creative processes and the collection of experiences.

13.3   The Importance of Product Sense

A few years ago, the responsible decision-makers of a large German technology company decided to launch a new product for an existing target group. They had collected all possible data and facts and carefully analyzed the market. The decision-makers were convinced that the product would triple revenues in the relevant customer segment in no time. So, the product manager and her development team immediately began designing and implementing the requirements and all necessary features they had identified based on their research. They were sure that the new product would be a complete success. After a few months, the product was finally ready and prepared for market entry. The marketing department launched a large advertising campaign to promote the new product among existing customers. Everyone involved was convinced that it would be a great success. Unfortunately, the opposite was the case. The customers did not respond at all to the new product and it sold very poorly. The team was confused and wondered what had gone wrong. Eventually, they found out that they had focused too much on implementing the requirements during the development of the product and had little sense for the product and its impact on customers and business. They had not thought about whether the product would really offer what the customers needed and whether the resources used could influence sales at all.

This is a purely fictional story. But in our experience, it happens in companies in a similar way. It is a vivid example of why a good product sense is of great importance for decisions in product management.

In organizations where there is little understanding of the product, product managers in practice are often responsible for the mere implementation of external requirements. In this case, neither can they think further into the future, nor are requirements questioned or plausibilized for their effectiveness. For product managers, it is difficult to make good and future-oriented decisions in such environments. Product management has little opportunity to develop an imagination of what effect individual requirements can have on users, customers, the product, or the business model as a whole.

Therefore, it is important that product sense is developed in product management. A good product sense helps product managers and other decision-makers to ask the right questions and to better classify requirements. This way, good decisions can be made regarding the desired effect and costly misdevelopments can be avoided.

A good product sense helps product managers to...

1. better understand causal relationships,
2. be able to estimate potential impacts in complex systems,
3. identify risks early,
4. achieve more impact for customers and their own company,
5. ask good, purposeful questions and
6. make correct decisions. ◀

Even though the ability of product sense primarily benefits decision-makers in digital product development—essentially the product managers—this ability can also be useful for other roles around product development: From engineering to design to marketing, sales and customer support, a strong product sense can be helpful to get more involved in product development and to actively participate in the design of the product. Accordingly, the development of product sense is of great advantage for everyone who has to make product decisions or wants to co-design.

13.4 How Product Sense Can Be Developed

Those who develop product sense simultaneously form a strong opinion. From initially incomplete information, hypotheses or arguments are derived that allow a conclusion or new perspective. This is important in order to be able to make good decisions. On the other hand, one's own opinion can also change with new insights. It must be continuously checked for its validity: Are the hypotheses still correct or are there refuting indications? What are the perspectives of the other team members? Have tendencies formed that stand in the way of an objective opinion? As soon as basic hypotheses no longer apply, what has been learned must also be consciously unlearned. The more informed the intuition, the better.

It is a paradox: the ability to have confidence in one's own ideas, and the humility to doubt what one knows (Meddlers n.d.). Product sense is a strong opinion, but it should not be unshakeable.

> "[…] my mantra for this process is 'strong opinions, weakly held.' Allow your intuition to guide you to a conclusion, no matter how imperfect – this is the 'strong opinion' part. Then – and this is the 'weakly held' part – prove yourself wrong." (Saffo 2008)

The more experience product managers gather in their career, the more likely they are to have developed a deep understanding and a good sense for products. The presence of product sense is thus one of the essential factors that distinguishes senior from junior product managers.

However, this ability does not simply come by itself, but must be actively formed and continuously developed. As already mentioned, this requires above all empathy and a deep, holistic understanding of product, business, and domain.

13.4.1 Building Empathy

Building empathy is a crucial skill for developing product sense. Product managers need to deeply understand their target audience(s), put themselves in their shoes, and empathize with their world. Only then are they capable of assessing the effectiveness of product features in terms of business potential and added value for the customers.

Empathy must be trained and actively developed. Product managers are not "normal" users or customers of the product they are developing—this also applies when they use the product themselves. Therefore, product managers need to speak directly and regularly with users or customers to understand them and recognize patterns. It is not enough to be informed only by the customer support or research team. On the one hand, the opportunity to ask for a better understanding and additional context is lost. On the other hand, recurring and regular interaction is also important, as customer needs and usage behavior can change over time. A user statement that seemed interesting yesterday may already be obsolete today.

In addition, observing usage behavior and measuring interactions with the product provide helpful clues about the needs of the end users. Marrying qualitative observations with quantitative data further enhances empathy (Rachitsky 2022). Therefore, product managers must be integrated into research or carry it out themselves in order to develop product sense.

> "It's time to stop letting the research butter be taken off your bread! Let the Biz Devs and market researchers do whatever they want, you need to define and execute your early phase research—based on your specific product management questions." (Becker 2016)

To continuously engage with users or customers, subjects for interviews and tests need to be found. The search for subjects for a B2C product with a large user base is naturally much easier than for a B2B product for specialists.

To get feedback on the interface of a B2C product, it is usually enough to go to the nearest coffee shop and ask a handful of people if they know and use the product. This way, subjects can be easily found without having to make any further effort. Finding users of B2B products, on the other hand, is much more difficult. A good start is to talk to users within your own company. Colleagues often know potential conversation partners in other companies who can be recruited as subjects.

Special attention must be paid to personal inclinations when developing intuition. All people are biased, this is inevitable. Product managers are influenced by, among other things:

- Confirmation Bias: the action is aimed at confirming one's own viewpoint and ignoring contradictory evidence
- Law of Small Numbers: the belief that small samples represent a total population or also
- Recency Bias: the preference for events and results that have just occurred.

To counteract the influence of these effects, one's own positions must be constantly reviewed. But product managers are not alone in this. They can draw from the various perspectives in their team and existing data and facts.

In addition to empathy for customers and users, empathy is also needed for the internal and external stakeholders of a product. Because a product is value creation for both customers and the company. Without real customer benefit, there is no business and without business, there is no investment in customer benefit. One of the main tasks of a product manager is therefore often to balance the needs of these two sides.

13.4.2 Strengthening Product and Domain Knowledge

Another essential key competence for acquiring a good product sense is the knowledge of how successful solutions for one's own business and customers can work in the market. This requires, on the one hand, a universal understanding of products and the building of product knowledge. On the other hand, the specific domain in the respective field of expertise must be understood and sufficient domain knowledge must be built up. This means that product managers must not only bring with them an understanding of the structure and basic elements of a product in general, but also knowledge about the respective market, the competition, the technology used, and the industry in particular.

13.4.2.1 Basic Product Knowledge

The most important question in product management is probably what a product is and what defines it. Often a product is described as a collection of functionalities (features) that solve a problem. In the best case, however, this only satisfies one side: the customer side. To satisfy the company as well, the product must also cover its costs and generate a profit. At the core of every product, therefore, is the exchange of value between consumers and providers. Providers create added value for their customers, who in turn give back to the provider, for example in the form of monetary values. A product is thus much more.

> "Building a product is NOT 'the product' of your startup. Your business model is 'the product'." (Maurya 2011)

The business model is the blueprint of the product. It describes on the customer side the target group(s), the corresponding value proposition, which is described by the problem solution, and the channels through which customers and users become aware of the product. On the business side, in addition to the financial model, consisting of cost structure and revenue streams, the company's competitive advantage is described (Maurya 2012).

Viewed holistically, a product is more than just the sum of its functionalities. A successful product combines a solution for the customer, for the business, and also for the technology (Cagan 2019).

A general understanding of the business model, the customers, the solution, the technology, and the resources to be used is therefore the basis for all product-relevant decisions. These correspond at the same time to the four major risks in product development: the risks of usability, feasibility, business success, and added value for the users or customers.

> "So don't let anyone try to tell you it's all about the business, or it's all about the customer, or it's all about the technology. Product is harder than that. It's all about all three." (Cagan 2019)

To better understand the business models of products, it is recommended to learn more about their structure. A helpful exercise is the deconstruction or deciphering of everyday products. It is always worth being curious, trying out new products, and breaking them down into their individual parts and analyzing them based on product knowledge. The insights can then be shared and discussed with other product enthusiasts or colleagues.

13.4.2.2 Specific Domain Knowledge

In addition to basic product knowledge, domain knowledge is also essential for a good product sense. This means, on the one hand, deeply knowing and understanding one's own company, product, business model, and customers, and on the other hand, knowing the market, the competition, and general trends and technology developments.

> "I argue that strong product sense is better described as deep product knowledge, and is the result of truly immersing yourself into a specific product space." (Cagan 2022)

To understand the vision and strategy of the main competitors, it can be helpful to regularly use their products and talk to their customers. This can better identify strengths and weaknesses.

In addition to competitor analysis, there are other ways to build domain knowledge: Collaborating with so-called Subject Matter Experts, i.e., real experts in a domain, is very valuable according to our experience in gaining own expertise. These can be existing customers or external consultants. Often, experienced experts can also be found among one's own colleagues. To learn more about one's own product, customers, and business, it is also worthwhile to exchange ideas with experts from other areas of the company. Whether it's Sales, Customer Success, Marketing, or Business Development, they all have valuable insights that can give product managers a better understanding of the domain.

13.5 Product Sense Quick Start

Regardless of whether you are very experienced or completely new to product management: In a new job—possibly also in a new industry—product managers initially have little or no empathy for customers or stakeholders. Knowledge about the business, industry, and the product is also not very extensive yet. Product managers face the challenge of having to develop a product sense in the shortest possible time in order to make good decisions.

Ultimately, Product Sense provides security. And that is urgently important in a new job. The sooner Product Sense is built up, the sooner confidence in decision-making also sets in. From our point of view, the formation of Product Sense should therefore be considered as part of the onboarding process and planned from the start.

The following list describes the activities that, in our experience, can help to build up Product Sense quickly. The chronological order can vary from case to case. Of course, the list can be supplemented by individual needs and requirements.

Firstly:

- Regularly block time in the calendar to speak with users and customers.
- Read product and team documentation.
- Understand and comprehend the business model and value proposition.
- Quantitative evaluation of analytics data; view performance data of individual functions and similar.
- Understand the technical landscape and possibilities or limitations.

Immediately after

- Conduct stakeholder interviews to understand needs and find points of connection.
- Get to know perspectives and needs of adjacent areas, such as Sales, Marketing, Biz Dev, Customer Support.
- Set up product KPIs and align them with other areas.
- Learn more about customer needs from other product managers, UX design, Customer Support, Sales, Marketing, etc.
- Research the company's vision and mission, goals, strategy, positioning, and differentiation.
- Subscribe to or attend newsletters, podcasts, conferences, webinars, communities of practice, meetups on product topics.

Somewhat later

- Carry out evaluation of initial prototypes with users or customers.
- Conduct conversations with subject matter experts to build domain knowledge.
- Exchange with competitors and/or industry experts.
- Deconstruct and analyze foreign products.
- Examine data collections and usage data of the industry.
- Keep an eye on the market, competition, trends, and venture capital investments.
- Read industry reports and visit industry trade fairs.

References

Becker, C. 2016. Reclaim your research! https://www.produktbezogen.de/reclaim-your-resarch/.

Cagan, M. 2019. What is a product? https://www.svpg.com/what-is-a-product/.

Cagan, M. 2022. Product sense demystified. https://www.svpg.com/product-sense-demystified/.

Maurya, A. 2011. Your product is NOT "The product". https://blog.leanstack.com/your-product-is-not-the-product/.

Maurya, A. 2012. Why lean canvas vs business model canvas? https://blog.leanstack.com/why-lean-canvas-vs-business-model-canvas/.

Meddlers. o. D. Having strong opinions, Gently Held. https://www.meddlers.com/resources/having-strong-opinions-gently-held.

Rachitsky, L. 2020. A comprehensive survey of product management. https://www.lennysnewsletter.com/p/product-management-survey?s=w#:~:text=BeingaProductManager.

Rachitsky, L. 2021. Twitter. https://twitter.com/lennysan/status/1466903466299715587.

Rachitsky, L. 2022. Julie Zhuo on accelerating your career, impostor syndrome, writing, building product sense, using intuition vs. data, hiring designers, and moving into management. 00:37:55–00:42:57. https://www.lennysnewsletter.com/p/episode-2-julie-zhuo#details.

Saffo, P. 2008. Strong opinions weakly held. https://www.saffo.com/02008/07/26/strong-opinions-weakly-held/.

Walter, J. 2022. How to develop product sendse. https://www.lennysnewsletter.com/p/product-sense.

Robert Schulke is a Senior Product Manager. His current focus is on Product Discovery. He has worked on finding new opportunities, developing digital platforms for adult education, and accompanying strategic initiatives to spin-off. From his long-term activity as a Product Designer (including at XING), he brings deep empathy for users and needs, without losing sight of the necessary value creation for customers and companies. His extensive professional experience covers various industries and markets, from mass-market products in the B2C sector to specialized professional information products in the B2B sector.
Contact: www.robertschulke.de

Nikkel Blaase is a Product Lead and Discovery Coach with a deep passion for innovation and a strong background in User Experience Design. He specializes in Product Discovery and Innovation. His passion is discovering real user problems and designing relevant products that cater to people's needs while achieving the right business results. He loves learning and enjoys sharing his knowledge in blogs, conferences, podcasts, or workshops.
Contact: www.nikkel-blaase.com

Product Leadership

Lateral and Disciplinary Leadership in Modern Product Organizations

Tobias Freudenreich

Abstract

This article is aimed at all product people who want to contribute to a strong product organization. Both individual product managers and their superiors will learn how they can best fulfill their various leadership roles. The first part explains how product managers can utilize the tools of lateral leadership to be effective within their product teams. The second part informs disciplinary leaders about how they can be effectively impactful in modern product organizations and how they can empower their product teams, rather than commanding them.

The requirements for product people in modern product organizations can sometimes seem overwhelming. Organizations demand from them to develop scalable business models, while understanding the individual needs of their users and analytically exploring their behavior. In addition, they should have an overview of both market trends and the latest technological developments, as well as the potential arising from them. At the same time, it is necessary to focus on one's own product vision, strategy, and goals, and to confidently manage countless stakeholders and their conflicting requirements. We expect them to lead interdisciplinary teams and ensure that these teams not only deliver the desired products *(Outputs)*, but also achieve the targeted results *(Outcomes)* in order

---

T. Freudenreich (✉)
Product Leadership Coach & Consultant, Hamburg, Germany
e-mail: office@tobiasfreudenreich.de

© The Author(s), under exclusive license to Springer Fachmedien Wiesbaden GmbH, part of Springer Nature 2024
S. Hoffmann (ed.), *Digital Product Management*,
https://doi.org/10.1007/978-3-658-44276-7_14

Fig. 14.1 Two directions of leadership. (*Source*: Own illustration)

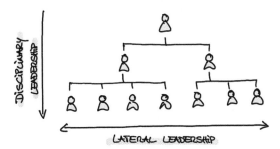

to generate as much impact for the company *(Impact)* as possible (Seiden 2019). And because *New Work* is on everyone's lips, they should always maintain their *Work-Life-Balance* in order to remain physically and mentally healthy and efficient in the long term.

To meet this spectrum of requirements, strong, self-organized teams are needed that complement each other and pull together in one direction. Clarity and focus in leadership are needed to set the right target corridors and thus reduce complexity as much as possible. This leadership takes place in modern product organizations in two directions: laterally within the product teams by product managers and disciplinarily by the superiors of these product managers, see Fig. 14.1.

This article illuminates the lateral leadership role in the first part, as exercised by product managers within their product teams. The disciplinary leadership is examined more closely in the second part.

▶ In this article, modern product organizations are understood to be organizations that are led according to the *Empowered Teams Model* (Cagan and Jones 2021). One of the characteristics of this model is autonomous, interdisciplinary product teams that bear end-to-end responsibility for their product area and are led in an *outcome-centric* manner. This article describes product leadership in companies that need a multitude of teams to develop a larger digital product. The essential characteristics of this leadership can also be applied to startup contexts, where sometimes only a single team is responsible for the entire product.

▶ Whenever this article refers to *executives*, it means disciplinary executives, i.e., the superiors of product managers, who in practice bear titles such as *Teamlead Product, Head of Product* or *Director Product*. To distinguish, the leadership role of product managers without personnel responsibility is consistently referred to as *lateral leadership*.

14 Product Leadership

14.1 Lateral Leadership

In modern product organizations, product teams consist of equal team members from various disciplines—we speak of *interdisciplinary teams*.

▶ The core of such an interdisciplinary team in the development of digital products usually consists of the disciplines *Software Development (Engineering), Product Management* and *User Experience (UX) Design* (see also Chap. 18 by Inken Petersen). Often this core is extended by the role of *Agile Coaching* to promote the team's development towards self-organization and agility. Depending on the context, however, *Marketing, Analytics, Customer Support* or *User Research* are also added. The crucial point is that the team has all the competencies necessary to take end-to-end responsibility for its own product area and to continuously create value for both users and the company.

Product managers do not lead these teams, but rather align themselves as equals with every other team member. Nevertheless, they are expected to lead the team in terms of content and ensure the success of the joint product work. Without formally granted power, this means that they must become effective as lateral leaders within the team. In other words, they must lead laterally, not hierarchically in a vertical direction.

Organizational sociologist Prof. Dr. Stefan Kühl names the three mechanisms of influence in lateral leadership as *understanding, power and trust* (Kühl 2017). *Power* seems initially unintuitive, as it is explicitly a leadership role without formal power, which is reserved for superiors with directive authority due to their title or position in the company hierarchy. However, product managers can use informal power to fulfill their role in the product team.

14.1.1 Lateral Leadership through Communication

The purpose and goal of interdisciplinary teams is the close interlocking of diverse skills to find creative and innovative problem solutions. The aim is to conceive products that are *usable, feasible, valuable* and economically profitable as well as legally and ethically justifiable *(viable)* (Cagan 2018).

Through close interdisciplinary collaboration, we aim to benefit from the different perspectives of team members at every stage of product development. While the engineers in the team usually focus on technical feasibility, UX designers can bring their expertise primarily in terms of usability. Product managers focus particularly on the user-side value contribution, economic profitability, and the legal and ethical justifiability of the product. In particularly high-performing teams, however, these boundaries blur and each team member feels equally responsible for all four dimensions.

Key to the success of this interdisciplinary collaboration is good communication flow within the team. *Agile Coaches* can make a valuable contribution by shaping team processes, but it remains a crucial role of product managers to actively shape communication within the team at a content level and ensure that the different perspectives of the disciplines are continuously taken into account.

Product managers become effective through lateral leadership by creating spaces for open and transparent communication. They should ensure that the different views of team members are heard and taken into account in the team's opinion formation. Strong product managers are by no means the opinion leaders within their team, but rather moderators of team communication with the aim of activating the individual views and experiences of team members.

▶ Product managers should be outstanding listeners and model active listening in their team. Those who listen to understand, rather than to respond, create a culture in which genuine and profound understanding is enabled through continuous changes in perspective.

In addition to this moderating role, product managers should also make their own substantive contribution to understanding. This includes the continuous communication of the product vision and strategy, the explanation of the business model, or the translation of the views of various stakeholders. Making this context knowledge available and understandable for the team is a significant contribution of product managers to understanding within the team.

Product managers who use the superpower of visualization go a step further. Especially technical discussions are often so abstract that schematic representations help all participants to understand the other's perspectives, recognize differences, and achieve genuine understanding. Whiteboard, flipchart, or Miro board should therefore be used in every discussion to visualize one's own understanding and thus make it tangible for others.

▶ In practice, the establishment of so-called *Product Trios* has proven to be helpful (Torres 2021). The product manager, UX designer, and the most experienced developer in the team form this trio, which simplifies communication paths: not all team members have to continuously communicate with everyone, but the trio bundles aspects of this communication. It is crucial that the trio itself does not fall into a hierarchical leadership role. It is important to avoid making decisions over the heads of the other team members, but rather to prepare decisions in such a way that they can be made efficiently together in the team. The trio itself is thus assigned a lateral leadership role.

14.1.2 Lateral Leadership through Power

As initially described, power as an instrument of lateral leadership seems counterintuitive, as these leadership roles explicitly do without formal power. However, alongside the classic disciplinary, formal power, informal forms of power also coexist. For example, power can also arise from exclusive access to resources—in product management, for instance, through sole access to key stakeholders, executives, or even information sources, such as analysis data.

Mastery of informal communication channels, i.e., good networking within the company, also gives product managers power. Last but not least, technical authority is a significant form of informal power. All these non-disciplinary forms of power have in common that they must not be granted from the outside, but must be acquired independently, which often equips them with even greater authority. Because ultimately, for all forms of power, power must be recognized to be effective. The followers must acknowledge and thus legitimize the power of the leaders, otherwise the leaders remain powerless.

Interestingly, some methods of disciplinary leadership also work in the lateral context. Strong product managers, for example, use servant leadership to fulfill their role within the team. They make themselves useful to their team, which over time rewards this with the recognition of informal power. This can be achieved, for example, by taking seemingly annoying tasks such as stakeholder communication off the team members or making analysis data accessible. However, it is important to find the right balance: if product managers occupy too many information channels or resources, they make the team dependent on them and build up knowledge of domination. This harms the team's ability to self-organize and leads to an increasing demand on the product managers in the medium term. They become a bottleneck for their team. Strong lateral leaders, therefore, make themselves useful by empowering their team members, rather than making them dependent on themselves.

The most natural form of lateral power is the already mentioned technical authority. It is not granted either, but must be acquired. Competent product managers learn this at the latest when they switch to a new team: the previously built-up technical authority must be reworked and acquired again.

But what characterizes the technical authority of product managers? On the one hand, it is the deep knowledge of the product domain: How does the market tick? How does the competition act? Which trends are relevant? How does the business model work? What technical challenges are there? What needs do the users have? Which vision, strategy, and goals need to be pursued? At the same time, the technical authority of product managers also arises from a good process knowledge: How does Product Discovery work? How should the Delivery be managed? What is the next step? What is the purpose of the current activity?

Strong product managers, therefore, not only penetrate the content aspects of their product but can also confidently guide their team through all phases of product development. Over time, this leads to technical authority and thus informal power.

14.1.3 Lateral Leadership through Trust

In the context of lateral leadership, as in disciplinary leadership, it is important to understand that the relationship level plays an immensely large role. The assumption that we mutate into rational beings at work and decisions are predominantly made objectively does not stand up to critical examination. A good discussion at the factual level therefore always requires an intact relationship level among the discussants, which in turn is based on mutual trust.

Trust, like informal power, must first be earned by product managers. Past successes count little here: In every new or changed team, trust must be re-established.

But how is trust created? Basically, by initially taking a risk and giving another person a trust advance, which hopefully proves worthy. If we have a positive experience, we repeat this process over and over again, building trust bit by bit until a solid basis, a long-term trust relationship, is established. Building trust is therefore an iterative process that takes time—strong teams do not emerge overnight.

Once we have created a stable and resilient basis of trust, it allows us a certain flexibility in dealing with each other. We are no longer dependent on every interaction immediately paying off and both sides benefiting equally. We are more willing to take risks for each other and help each other because we can rely on this paying off for both parties in the long term. Trust thus becomes an instrument of lateral leadership.

In practice, product managers should therefore continuously work on a good, stable relationship with all team members. It certainly helps to get to know each other personally and to strengthen the bond among team members through team events. However, it is even more important to prove oneself trustworthy in daily work. This can be achieved, for example, by absolute reliability: If product managers promise their team that there will be an opportunity to reduce technical debt after the release of the time-critical feature, this promise must be kept. If they argue for the quick launch of a solution with the argument that design problems can be solved in a subsequent iteration, they must ensure that this happens. If these promises cannot be guaranteed because, for example, stakeholders do not grant the necessary degrees of freedom, product managers should not make these promises.

Because it is important to understand that every trusting relationship always remains fragile. Although we may have built trust through countless positive interactions, the smallest breach of trust is enough to destroy this basis and turn it into mistrust. Product managers should be aware of this and do everything they can to keep their trust base within the team stable.

This insight is particularly essential in the event of a conflict: We often fail to resolve conflicts at the factual level because we do not recognize that a disturbed interpersonal level

14 Product Leadership

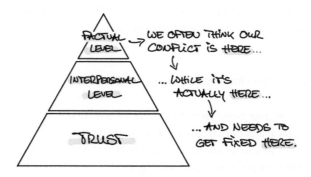

Fig. 14.2 Utilizing relationship levels in case of conflict. (*Source*: Own illustration)

is fueling the conflict, see Fig. 14.2. If we manage to pause in these situations and recognize the core of the problem, this will not only facilitate the resolution of the current conflict, but can also help to strengthen our relationship for the future. Through newly gained trust, smoother collaboration becomes possible and lateral leadership significantly easier.

▶   Communication is a core competence of strong product managers. Those who master clear and target group-oriented communication can develop into a strong lateral leadership force. The claim to lateral leadership often proves itself in the event of a conflict: Those who manage to identify, address and constructively resolve conflicts in the team will gain lasting trust.

14.1.4 The Interplay of Communication, Power, and Trust

The mechanisms of communication, power, and trust can be used independently of each other for the purpose of lateral leadership. However, particularly strong product managers use them in combination and modulate them situationally. It depends on a skillful interplay: It is easy to see that the exercise of power can hinder the building of trust. Conversely, a solid basis of trust can favor the well-dosed use of power or facilitate communication. If we trust each other, we are more likely to adopt the perspective of our counterpart and it is easier for us to acknowledge their professional authority.

It is also noteworthy that the factors communication, power, and trust can even substitute each other (Kühl 2017): Where at the beginning communication was necessary for mutual persuasion, trust may take this place at a later stage of team development. Because team members trust each other blindly, they are more likely to accept the suggestions of others and less communication is needed. As a team grows closer over time, decision-making ability and thus productivity increase immensely.

Product managers should therefore also have a great interest in team development as lateral leaders and be aware of their own role in it, instead of seeing this task only in their *Agile Coaches*. Organizations, in turn, should become aware of the value of stable teams and refrain from too frequent restructurings.

> **Tip**
> It helps to reflect from time to time on how one appears to the team:
>
> - Do I ensure deep understanding in the team by promoting genuine exchange and perspective changes in discussions?
> - Is my professional authority recognized in the team or do I need to catch up in a field to close my professional gaps?
> - Do I invest enough in good, trustful relationships with all team members? Can I trust everyone? Can everyone trust me?

14.2 Disciplinary Leadership

Disciplinary leadership in modern digital product organizations has little in common with a classic understanding of leadership. Anyone trying to drive product teams to peak performance through an authoritarian leadership style will hardly be successful in the long term and will not be able to develop outstanding product teams. Instead of leading authoritatively, product leaders are now required to enable self-organized teams. This means, among other things, that the methods of lateral leadership also help disciplinary leaders to greater success. It is their task to develop a system within which the teams are able to make the right decisions themselves, instead of making detailed decisions for the product teams.

Jeff Redfern uses the metaphor of a shipyard to illustrate this: The task of leaders is to build better shipyards. Shipyards where teams are enabled to build the best ships (Redfern 2019), see Fig. 14.3. Anyone who wants to get their hands on shipbuilding should reconsider whether a professional career is not more fulfilling than climbing the hierarchy. Because enabling teams also includes allowing them to learn and grow from their own wrong decisions.

When the pressure to deliver results increases, many leaders are put to a tough test: Should they interfere with the team to accelerate the release of a feature and thus risk inhibiting the team's development? Or do they withstand the pressure and risk a delay because they want to benefit from a strong team in the medium to long term?[1]

---

[1] This is a typical dilemma of leadership in modern work environments, as described by Christian Gärtner in "Ambivalences and Dilemmas in Digitally Transformed Work Environments" (Gärtner 2019).

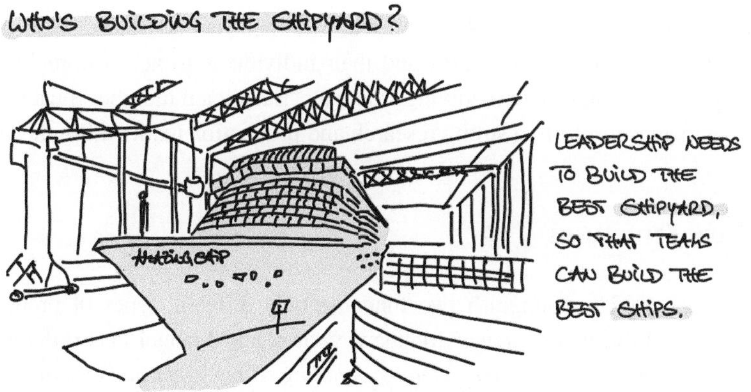

Fig. 14.3 Leaders must build the shipyard, not the ship. (*Source*: Own illustration)

In these pressure situations, it is tempting to choose the seemingly faster solution of interfering and thus efficiently working off open topics. Over time, however, the teams will lose their ability to think and decide for themselves and will instead orient themselves towards the leader. It is therefore important for every leader to realize that an instructive leadership style over time leads to becoming a bottleneck oneself. This insight should protect against repeatedly getting involved in shipbuilding and losing sight of the shipyard.

However, we should not overstretch the metaphor of the shipyard. Shipbuilding today is at best still a complicated, but by no means a complex problem. Engineers know how to build a ship, there are standardized technologies and proven procedures. Technical specifications can be worked off in a division of labor and assemblers can be guided with detailed instructions.

Digital product development, however, is a complex problem across all industries: While we are working on a solution, the market is dynamically evolving. The interests, desires, and needs of our users are also constantly changing. The same applies to the technologies we use for product development. Since we fail to analytically penetrate the problem space in complex systems and derive suitable solutions from this analysis, we are asked for other problem-solving strategies. We are encouraged to introduce experiments into the system, observe their results, and derive the next steps from them (Snowden and Boone 2007).

Modern product organizations are therefore not industrial assembly lines—they are rather research institutions of applied sciences and manufacturing at the same time. Product teams must not only be excellent software producers, but also top researchers, in order to continuously conceive and produce competitive products.

How can leaders best be effective here and enable teams to have this competence? Firstly, it is important to reduce complexity as much as possible. While the complexity inherent in the matter cannot be influenced, the complexity of one's own organization can. Therefore, clear structures and objectives are needed for product teams. Product leaders must set the right framework to enable their teams, rather than command them. Secondly, it is necessary to enable product teams and their individuals to act in complex environments and apply the right problem-solving strategies. Each team member must develop the necessary competence to form a strong research and production team within the team.

14.2.1 Clear Structures

Cagan and Jones (2021) distinguish two fundamentally different types of product teams: *platform teams* and *experience teams*. Matthew Skelton and Manuel Pais differentiate four different types of teams: *stream aligned teams, enabling teams, complicated subsystem teams* and also *platform teams* (Skelton and Pais 2019).

Regardless of which taxonomy one uses, it is important to create clarity about the team topology within the organization:

- Which teams bear end-to-end responsibility for the product experience of a user group?
- Which teams enable other teams by providing technical platforms on which they can build?
- Which teams encapsulate certain technical systems to reduce complexity for other teams?
- Which teams do not own their own program code, but support others by conveying knowledge or keeping an eye on overarching topics, such as system architecture?

Depending on their topology, teams need different competencies: While those teams that work close to the users must absolutely master methods of qualitative and quantitative research, it is usually sufficient for platform teams to regularly talk to those who use their internal product.

Leaders should ensure that the teams are aware of the topology and especially that there is clarity about the interaction mode in cross-team collaboration: Is it, for example, the platform team that determines the roadmap of platform development and informs the user experience teams about new features of the platform? Or is it rather the user experience teams that formulate specifications for the further development of the platform based on their knowledge of user requirements?

Creating clarity here significantly reduces the complexity of cross-team collaboration and helps teams to put all their energy into actual product development.

14.2.2 A Clear Goal Corridor

With the *Decision Stack*, Martin Eriksson (2021) has presented a mental model that helps product leaders create the necessary clarity within their product organization. Eriksson shows how product *vision, strategy, objectives, opportunities,* and *product principles* interlock and how these artifacts help us make difficult decisions quickly, see Fig. 14.4.

Product Vision The task of the product vision is to convey an idea of the long-term goal: What problem do we want to have solved in five years? The time horizon may vary depending on the context, but the task of the vision remains the same: It should inspire and motivate all participants by conveying the idea of a desirable state in the future. The vision does not answer how to reach this future state.

Product Strategy The product strategy explains what needs to be done to come sufficiently close to the set vision. In practice, the strategy often covers a time frame of four planning intervals—in most companies, therefore, four quarters, or one year. The strategy aims to put the next steps in a plausible sequence.

By no means should a product strategy in modern organizations dictate which features are to be developed by the teams. Instead, it should outline which user needs are to be addressed, for example, which major user problems are to be tackled in which order. The strategy thus describes which values are to be created for users *(Outcomes)* and also outlines which positive value contribution is expected for the company *(Impact)* as a result. This linkage is the *strategic hypothesis,* which is the responsibility of the management team, see Fig. 14.5.

Objectives The objectives, in turn, should specify for each individual product team which values for users *(Outcomes)* are to be focused on. They are directly derived from the strategy. The magic of the *Decision Stacks* is the linkage of all levels through the question of *Why* or in reverse direction after the *How*. This way, product teams gain the necessary contextual knowledge: They not only see the strategic sense of pursuing their objectives, but also how local activity contributes to achieving the vision.

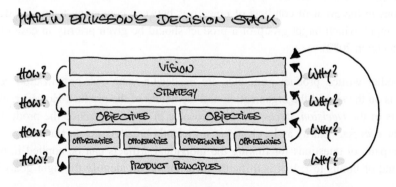

Fig. 14.4 Decision Stack according to Martin Eriksson. (*Source*: Own illustration)

Fig. 14.5 The tactical hypothesis is the responsibility of the product team, the strategic hypothesis is the responsibility of the management team. (*Source*: Own illustration)

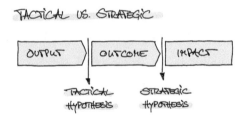

Opportunities Once the product team knows which values are to be created for users, it can begin the actual *Product Discovery*. The task is to find out which *Opportunities* are suitable for producing the desired result. The fixed term *Opportunities* in this context means according to Teresa Torres (2021) both user *needs,* as well as *desires* or *pain points*—provided their addressing is suitable to deliver the hoped-for value.

The research assignment for the product team is now to identify these *Opportunities* and to develop solutions through an iterative, experimental approach that satisfy these customer interests. The tactical hypothesis, which products *(Outputs)* are suitable for achieving the desired results *(Outcomes)*, is thus the responsibility of the product team, see Fig. 14.5.

▶ The strategic hypothesis is the responsibility of the management team and is important contextual knowledge for the product teams. The task of the product teams, in turn, is the elaboration and pursuit of the tactical hypothesis.

Product Principles Especially in larger organizations, where a multitude of product teams are working on a common product, the *Alignment* (see Chap. 15 by Arne Kittler) of the teams becomes highly important. Although we advocate autonomous teams in modern product organizations, there are limits to this autonomy. There needs to be an agreement on common principles to ensure that the sum of the parts ultimately forms a coherent whole for the users. Well-chosen product principles can also help to make decisions in the event of conflicts of objectives between competing teams, by defining, for example, which target group of a product should be given priority in case of doubt (Freudenreich 2022).

Whether written product principles are needed in your own organization certainly depends on the size of the organization and the nature of the product. However, all other artifacts of the *Decision Stacks* are indispensable in order to provide the product teams with the necessary clarity and a clear, yet sufficiently broad, target corridor.

The pairs of questions for linking the individual artifacts can be applied in practice as a kind of litmus test: If it is difficult, for example, to identify the right goals for the coming quarter and to coordinate them with the teams, this is often because the question of *Why* cannot be answered. This is a sign that there is a lack of a clear product strategy and that action needs to be taken at this level. Once a clear strategy is in place, it will be easy to derive the right goals.

▶ **Tip**
The terminology "product team" carries a risk in practice: Because both product vision and strategy each have "product" in their name, it is often misinterpreted that each product team should also have its own vision and strategy. This inevitably leads to confusion in larger organizations: Vision and strategy are important artifacts for developing a future-proof product. If several teams work together on a product, these artifacts serve the *alignment* of the teams—however, individual visions and strategies at the team level would counteract this purpose.

Nevertheless, it is understandable that product teams want to assure themselves of their own role and record what their contribution to the bigger picture is. If clearly formulated objectives derived from the strategy are not sufficient, it is recommended to work with *team mission statements* to avoid diluting the role of vision and strategy unnecessarily (Cessan 2019).

14.2.3 Competent Product Managers

Developing one's own employees must be the top priority of any manager with personnel responsibility. Only those who manage to support employees in their development, to challenge and promote them equally, and thus to open up career opportunities for them, justify their high salary in management. Therefore, the top priority of product leaders should be to strengthen the strengths of their product managers and help them overcome learning fields. This presupposes that leaders have a clear understanding of what competence actually means in their own context.

Petra Wille (2020) calls this understanding *Definition of Good*. Leaders must know what *"good"* or *"competent"* looks like in the respective job role in order to be able to develop employees at all. To be linguistically precise, it is never the leaders who *develop* their employees. That would be a rather Frankenstein-like understanding of leadership. No: it is always the employees themselves who develop—the task of leadership is to show them development opportunities, provide resources and define development goals together with the employees.

As a starting point for developing your own *Definition of Good*, the *PMWheel* also presented by Petra Wille is suitable (Wille 2022). This "product management wheel" is a spider chart that spans eight dimensions for assessing the competence of product managers:

1. *Understand the problem*—The qualification to identify user needs and derive potentials for your own product development from them.
2. *Find a solution*—The ability to develop solutions that are suitable for addressing the identified needs.
3. *Do some planning*—The competence to structure and plan the product work of the team.
4. *Get it done*—The ability to motivate oneself and the team to complete the task.
5. *Listen & learn*—The trait of listening and learning from it.
6. *Team*—The lateral leadership quality and one's own suitability as a team player.
7. *Grow*—The continuous endeavor to develop oneself further.
8. *Agile*—The understanding of agile methods and the ability to promote them in the team.

Now, it should not just be about applying this framework in your own context and assessing your own employees based on exactly these eight dimensions. Rather, it is about developing an individual version of the *PMWheel* for your own environment. To do this, it helps to reflect on the following questions:

- What personality traits are helpful for being successful in the role of product manager? Which ones are rather hindering?
- What knowledge and skills are needed?
- What ways of thinking *(Mindset)* and what values should product managers represent in the organization?

Once your own *Definition of Good* has been found, it simplifies several aspects in the development of competent product managers. For one thing, it helps to hire the right candidates. Therefore, every hiring process should start with this and job advertisements should be derived from the *Definition of Good*.

Furthermore, the definition helps to create transparency and a common understanding of the claim for the employees. This enables development discussions on an equal footing—an important prerequisite for effective employee development. Based on this, continuous feedback discussions and the annual discussion ritualized in many companies are greatly facilitated.

Individual development potentials arise from the difference between role claim *(Definition of Good)* and the current degree of fulfillment of this claim by the employee. Once these potentials are identified, the manager can develop the right measures for further development in dialogue with the employee and set corresponding goals. If there is a lack of technical skills, for example, training or further education may help to work on this learning field. Perhaps there is also the opportunity to learn new competencies in other areas of the company. If there is a lack of empathy for the users, for example, a job shadowing in customer support may help to get a better feel for the problems of the target group.

14 Product Leadership

Of course, it remains the most important task of every manager to individually support their employees in their further development. Therefore, *Coaching* absolutely belongs in the toolbox of every modern manager. At its core, it's about leading employees not through instructions, but by stimulating their own problem-solving skills through questions. If employees receive pure instructions, this will in most cases lead to the expected results in the short term. However, it does not lead to employees learning to help themselves—they grow little if they only follow instructions. If, on the other hand, managers help them through good questions to find their own answers, they promote the long-term growth of their employees.

An acute problem will be solved slower in doubt—which, as initially described, triggers a sometimes hard to bear conflict for managers: Is the quick problem solution or the long-term growth of the employees to be prioritized?

Good coaching is characterized by choosing the individually and situationally appropriate methods. Career starters are certainly not helped if they are led by questioning. They need instructions, guidance, and concrete assistance. However, if the same methods are applied to the most experienced employees, their motivation will quickly collapse. The goal of every coaching relationship should therefore be to gradually move from an instructive to a questioning approach. This can be achieved, for example, through intermediate stages such as expressing recommendations or constructive feedback, see Fig. 14.6.

▶ In order for managers to be able to coach their employees efficiently, they should be able to experience their daily work. Just as a football coach needs to observe the players in the game in order to be able to develop them further, managers also need these observation points. For this reason, we should critically question the

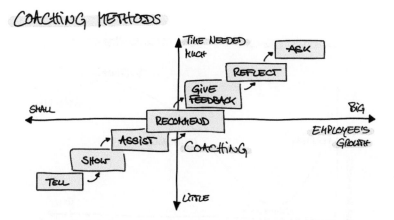

Fig. 14.6 The goal of coaching is the development from an instructive to a questioning leadership style. (*Source*: Own illustration)

matrix organizational form: Is the separation of technical and disciplinary leadership really suitable for producing strong product teams? Last but not least, Spotify also critically questioned this aspect in an iteration of their much-cited 2012 organizational model and moved the disciplinary managers closer to the daily work of their employees. (Lee 2020)

As shown, it is the task of managers to give employees development opportunities, resources, and goals and to support them in their own development in the sense of a good coach. But the painful truth of leadership also includes that managers must act when employees do not develop successfully in the given context. Regardless of whether they cannot or do not want to develop the necessary competencies. It is then the task of the manager to dismiss the employee from this context and to show them other development opportunities within or outside the company. Managers who avoid this difficult process cause lasting damage to their own company and promote a culture in which goals and requirements count for nothing. They also undermine their own leadership claim and damage the performance and especially the willingness to perform of their teams. Ultimately, they also harm the affected employees, because people are not happy in roles whose requirements they cannot fulfill.

14.2.4 Strong Product Teams

The American psychologist Bruce W. Tuckman developed a model as early as 1965 that describes the basic developmental stages of teams. This model includes the four stages Forming, Storming, Norming, and Performing (Tuckman 1965). In a later study, Tuckman, together with Mary Ann C. Jensen, expanded the model to include the fifth stage Adjourning (Tuckman and Jensen 1977), see Fig. 14.7.

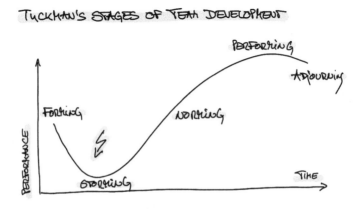

Fig. 14.7 Stages of team development according to Tuckman. (*Source*: Own illustration)

The model shows that teams must overcome some preliminary phases before they can reach their peak performance. After the team is assembled *(Forming)*, they typically go through a phase characterized by conflicts—the so-called *Storming*. Different ideas of work methods, conflicting values, and cultural imprints collide. Teams must now manage to agree on common work methods and values. They must agree on their own norms. Tuckman therefore refers to this phase as *Norming*. Only when the norming is achieved can the team grow to peak performance and finally arrive at *Performing*. Once a team has fulfilled its founding purpose, the phase of *Adjourning* begins—the collaboration is ended. In this final phase, the team is busy winding up its own work, causing productivity to collapse. For product teams, this last phase is less relevant, as they are designed as permanently stable teams, unlike project teams, and are only dissolved when the product is discontinued.

Understanding this model helps to build strong product teams. It is immediately clear why it is not enough to simply throw teams together and send them on their way. They then run the risk of getting stuck in the *Storming* or spending unnecessarily long time in this phase. The goal of every leader must therefore be to quickly guide a team through the *Storming phase* towards *Norming*.

It is therefore a leadership task to closely accompany newly formed or reformed teams in the first weeks. Intensive kick-off workshops can help, among other things, to give the team the necessary context and to give team members the opportunity to get to know and exchange ideas. Tools such as retrospectives, role and value workshops can—if well moderated—help to quickly identify and resolve conflicts.

Many teams work out a common set of rules for collaboration and document this in the form of a *team charter* or *working agreements*. If this happens, the *Norming* has already been reached and the team is well on its way to *Performing*.

Once in the *Performing* phase, staying in this phase is unfortunately not guaranteed. If, for example, individual team members change, new areas of responsibility are added, or there is a conflict within the team, it can quickly fall back into the *Storming*. Leaders must recognize these moments and, if necessary, intervene to help teams back through the necessary phases and back into the *Performing*.

14.2.5 Interdisciplinary Leadership

Although interdisciplinary product teams are long standard in the digital industry, interdisciplinary collaboration at the leadership level often appears underrepresented in practice. Many leaders continue to operate in interdisciplinary environments as if they were leaders in a functionally structured organization. For example, product leaders develop their product strategy exclusively in the circle of product managers, while their colleagues in engineering work alone on a tech strategy and consider how the large mountain of *technical debt* can finally be paid off. The result is often competing strategy artifacts, e.g., a product strategy, a tech strategy, and a UX strategy, see Fig. 14.8.

While all these artifacts may contain valid and important strategic considerations, the question remains: What should an interdisciplinary product team do with them? How should team members deal with conflicting statements from the various documents?

It is absolutely necessary to avoid team members having to spend precious time and energy trying to hear the right tone from a cacophony of voices. There is therefore no way around working collaboratively in an interdisciplinary manner at the leadership level as well. It is necessary to resolve prioritization conflicts already at the leadership level and, if necessary, to merge separately existing tech, UX, and product strategies into a common strategy.

The term "product strategy" is often a hindrance, as it easily gives the impression that it is a strategy exclusively for product managers. However, a product strategy should be holistic: after all, every product needs a competitive *User Experience* and in the digital world, there is simply no product without technology. It is therefore imperative that the leaders of all disciplines work together to lead the product teams with one voice and provide them with the necessary clarity.

Four measures can help in practice to form a strong interdisciplinary leadership team:

1. Regular coordination
2. Role-reversed communication
3. Interdisciplinary coordinated goals
4. Interdisciplinary tactical meetings

Regular Coordination Product leaders should ensure that they spend enough time per week with the leaders of the other disciplines. In weekly jour-fixe meetings, leadership teams should continuously coordinate on the three crucial dimensions of *people, process, and product*:

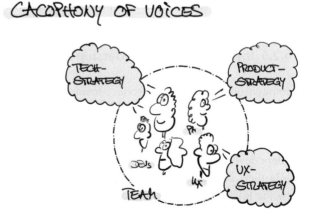

Fig. 14.8 The cacophony of competing strategies leads to misunderstandings and inefficiencies. (*Source*: Own illustration)

- *People:* Are there any updates on filling open positions? Are critical departures or longer absences imminent? What do the employee retention metrics look like? What should the focus of the leadership team be?
- *Process:* How is the health of the teams? What about *agile maturity)*? Can process-related experiences of one team be used profitably for other teams? How is the next quarterly planning approached?
- *Product:* How well is the current strategy being implemented? Are the desired results *(Outcomes)* achieved and have they had the hoped-for effect *(Impact)*? If not: What should be done to correct the course?

Role-Reversed Communication Leading by example is probably the most powerful tool in any leader's toolbox. If we demand that engineers commit to the value contribution of the developed product and product managers do not lose sight of the *technical debt*, then this must also be lived by the leaders. A very effective means of doing this is to swap roles on the internal stages from time to time. If the engineering leader presents the product strategy at the next *All-Hands Meeting*, while the product leader explains the next big tech initiative, this will have far more impact in promoting a true interdisciplinary culture than any well-intentioned declaration of intent.

Interdisciplinary Coordinated Goals Regardless of the framework used for goal setting, it is important to ensure that goals are always coordinated in interdisciplinary rounds. Many companies nowadays use the *OKR framework* (see Chap. 4 by Cansel Sörgens) for quarterly goal setting. In the course of this, the leadership level and team level come together and agree on the right objectives for the upcoming quarter. This should be done in an open dialogue to weigh the perspectives of all disciplines in the goal setting. Only in this way can it be ensured that the goals within a team are identical and there is a common understanding of the priorities.

Interdisciplinary Tactical Meetings Even more important than agreeing on the right goals, however, is the continuous pursuit of these (Wodtke 2021). Vision, strategy, and goal agreements have no value in themselves. Their value only arises in the execution by the product teams. To best support these, leaders and teams should regularly come together and discuss degrees of goal achievement as well as resulting insights and possibly necessary measures.

This should always be interdisciplinary and not take place in the silos of professional functions. Only in this way can it be ensured that all employees are clear about the priorities and all have the necessary contextual knowledge to make their best possible contribution to achieving the goals. Ultimately, the aim is to learn together whether the tactical hypotheses (see Fig. 14.5) are fulfilled—whether the delivered *output* had the envisaged result *(Outcome)*. Regular tactical meetings can help to become better at forming and pursuing these hypotheses across all disciplines. In the dialogue between team representatives and the leadership team, any blockers can be quickly identified and eliminated.

14.2.6 Final Considerations

In every organization, the actual value creation does not take place in management, but in the operational teams. It is the product teams that conceive digital solutions in a modern product organization, with which users are delighted and, in the best case, converted into paying customers of the company.

Organizational development in modern organizations should therefore always be thought of from the bottom up: What do interdisciplinary teams need to do their best work? What knowledge, resources, competencies, processes, and environments are necessary to empower strong teams? These guiding questions should determine the thinking and actions of all leaders and motivate them to create a system in which interdisciplinary teams are enabled to create the best digital products.

References

Cagan, M. 2018. *Inspired: How to create tech products customers love*. 2nd ed. Wiley.
Cagan, M., and C. Jones. 2021. *Empowered: Ordinary people, extraordinary products*. Wiley.
Cessan, V. 2019. https://www.viktorcessan.com/team-mission-statements/.
Eriksson, M. 2021. The decision stack. https://www.youtube.com/watch?v=L4jzhUCfOhM&t=897s.
Freudenreich, T. 2022. https://www.mindtheproduct.com/overcoming-decision-overload-using-principles-to-make-better-decisions-faster-by-martin-eriksson/.
Gärtner, C. 2019. Ambivalenzen und Dilemmata in digital transformierten Arbeitswelten. *Supervision: Mensch – Arbeit – Organisation* 37(4):10–17.
Kühl, S. 2017. *Laterales Führen: Eine kurze organisationstheoretisch informierte Handreichung*. Springer VS.
Lee, J. 2020. https://www.jeremiahlee.com/posts/failed-squad-goals/.
Redfern, J. 2019. A Better Shipyard – Joff Redfern on The Product Experience: https://www.mindtheproduct.com/a-better-shipyard-joff-redfern-on-the-product-experience/.
Seiden, J. 2019. *Outcomes over output: Why customer behavior is the key metric for business success*. Sense & Respond Press.
Skelton, M., and M. Pais. 2019. *Team topologies: Organizing business and technology teams for fast flow*. IT Revolution Press.
Snowden, D. J., and M. E. Boone. 2007. https://hbr.org/2007/11/a-leaders-framework-for-decision-making.
Torres, T. 2021. *Continuous discovery habits: Discover products that create customer value and business value*. Product Talk LLC.
Tuckman, B. W. 1965. Developmental sequence in small groups. *Psychological Bulletin* 63(6):384–399. https://doi.org/10.1037/h0022100.
Tuckman, B. W., and M. A. C. Jensen. 1977. Stages of small-group development revisited. *Group & Organization Studies* 2(4):419–427. https://doi.org/10.1177/105960117700200404.
Wille, P. 2020. *Strong product people: A complete guide to developing great product managers*. Petra Wille.
Wille, P. 2022. https://www.strongproductpeople.com/pmwheel.
Wodtke, C. 2021. *Radical focus: Achieving your most important goals with objectives and key results*. 2nd ed. Cucina Media LLC.

Tobias Freudenreich has been working in the digital industry for over 20 years and has held various product management and leadership roles over the years. Today, he helps product people and their organizations as a freelance *Product Leadership Coach and Consultant* to continuously grow and develop successful products. In addition, Tobias is a co-organizer of the *MTP ProductTank Hamburg,* co-moderator of the *Product at Heart* conference, and host of the podcast *Produktmenschen.*
Contact: office@tobiasfreudenreich.de

Alignment 15

Why Good Alignment is So Important—and How to Achieve It

Arne Kittler

Abstract

Being well-aligned is important for product managers—this applies regardless of the size of the company or the industry in which one works. Good alignment is a necessary prerequisite for product managers to gain trust. And trust, in turn, is the basis for many success factors of modern product management, such as an ideally autonomous iterative working method as a product team or efficient decision-making. The following article describes in more detail why and in which situations alignment is important and how to achieve it.

15.1 Why is Alignment Important in the Context of Modern Product Development?

When we talk about alignment in this post, it means that as a product manager, you have established clarity with relevant people in your environment about what you intend to do and why, and how this fits in with what the other participants intend to do. It does not mean that all actors necessarily agree with the plans of others, but it is primarily about achieving the greatest possible clarity—possibly even in dissent. This clarity is a necessary basis for trust. It also helps to reduce the risk of unnecessary work ("waste") and to make decisions.

A. Kittler (✉)
Product at Heart, Hamburg, Germany
e-mail: mail@arnekittler.de

© The Author(s), under exclusive license to Springer Fachmedien Wiesbaden GmbH, part of Springer Nature 2024
S. Hoffmann (ed.), *Digital Product Management*,
https://doi.org/10.1007/978-3-658-44276-7_15

15.1.1 Alignment Creates Trust

In contrast to traditional "Command & Control" leadership styles, where very specific instructions are given hierarchically and their compliance is checked, modern product organizations operate with a much more open leadership style. But even with this leadership style, product teams are expected to align their work with overarching company goals, long-term visions, strategies, etc. Regarding the question of WHAT they do specifically and above all, HOW they do it, product teams ideally enjoy a high degree of decision-making space and autonomy. Only with these freedoms are product teams really empowered to develop the best solutions for the users and the company using iterative and agile working methods (Cagan 2018).

The mandate to act largely independently as a team in product development cannot simply be claimed by a team in practice, but will only be obtained if all relevant actors in the environment of the respective team have sufficient trust in the team and its approach.

If this trust is lacking, higher-level decision-makers will usually have a more concrete influence on the team's working methods than it is comfortable with, and cooperation with other actors will at least require significantly more coordination or may not even occur at all. By aligning themselves early with their environment, product managers can make a significant contribution to building trust in their own work and the work of their own team.

15.1.2 Alignment Helps to Avoid Waste of Resources

If there is a lack of sensible alignment, situations like the following can easily arise:

- After the launch of a product, there is disagreement about whether the results achieved are to be considered a success or not. Important decision-makers question whether the effort expended was worthwhile in view of the result.
- Shortly before the completion of an important product launch, the affected teams realize that although they have all worked intensively towards the launch, due to a lack of alignment their partial results do not make sense together and can only be integrated with considerable additional effort.

The two examples illustrate that the work of teams either does not contribute to the overall result as planned or is at least not rewarded. Both lead to less capacity than theoretically available being used for the best possible product solution in the interest of the users.

A vivid example of the cost of lack of coordination is provided by long-time Spotify coach Henrik Kniberg (2016) in his drawing (Fig. 15.1).

15 Alignment

Fig. 15.1 Misalignment. (*Source*: Kniberg 2016)

15.1.3 Alignment Helps to Make Decisions

As mentioned at the beginning, product managers' alignment is not necessarily about achieving comprehensive consensus. Due to different perspectives or in extreme cases even due to conflicting goals, it is often unavoidable that product managers have a different view of a product development project than their counterpart. This can be the case in larger organizations, for example, in the cooperation between product managers who want to get the maximum out of individual sub-products, and platform product managers who have a more holistic perspective than local optima in mind.

Not only to endure these conflicts, but to resolve them independently or to lead to a decision promptly by regulated escalation (see Sect. 15.7) is a central responsibility of product managers.

If disagreements are not brought to a successful clarification, this has a negative effect on mutual trust in cooperation. Often, unresolved or delayed decisions also lead to product development being blocked or at least negatively affected.

For the reasons mentioned, it is so important that product managers establish clarity with their environment through sensible alignment.

15.2 Who Should a Product Manager Actively Align With?

As a product manager, alignment in three dimensions is important: vertical, lateral, and with your own team.

The most obvious is the importance of successful **vertical alignment** with superiors and other higher-level decision-makers: It is in the interest of product managers that superiors understand why one acts in a certain way and what one plans to do, so that they can grant the necessary trust to the product manager and their team to decide independently how they proceed.

In the course of this alignment, it may be found that superiors have a completely different idea and therefore one has to question one's own approach again. This may be inconvenient in the short term, but it is typically more sensible and efficient to find out different ideas as early as possible and not to start "secretly" and without alignment, risking that the acting teams work in vain due to later changes.

Especially in larger organizations with several product teams or strong teams in other functional areas, such as sales or marketing, good **lateral coordination** is particularly important. Lateral means to exchange and coordinate at the same "hierarchical level". Because only in this way can one ensure early on that overarching cooperation ultimately fits together, or one quickly realizes if there are conflicts of interest that can only be resolved by escalating to a higher hierarchical level.

And finally, it is equally important that product managers are also well aligned **with their own team** as to why they are pursuing product development and what they roughly plan to do. Only when team members understand this context can they contribute meaningfully from their respective professional perspective to the best possible solution. And it is also motivational for all team members to understand how their work contributes to the success of the company. Clarity about this is much better achieved with systematic alignment than purely informally.

15.3 In Which Contexts is Alignment Particularly Important?

Thorough and systematic alignment means an additional effort for all involved at first. However, the effort of early alignment is generally worthwhile because it helps to avoid later inefficiencies, misunderstandings, or problems that can no longer be solved at a later stage.

Important indications for product managers to strive for active alignment include the following situations:

- A planned initiative is of high relevance to many, especially heterogeneous decision-makers in the company.
- A planned initiative requires collaboration with other teams or supporting specialists such as analysts, data science, or marketing.

15 Alignment

- A planned initiative represents a significant development effort for the own team and possibly also for other affected teams and specialists.

Whenever product managers find themselves in a situation where at least one of these criteria applies, it is advisable to clarify the context more actively through systematic alignment of the planned initiative.

15.4 When Should Systematic Alignment Ideally Take Place?

In principle, alignment should take place as early as possible in an initiative to keep the risk of later changes in direction and thus inefficient use of resources as low as possible.

Experience shows that , especially with new developments at an early stage, there is a high degree of uncertainty about the context of the product initiative and one may not yet be completely clear about one's own attitude towards further action. The fact that one knows how much one actually does not yet know should not prevent product managers from seeking early joint clarification and in this way also gaining more clarity for themselves.

15.5 What Approaches Help in Alignment?

How exactly one as a product manager can best achieve successful alignment often depends on specific context factors, such as the corporate culture and the importance given to product management. However, it generally helps to consider the following aspects:

15.5.1 The Right Conversation Partners in the Right Order

As described in Sect. 15.2, it is helpful to coordinate with a variety of people (groups). However, of course, one cannot speak with everyone at the same time. Therefore, it makes sense to initially—and also repeatedly during the course of an alignment process—consciously consider who should be involved and in what constellations and sequences this is best done.

In the interest of a trusting collaboration with other teams, it can help, for example, to first go laterally into alignment and only afterwards—and possibly together—involve hierarchically superior stakeholders or decision-makers.

However, if one perceives contradictory signals from the direction of several decision-makers, it is most important to first resolve this ambiguity before going into more operational alignment. And if, as a product manager, one does not have sufficient clarity about the details of the product to be coordinated, it is generally helpful to first go into alignment with one's own team and thus lay a more solid foundation for all further coordination outside the team. Since product managers often act as the "foreign minister" of their team in alignment, it is important to know the context well and also to know the team's attitude, so that the team feels adequately represented.

15.5.2 Sensible Constellations and Methods for Active Alignment

No matter with whom and in what order one speaks, it is helpful to consciously choose the respective group constellations. On the one hand, product managers will hardly have time to align separately with all relevant persons (especially since this would often not make sense in the interest of mutual understanding of the respective perspectives). On the other hand, a group that is too large or too heterogeneous can also make conversations more difficult, for example because too many people do not actively participate or because the "flight level" of the topics discussed does not fit.

Depending on the method and composition, a group of 2 to 6 participants usually offers a good opportunity to gain a common view with several participants at the same time and to keep the energy level high. Active participation of all present in a coordination is important because only active participants reveal their position. And only when they do this, does the coordination move forward. In other words: A meeting to which too many people are invited and during which many are then not actively involved, is poorly invested time for all participants.

In addition to the group size, it also helps to consciously choose formats for alignment meetings that invite active participation, for example by asking all participants to contribute their perspective via self-written post-its. This is one of the reasons why canvas-based coordination frameworks (see Sect. 15.8) are well suited as aids for coordination. In addition to the active involvement of all participants, the use of a canvas has two other major advantages:

- The participants are encouraged to externalize their thoughts on the product initiative being discussed and thus make them transparent and "manageable" for others;
- It helps to structure the coordination and thus, for example, to ensure that difficult or critical questions are not forgotten or avoided.

15.6 Important Questions to Clarify in the Context of Alignment

The worst enemy of effective alignment is an apparent consensus in which the critical issues are left out. This is because the actual need for clarification is ultimately only postponed to a later point in time, at which the consequences are typically more serious.

To avoid this, it helps to explicitly address some conflict-prone questions in the context of coordination in order to either achieve a consensus or identify a need for escalation. The following questions are based on the most important aspects of the "Auftragsklärung" alignment framework practiced at XING since 2016 (see Sect. 15.8 in detail), but they can also serve as a guide on the way to effective alignment independently of this.

15.6.1 Initial Situation from the User's Perspective

In order to be able to exchange ideas sensibly, it is important that all participants have important information about the initial situation:

- What is the current user perception of the relevant facts—and how many users are affected by it?
- What other relevant information from qualitative and quantitative user research should all participants know?
- What major user research projects are already planned and what exactly is to be investigated?

15.6.2 Vision from the User's Perspective

It will come as little surprise that it is helpful to achieve a common understanding of the desired end state in the context of early coordination of a product initiative. To avoid a company-centered view, it is helpful to describe the vision not from the internal perspective or in the form of implemented features, but to consciously put the user's perspective in the foreground: How will the result of the planned initiative feel for the affected users when we are finished?

For this external perspective of the future, one can, for example, orient oneself on the "working backwards" format often associated with Amazon, with which one tries to describe in advance, using a fictitious press release, what the emotional and functional added value of an initiative will be for the target users (Bariso 2019).

15.6.3 Hypotheses

Preferences regarding future approaches and priorities typically feed not only on facts, but also to a considerable extent on individual assumptions about future cause-and-effect relationships. As long as one does not know the assumptions of the other participants in their actions, it is difficult to understand the other behaviors and to collaborate meaningfully.

In an alignment process, it is therefore valuable to make the personal assumptions of the participants explicit and to agree on a central set of hypotheses: Which assumptions must prove to be correct in order for the initiative to have the desired effect on the users?

A common understanding of central hypotheses can also subsequently facilitate the prioritization of important product experiments, with which one ideally tests particularly success-critical hypotheses.

15.6.4 Input—and Roles

It makes sense to discuss at an early stage the respective ideas of what inputs—in terms of resource allocation or work capacity—one intends to use for the initiative. Especially when coordinating with higher-level decision-makers, this serves to make an early decision as to whether the intended investment is in a healthy ratio to the expected result. A good unit for quantifying expected development efforts, for example, could be person-months.

Another important aspect in the context of clarification is making explicit the respective roles of the individual participants in the joint project. This helps, among other things, with the question of who it makes sense to coordinate with. As a rule of thumb, one should involve all participating departments from which one expects a significant contribution, specifically in this clarification.

15.6.5 Output—and Boundaries

Even if one should ideally still be open to the best possible results of a discovery phase at an early stage, all those affected will already have a certain idea of what tangible results—in terms of concrete artifacts in front of internal or external users—will come out of the initiative: So, for example, is it assumed that a new native app will be developed? Or is it about expanding a service within an existing web offer? The challenge in coordination is to be sufficiently open to results, but at the same time to share one's own expectations with others, so that it is quickly apparent whether one basically has the same ideas.

As with the outcome, it makes sense to set explicit boundaries for the output: In this case, however, it is more about naming what is explicitly out of scope. Especially with long-term initiatives involving heterogeneous participants, it is important to clarify what one is expressly not concerned with, or at least not concerned with in a first phase. In this way, the risk of misunderstandings and later disappointments can be reduced.

15.6.6 Outcome—and Limits

Clarity about what an initiative should change is central to achieving consensus on when to consider the initiative a success. This is one of the key questions of the canvas. It's not about the visible result (output), but about the change for the users and/or the company (outcome).[1]

It is important to specify as precisely as possible which metrics you want to move and how large the change should ideally be by which point in time.

In the best case, you identify metrics that can be directly influenced by the planned initiative. Instead of the general development of weekly active users (which many initiatives in most companies work towards in parallel), you could, for example, rather use the return rate of a specific user segment as a success criterion.

Especially when the vote takes place at an early stage, it can sometimes be difficult to reliably predict specific target values. However, in the interest of mutual expectation clarification, it makes sense to name target values during the vote, even if they only originate from your own gut feeling. Because with this, you can initiate a fruitful dialogue about which target values different voting partners would be satisfied with the result of the initiative. If you find out on this occasion, for example, that important stakeholders only find the initiative worthwhile if the target metric is multiplied by ten, but you only consider a doubling possible, it is important to notice this early on and make it explicit.

In addition to the target value, it is also important to specify by when you believe you can achieve this and ideally also how the target metric should develop in the meantime. With this, you create the basis to be able to determine early in the process whether you are still on track.

In addition to the planned target metrics, it is important to also explicitly state whether there are unintended side effects that must be avoided at all costs. For example, it could be that an improvement in the sign-up process for existing users must not be at the expense of the registration rate of new users. Or that when integrating additional advertising spaces, the click rate of the actual content may only be impaired up to a certain threshold.

15.7 Identify Conflicts and Bring Them to Resolution

As mentioned at the beginning, clarification does not necessarily mean agreeing with all participants immediately. On the contrary, the value of early alignment, especially in more complex product development projects, often lies in identifying potential conflicts

---

[1] For the difference between outcome and output, see Gothelf and Seiden in detail (2017).

at a time when you still have options for action and can therefore address them. Accordingly, in the context of clarification, it is not the task of product managers to please everyone, but to identify conflicts early on and bring them to resolution. The following rules can help, which are based on the "Clarification Manifesto" used at XING (Kittler 2018):

Agree That You Can't Agree
When you realize in votes that conflicts are not just based on misunderstandings, it is the responsibility of the involved product managers to quickly and explicitly name the conflict as such and agree with the other party that you currently do not agree and probably will not agree without further clarification of the boundary conditions ("Agree to disagree").

Escalate Together
The term escalation has a negative connotation for many, although it actually only says that things that cannot be clarified at your own level are taken to a higher hierarchy level to ask for support in clarification there. So basically a completely normal, value-neutral process. The negative association probably comes mainly from the fact that escalations often occur unilaterally and behind the backs of individual participants, which makes the hierarchically superior intervention come unexpectedly for those affected and can therefore be difficult for them to accept. Much less negative, on the other hand, is an escalation that is initiated together by those who disagree. Two product managers who agree that they cannot agree can therefore escalate together to their respective product leadership.

Clearly State the Need for Clarification
In a joint and thus transparent escalation, it is helpful if the escalators can clearly state in what respect they need help with the clarification ("Be clear about what's unclear"). Instead of laying out the complete course of the clarification process to the managers, it will usually be more helpful to make very explicit which framework conditions or basic decisions the product managers need in order to be able to continue the clarification ideally on their own afterwards.

Leave Responsibility Where It Belongs
In the sense described above, the involved managers should only provide the necessary clarification assistance. The product managers should then (again) take responsibility for further clarification. If the managers involved misunderstand the requested clarification assistance as a basic delegation and start micromanaging, it may be necessary for the product manager to actively reclaim the task.

15.8 Alignment in Practice: "Auftragsklärung" at XING

Many of the considerations described for the alignment of product managers are based on the author's experiences as a product leader at XING. There, alignment was identified as one of the main challenges by the internal product community a few years ago, and the **mission statement or "Auftragsklärung"** was established as a method that is now also referenced worldwide within the product management discourse, for example by Martin Eriksson, the founder of Mind The Product and co-author of the book Product Leadership (Banfield et al. 2017). XING's team consciously chose to use the German term "Auftragsklärung" also in English as a reference to the Prussian "Auftragstaktik" established by Helmuth von Moltke.

The following excursion to the Auftragsklärung is intended as a suggestion, not with the claim that an Auftragsklärung à la XING is the best method of alignment for every context.

15.8.1 Origin and Development of the Mission Statement

After the product organization at XING had grown significantly to over 30 product managers between 2010 and 2015, a professional community ("Community of Practice") was established to pursue systematic exchange and joint alignment. Because even though XING operates with methods of agile software development and thus also the ideal of as autonomous teams as possible, there were and are numerous mutual dependencies and synergy potentials due to the close interlocking of individual products. In the course of an initial assessment, it was identified that cross-departmental alignment was one of the topics that many of the product employees found particularly challenging.

As a common method, the "Auftragsklärung" was established as a uniform coordination format in all product departments of the company. After initial attempts with formulated, longer text documents, the format was revised to a much more participatory canvas, which was then rolled out communicatively both within and outside of XING. As an example, reference is made to the presentation by Marc Kadish at ProductTank London (Kadish 2016).

After several years of use, the format was revised in 2019 to more explicitly include the user perspective and to provide better assistance in application through restructuring and help texts (New Work SE 2019).

15.8.2 Essential Artifacts and Common Practices

At the heart of the Auftragsklärung is the canvas, as it is particularly useful as a tool in coordination meetings and helps to encourage participants to externalize their respective positions. However, it is important in application that the canvas and all other artifacts

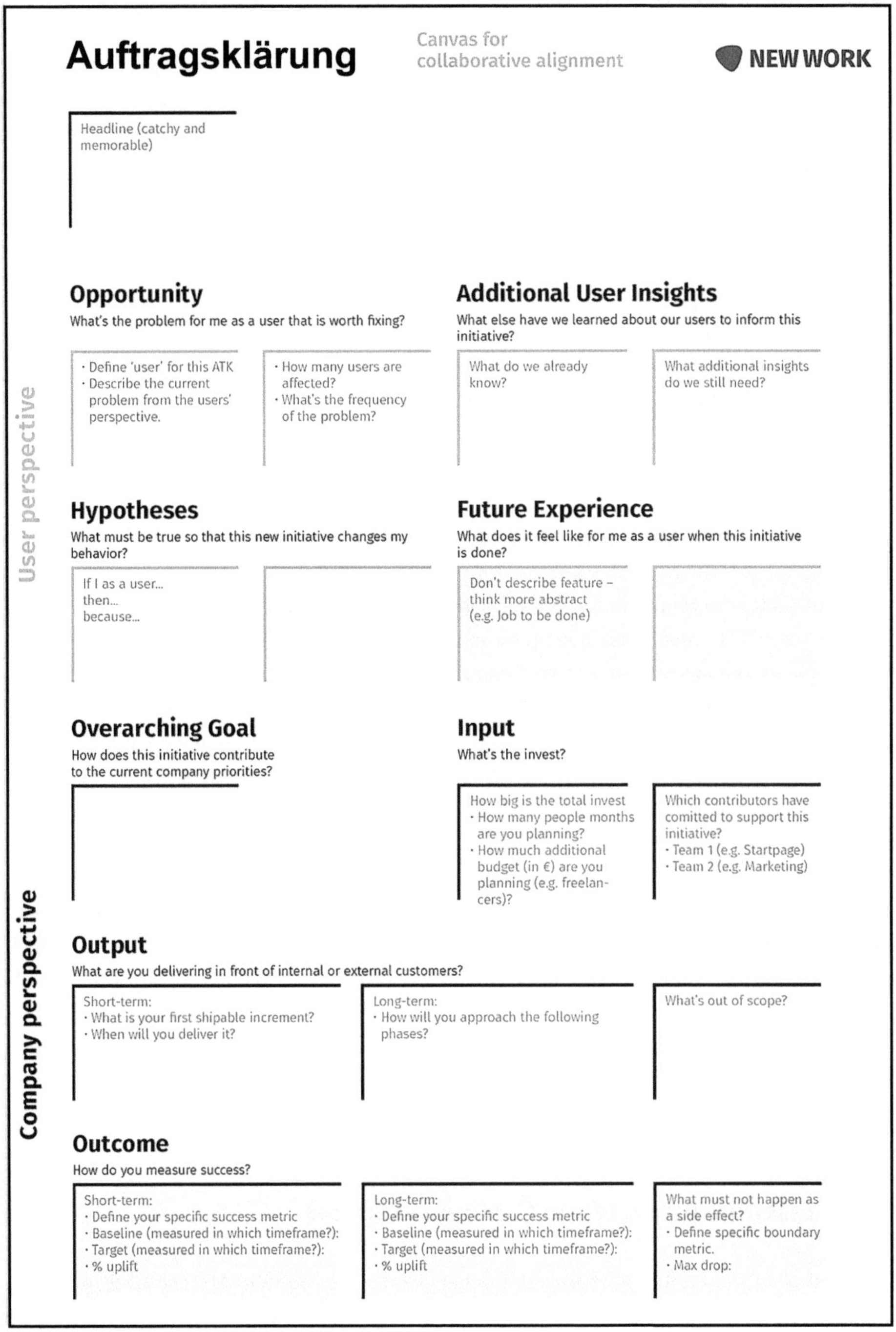

Auftragsklärung Canvas for collaborative alignment — NEW WORK

Headline (catchy and memorable)

User perspective

Opportunity
What's the problem for me as a user that is worth fixing?

- Define 'user' for this ATK
- Describe the current problem from the users' perspective.

- How many users are affected?
- What's the frequency of the problem?

Additional User Insights
What else have we learned about our users to inform this initiative?

What do we already know?

What additional insights do we still need?

Hypotheses
What must be true so that this new initiative changes my behavior?

If I as a user...
then...
because...

Future Experience
What does it feel like for me as a user when this initiative is done?

Don't describe feature – think more abstract (e.g. Job to be done)

Company perspective

Overarching Goal
How does this initiative contribute to the current company priorities?

Input
What's the invest?

How big is the total invest
- How many people months are you planning?
- How much additional budget (in €) are you planning (e.g. freelancers)?

Which contributors have comitted to support this initiative?
- Team 1 (e.g. Startpage)
- Team 2 (e.g. Marketing)

Output
What are you delivering in front of internal or external customers?

Short-term:
- What is your first shipable increment?
- When will you deliver it?

Long-term:
- How will you approach the following phases?

What's out of scope?

Outcome
How do you measure success?

Short-term:
- Define your specific success metric
- Baseline (measured in which timeframe?):
- Target (measured in which timeframe?):
- % uplift

Long-term:
- Define your specific success metric
- Baseline (measured in which timeframe?):
- Target (measured in which timeframe?):
- % uplift

What must not happen as a side effect?
- Define specific boundary metric.
- Max drop:

Fig. 15.2 Auftragsklärung (*Source*: New Work SE 2019)

ultimately only serve the actual purpose of the Auftragsklärung, namely early, collaborative alignment.

Typically, the Auftragsklärung at XING is initiated by the product managers responsible for an initiative and detailed using the canvas in several iterations. The resulting canvas often hung as a reference in the office of the affected teams. Due to the increasingly cross-location working method at XING locations, experiments are currently also being carried out with remote-suitable formats of the Auftragsklärung, e.g. using the Miro software.

15.8.3 Introduction, Application and Misunderstandings

After an initial pilot phase, there were several waves of training phases at XING in which all product managers were trained in the use of the Auftragsklärung. These trainings helped to establish the framework and contributed to the Auftragsklärung becoming firmly established in product work at XING and increasingly being requested as a reference in collaboration ("I'm new to the topic. Can you please show me the Auftragsklärung?"). And even outside the product departments, the Auftragsklärung was increasingly used, but was sometimes applied differently than intended due to the lack of systematic training and support. As a result, for example, long-formulated written documents were created in the structure of the Auftragsklärung to advertise for internal initiatives. However, these formats miss the actual purpose of the Auftragsklärung , namely to serve as a tool in a dialogue and thus help to address critical issues at an early stage. XING is therefore currently considering expanding training on the Auftragsklärung beyond the product organization.

15.9 Limits of Sensible Alignment

The importance of good and early coordination has already been explained. However, it is also important to keep in mind that an "alignment fetish" does not develop within an organization, which contradicts the intention formulated here.

This would be the case, for example, if too many operational details are fixed early on and therefore a sensible scope for iteration is lacking. Or if product managers spend so much time in alignment that there is no more time left for collaborative work on good user solutions.

Therefore, it makes sense not to make clarification an end in itself, but to question the need for clarification of each initiative in relation to the respective situation and, if necessary, to consciously decide against alignment.

References

Banfield, R., M. Eriksson, and N. Walkingshaw. 2017. *Product leadership*. Sebastopol: O'Reilly.
Bariso, J. 2019. Amazon has a secret weapon known as „Working Backwards"—and it will transform the way you work. https://www.inc.com/justin-bariso/amazon-uses-a-secret-process-for-launching-new-ideas-and-it-can-transform-way-you-work.html.
Cagan, M. 2018. Empowered product teams. https://svpg.com/empowered-product-teams.
Gothelf, J., and J. Seiden. 2017. You need to manage digital projects for outcomes not outputs. https://hbr.org/2017/02/you-need-to-manage-digital-projects-for-outcomes-not-outputs.
Kadish, M. 2016. Collaborative alignment—the ‚Auftragsklärung' framework. https://www.mindtheproduct.com/alignment-framework-managing-stakeholder-communications.
Kittler, A. 2018. Clarity in collaboration. https://youtu.be/T5Ta6TJtQKs.
Kniberg, H. 2016. Misalignment. https://blog.crisp.se/2016/05/30/henrikkniberg/misalignment.
New Work SE. 2019. Auftragsklärung. https://auftragsklaerung.com.

Arne Kittler has a background in interdisciplinary media economics and graduated from Universität Siegen as a Media Economist ("Diplom Medienwirt"). In various roles he has been involved in building digital products, services & communication solutions for 25 years in B2B and B2C contexts and many differnt domains. For over 12 years he has actively established and lead product organizations. This included his role as VP of Product Management at XING, then the leading professional social network in the German speaking markets, and Chief Product Officer at Facelift, one of the pioneers in the SaaS Marketing Technology space. Meanwhile he's a product transformation consultant & product coach and helps individuals and organizations on their journey to more impact through good product management. As a passionate community-player, Arne also is the co-founder of Product at Heart, a conference for curious product people (www.productatheart.com).
Contact: mail@arnekittler.de

Product Evangelizing and Storytelling

How Product Managers Convince with Good Stories

Petra Wille

Abstract

Stories are an incredibly powerful tool for convincing others to collaborate with us, especially when it comes to solving problems as a group. Consequently, the ability to conceive and tell a coherent and relevant story is essential for product people. Giving more space to this ability may feel strange at first. After all, we have been able to tell stories since we were young, but we often have not used this ability or even let it atrophy. We are so accustomed to our professional corporate speak that many people find it difficult to send a clear, unambiguous message. Nevertheless, we know about the power that a well-told story can have. Think of the examples of Nike, BMW, and Apple. Or simply the moments when we have let ourselves be carried away by colleagues or superiors. Conceiving and writing a story is a lot of work, but if done correctly, the same story can be used months or even years later.

16.1 Why Storytelling is Important in Product Management

Almost 15 years ago, when I was still a product manager myself, I found myself in a strange situation: I thought I was doing my job well. I had backlog management and prioritization under control, and our team meetings (then according to Scrum) were always well prepared. The team's performance was good. The team could "ship": feature by feature, sprint by sprint, we constantly released new things for our customers. But somehow

P. Wille (✉)
Strong Product People, Hamburg, Germany
e-mail: info@petra-wille.de

© The Author(s), under exclusive license to Springer Fachmedien Wiesbaden GmbH, part of Springer Nature 2024
S. Hoffmann (ed.), *Digital Product Management*,
https://doi.org/10.1007/978-3-658-44276-7_16

the things we put out made no difference at all. Nothing really took off. None of our KPIs moved in the desired direction. None of the features really changed the lives of our users in a sustainable way. We were not measurably successful.

And of course, it couldn't go on like this. Our stakeholders (then mainly Sales, Customer Care, and Marketing) were getting nervous, and my then supervisor had already signaled that "they would now take a closer look". So I knew: something had to happen, and quickly.

Of course, we had noticed before our colleagues that something was wrong, and we had already carried out some product discovery initiatives (which in retrospect helped us a lot to understand our users much better over time), but that too had not brought a breakthrough in the short term. We were still just releasing "stuff". I was frustrated and didn't know what else we could have done to finally be able to demonstrate measurable success. Why didn't the users use features that we had built based on their feedback and the analysis of their needs?

Fortunately, I was privileged to work with a product coach at that time who had brought a lot of experience from Silicon Valley. So I thought: This is the perfect topic for my next coaching session.

When I explained my problem to him, he had to smile, because for him it was probably obvious what we were lacking. And after our session, it was clear to me too: We lacked a common thread, a good narrative that linked the learnings from our product discovery into a story. A story that coherently explained where the product should develop and how the product should change the lives of our users for the better. A story that could convey to both the development team and Marketing, Sales, the company management, and even our existing customers what the future could look like.

But what needed to change in our way of working? What had we or what had I done wrong so far?

So far, I had done all the discovery work with my interaction designer and an engineer almost "behind closed doors". And I had not been able to adequately explain to the team and the rest of the company what we had learned. Important information was lost, the spark did not jump, and the team was neither inspired nor motivated by what we told them about our findings.

My coach recommended that I read the book *Selling the Dream* by former Macintosh evangelist Guy Kawasaki (1991). And that's exactly what I did. After reading it, I realized how important it is to get better at creating coherent stories and being able to tell them well. And—and this is the main learning from the book—I realized how seriously this skill is taken in successful American companies. They really invest time in this topic and often have entire departments that take care of it. So it was clear to me: This will be work.

I started paying more attention to the topic of storytelling, continued reading, and a few weeks later I had built a coherent, inspiring, and humorous story from our research results. One that put our users at the center and that I could tell well and freely to different target groups in the company.

The positive feedback from all areas, as soon as I started actively telling the story, exceeded my wildest expectations. From then on, it was much easier for the team to prioritize, as they now always had the users from the story in mind, and discussions about the sense and nonsense of individual functions decreased significantly. Because suddenly our stakeholders could remember what we all wanted to achieve together and censored themselves: If an idea did not fit the goal (outcome) conveyed in the story, they often discarded the idea themselves or only approached it as: "Once we have achieved outcome A, that would be something we could think about again". In short: my PM life became much easier and I felt better prepared and armed with my story in the background.

The development of the ability to tell stories and product evangelizing also changed the rest of my career. I started telling stories more and more often that united my product development team, convinced stakeholders, helped marketing sell the product, and—most importantly—I found out what was really important to our users by putting them at the center of the stories.

And if all this sounds tempting, then keep reading here. Because in the following, I will illuminate why we are born storytellers, why our human brains love stories, and how product managers can succeed in creating and telling good stories.

16.2 Why Our Brains Love Stories

We've all experienced it: Some people manage to move mountains with their stories. With a few clear words, they inspire teams, entire companies, or even worldwide movements.

Which person, in your opinion, consistently manages to reach not only the minds but also the hearts of people? Which charismatic personality comes to mind when you think about storytelling in a professional context? In my workshops and coaching sessions, the answers are often something like: Barack Obama, Steve Jobs, Annalena Baerbock, Elon Musk, or Greta Thunberg.

On this list, there are already two entrepreneurs who have undoubtedly managed (and you don't have to appreciate them as individuals for this) to talk about their companies and especially their products in such a way that they could generate great interest, great curiosity, and even a real hype. And with my very personal introduction and the aforementioned leading figures in mind, I think it is undisputed when I say: The ability of storytelling, of product evangelism, is one that is important for the success of a team, a company, or a product. And thus, it is also an important skill for everyone who works in product management.

But when I talk to product managers about the ability to tell stories, they find that they have

- little in common with the aforementioned individuals and their rhetorical talents, or are
- not even aware that storytelling is an important skill for them as product managers.

My goal is to address both aspects in this article. Because the ability to tell good stories is, from my experience, a critical success factor for a successful career in product management. And the best part: The ability to tell good stories is inherent in every person. You don't have to learn it. You just have to professionalize it.

How I Justify This Claim
We humans are born storytellers (even though we obviously can't speak from day one). The ability to do so is virtually ingrained in our DNA. Because we learn from an early age that a good story helps us get what we want: We can influence other people with a good story.

Like my 4-year-old daughter did some time ago: Thanks to a good story, I allowed her to go to kindergarten in winter boots in the middle of summer at 30 degrees and bright sunshine.

She had convinced me that she and her friend wanted to play Elsa and Anna from Disney's Frozen and that it required a bit of winter equipment. Since the story was coherent and convincingly presented, she naturally had me in her pocket and I was willing to endure the strange looks of passers-by on the way to kindergarten.

Do you perhaps know similar stories from your environment? When was the last time you did something because another person inspired you to do so with a coherent, emotional story (or even just an anecdote)?

But it's not just the active telling of stories, as my daughter did, that is innate to us. No, it's also the listening. From an early age, we love to hear stories because they captivate us, entertain us, and help us gain new insights. We learn new things from stories. We humans have been passing on knowledge through the spoken word for thousands of years. Long before we had invented this character/letter/writing thing, that was the only possibility.

And since stories brought a knowledge or even evolutionary advantage, good stories also have a biological effect on us. They demonstrably (Phillips 2017) trigger the release of hormones in our body, in our brain. And hormones, as we all know, have a great effect on us. Specifically, these are the hormones:

- Oxytocin, which creates trust, generosity, and a personal connection to other people in us.
- Endorphins, which make us laugh or help us deal with fear, pain, or uncertainty.
- Dopamine, which triggers the desire to find out how something continues. Especially with stories with ups and downs. With stories that lead to cliffhangers, we remain curious about the end due to the release of dopamine.

As Carl Alviani (2018) once emphasized in an article, "…we think in stories, remember in stories, and turn pretty much everything we experience into a story …".

Often simply to remember things better.

This ability to convince others to work with us through stories, especially to solve problems as a group, has given our species, Homo sapiens, a unique evolutionary advantage.

16 Product Evangelizing and Storytelling

Fig. 16.1 Convincing with words: a story from thousands of years ago

And this advantage has enabled us to survive and evolve on this planet. Thousands of years ago, as shown in Fig. 16.1, we worked together to hunt our dinner. Today, we work together to combat pandemics or to build digital products in small teams in a corporate context.

16.3 What Stories can Achieve in a Professional Context

Throughout their professional lives, most people can observe several times how good storytelling can unite a group of people—from a small product development team to an entire company. In this case, stories are the tool with which a person can inspire others to use their skills, knowledge, and time to solve a difficult problem.

And this is exactly what stories in a professional environment must achieve, because only then can they be described as good, functioning stories.

16.3.1 Elements of a Good Story

All stories that are capable of uniting people and bringing them into action (i.e., not just remaining listeners, but then also getting into active doing) have some things in common. They exhibit the following key elements:

- They paint a picture of a desirable (better) future in the minds of the listeners.
- They make it clear why one should become part of this future.
- They acknowledge the current situation (of the listeners, the company, …) and at the same time describe the potential difficulties that can arise and why it is worth overcoming them.

- They propose a common goal and provide enough information that the next steps are clear to the listeners.
- And at the end, they call for taking the first necessary step and convey a certain urgency in a convincing way.

Companies with strong brands often manage to include all these elements in the shortest slogans. They are masters at telling such stories. Their slogans can evoke images in the minds of customers that encourage them to look into a better future (which of course also includes buying the company's product). Consider, for example, Nike's "Just do it", Apple's "Think different" or BMW's "Joy of driving" (In English, by the way, "The ultimate driving machine" or "Sheer Driving Pleasure" (BMW 2020).

And it doesn't stop at the slogan. The slogans are expanded into larger stories and are told in elaborate campaigns. And for the telling of the stories, companies often employ charismatic personalities (we think of the aforementioned Macintosh evangelist Guy Kawasaki or currently Amplitude's John Cutler (Hayward 2019) or public figures, such as athletes and celebrities. These help to carry the message of the big brands and their stories out into the world or to spread them within the company.

But not every company takes the trouble to develop such motivating stories, and not every company is able to tell the stories in an appealing way. Thus, I have unfortunately seen (too) many products that never saw the light of day because those responsible (indeed often the product manager) were not able to describe convincingly and in clear words what the product would achieve in the world and why it is worth as a company/team to do everything to make the product a reality.

If a product manager lacks this talent, the result is often: An uninspired product team that fails to work together on a topic, that struggles with alignment with other teams and departments, and you often find internal stakeholders who are not particularly convinced to support the team in their efforts as best as possible. In my introductory review of my storytelling awakening, I did not consider the success factors mentioned and therefore found myself in this situation. But armed with a story that included the key aspects mentioned, I was able to completely change the climate and mood in the team and company for the better. So it is worth investing the time.

But before we delve deeper into the topic of "building a story", I would like to provide a hopefully helpful standpoint in the following: A look at storytelling that encourages you to just get started.

16.3.2 Stories are the Perfect Design Tool

Stories: a perfect design tool. Steep thesis? I am very happy to justify it.

As we have already learned in the course of this chapter, everyone is capable of inventing a story and telling it. Apart from pen and paper or a text file, you don't initially need any expensive tools to get started. So there is hardly any entry barrier. And if you stick to the spoken word exclusively at the beginning of the creation process, you can tell the story in slight variations to see in which form and with which information it triggers what is important to us in the audience.

If we do our job as storytellers well, then a story brings clarity, promotes team buy-in, is motivating and all in a way that ensures that people remember the story and it works into their work as orientation and guiding star.

And whether a story does this, we test by telling, optimizing the story, telling again, etc. Building stories is therefore a bit like creating a prototype for the next usability test. Only much easier, because less tooling is involved.

However, it is still important to acquire the right tools. To know about different story structures (also called schemas) or plots. It is also important to handle language carefully: avoid abbreviations and technical terms (they do not trigger hormone release in the brain), use natural language and leave out everything unnecessary: no empty business phrases and no bullshit bingo. Because people become numb to these empty words and simply stop hearing them.

But how to get started with storytelling now? We will explore this in the following paragraph.

16.4 How to Conceive and Tell Good Stories

A good story has a **clearly defined structure,** which makes it easy for people to follow the story. One of the most well-known schemas is the "hero's journey," which was first described in detail by literature professor Joseph Campbell (1949). And it, here I anticipate, is perfectly suited for product stories.

The hero's journey begins in a very ordinary world on a very normal day, see Fig. 16.2. And on this day, the call to adventure follows for the hero or heroine. This often happens in the form of a big nocturnal dream, in which a desirable future appears. Or through an extraordinary event.

The hero then embarks on a journey that leads past a series of challenges, tests, trials, and setbacks to the final, promising goal. When the hero reaches their goal, a transformation usually occurs. In fairy tales, this transformation is often physical in nature (the frog becomes a prince) and is seen as a metaphor. In other stories, the transformation is more related to character traits. It is then about an inner change or maturity. In some hero*ine stories, the hero's introspection and the sharing of what has been learned with the readership or audience then follows.

16.4.1 What Does all This Have to do With Product Management?

Well, with a little creativity and imagination, this structure can be easily applied to our work. Because in the end, product development is always the promise of a better future.

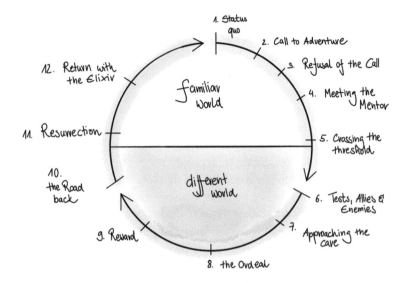

Fig. 16.2 The hero's journey: a good template for product stories

A future in which problems and challenges that our users* have now will simply have disappeared. Because our product is the solution to the problem!

The story starts, for example, on a normal office day when the hero*ine might get a task that he*she has never had before. And then the figure sets off to solve this big, almost inhuman task. This is essentially the call to adventure.

Along the way, there are all kinds of resistances (bad tools, dismissive colleagues, time pressure...) and when things look very bleak, the hero stumbles upon our solution, our product. And with it, they manage to solve the task and thus help the team, the company, or even the whole world. And yes: a little pathos is simply part of it if you want to charge a story emotionally. Here it is important to find a middle ground: too much exaggeration seems artificial.

Our goal as product managers* must therefore be to use the proven structure of the hero's story in such a way that our vision for the product is clearly recognizable to everyone in it. Because only in this way can the story bring the motivation, clarity, and alignment that we hope for from it.

▶ A note at this point: Sometimes a story that puts users/customers at the center does not have the desired effect. Especially with B2B products, where individual team members find it difficult to put themselves in the shoes of the end users, it can be a good trick to put the product team at the center of the story. Then they are the hero of the story and they are called to adventure.

16 Product Evangelizing and Storytelling

But if the hero's journey puts users* at the center, it is often necessary to link this story with the team's reality, the colleagues' reality, and to put it in relation. Then the actual hero's journey is only a part of the overall story.

With the end result, the entire narrative should achieve the following:

- We should be able to advertise for more support for our product development (be it more budget, management attention, or simply more headcount).
- We should be able to get other teams/departments to support our project and
- we should be able to make difficult compromises or decisions faster.
- In addition, a certain roadmap should be readable from the story. This applies both to processes and work steps of the hero (here you can super incorporate your jobs-to-be-done or story mapping insights) as well as to the order in which the development team should implement these work steps or the hint of a roadmap.

If all these components are integrated successfully, it is time to test the story. And we do this by starting to tell it and share it with others. If a story works well and you have considered everything, the following happens quite naturally:

- Explain the value of the product to non-customers, hopefully making them new customers;
- sketch a roadmap for the next steps and thus provide more clarity in the team and for stakeholders;
- acknowledge the team, the people behind the product, and their achievements by clearly naming and illustrating the challenges in the story and what is needed to overcome them;
- establish trust in the storyteller (and possibly even build the personal brand of the storyteller), because good stories promote this trust (Keltner, Dacher 2016).
- And in the end, it succeeds in inspiring others to do the right and necessary thing to achieve the common goal.

And to make this easy, here is a checklist that is valid regardless of the chosen schema:

- It is important to define and communicate the desirable future/the big dream convincingly.
- It is important to clearly state why each individual listener (from the team, stakeholders, users…) should become part of this future.
  In doing so, it is necessary to cover three perspectives to ensure sustainable motivation:
    - Why it is good **for me** as an individual in the audience to become part of the story;
    - why it is good **for us** as a team or for us as a company and
    - why it is good **for all of us** in the sense of "the world" in the broadest sense. Often this refers to a certain social class, a certain user group, customers of a certain community.

- With every product development, there are also obstacles and challenges. And not describing these makes a story unbelievable. So it is necessary to clearly name and explain expected difficulties and why it is worth overcoming the obstacles. The story must clearly show that the audience's reservations and concerns ("We have so much legacy code, how are we supposed to manage that?", "Some customers will not be satisfied if this is the new strategic direction!") are taken seriously and addressed wherever possible. It is important to express understanding for the listeners' concerns.
- A good story proposes a common goal that the listeners then adopt ("In the end, through our joint effort, we will have achieved the following…") and provides just enough information to make clear to the listeners their next step, their part in the story.
- And in the end, it is also important to create a sense of urgency. But of course not by ending the story with sentences like "and we have to have achieved all this by September". Instead, the urgency must become clear from the story itself. Do we need to get ahead of a (nasty) competitor? Or is the users' work unbearably complicated until the team finally develops a good solution to support them? Whatever it is, it must put the teams into action almost immediately. If this is not the case, the story needs to be optimized.

16.4.2 Overcoming the Fear of the Blank Page

But how to start now? To overcome the often paralyzing fear of the blank page, I like to give PMs the following fill-in-the-blank text. They should first fill in the blanks sensibly with a few sentences. Often, a larger story slowly but surely emerges from this basis.

> For these people (users, customers, ---)
> _____
>
> we (as a team/organization/company) want to achieve that
> _____
>
> This enables/improves the following for this group of people:
> _____
>
> Because if we don't do that, then (bad consequences)
> _____

In the next step, I ask the PMs to gather and review everything they already know from their product discovery efforts and everything that exists in the company in terms of framing (vision, strategy, goals/objectives). This information should be used and sensibly woven into the story.

Then the actual process of creating stories begins. The illustration inserted above and the checklist are helpful in this process.

16.5 How to Anchor the Message Sustainably

As described in the previous sections, a good story (remember, a good story promotes the release of certain hormones) ensures that we take more from a story at the moment of listening. But does this effect last? Do we still remember details weeks later?

The answer is unfortunately: no. Although our colleagues, superiors, listeners remember the essence, the "moral of the story", they no longer remember the details. Or they were captivated by what we had told at the moment of listening, but this could not have an impact on their daily work.

But that's exactly what we wanted to achieve. We wanted more:

- **Alignment:** A sufficiently similar picture of a desirable future is created in all minds.
- **Buy-In:** The listeners understand why they should be part of this future and what their contribution would be. They are sustainably convinced.
- **Decision Making & Actions:** Ultimately, we want to work together and with united forces on something bigger. For this, it is not only necessary to convey to all parties what their contribution would be, but also to motivate real actions in this direction. And we need to enable all participants to make decisions that benefit the common goal.

Especially the latter cannot be achieved with a one-time presentation, with the one-time telling of our story. So what to do? How to encourage people to act in a goal-oriented manner? How to give them guidelines for their decisions?

Many would now say: With a good product strategy and good product principles. And here I would not disagree. Nevertheless, I want to break down the question of anchoring a little bit into individual components and think from the perspective of "telling stories".

The key to anchoring a message lies in the **repetition of the same message in different formats.**

Of course, people are inspired by lectures, speeches—in short, the spoken word. But drawings, illustrations, or well-written texts also reach the minds and hearts of our colleagues. It's not for nothing that the saying goes, "A picture is worth a thousand words".

From my work with coaching clients, I know that not every one of the formats mentioned above is usually catered for. So, I often work with my coachees to create the missing format (written, spoken, illustrated) from the three. Often, a presentation that had to be given somewhere in the recent past (at a board meeting, quarterly leadership offsite, portfolio alignment session, or just a meeting with your own development team to plan the next few months in more detail) serves as a starting point. So, there are a few slides and someone who can present these slides convincingly. This is the perfect starting point to first optimize the story and then derive other formats from it.

Helpful questions include:

- What could a drawing for this presentation look like if you couldn't use the slide set? If there was only a whiteboard or flipchart: How would you then visually support the spoken word so that others can firstly follow and secondly reproduce what was said afterwards?
- How do you ensure that all interested colleagues can read or understand the story again?

In addition, it is important to prepare the story in very different lengths. Let's imagine a product manager has been thinking about an updated product strategy with the team, stakeholders, and management for weeks. This strategy is now to be rolled out. Of course, this requires real roll-out planning. Because we want to achieve alignment, buy-in, decisions & actions along this strategy. And this requires repetition.

For the first presentation, you might use 20 minutes of time in the company all-hands meeting. Afterwards, you want to talk to the affected teams about what impact this now has and how to get into action. For the presentation, you might have 5-6 minutes at the beginning of a meeting. And finally, you need a distillate of it so that you can occasionally remind people of the common goal in the daily stand-up ("That's why we're doing all this, and that's why it's worth it!").

I always guide my clients to prepare their story in three different lengths—**short, medium, and long:**

- **Short** corresponds to an elevator pitch: no more than about 150 words or about 75 seconds. Studies have shown that the attention span of executives being told a short story online is a maximum of 75 seconds (Connell-Waite 2019). And I assume this is not only the case for executives.
- **Medium** is significantly longer: about 900 words or 6 minutes of spoken word. A text of this length should already be divided into three parts. Like the acts of a play, each part can have its own message. Or—if the story is written in the form of a hero's journey—the three acts are already given. Either way, that's about 300 words per part. A simple trick, if you can't think of a good structure, is: Tell people what you're going to tell them, then tell them, and then conclude with a repetition of what you've said. Texts of this length are also perfect for templates in the style of the Amazon Six-Pager[1].

---

[1] The Six-Pager is an internal template document used at Amazon to prepare for decisions. It covers six pages and contains a detailed description of the product or project as well as an analysis of market opportunities and potential risks. The Six-Pager is written by an employee before a meeting, read by all participants in a meeting, and thus serves as a standardized basis for discussions and decisions in leadership meetings (Amazon 2018).

- **The long version** is intended for cases where a short or medium version is not sufficient to tell the desired story in a captivating way. Because often, especially when we tell a story for the first time, we need a bit more context for the audience. Here too, you should think in acts. In this case, there are three acts with about 800 words each and a total of about 18 spoken minutes. It's no coincidence that TED talks are limited to just these 18 minutes. TED curator Chris Anderson says: "It [18 minutes] is long enough to be serious and short enough to hold people's attention. By forcing speakers who are used to going on for 45 minutes to bring it down to 18, you get them to really think about what they want to say" (Gallo 2014).

I am an enthusiastic follower of simple illustrations, drawings, and other visual elements that help to convey a story or highlight and underline key elements of it.

So I raise the question again: What flipchart drawing, what illustrated slide would be helpful in telling your story? What diagram, what illustration can be quickly reproduced on a whiteboard and would enhance the emotional access to the story for others (and thus anchor it more strongly)? And what visualization would summarize important aspects of the story again?

It may initially be unusual to think about this. And the first pictorial representations of a product strategy or the next sprint goal may not be perfect. But the more we think in pictures, the stronger our stories become. And over time, it becomes easier and faster to find the central visualization.

Those who want to delve deeper into this topic should look into sketchnoting. In sketchnoting courses, you are taught simple drawing vocabulary to be able to visualize things successfully and uncomplicatedly in a business context.

Here are the dos and don'ts for product people when writing and sharing a coherent, appealing story that unites the team and inspires the rest of the company:

Dos
- It is important to trigger something in the listeners' brains. So how do we get the neurons to fire and the brain to light up?
  - Use words that evoke emotions.
  - Use words that appeal to the listeners' senses (smell, touch, sight, sound, and even taste).
  - If possible, make the audience laugh.
- Check the story for consistency. For example, with the three criteria that David Axelrod, speechwriter for Obama, always used: He always made sure that everything about the story of a speech was relevant, important, and true (Axelrod and Rove n.d.).
- It is important to ensure that you can present the story with curiosity, passion, and a certain vulnerability. Because no one knows the answers to everything at the beginning of an adventure. It is about embarking on an adventure with an uncertain outcome together.

- Does the story succeed in not only addressing the heads, but also the hearts of the audience? It should be more important to inspire them to take the right action than to convince them of something specific (your worldview, following your advice, buying a product, etc.).

Don'ts
- Avoid words that are constantly used within the company/team. Terms such as "Digital Transformation" or "Product Discovery" will cause people to tune out when listening. This is similar to banner blindness.
- The use of buzzwords, tool names or abbreviations should be reduced to a minimum. These terms appear too "technical" and often disrupt the flow of the story.
- No manipulation! Storytelling can be misused—especially in a time when people pay less attention to data and science and tend to believe any fake news presented to them as long as it is somewhat convincing.

16.6 My Conclusion

Each of us has the ability to tell stories. However, we often do not make enough use of it in a professional context. Storytelling plays a particularly important role in product management. Because with a vivid, coherent story, it is almost effortless to gather the team behind a common goal and inspire colleagues, stakeholders, and customers.

Product managers should therefore consciously focus more on their innate ability to tell stories and develop it further. I hope I have succeeded in providing some tools and approaches for this. If you want to read more on the topic, I have provided links to videos and online articles on my website: https://www.petra-wille.com/springerstorytelling.

References

Alviani, C. 2018. The science behind storytelling. https://medium.com/the-protagonist/the-science-behind-storytelling-51169758b22c.
Amazon. 2018. 2017 letter to shareholders. Retrieved from https://blog.aboutamazon.com/company-news/2017-letter-to-shareholders/.
Axelrod, D., and K. Rove. o. D. The campaign message. https://www.masterclass.com/classes/david-axelrod-and-karl-rove-teach-campaign-strategy-and-messaging/chapters/the-campaign-message.
BMW. 2020. Freude am Fahren. https://www.bmw.com/de/automotive-life/die-geschichte-des-bmw-slogan.html.
BMW Webseite. „Freude am Fahren": die Geschichte des BMW Slogans. https://www.bmw.com/de/automotive-life/die-geschichte-des-bmw-slogan.html#:~:text=So%20hieß%20es%20in%20englischsprachigen,„For%20sheer%20driving%20pleasure.
Campbell, J. 1949. *The hero with a thousand faces*. New York.

Connell-Waite, J. 2019. The 72 rules of commercial storytelling. https://www.linkedin.com/pulse/72-rules-commercial-storytelling-jeremy-waite/.

Gallo, C. 2014. The science behind TED's 18-minute rule. Retrieved from https://www.linkedin.com/pulse/20140313205730-5711504-the-science-behind-ted-s-18-minute-rule/.

Hayward, E. 2019. The unintentional career of John Cutler. https://www.mindtheproduct.com/the-unintentional-career-of-john-cutler/.

Kawasaki, G. 1991. *Selling the dream*. New York.

Keltner, D. 2016. Good leaders tell stories that make people trust them with power. https://qz.com/685562/good-leaders-tell-stories-that-make-people-trust-them-with-power.

Phillips, D. J. P. 2017. The magical science of storytelling. https://youtu.be/Nj-hdQMa3uA and empathy, neurochemistry, and the dramatic arc: Paul Zak at the future of storytelling 2012 via https://www.youtube.com/watch?v=q1a7tiA1Qzo.

Petra Wille is an independent Product Leadership Coach, author, and co-organizer of Product at Heart, a conference for product managers in Hamburg.

Petra began her career as a software developer at one of Germany's largest publishing houses (Hubert Burda Media), made a stop at SAP, and finally came to product management at XING. After her time at XING, Petra first became Head of Product and later Managing Director of the translation startup tolingo.

In 2013, she began working as an independent consultant and Product Discovery Coach. Since 2019, Petra has been focusing on working with Heads of Product, CPOs, Product Team Leads, in short, with executives in product management.

From her coaching work, the coaching card set "#52questions", an assessment for PMs named "PMwheel", and the book "STRONG Product People: A Complete Guide to Developing Great Product Managers" were created.

Contact: info@petra-wille.de

Product Owner and Scrum Master

Two Roles—One Successful Team

Jan Köster and Florian Meyer

Abstract

Scrum Masters and Product Owners jointly lead expert teams without being hierarchically superior. This tension often leads to conflicts in everyday life, but it can also turn the two into a real team if they heed some tips given in this chapter.

17.1 More than a Role Model from a Framework

In a setup where complicated problems, i.e., problems that have occurred in one way or another before, are to be solved, a person, such as a project manager, can set up a plan with a specific goal and orient themselves towards "best practices". The execution of the plan can then be arranged hierarchically and solved by a team in the given steps.

In contrast to working on complex problems, where the leader not only leads with a "why", but also dictates "what" and "how" a problem is solved, in agile systems the solution is found by the experts who work together to develop the solutions, as only they have the necessary knowledge and skills. They develop the "how" from within themselves. In this case, leaders cannot lead with their expertise, but only with the "why" something needs to be done. They set the framework conditions and, depending on the maturity level of the development team, also specify "what" needs to be done.

J. Köster (✉) · F. Meyer
Gruner + Jahr, Hamburg, Germany
e-mail: jan@lernendeteams.de

F. Meyer
e-mail: florian@lernendeteams.de

In most agile setups, the team is laterally led by two roles. In Scrum, as the most widely used system of agile product development, these are the Product Owner and the Scrum Master.[1] The Product Owner (PO) is responsible for the team's value creation. He is responsible for ensuring that the team delivers the maximum value with the given resources and means. The Scrum Master (SM), or the "processual leader", is responsible for ensuring that the expert team, consisting of PO, software developers, and Scrum Master, can work under the best possible conditions, reflect on their system, and improve it bit by bit.

One cannot go without the other. A team becomes a team through a common goal, which the PO conveys to them. And the individual members only become a true team through working on the system, where the Scrum Master leads through impulses, feedback, and reflection.

▶ The Product Owner leads "in the system" by specifying what should be worked on with which priority. He does this, among other things, through the prioritizations in the Product Backlog, which defines what should be implemented next by the expert team. The Scrum Master, on the other hand, leads the team "on the system" to gain insights and better system understanding, to improve the system itself step by step. For this, he uses different methods. The most important of these is the retrospective, in which the expert team looks back at the last sprint and identifies how it can improve.

From this setup, major conflicts can arise between the Product Owner and Scrum Master, which the two roles have with each other: On the one hand, they lead a team from within the team on an equal footing, and on the other hand, they work simultaneously on a product and a team. And they do this without being hierarchically superior to the experts.

17.2 How Good Collaboration Can Succeed

How a team of Scrum Master and Product Owner approaches this challenge, how it develops solutions for it, checks these, and learns in the process, determines whether the team fails, is average, or becomes a duo that masters every challenge.

---

[1] For the sake of completeness, it should be mentioned that there are indeed agile team setups where the two roles are supplemented by another, usually technically oriented, role, e.g., architect, system manager, senior developer, or similar. This construct will not be examined in more detail in the following.

17.2.1 Start with Why

The basis of every team is a shared vision and mutual trust. These are therefore the first things you should work on as a PO-SM team. Ask yourselves why you are working together in this particular constellation and why you want to work in this agile setup. Together, consider the **Cynefin Framework** (Snowden 2000) from Fig. 17.1 and check whether your project or your way of working can actually be found in the complex area where agile work makes sense.

The **Cynefin Framework** by Welsh researcher and knowledge management consultant David J. Snowden (2000) divides systems into 5 different fields: simple, complicated, complex, chaotic, and confused.

Every problem or project can be sorted into one of these fields:

- **Simple problems** are characterized by a clear cause-effect principle. These are problems that an expert can solve alone, often has already solved, and for whose problem solution only simple tools are needed (e.g., a checklist).
- **Complicated problems** are like simple problems describable by a clear cause-effect principle. However, the number of cause-effect relationships is diverse and the solutions must be structured. Expert knowledge is needed to develop solutions, but there are best cases that an expert can follow. Also, there is a clear goal for solving the problem. The expert who creates the plan to solve the problem uses various tools. Here, classic project management methods are ideally applied.
- **Complex problems** differ significantly from complicated ones in that there is no clear, previously recognizable cause-effect relationship. If at all, such relationships can only be identified in retrospect. To develop solutions, a group of experts must experiment and step by step find a way to the solution and learn from it. There is no best case and no possibility to sketch an exact solution in advance. These problems can only be solved with agile methods.

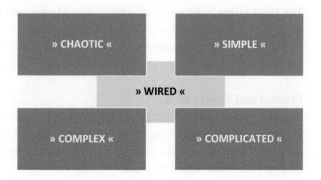

Fig. 17.1 The cynefin framework. *Source* Own representation

- **Chaotic problems** are like complex ones without a clear cause-effect principle. But here, the same inputs can generate different outputs, so even a subsequent analysis of the solution path does not provide a reproducible result in the future.
- **Confused problems**: Projects, systems, or processes that cannot be clearly assigned to one of the above fields are referred to as "confused". Often, wrong methods are used here to cope with complexity—e.g., an attempt is made to manage a complex project with classic project management.

To clarify whether you are really in a complex problem situation, three short questions can help:

- Can you describe only a vision or a goal, but not a clear goal where the product is completely defined?
- Are there no best practices that you can copy?
- Do you agree that you need to proceed iteratively and learn together with your customers from product increments how you can reach the target area?

If you answer the questions together with yes, you have made the first big step. You have clarified the "why an agile setup is necessary" for you and your team.

WHY-Poster
Create a poster for your project room and describe in one sentence: Why are we working agile in our project?

17.2.2 Shared Visions

Next, as Product Owner and Scrum Master, you work together to develop visions that should guide you and the team. The **product vision,** with the PO in the lead, defines what the system is working towards with the team, i.e., the target area of the product. The **team vision,** whose owner is the Scrum Master, defines what is being worked on in the system, i.e., the target area of team development.

The other person supports the development of the vision and serves as a sparring partner who contributes to gaining insights through critical questions.

Product and Team Vision
Develop your vision and then ask your partner to question it. Start with the "why" and then describe the target image, i.e., where the team or the product should develop. To question the vision, choose particularly critical stakeholders or team members and take on their role. What would they ask?

Complex problems and challenges can only be solved through experiments. These experiments must be thought of courageously and outside the usual solution paths, and controlled failure is just as likely and useful as a successful experiment. Teams that openly discuss their mistakes and learn from them become more performant and courageous, thereby finding better solutions.

17.2.3 Trust

Once you have clarified why you are working agile and have defined and agreed on the technical target areas, it is about laying the foundation for good teamwork. The basis of any good collaboration is trust. A trust that stands for each team member being in a safe environment and where there is an open feedback or error culture.

Trust develops from shared experiences and personal knowledge about the other team members. It's about getting to know each other on a human level. The focus should not only be on strengths. Especially the revelation of mistakes or own weaknesses creates a deep trust. As a Product Owner and Scrum Master, you should therefore master shared experiences and situations and grow from them. Step out of the comfort zone of your work environment and get to know each other personally. A first step can be an experience curve, a shared activity, or creating a shared work environment.

The Experience Curve
Draw a scale on a piece of paper on the y-axis from "particularly nice" to "particularly sad". The x-axis represents your years of life. Now draw your life line. When was it particularly nice and when not?

Now label 7 events that have shaped you a lot and that you want to share with each other. Take your time for this and question yourself—afterwards, present your curves to each other.

Don't Write
In many, especially larger organizations, every form of communication is recorded in writing in order to be able to refer to it later in case of doubt and to protect oneself. As a team of Scrum Master and Product Owner, however, you should move away from this. Trust each other, don't secure yourselves, but talk to each other.

This is not about no longer taking useful notes or not visualizing theses and goals. It's more about consciously tearing down your personal safety net of PowerPoint presentations, meeting minutes, and responsibility matrices and realizing that you either shine as a team or go down together.

17.2.4 Agile Principles

The Agile Manifesto and its principles define the values needed to work in complexity. They can serve as guiding principles and provide you with orientation. Often, however, these principles are interpreted differently or over-interpreted, almost dogmatically recited. It is overlooked that the manifesto is now somewhat outdated. Therefore, use it consciously as a basis for discussion to define common values and demonstrate these to your team. It's primarily about an attitude and less about strict rules to be followed.

Agile Principles
Print out the agile principles and arrange them—initially each for yourself—from the most important principle to the least important in an order. Then present your results to each other and explain to each other how you arrived at the respective result. This is not about consensus, but rather about understanding the other person.

17.2.5 When do we Stop?

A common area of conflict between Product Owner and Scrum Master are time-intensive rituals, which especially in later product development seem to be no longer needed. Therefore, always be aware that agile working is not an end in itself. It is a way of working, not a religion. At the beginning of your collaboration, determine when you will notice that working methods and the associated rituals may become superfluous and you no longer need them. This helps to ensure that you have a set of rules throughout the collaboration that reminds you to question your way of working.

When do we stop?
Stick three large post-its on your poster: "Why we work agile", each with an indication that would make you realize that agile working no longer makes sense and you have enough information to set a clear goal and work out a plan with all necessary steps. If this is the case, other methods are more efficient and appropriate.

17.2.6 Why do you do it that Way?

Understand yourselves as a true team and accept that you have no idea about the other's work, even if you may have taken on a similar task in a different context. Just as only the Product Owner knows the product and its stakeholders, sets the priorities and takes responsibility for value creation, so only the Scrum Master knows the team, the priorities for working on the system and takes responsibility for good cooperation.

17 Product Owner and Scrum Master

This does not mean that you should not critically question the other's actions or have them explain why your partner makes certain decisions and sets priorities. On the contrary: your partner is even encouraged to question you critically at all times and to point out deficiencies to you. However, this should always happen in a trusting environment at eye level, without it seeming as if you wanted to elevate yourself over the other in a group.

Why do you do it that way?
Give your partner the feeling that you appreciate him as an expert and ask him at least once a week why he does certain things in his way. Give him space to convince you of his expertise and to explain his actions to you.

17.2.7 Be Partners

You should work as a real team. It helps if you understand each other so well that you first see yourselves as a team in the system. Many find the comparison with police partners from American films helpful: they watch each other's backs, support each other in difficult situations, joke about each other, and know they can rely on each other at any time.

Be Partners: Good Cop—Bad Cop
Briefly discuss what you expect from a meeting and how you can achieve the planned together. Often it helps if you prepare conversations together and agree on roles—these can be, for example, the classic role distribution between Good and Bad Cop or the team and customer protector.

17.2.8 Shared Rituals

Shared rituals help to become a team. The daily exchange is comparable to the stand-up of your development team. And the rituals in which you work together as a PO-SM team are comparable to the Scrum cycles.

Daily rituals are based on the agile principles that experts and requesters should work closely together and that the most efficient and effective method is to convey information in face-to-face conversations. Create a ritual for this. It doesn't matter whether it's the coffee after the team stand-up, shared lunches, a meeting in the coffee kitchen, or a fixed jour-fixe appointment. The main thing is that you have at least one shared ritual every day. This gives you the opportunity to address problems immediately and react directly to them. This also demonstrates to your team how important direct communication is and how closely you work together.

Walking

Block 15 minutes in your calendars every day after your team's stand-up. Be first available for your expert team and use the remaining minutes to take a walk together. The walk doesn't even have to be outside the building. Stroll down the corridor and briefly discuss the most important findings from the stand-up.

Feedback

Use the daily regular meetings to give each other ritualized feedback. Describe to the other how you perceived them in a situation, what it triggered in you, and what your impulse to them would be.

Example: "I noticed in the stand-up that you had your phone in your hand. This gave me the feeling that you were not taking the meeting seriously and I would like you to be fully concentrated for the 15 minutes, or tell us what is distracting you so that we can understand your actions."

A feedback ritual makes you better together, practices structured feedback giving, and you demonstrate to your team the importance of feedback. It also strengthens your mutual commitment and trust in each other, as the other person openly shares their thoughts with you.

17.2.9 Your PDCA Cycle

After the daily joint ritual has hopefully become a firm part of your work, consider what an overarching PDCA cycle could look like for you. A **PDCA cycle** or Deming circle is the basis of any agile work and describes the recurring sequence of planning, execution, checking, and action, see Fig. 17.2. The PDCA cycle ensures continuous improvement: First, hypotheses and work packages are planned (Plan). These are then implemented

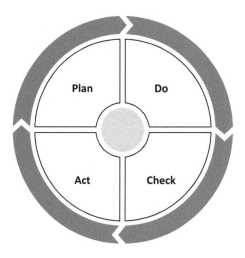

Fig. 17.2 The PDCA cycle. *Source* Based on Shewhart 1939

and delivered as an increment (DO). The increment and the underlying hypotheses are then checked (CHECK) and deductions are made for the next cycle from what has been learned (ACT). It is important in the cycle, among other things, that the checks are already taken into account in the planning (Scholtes 1998).

In the PO-SM constellation, the individual phases of the PDCA cycle have the following meaning:

- **Plan:** Consider for whom you are doing what and in what priority. Try to pay special attention to ensuring that none of your three major stakeholders are neglected: You as a PO-SM team, your implementation team with whom you are working on the product, and also the customer for whom you are developing the product.
- **Do:** Implement the measures. Pay particular attention to transparency about who is currently working on which to-do and whether they need the help of their partner.
- **Check:** Check whether you have achieved your goals with the measures, give each other feedback and reflect on what you have learned from the past cycle and the results. You should particularly look at how well these measures could be reconciled with working on the product. Also look at your checklist "Does Agile Work Still Make Sense?". Hold each other accountable and be your strongest critics, because it is in this phase that you gain the insights that make you, your development team, and your product better.
- **Act:** Derive new measures from what you have learned and possibly correct your target space or your team vision.

Your PDCA cycle should of course not be as short as that of your teams while they are working on the product. But it should also not be so long that it feels more like a roadmap for the next few months.

The Length of Your PDCA Cycle
A PO-SM PDCA cycle of 6 weeks has proven to be effective. Plan a weekly meeting (Weekly) and set specific goals for how you want to work on the team and product vision. Set up a review and reflect afterwards whether you have come significantly closer to your goals.

17.2.10 Leading through Why and Transparency

Scrum Masters and Product Owners are lateral leaders in agile work. They delegate, moderate, and lead through feedback. They set the framework and explain the meaning of the team's tasks, classify "why" something needs to be done and explain the significance for the overall organization. They lead together operationally at eye level with the team. Their task is to create transparency about the work internally and externally and to ensure a working environment in which the experts can work as well as possible. In each stand-up, they collect the important information and with the question "What is hindering you" items that they solve as quickly as possible together or report on the current status the next day.

Why? Why? Why?
Encourage your development team to challenge you and make them your critics who question every one of your decisions with a why. Because only when everyone has the same understanding will you be successful together. As soon as each expert knows how he can lead the whole to success with his actions and has internalized the priorities, he can bring his full potential, act in the interest of the product and think along.

Show What You Are Working On
Write all obstacles on post-its and bring them to your team's sprint board. If your implementation team uses a digital board, make it transparent there as well. Let the team prioritize the post-its and assign them to the correct columns. Move them in the daily stand-up if you were able to solve something or clearly state why you are not making progress on a topic. This shows your team that you make your work as transparent as you expect from them.

17.2.11 Leading through Attitude

As Scrum Master and Product Owner, you lead through attitude. This means that you must be aware that every one of your actions serves as a role model. Whether you arrive late to the stand-up, suggest skipping the retro, or leave your coffee cup on the meeting table: your actions serve as a guide. You show that the stand-up is not important to you, or that your time is more valuable than others', if you are not punctual. You diminish the importance of the retro and make it clear to the team that you do not value its measures if you let it fall through. And you show everyone that you supposedly think you're better when you leave your cup and expect someone else to clean it up for you. And even if you don't mean it that way, it can be interpreted that way.

Be each other's biggest critic
In our daily actions, we cannot pay attention to everything—leading through attitude is difficult. But this is where the team of Product Owner and Scrum Master has a decisive advantage. You can be each other's biggest critic and point out each other's attitude or show how it could be interpreted.

17.2.12 Shared Leadership

You lead a team of experts who know much more in their field than you do. And each individual is indispensable for collective success. Therefore, treat everyone with respect and lead on an equal footing.

But only you can find your way to challenge your team in such a way that it delivers the best possible result for the common goal, without overburdening the experts or them overburdening themselves.

Shared leadership is particularly challenging. You must appear as a unit—even if you do not always agree. If this is the case, never argue in front of the team; still appear together and try not to contradict each other. Support each other in difficult situations and initially assume that the other is acting in the best interests of the team and to the best of their knowledge and belief.

Work with your team on a daily basis. Be approachable, constantly present and not rushed. Participate in all team rituals and learn together with the team. Even though the Scrum Guide states that participation in rituals is optional, practice has shown that this should not be an option for a productive team.

As Scrum Master and Product Owner, make it clear that the team you lead is successful when the project is successfully completed. If this is not the case, then the team is not responsible for the failure, but you are.

To prevent a separation between the team, Product Owner, and Scrum Master, one thing should be clear to you at all times: To achieve the common visions, everyone from the large team is needed. None of you will succeed alone in the complex. And whether it's the product or team vision: the solution can only be worked out together by the expert team. Product Owner and Scrum Master serve as lateral leaders—they lead from within the team.

"We"
To make the team aspect clear to you at all times, never say "the team must", but always speak of "We".

17.3 What's Next?

What should you as a Product Owner or Scrum Master take away from this? Above all, orient yourself to the three guiding principles that make the difference:

1. Be a PO-SM team
2. Be leaders
3. Be part of the entire team

Then you will together realize your product and team vision, lead your team efficiently and accompany it in mastering every challenge. The biggest mistake you can make is not to work with each other, but against each other. Understand the previous tips as suggestions and not as strict solutions, because the best architectures, requirements, and designs emerge from self-organized teams—and that's you in this case.

Also, keep learning. Try to always get better as a team and develop further. Experiment, make mistakes, fall down, get up again and keep going. Just do it and fail fast— agile work lives from small experiments, failure, and learning. As a team of Product

Owner and Scrum Master, you always have someone by your side who pats you on the shoulder when an experiment is successful. And much more importantly, someone who helps you up when you have failed with one. Don't lose sight of your visions and make sure that you are the best team you have ever worked in.

17.4 Learning Teams

Always be aware that as a Product Owner and Scrum Master, you are only part of a team of experts. For the expertise of each employee to complement each other as well as possible and to create a coherent overall picture of the challenge, the feeling of ***community*** in the team is an important, supporting pillar. A strong sense of community ensures that the experts can rely on each other and grow together. It thus provides support and a strong identification within the team.

In addition, teams, especially in complex environments, need ***orientation,*** so that they always know what they are doing and why, and how their work contributes to the overarching goal (for example, a new product). Orientation includes both an outward view (e.g., competitive environment, competition) and an inward view (team issues and collaboration), so that the *why* is always clarified.

The third core value that teams need is ***autonomy***—the ability to adapt their own system of collaboration to meet their own conditions. For this, team members consider their own competence boundaries and learn to improve their processes step by step and continuously.

To meet the complex challenges in digital product management, teams must constantly learn—but how do they do this specifically? First of all, learning is to be understood in two ways. Teams can and must learn on two levels: content and process. The obvious learning is the **content learning:** Teams learn, for example, in product development through market research or product tests, which helps them improve their product. The second level of learning, which often gets overlooked but is becoming increasingly important, is the **process learning:** Teams must learn how to work well together, what they (need from each other) and how to design their system. In this process, they develop, for example, rules of interaction with each other or create and shape common rituals (weekly meetings, etc.).

Learning teams create their own culture, which contributes to their way of working and is positively shaped by it. It should be characterized by trust, responsibility, and transparency. In learning teams, members should openly address and resolve conflicts in the matter, always dealing with each other solution-oriented and on an equal footing. The handling of mistakes is also part of the culture of learning teams, as mistakes are seen as a natural part of experimental collaboration.

To develop learning teams in product organizations, we provide numerous tips and impulses on the (German) website www.lernendeteams.de.

References

Scholtes, P. R. 1998. *The leader's handbook—Making things happen, getting things done*. New York et al.: McGraw Hill Professional.

Shewhart, W. A. 1939. *Statistical method from the viewpoint of quality control*. New York: Graduate School Department of Agriculture.

Snowden, D. 2000. The social ecology of knowledge management. Cynefin: A sense of time and place. In *Knowledge horizons: The present and the promise of knowledge management*, Editor C. Despres and D. Chauvel. Oxford: Butterworth-Heinemann.

Jan Köster As Vice President of Transformation, he shapes the transformation of Gruner+Jahr and leads the company into the future together with the management and other responsible parties. As a publishing child, he developed with training as a media designer at Axel Springer, a civil service at Hinz&Kunzt, a degree in media informatics, as a consultant for various publishers, product developer, Scrum Master, Agile Coach, Chapter Lead and further iterations just as constantly as the systems he accompanies. Together with other experts, he solves the challenges of a complex world and creates an environment for the organization in which they can work and grow together as learning teams.
Contact: jan@lernendeteams.de

Florian Meyer serves as an Agile Coach in the transformation of Gruner + Jahr. His journalistic background with experiences in tabloid, online, and entertainment journalism has laid the foundation for his understanding of the media business. His training as an Agile Coach, long-term team support, and the guidance of the organization through the pandemic, various changes, and the challenges of the economic crises at the beginning of the 2020s have always allowed him to grow with new challenges.
Contact: florian@lernendeteams.de

Jan Köster and Florian Meyer have developed the "Learning Teams" model and together they run the podcast "Method Monday", in which they present specific methods for workshop moderation and team support every week.

Understanding User Experience

Successfully Using UX Teams in Digital Product Development

Inken Petersen

Abstract

Digital products and services are part of our everyday life. With increasing digital competence, users' awareness and expectations rise. They engage intensively with the expected product benefits—even before downloading or registering. The user experience (short UX) during product use has an increasingly significant influence on the decision for or against a product. Many companies have recognized this and invest specifically in a good user experience of their products. They employ UX teams and various UX specialists who are dedicated to researching and designing the best user experience every day. However, product managers often lack clarity on how the individual disciplines in a UX team interact and how best to use a UX team in product development. Therefore, this article builds a basic understanding of the importance of UX, the individual UX disciplines, and the best integration of UX teams.

18.1 The Importance of a Positive User Experience

User Experience, according to Don Norman, encompasses "all aspects of the user's interaction with the company, its products, and its services" (Norman and Nielsen 2016). Don Norman was the first UX Architect at Apple in 1993—a company that recognized the importance of UX very early on.

I. Petersen (✉)
Hamburg, Deutschland
e-mail: contact@inkenpetersen.com

A positive user experience does not start only at the purchase of an app or after registration, but already at the first contact with the brand through a recommendation or a hit in a search engine. This holistic approach is now also defined as a standard in the corresponding ISO standard 9241-210 (International Organization for Standardization 2019). The focus for the user is the question of how much the product really offers a benefit. Only after that do aspects such as simplicity, aesthetics, or joy come into play. A product that is easy to use and beautiful but without benefit will not find customers.

Good UX goes beyond the **User Interface** (UI), i.e., the pure surface design of the product. Even a perfect user interface does not help a user if he needs functions or services that the product cannot provide. If the user needs a product by express delivery, but the delivery time is 2 weeks, he will leave the online shop dissatisfied and shop elsewhere. If he would like to share videos with his friends but can only share photos, he will also be dissatisfied.

For outstanding UX, one must always be one step ahead of the user. It is therefore not enough to work through checklists of desired features from surveys and user tests. It is more about all functions in the company—such as marketing, sales, engineering, product management, UX design, etc.—becoming customer understanders and actively co-designing the perfect user experience.

The UX design process thus gains relevance as a procedure beyond the UX team and product development. Because the philosophy behind the design process can also be transferred to projects in marketing and sales.

18.2 The Iterative UX Design Process

The UX design process is an iterative and rapid process that has evolved in the environment of agile product development and is based on well-known design approaches and philosophies such as "Design Thinking" and "User Centered Design".[1]

The focus in the UX design process is on holistic product design, which includes the entire customer lifecycle and all interaction points between customers and the product or service. In addition, the UX design process (similar to Design Thinking) is characterized by fast and easily implementable methods to fit into the pace of modern agile product development.

The iterative UX design process, as illustrated in Fig. 18.1, consists of 4 steps that build on each other and are repeated cyclically: **Understanding, Prototyping, Reviewing** and

---

[1] More on the topic of Design Thinking can be found in the "Change by Design" book by design thinking pioneer Tim Brown (2009). More about the "User Centered Design Process" can be found in Don Norman's book "User-Centered System Design: New Perspectives on Human–Computer Interaction" (Norman 1986).

18 Understanding User Experience

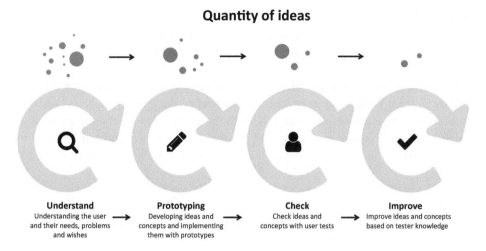

Fig. 18.1 The iterative UX design process. (*Source*: Own illustration)

Improving. Over the course of these steps, a multitude of ideas and solution approaches are generated and then reduced to the best ideas. The iterative and rapid approach is based on the Lean Startup principle, which was coined by Eric Ries (2011).

(1) Understanding
At the center of the UX design process are always the users—the current and the future ones. At the beginning of each project, user behavior is analyzed with observations or surveys. These insights are condensed into models, such as personas or user scenarios, which provide a good overview of the target group and the usage situations with the product or service. In this phase, ideas and solution approaches sprout, as dealing with the user at this level is very inspiring.

(2) Prototyping
The next step is prototyping, i.e., creating models for the new product, the new service, or the new features. In UX design, there are a multitude of prototyping methods such as paper prototyping, wireframes, and click dummies, which help to visualize the ideas and future system behavior. The prototypes form the basis for communicating the new ideas and validating the ideas with the target group.

(3) Reviewing
The ideas, hypotheses, and design approaches in the prototypes are checked and validated using user feedback. Critical UX or usability problems can thus be solved before a technical implementation and the risk of developing products that nobody wants or needs is reduced. There are a multitude of methods for reviewing—from the classic test in the user lab to the A/B test with a programmed version of the prototype.

(4) Improving
The test findings obtained are usually prioritized in the team and then transferred to the prototypes. Depending on the test result, the ideas and concepts are radically changed or slightly optimized in this step.

The UX area takes on a special role as a specialist unit here, as many of the tasks are done in the UX team—in close coordination with product management and software engineering. UXers are familiar with UX methods and tools to generate many ideas in a short time, design quick prototypes, and check them. Since all these tasks can hardly be accommodated in one role, three core disciplines have developed in the UX area in recent years.

18.3 The Core Disciplines in the User Experience Field

A modern **User Experience team** typically consists of the three areas of UX Design, Visual Design, and User Research. All are concerned with making the user experience of a digital product as pleasant, satisfying, motivating, efficient, and productive as possible. They consider, for example, whether a website navigation is intuitively understandable or whether the smartphone app leaves a visually appealing impression. They use a variety of different methods and tools to analyze user behavior before, during, and after use and to design the product or service based on this. Each discipline has its own focus as well as its own methods and tools.

18.3.1 The UX Designer

The **UX Designer** is probably the best-known discipline in the UX team. Nowadays, the UX Designer is often also referred to as a **Product Designer**. The focus of the UX Designer is on the conception of useful and well-functioning products, rather than on aesthetics.

The tasks of the UX Designer include:

- Understanding how the user behaves, what problems they have, and what they need;
- Creating user models, such as User Journeys and Personas, as a basis for product design;
- Designing easy-to-use and well-functioning product concepts with paper prototypes, wireframes, and interactive prototypes;
- Checking the product concepts using user feedback from UX tests, usability tests, customer interviews, A/B tests, etc.

Some examples from the toolbox of a UX Designer include: application scenarios, functionality, usability, navigation, information architecture, personas, screen structure, user journeys, wireframes, prototypes, etc. The book "101 Design Methods" by Vijay Kumar provides a good overview of common design methods (Kumar 2012).

18.3.2 The Visual Designer

The Visual Designer takes care of the contemporary aesthetics of a product and its visual consistency. Their designs aim to be beautiful and easy to use, as well as to fit the technical requirements. They are often also referred to as a **User Interface Designer** (UI Designer).

The tasks of the Visual Designer include:

- Understanding which visual style fits the brand and the users of the product;
- Developing the visual user interface of the product;
- Designing the visual user interface to fit the technology, such as responsive websites or native apps;
- Ensuring that the interface elements are used consistently

Some examples from the toolbox of a Visual Designer include: the visual design of interaction elements such as buttons and input fields, visual design of the user interface with fonts, colors, and icons to match the brand, development of animations for e.g. teasers, creation of visual style guides, creation of visual design templates in Sketch or Photoshop as a basis for technical implementation, etc.

18.3.3 The User Researcher

The **User Researcher** is the internal expert for all questions related to user tests. They know a multitude of suitable test methods and test tools and carry out the appropriate UX research method in the project. They are also referred to as a **UX Researcher**.

The tasks of the User Researcher include:

- Defining the hypotheses to be tested for the user tests;
- Selecting the test methods and test tools that are best suited for the respective context, such as interviews, UX tests, surveys, usability tests, remote tests, etc.;
- Preparing, conducting, and evaluating the tests;
- Compiling the findings from several tests as a knowledge base.

Some examples from the toolbox of a User Researcher include: user observation, user surveys, usability tests, test software, test guide, feedback tools, data analysis. The methods of the User Researcher are well described in the book by Tomer Sharon "Validating Product Ideas: Through Lean User Research" (Sharon 2016).

18.4 The Different Types of UX Teams

A variety of different tasks fall within the UX team. Many of these tasks are interdependent or build upon each other. This makes UX a team sport and the flow of information and exchange within the team very important. Depending on the size of the company and the competencies of the team members, it may make sense to combine certain disciplines into one role. Each organizational structure has its advantages and disadvantages, which should be considered when deciding for or against a division.

18.4.1 The Classic UX Team

In the classic UX team, there is a clear division of tasks among the individual disciplines of UX design, visual design, and user research.

Advantages of the classic solution are
- clear responsibilities;
- knowledge and competence building at a high level possible;
- task division fits very well with the requirements in product development.

Disadvantages of the classic solution are
- information exchange is not easy;
- the organization of work takes more time as more disciplines are involved;
- specialization can promote tunnel vision.

For most companies, the classic structure is the best solution due to its clarity. In addition, finding suitable designers is easier, as there are, for example, very few designers who can cover both the UX design and the visual design area at a very high quality.

18.4.2 The "UX Team of One"

In the "UX Team of One", one person takes on all tasks of the three different UX disciplines.

Advantages of the "UX Team of One" are
- a very good overview and good knowledge of all UX topics;
- very flexible use of UX expertise.

Disadvantages of the "UX Team of One" are
- covering the various tasks and projects alone is a challenge;
- many tasks cannot be done in parallel and the UX of the product suffers as a result.

The "UX Team of One" can be a pragmatic initial solution in small startups or companies that are starting with a professional UX area.

18.4.3 The Hybrid "UX & Visual Design Team" with Separate User Research Dimension

In this solution, there are no separate design disciplines. The designer takes on all UX and visual design tasks. However, separate user researchers ensure that the testing of hypotheses and concepts is not neglected.

Advantages of the hybrid solution are
- No handover from the UX designer to the visual designer is necessary during the project;
- due to the separate research discipline, there is still enough time to thoroughly test hypotheses and concepts.

Disadvantages of the hybrid solution are
- Covering the various tasks of UX design and visual design is not easy, as many designers usually have their strengths in only one discipline.
- The hybrid solution can work if the designers in the team can cover the tasks from UX design and visual design well or can support each other in their special disciplines through "design pairs", i.e., close cooperation in a team of two.

18.5 The Best Organizational Form

In addition to assembling the UX team, product and UX managers also have to deal with the question of the best integration into the agile product development organization. Currently, two opposing approaches are mainly evident in practice: the distributed UX team and the centralized UX team.

The Distributed UX Team
In this approach, the UX team works decentralized and distributed in so-called **Cross Functional Teams,** i.e., in cross-functional agile product teams. The UX and visual designers sit directly with a product team and are mainly active for this team. The advantages of this solution are very efficient and good cooperation with the product managers and software developers and a greater thematic proximity of the designers. A disadvantage is the often lacking cross-functional exchange of UX and visual designers among themselves. Lack of feedback and the view beyond the horizon often lead to dissatisfaction among the designers in the long term, as their own development suffers.

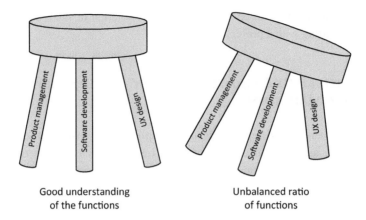

Fig. 18.2 The three-legged stool in product development. (*Source*: Based on Schleifer 2018)

The Centralized UX Team
The opposite approach is the centralized UX team, which works like an internal design agency. The UX team sits together in one place and works on projects from different product teams. The advantages of this solution are the good exchange within the UX team and the good opportunities for personal development through, for example, feedback from other designers. A major disadvantage is the more difficult cooperation with the agile product teams, which often leads to the user experience being simply neglected in projects. Therefore, the centralized UX team is usually only suitable for companies that already have a pronounced UX culture and where the user experience is simply part of the work process.

The organizational form should therefore always be chosen depending on the overall context and can change over the years. In addition to the organizational form, the UX team also always faces the question of the necessary number of designers and researchers. Best practices have been established for this in recent years.

18.6 The Right Amount of UX

Anyone who wants a product with an excellent user experience must invest in UX. Equal integration of UX into work processes and decisions is important. Unfortunately, UX disciplines are often equated with "beautifying" the surface. When this happens, however, companies deprive themselves of important opportunities and potentials in product development.

When building up employees in product management and software development, one should therefore follow the model of the **Three-Legged Stool**, see Fig. 18.2: An optimal balance between all functions is ideal. A leg that is too short in one of the functions leads to a wobbly stool or a wobbly product. In companies like AirBnB, the model of the three-legged stool has already proven itself (Schleifer 2018).

The appropriate ratio, i.e., the relationship of UX to the other functions, varies for the individual UX disciplines. The following rules of thumb have proven successful for both the distributed and the centralized UX team model:

- UX Design Ratio: 0.5 to 1 UX designer per product team
- Visual Design Ratio: 0.25 to 0.5 visual designers per product team
- User Researcher Ratio: 0.25 user researcher per product team

The ratios are based on the recommendation of Marty Cagan, the founder of the Silicon Valley Product Group (Cagan 2007).

It is important to note that the hybrid designer model, i.e., UX designer and visual designer in one person, does not mean that designers can be saved. At least not without losses in speed or quality. The ratio remains the same.

18.7 The Future of UX

Technical products are becoming increasingly complex and topics such as artificial intelligence, voice input, links between physical products and digital products (example: tracking bracelets with digital apps) as well as more and more end devices are constantly changing the requirements for the user experience. At the same time, the UX factor is becoming increasingly important for users in this complex technical world.

Unfortunately, the added value of good UX teams is often underestimated or not understood. And the UX community itself shows too little presence to the outside world or has difficulty selling its own added value well and making it clear. One reason for this is certainly that the tasks of the three core disciplines have been very much in motion in recent years. With the more complex tasks, the requirements grow, and the job profiles change. And these changes are not yet complete. Universities and possible training paths are lagging behind—especially in Germany. Therefore, finding good UX employees in the digital environment is a major challenge.

For all UX designers, visual designers, and user researchers, this means continuous further education and questioning of current work processes and tools. And taking time for the external presentation of and education about UX. For everyone who deals with UX in their projects, this means being familiar with the basics of good UX. This is simply part of the basic knowledge for everyone who works in digital product development. Hopefully, this article is a push in the right direction.

References

Brown, T. 2009. *Change by design—How design thinking transforms organizations and inspires innovation*. New York: HarperCollins.
Cagan, M. 2007. Roles and ratios. https://svpg.com/roles-and-ratios.
International Organization for Standardization (ISO). 2019. *Ergonomics of human-system interaction—Part 210: Human–centred design for interactive systems*. Genua: International Organization for Standardization (ISO).
Kumar, V. 2012. *101 Design methods: A structure approach for driving innovation in your organisation*. Hoboken: Wiley.
Norman, D. 1986. *User centered system design: New perspectives on human–computer interaction*. Boca Raton: CRC Press.
Norman, D., and J. Nielsen. 2016. The definition of User Experience (UX). www.nngroup.com/articles/definition-user-experience.
Ries, E. 2011. *The lean startup: How today's entrepreneurs use continuous innovation to create radically successful businesses*. New York: Crown Business.
Schleifer, A. 2018. Defining product design: A dispatch from Airbnb's design chief. https://firstround.com/review/defining-product-design-a-dispatch-from-airbnbs-design-chief.
Sharon, T. 2016. *Validating product ideas: Through lean user research*. Brooklyn: Rosenfeld Media.

Inken Petersen has held many different roles within and outside of UX teams throughout her career as a UX designer, Information Architect, UX Lead, and Product Owner. Her passion is products and services with outstanding user experience. As a freelance UX consultant, she coaches her clients on UX strategy, UX management, Product Discovery, and Continuous Product Discovery. For new products and larger relaunches, she creates design visions with vision prototypes and builds new and efficient design systems. She is a co-founder of the Product & UX community blog produktbezogen.de.
Contact: contact@inkenpetersen.com

Data Analytics

Challenges in Working with Data

Jan Martens

Abstract

Some may expect to find solutions in this chapter for the right KPI, the right analysis strategy, or the right technical data platform. In my opinion, however, almost all challenges lie in the communication between product manager and analyst: What is the right question and how do we arrive at an answer that is promising and business-relevant and contains an actionable step? Only when you and your organization are prepared to meet this communicative challenge with the right attitudes and the necessary dose of self-criticism, will you be able to reap the expected analytical value. How this can be achieved is outlined in the present contribution.

19.1 Introduction

The relationship of the product manager to data and its "processors" is complex. When I was asked to contribute a chapter to this book, I myself had no idea how best to describe the challenges of this working relationship. Originally, I wanted to write down a kind of guide; a manual, to work by recipe. However, this quickly proved to be not useful: Neither is a product manager on the green field, where he can completely rebuild his data landscape, nor are the initial conditions similar enough that a one-size-fits-all recipe could create effective solutions.

J. Martens (✉)
Lotto24 AG, Hamburg, Deutschland
e-mail: martens.jan@gmx.de

© The Author(s), under exclusive license to Springer Fachmedien Wiesbaden GmbH, part of Springer Nature 2024
S. Hoffmann (ed.), *Digital Product Management*,
https://doi.org/10.1007/978-3-658-44276-7_19

Instead, I decided to provide a collection of problem descriptions, because of which one often does not work as successfully with data in practice as one would like and could. In doing so, I show—where possible—ways to circumvent or solve the respective problem.

It is up to your analysis to determine which of the challenges particularly apply to you. I consider it conceivable and likely that many may be latently affected by several problems at the same time—consecutively or even simultaneously.

19.2 Roles and Organizations

Analyst or Scientist, what's the difference? There is plenty of material on this topic on the internet. However, the picture is not uniform and often the job titles and requirements overlap more or less strongly.

The **Data Analyst** is often described as working "on site" with the product team, with frequent direct contacts to the product manager (or other stakeholders). His tasks are often more detailed, rather descriptive, backward-looking. He is supposed to report and answer direct inquiries. The **Data Scientist**, on the other hand, is often described as a person who works on tasks centrally in a team of like-minded people, which are often more extensive and have a project character. Common examples are modeling and forecasts that are intended to predict future decisions by customers or other influences.

When I speak of the analyst in the following pages, I always mean the whole group of analytical roles, whether Business Analyst, Data Scientist, BI Analyst, BI Manager or related role names. Also, my remarks are meant for both employees in central organizations and those integrated directly into your team.

19.3 The Pitfalls

Let's get to my top 12 of analytical challenges, which are not sorted by severity or frequency of occurrence. First, I focus on the causes in the area of stakeholders, followed by the challenges that have their starting point more with the analyst. When you compare your own problems with these pitfalls, please keep in mind that there is often no clear assignment and you should also consider being affected by several pitfalls at the same time.

19.3.1 The Feel-Good Analysis

Have you ever asked your analyst how successful and effective one of your decisions was? You certainly have! It is the classic among the pitfalls discussed here and we are all latently affected by it. Who is not looking for confirmation, wants to verify his work, wants to have confirmation for future decisions that the decisions made in the past were correct. The problem with such questions remains: What recommendations for action should emerge from them? Very often none at all.

The whole reporting system from standard reports to dashboards to business balance scorecards and quarterly reports basically serves to check the success of those responsible. Don't get me wrong: Such instruments are needed and have their purpose.

However, if you want to learn something from the data for future decisions, then please do not look into your reporting system. The answers are not in there. Therefore, avoid having your analyst dive into descriptive analyses and look for possible effects he can find to confirm you in the greatness of your decisions.

Instead, ask yourself what decisions you will face in the future and what you need to know before you make your decision. Work with your team to develop a list of hypotheses and prioritize the most important hypotheses so that your team focuses on answering these hypotheses. Developing the right hypotheses is not a matter of course, as many are often formulated from the perspective of the entrepreneur and not from the perspective of the customer.

19.3.2 The Justification Analysis

A variant or escalation of the aforementioned phenomenon is the justification analysis, where a pressure to prove success rests on the product manager and he tries to prescribe solutions to the analyst. The analyst often (too) frequently bows to the pressure in practice and delivers as ordered, but no longer brings his problem-solving competence into play.

As a result, results are often embellished, with interpretations of trend lines where there is actually no effect, or even faked by good-looking apples-to-oranges comparisons or other instruments from the category "Don't trust any statistics you didn't fake yourself".

Especially when the analyst is in the reporting line, it is difficult for him to offer real opposition and participates in the embellishment of the results for lack of alternatives. Here it is difficult for the product manager to create solutions single-handedly, because this is almost an organizational fault. In this case, try not to pass on the pressure on you to your analyst, so that he can continue to serve you the unvarnished truth as best he can.

19.3.3 The Symptom Analysis

In every company, there is a reporting system (see Sect. 19.3.1 Feel-Good Analysis). All these dashboards show business-relevant key figures almost exclusively in time series over different periods, often compared to past periods or set goals. Inevitably, these time series are interpreted, and both untrained and trained eyes ask the question when key figures are falling or "not rising enough": "Do we have a problem?"

You can keep entire analysis departments busy with such questions for months and you can already guess: This could be quite ineffective. Why is that? Either the problems are external or homemade. Many external problems or challenges can hardly be analyzed from internal data, while internal problems should actually be found with quality control tools, e.g. watchdogs, software tests or milestones in project controlling. Symptom analysis is expensive, because errors should not be discovered afterwards, but avoided beforehand.

The hunt for the undiscovered problem is questionable in several respects, but if you are already doing it (have to), then at least develop all relevant hypotheses for possible causes in a brainstorming session and systematically work through the hypotheses afterwards. Accept that the answer to many hypotheses will be: "Within the possible measurement accuracy, no effect can be seen."

Once all hypotheses have been questioned, do not send your analyst on the hunt for the unknown problem that may not even exist. Be satisfied with the answers to the hypotheses and focus again on the upcoming decisions of the future.

19.3.4 Simple Questions, Complex Answers

The first three conflict areas dealt with questions which, in my view, were asked for the wrong motives of the product manager. But there is another conflict area, which comes from the category "Product manager asks question, analyst answers": Product managers often expect answers to their questions as soon as possible, especially when decisions need to be made in the current sprint in agile environments. However, the expectation of simple and immediately available answers often contradicts the availability of the analyst or his estimate of how long the complex answer would take in his view. In this area of tension, the analyst often has no choice but to deliver no answer, an insufficient answer, or a late answer.

> **Example**
>
> A product team is working on a feature that it hopes will provide an uplift. The analyst points out that without an A/B test and additional data fields, the hypothesis cannot be answered. But it's too late for that, because the feature is already in production. It would be better to anticipate and clarify the analytical questions before the actual product development and to determine which questions are worth testing and answering. ◀

This conflict can only be resolved if, on the one hand, expectations and solutions are agreed upon that both sides understand and agree to, and on the other hand, analytical questions are anticipated far enough in advance so that needed solutions are available when decisions are pending.

19.3.5 Overconfidence

Have you ever done something with full conviction and then it didn't work? This cognitive bias, also known as Overconfidence Bias in English, hits everyone sooner or later. In business environments, decisions made out of overconfidence often lead to poor performance and risks for the company.

In our context, the product manager is convinced of his ideas, implements them, but the expected positive result does not occur. An analysis that may have already been carried out—unfortunately executed incorrectly—confirms the product manager in his idea. But at the latest in the sales or profit figures, a correspondingly equivalent result cannot be found, leaving the question open as to why the analysis came to a much more positive result. The error in the analysis was not noticed because one was too convinced of the original idea and no longer critically questioned the result.

In the better case, the analysis already delivers the correct result, that the expectations were not met and the effect is much smaller, probably below the measurement accuracy, and therefore not visible. Overconfidence can be corrected: A practical tool is the reflection of expectations in the team before the feature is implemented. Each team member gives his own estimate of effectiveness by expressing his expectation in the increase of the target KPI. If all important decisions of a team are documented in this way, the overconfidence of individuals or the whole team becomes apparent after some time and one can try more realistic estimates or devote oneself to the question of whether other actions would be more sensible if the decisions of the past were so ineffective.

19.3.6 Narcissism

After having thoroughly criticized your potential own mistakes, it's time to not spare my own profession: analysts and data scientists have great tools, which are often not really understood in terms of content, right? How could they be? They are complex and it's the analyst's job to understand and use them correctly. It regularly happens that the analyst uses the tool that he enjoys the most, which he always wanted to try out, which educates him the most personally or with which he wants to gain experience. The prioritization is not based on effectiveness, but on preference. Thus, instead of a simple forecasting method, such as a simple decision tree, a neural network or other innovative methods are quickly used. The added value of such advanced tools is hardly discernible from the outside. Therefore, it is necessary that the analysis department can justify its tool choice in a self-reflective manner and provide information on how much better a complex method is compared to a standard method. However, all of this must be economically viable.

▶ Feel free to challenge your analyst and demand that he explains why he chose one solution. Have him explain why the more complex solution is the better one and don't be satisfied with the answer that it's a black box and you have to blindly trust the model's recommendation. For your next steps, you need to understand what the black box can and cannot do anyway.

19.3.7 Simply Wrong

In the past, I have seen numerous analyses in which small but consequential errors were present. They can appear at various stages of an analysis: during the conception, data collection and cleaning, or in the presentation or interpretation of results.

Every development department tests their software code, and so every analytical department should check their analyses for correctness. However, this is easier said than done, as the errors manifest themselves in distorted results, which by definition no one knows whether they are right or wrong. Suddenly, an A/B test with a surprising result is highly significant and the product is implemented accordingly. Here too, one wonders months later why no corresponding effect can be seen in the company's results.

Error detection in analytics is challenging. The only way is to transfer scientific tools to the operation in the company: internal revision of analytical results, 4- or even better 6-eye principle, code review, independence of the analysis, redundancy and repeatability. All of this unfortunately costs money and time and is therefore often criticized for underperformance or slowness.

In practice, I use the following tools to minimize these risks: The more relevant and surprising a result is, the more time and effort we spend on the internal control process. We have already rewritten SQL queries independently a second time to verify their correctness.

Product managers often try to snatch intermediate results, which tend to take on a life of their own and make the rounds before the result is coherent. If the final result looks different, the surprise is great and sometimes painful. So be patient! If your analyst says, "We'll check that again," there's probably a good reason for it.

I'm not a fan of centralized data teams and would rather see analysts sitting and working in the product teams. However, they should be able to work in pairs there, if at all possible, to enable control processes in daily work, i.e., in as short iteration cycles as possible: A complex multivariate A/B test should not only be checked for errors when everything is beautifully written, but should be checked early and easily by the person sitting next to you. This challenge is of course greater the smaller the company and the number of analysts are.

And what if there is only one analyst? How does he check himself? I have not yet found a satisfactory answer to these questions.

19.3.8 "Not Significant"

"Not significant" is a response I've often heard from analysts, and it initially leads to recommendations for action such as "no result" or "no recommendation". In my view, this is too short-sighted. A simple change in the product manager's perspective usually makes it clear to the analyst that a decision is always made, even if it's just the decision to leave everything as it is. Leaving the product manager alone with his decision and shirking responsibility may seem tempting at times, but it's not a business solution.

Therefore, every recommendation for action should consider the possible options in the context of value and risk. Even a non-significant result always leads to a recommendation for action that takes into account the product conditions and the relevance of the decision. If the analyst can't manage this, he's not doing his job properly. As a consequence, the final interpretation of the results is taken over by the product manager again, as the recommendations for action are not consistent for him.

But there is also the opposite problem: The analyst rightly gives the feedback that a recommendation for action cannot be given, as the data only pretends to signal randomly. As a product manager, therefore, familiarize yourself with the language of statistics and ask what is meant by "significant" or "not significant" in terms of content. How much reliability is in the analyst's recommendations should always be part of your decision-making process.

▶ What is significant and what is relevant? A ten percent increase in sales is very likely relevant in many business areas. If it's only 0.1%, many will already say that it's not important enough. I would translate relevance simply as importance. Nevertheless, the 10% could be random, i.e., not significant, but the 0.1% significant, and thus a reliable statement.

19.3.9 Too Demanding

The job profile of an analyst is very broad and ranges from communication tailored to the recipient with analytically non-experts and project management skills to a deep understanding of the product, mathematical-statistical skills, and expertise in different programming languages.

This profile is demanding and many struggle to achieve good results in all areas. Rarely (actually never) do you find applicants who are already comprehensively trained for this profile. Despite all training efforts, I still find that this profile is so demanding that I have a high rejection rate in personnel selection. Therefore, there needs to be an internal training concept that someone knowledgeable must supervise. This person often does not exist, and so the analytical team has to train each other or buy in the necessary knowledge.

Nevertheless, I recommend that you question and optimize the quality of your analytical colleagues. As a product manager, you may have only a few opportunities to influence this. However, try to convince the responsible hiring person of the breadth of the job profile and not to focus only on the technical-mathematical skills. In addition, you should guide the analyst as if he were your junior product manager. He should be able to understand your patterns of action and motives.

Another possible source of difficulties can be a too large spatial and often associated mental distance between the product manager and the analyst. If the two rarely see or meet each other in the operational business, the solutions proposed by the analyst may risk not addressing the real problems of the product manager. Conversely, the product manager may not be able to understand all the framework conditions of the analyst. Particularly at risk are centrally organized data science teams, which are often perceived as business-foreign due to their spatial placement. They then do not generate the hoped-for added value, as a consequence of which the product manager hires his own analyst on site. This often leads in practice to the separation of data science and data analytics, with the individual "on-site analyst" quickly being overwhelmed by the questions, as he often lacks the above-mentioned tools and further training opportunities. Therefore, in the event that the analysts in your team regularly show up, demand from your central department that they are locally integrated into your team, not just for meetings but on a daily or weekly basis.

19.3.10 Lack of Distance—Sunk Costs

Especially in small teams and startups, there is often no real separation between product manager and analyst. It is also common for these roles to be combined in one person. Then there is often little room for distance and criticism, because the analyst also acts success-oriented and falls prey to the same potential challenges and is not critical enough of his own analytical activity.

Sometimes the analysts are also directly subordinate to the product manager. This makes them dependent and biased in their activity and restricts them from dealing critically with challenges. If your analyst is directly subordinate to you or your department, consider granting your analyst a certain degree of "fool's freedom" and affording his views some "minority protection". Otherwise, the product managers will only reinforce themselves in their decisions and revise wrong decisions too late.

19.3.11 Too Little Data

Mathematics and analytics cannot perform magic and there is simply an area where relevance and significance do not meet: in the valley of too small a sample. Especially in the new customer business of startups, data is expensive, because each customer has to be bought. If the analyst then says for the answer to a question, he would need X customers or Y clicks, then answering the hypotheses becomes a question of budget.

In the life cycle of product development, many analytical tools are therefore to be applied rather later, while many fundamental decisions are made rather early in the product life. This creates a tension that can only be partially resolved. "MVP", "Fail fast" or whatever the concepts may be called: All are supposed to enable the fundamental product decisions at an early (and cheap) point in time. However, there remains the conflict that one is always driven between the two poles of speed and thoroughness in the product life cycle. Any company with a sufficiently large reservoir of existing customers can consider itself lucky to be able to test alternatives comparatively easily.

Therefore, a fundamental challenge of analytics is contained here. The significance and relevance of analytical questions and answers are always in conflict. The micro-conversion of a website can be optimized significantly, but may not be relevant for business success. Successfully validating a test hypothesis to increase the customer lifetime value would of course be highly relevant, but a significant test design is extremely challenging to create. It remains the task of the analyst to mediate between these two extremes and to show a way that combines both sides.

19.4 Conclusion

From the previously described problems and challenges, I see the following recommendations for good cooperation between product managers and data analysts:

- Keep talking to your analyst. Continuously optimize communication with them.
- Speak to your analyst with a goal in mind. Explain to them what your problem is, not what solution you have in mind.
- Question the success and effectiveness of the delivered services.
- Understand data also as a tool for learning, not just for control: Data can justify or confirm decisions, but only the answer to a controversial hypothesis creates added value. Allow different opinions—even more: Demand different opinions.
- Accept the limits of analytics and data science. Every question needs its data source to be answered correctly. Demand from your analyst to clarify these limits in the sense of the decisions to be made.

If a company succeeds in creating a mutual genuine understanding between product managers and data analysts, this means an enormous added value for the customer benefit of the products and ultimately also for the company.

Jan Martens works as Director of Data Science and Analytics for Lotto24 AG. After studying physics, he worked in the semiconductor industry for 13 years. For the past 6 years, he has been leading analytical teams in e-commerce.
Contact: martens.jan@gmx.de

Product Organizations

How Successful Businesses Use Their Product Organization as a Competitive Advantage

Michael Schultheiß, David Gehrke and Lutz Göcke

Abstract

Efficient and effective product organizations are crucial to successful digital product development. No two organizations are the same, but there are certain patterns which successful digital product organizations have in common. In this chapter, we will analyze these characteristics and examine the structures, processes and roles at play in product organizations. This essay will provide an overview of the key features of a successful product organization with a view to providing impetus for potential change.

20.1 What is a Product Organization?

Digital product organization refers to the structures and processes that a company uses to design, test ("product discovery"), develop, expand, adapt ("product delivery") and, where applicable, discontinue digital products. Moreover, it encompasses the way in which product management, product design, software development, stakeholders and the company management cooperate with one another.

M. Schultheiß (✉)
McKinsey & Co, Berlin, Germany
e-mail: michael_schultheiss@mckinsey.com

D. Gehrke · L. Göcke
Nordhausen University of Applied Sciences, Nordhausen, Germany
e-mail: david.gehrke@hs-nordhausen.de

L. Göcke
e-mail: lutz.goecke@hs-nordhausen.de

© The Author(s), under exclusive license to Springer Fachmedien Wiesbaden GmbH, part of Springer Nature 2024
S. Hoffmann (ed.), *Digital Product Management*,
https://doi.org/10.1007/978-3-658-44276-7_20

The focus here is on product organizations that can develop and deliver digital products end to end, also referred to as product- and technology organizations (Cagan 2014). In this essay, therefore, the term *product organization* implies a more generalized meaning and refers to an organization with designers and software developers in addition to product managers.

These are contrasted with traditional IT or project organizations, agile organizations, i.e. those with enterprise-wide business agility, and product-centered organizational models whose scope of application extends beyond software development alone.

20.2 Five Features of Successful Product Organizations

Product organizations bring their entire value chain in line with the development of their digital products. Each digital product has a set of characteristics that affect their development; the product organization and business model must be precisely tailored to those specific features. Moreover, the distributed nature, interactivity, and re-programmability of digital products means that the operational and organizational structure of digital product organizations must fundamentally differ from that of traditional product organizations (Nambisan 2017; Yoo et al. 2012).

Despite all the differences between the various companies in the field of digital product development, successful product organizations share five common characteristics:

1. An outcome-focused approach: The (business) outcomes are the primary objective. The added value that the company is aiming for is achieved by changing user, customer or employee behavior. In this way, successful product organizations differ from project organizations, which draw on a specific input (such as finances, human resources, or time) to produce an output (such as functions, products, or services). Objectives and key results (OKRs) are useful instruments in the outcome-focused approach. Amazon's "working backwards" method can also be seen as outcome-focused (see Chap. 4 by Cansel Sörgens; Doerr 2018; Bryar and Carr 2021).
2. Decentralization of decisions: The basic assumption is that decisions are best made by those most familiar with the problem and its possible solutions. Usually, this comes into play at the team level. Strategic management is carried out by defining objectives or outcomes (Seiden 2019).
3. Risk mitigation through experimentation: Hypotheses and assumptions are tested continually. The main focus is on testing, generating new insights into the user and their behavior, and using those insights to optimize the product. Simple experiments include prototype testing or A/B testing (see Chap. 11 by Sascha Hoffmann; Torres 2021).

4. A team-focused approach: Having small teams set up along the value chain means flat hierarchies, small spans of control and decentralized decisions, which in turn significantly accelerates decision-making processes (Skelton and Pais 2019).
5. Adaptability and scalability: Decentralized decision-making, scalable structures, and an attuned company culture, make it easier for modern product organizations to shift their resources and focus in response to changing market conditions, such as the economic situation, technological developments and new competitor strategies (Bryar and Carr 2021).

Working backwards approach
Amazon's **working backwards approach** is a method of outcome-focused product development in which a team clarifies what they need to build by defining the desired outcome, the customer experience, and iteratively working backwards from that point. Planning begins with a fictional press release about the product launch and a list of frequently asked questions (FAQs). This process gives the product team a deeper insight into the target group, the problem to be solved, and the benefits of the product (Bryar and Carr 2021).

20.3 Structures, Processes, Employees

For the purposes of this essay, a simple three-layer model is used to describe and analyze product organizations. "Structure" and "Process" cover operational and organizational structures, while "Employees" explores the roles, skills, and culture within product organizations.

20.3.1 Structure

The cornerstone of a modern product organization is the empowered product team, also known as the product team or squad. It has specific characteristics derived from agile ways of working:

1. Cross-functionality: All skills and roles required to deliver the product and the desired outcome end to end are accounted for within the product team. This reduces handovers to other teams and leads to higher delivery speed. Cross-functional teams typically include a product manager, engineering manager, product designer and software developers (Cagan and Jones 2020). Moreover, the team members are assigned to their team full-time, while the teams themselves are set up for long-term stability.
2. Team size: The established ideal for the size of a team is seven plus/minus two (Miller 1956; Schwaber and Sutherland 2020). At Amazon this is known as a two-pizza team; in other words, two pizzas should be enough to feed everybody in the team. This

approach makes for more efficient communication and is based on Dunbar's number and Metcalfe's Law.
3. Product focus: To state the obvious, a product team is set up to develop a digital product. This means that the structures within the team are geared towards enabling it to create added value with that digital product. By contrast, feature or component teams focus on features or the building blocks for features. Ideally there is one team per product, which is often the case with start-ups. This ratio changes later on in the product lifecycle.

Dunbar's Number
Dunbar's number is the cognitive limit to the number of people with whom a person can maintain a personal relationship. Essentially it represents how many social relationships one person can have. For example, one can maintain intimate relationships with only about five people, and profoundly trusting relationships with some 15 people. **Metcalfe's Law** refers to a network effect, whereby the value of a network is proportional to the number of communication nodes (see Fig. 20.1). More communication nodes means more potential connections, which brings the disadvantage of greater network complexity (Dunbar and Dunbar 1993; Gilder 1993).

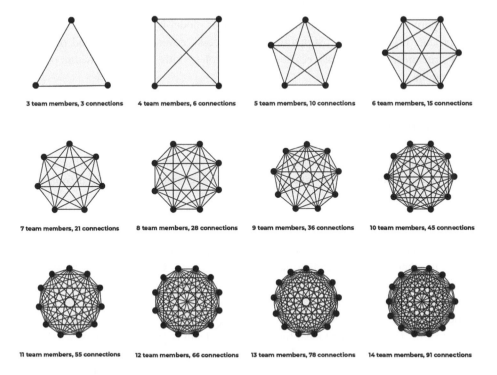

Fig. 20.1 Potential 1:1 communication connections in teams of increasing size

Feature and Platform Teams

Marty Cagan describes feature teams in contrast to empowered product teams, explaining that feature teams build features (the output) but are not responsible for business results (the outcome). Such teams carry out little to no product discovery (see Sect. 1.4.2.1; Cagan and Jones 2020).

The product-focused approach is also frequently used for shared services and components, i.e. internal products used by other teams within the company. The teams responsible for these products are known as platform teams. Common examples of what a platform team might work on include single sign-on, payment services or internal data services. Here, other teams become the customer, and APIs or component libraries become the product.

Figure 20.2 depicts an example chart for a product organization. This chart is the cross-functional view which does not necessarily represent reporting lines, which is one of the special characteristics of a digital product and technology organization: It has a cross-functional (per teams) and a functional (reporting lines) view. Management by a Chief Product Officer (CPO) or a Chief Product and Technology Office (CPTO) is typical, as is leadership of single or multiple product teams by managers from product management,

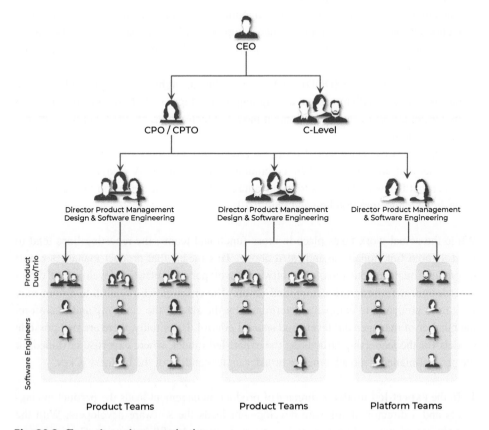

Fig. 20.2 Example product organization

software development and design (the product trio, or the product duo, in the absence of a designer, which is more common recently).

The graphic merely demonstrates the typical structures within a product organization and is not a blueprint for organizational design. Organizational adaptability is necessary for empowered product teams to work in an outcome-focused manner. An organization chart therefore tends to be nothing more than a snapshot, which would be reconfigured in a different context (Skelton and Pais 2019).

The exact structure of a product organization is heavily dependent on context and the value streams within the company. The following list gives a brief **overview of the methods** that can be used (where applicable, in combination with one another) to define **product and platform teams**:

Methods for Defining Product and Platform Teams in a Coherent Team Topology
1. Value stream mapping: This is a visual tool that demonstrates the flow of business value generation (via material or information flows) within a company. Value streams often give a good early indication of which products, sub-products or product lines can be cut (Osterling and Martin 2013).
2. Customer journey mapping: Journey mapping is a design-thinking tool which documents the experiences that a customer group has with a company's products (Patton and Economy 2014). In this approach, journeys and their respective personas are used to create the topology.
3. Domain-driven design (DDD): DDD is a technical architecture logic and software development paradigm aimed at aligning technology with business concepts. An important aspect of this is the domain model, which represents the functions within a business domain.
4. Inverse Conway Maneuver: Conway's Law states that companies build (software) systems that are copies of their communication structures. A company can use the effect that Conway describes to its advantage by building its teams on the basis of the desired architecture (Skelton and Pais 2019).

While the actual work takes place in cross-functional teams, the reporting lines tend to be structured functionally as indicated above. This means that product managers report to product management directors, software developers to software development directors, designers to design directors, and so on. The titles of who reports to whom may vary from company to company, determined by the size of the company and, therefore, the number of management layers and span of control. Essentially, there are two possible models for the leadership structures: the expert-led model, where expertise is valued, or the general-manager model, where a broader understanding of the business is key.

1. In the **expert-led model**, a director of product management leads the product managers and a director of software development leads the software developers. With the right experience and background, one person may also fill both roles. Depending on

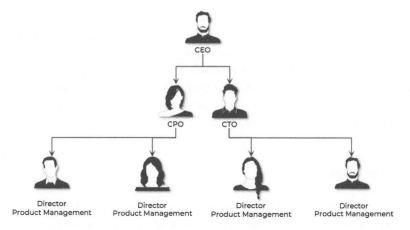

Fig. 20.3 Expert-led management model. (With reference to Venkateswaran et al. 2021)

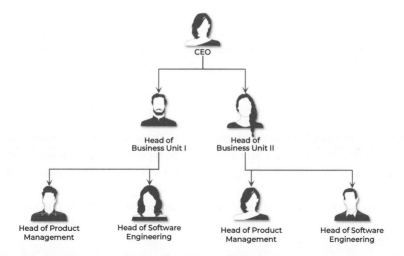

Fig. 20.4 General-manager model. (With reference to Venkateswaran et al. 2021)

the size of the company, these are VP- or C-level (CPO/CTO) roles, which report directly to the CEO or managing director. Occasionally there may be a product trio, made up of a product management director, a software development director, and a design director (see Fig. 20.3).

2. The **general-manager model** is more common in traditional companies undergoing a digital transformation. Here, a director of product management and a director of software development report to the corresponding department or division head. If there is a CTO in this model, they often have a dotted line to the different software development directors (see Fig. 20.4), who then gain a second reporting line.

In summary, the structural characteristics of a product organization at the team level are cross functionality, a team size of seven plus/minus two, and a product-focused approach. These characteristics do not just apply to product teams in the classic sense; platform or component teams can also benefit from this structure. The product trio or duo is the core component of a cross-functional team and offers a number of advantages at the management level. The actual organizational structure can be determined by various methods and should be adaptable.

20.3.2 Processes

This section provides an overview of the processes that are characteristic of a product organization. The activities themselves are described in more detail in other essays in this volume.

Product Discovery
Product discovery (see Chap. 6 by Philip Steen and Alexander Hipp) encompasses the activities carried out within a product organization to determine what product should be built.

> The purpose of product discovery is to quickly separate the good ideas from the bad. The output of product discovery is a validated product backlog. (Cagan 2018)

The purpose of product discovery is to minimize risks and uncertainties when answering one key question: should this product be built? The typical toolkit for product discovery draws on lean startup, design thinking, and the ever more popular continuous-discovery approach (Ries 2011; Torres 2021) and encapsulates all types of research and insight generation from testing and experimentation to ideation and validation methods.

Product Delivery
The product delivery processes (see Chap. 8 by Tim Adler) nowadays are essentially based on agile ways of working, values and principles, and are often heavily adapted to the context of the product organization and the company culture. Fundamentally, there are two distinct levels: the team level and a wider portfolio level.

1. **Team level:** Common methods include Scrum, Kanban, Scrumban and Extreme Programming, with Scrum by far the most known approach. What sets Scrum apart is its simplicity and its clear structure, with an internal logic and risk minimization that are easy to understand. The Kanban method, by contrast, applies a number of principles from Lean and the Toyota Production System and focuses on optimizing flow within a system. Scrumban describes any combination of the two methods, while Extreme Programming (XP) was a popular approach in the early 2000s in particular, and focused

Table 20.1 Comparison of selected agile scaling-up approaches

Scrum of scrums	Large-scale scrum	Scaled agile framework	Spotify model
Straightforward scaling and voting mechanism for teams by appointing one representative per team	Scaling framework that positions the product owner as the central element and introduces further roles such as the area product owner	Heavily descriptive and much-discussed scaling framework, which specifies process flows and is frequently used in large corporations	Matrix model focused on small, autonomous teams with end-to-end responsibility

on software-development practices. In practice, a combination of Scrum and XP is often used (Kniberg 2014a).

As maturity increases with respect to agility, another development can be observed: many start-ups and scale-ups do not impose any of these methods on their teams. Instead, the organizations adopt a variety of lightweight approaches under the maxim plan, build (iterate), ship. The common objective is to handle the planning, building and shipping process within only a few hours to days. The teams decide for themselves which elements of the different methods, if any, to adopt. This process offers the maximum flexibility and autonomy during development (see Chap. 21 by Stefan Roock; Orosz 2022).

2. The **portfolio level** is often shaped by scaled agile approaches. Scaled agility refers to all approaches that can be used to scale up the team's methods and frameworks. Well-known approaches are scrum of scrums, large-scale scrum (LeSS), scaled agile framework (SAFe) or the Spotify model (see Table 20.1). Interestingly, these models are rare outside of traditional companies.

Example: Spotify Model.

The **Spotify model** refers to a widely discussed agile scaling approach which arose in 2011 from the description of the culture and the operational and organizational structure of the streaming service Spotify. At the heart of the Spotify model is a focus on small, self-organized, cross-functional teams with end-to-end responsibility. This gives rise to scaled structures and processes that promote autonomy, cooperation and communication. The organizational structure can be depicted as a matrix. The agile cross-functional teams are called squads and are usually made up of eight people. Further organizational units are called tribes (multiple squads with a shared objective), chapters (cross-squad group of specialists) and guilds (voluntary community of people with a shared interest). Other distinctive features are the product trio and alliances, which are defined as a combination of multiple product trios from different tribes working towards a broader objective (Kniberg 2014b). ◄

Tab. 20.2 Comparison of digital-native configuration and scrum-focused configuration

	Digital-native configuration	Scrum-focused configuration
Typical line-up	Product trio (product manager, engineering manager, designer) and software developers	Product owner, scrum master, software developers, poss. designers
Product responsibility	Empowered product team	Product owner

In summary, product discovery seeks to answer the following question: What is the right product for a specific market problem? The purpose of product discovery is to ensure that right product is being built so that the development and delivery processes can operate as efficiently as possible. Both processes have a range of tried and tested frameworks and methods.

20.3.3 Employees

Following on from structures and processes, the third and final component under examination here is the employees. This section outlines the necessary roles and their corresponding career paths, along with the cultural characteristics of successful product organization.

Roles
There are two prevailing configurations with respect to the roles within a digital product organization's teams: the digital-native configuration and the scrum-focused configuration (see Table 20.2).

1. The digital-native configuration is modelled on product teams of companies that were founded in the digital era. In the digital-native configuration, the product is managed by a product manager, while the project management portion of the work is carried out by an engineering manager. This is the prevailing configuration in VC-backed and Silicon Valley oriented start-ups and scale-ups.
2. The scrum-focused configuration is strictly based on the scrum framework with the product owner and scrum master as two distinct roles (see Chap. 1 by Sascha Hoffmann; Schwaber and Sutherland 2020). This configuration is often found in more traditional companies.

The main difference between the two team configurations is the roles of product manager and product owner. According to the Scrum Guide, the product owner is responsible for maximizing the value of the product produced by the scrum team. The product owner's roles and responsibilities include defining the product goal, creating and communicating the product backlog, and representing the stakeholders.

In contrast, the responsibilities and the required skills of the product manager in the digital-native configuration are shaped by considerably broader and more intensive activities across the entire product lifecycle. Before product development proper can begin, a product manager primarily carries out strategy and discovery work. During product development, they might assume the roles and responsibilities of the product owner. Once the product has been launched on the market, more discovery work takes place, along with the associated validation of assumptions. In the product trio, the product manager is responsible for the business viability risk.

Difference Between Product Manager and Product Owner
It is often said that product manager is a job title, while product owner is a role within a scrum team. This means that a product manager may occupy the role of the product owner in a scrum team, but does not have to (Perri 2017).

Even within the job title, the scope of activities is not standardized and is heavily context dependent. In recent years, sub-types have emerged, such as technical product manager, growth product manager or generalist product manager (Mehta 2020).

The second fundamental difference is the roles of engineering manager and scrum master. Whereas in the digital-native configuration the engineering manager and the team take on a large portion of the project management from the product manager, Scrum introduces an additional role, the scrum master, who acts as an enabler, coach and facilitator within the team and removes obstacles. Ideally the digital-native configuration will enable the product manager to focus entirely on strategy as there is little to no need for them to write user stories.

Regardless of the configuration, design and technology roles with special expertise also come into play. The teams are completed, for example, by a designer. Even within the field of design there are various possible line-ups. Ideally the team will have a full-time product designer who works with the product manager and software developers on product discovery. However, design is often incorporated through an agency model, and depending on how it is implemented, this can lead to delays and bottlenecks (see Chap. 18 by Inken Petersen). Depending on the product, a researcher or a data scientist can take the place of a designer in the product trio alongside the product manager and the engineering manager.

Other common technical roles are software developers, DevOps engineers, site reliability engineers, data scientists and data engineers. Depending on the product, the software development roles in particular can be differentiated further. As in product roles tend to be conceived on a company-specific basis and are interpreted differently in different companies. Depending on the scale and focus of the organization, further specialist roles such as researchers or product ops may also play a part.

> **Specialist Roles**
> - **DevOps engineers** take care of the efficiency, speed and security of the software development, being responsible both for the development of the software (hence *Dev*) and its operation (hence *Ops*). The main roles and responsibilities

of a DevOps engineer are the programming and provision of automated applications and other tools for improving the workflow (GitLab 2022a).
- **Site reliability engineers**, like Dev Ops Engineers, are responsible for seamlessly connecting development and operations, with a focus on reliability (Microsoft n. d.).
- **Data scientists** gain insights relevant to the business or product from the organization's data sources. To do so, they make use of artificial intelligence, machine learning and statistics (see Chap. 19 by Jan Martens; IBM n. d.).
- **Data engineers** administrate the data infrastructure and data provision, thus forming the basis for a successful data product (GitLab 2022b).
- **Product Ops** support cross-functional product teams, for example by managing the required tools, user interviews, and research activities (Perri 2019).

Identifying the specific skills required and formalizing them into expert roles is another success factor of modern product organizations. Differentiation into dedicated expert roles demonstrates recognition and appreciation and influences both the employees' salaries and their career paths. That is why, in many organizations, there are two distinct development paths for the various roles over multiple levels: the individual contributor path or the management path. The idea behind this is to provide opportunities for career progression and further development to employees who are not interested in moving into management roles and being responsible for other personnel. Taking the product manager role as an example, Fig. 20.5 shows the possible development stages of a career that splits into the two different paths after a certain level of seniority. The development stages are analogous in software development and design.

Culture
Successful product organizations have established a unique culture that is appropriate to their market environment. Just like the product, this culture gives them a competitive advantage. In other words, a company's specific culture has a positive influence on its position in the market and sets its apart from the competition, which in turn influences the added value generated by the digital product. Such a company culture can increase employer appeal, make processes more efficient, or establish a group dynamic. The sum, therefore, generates greater value for customers or for the company than its individual parts.

Schein's (1984) iceberg model is a useful way to conceptualize the structure of company cultures. The tip, the visible part of the iceberg, is made up of artifacts. Underneath that are the company's values, which are only partially visible, and at the bottom are the basic assumptions:

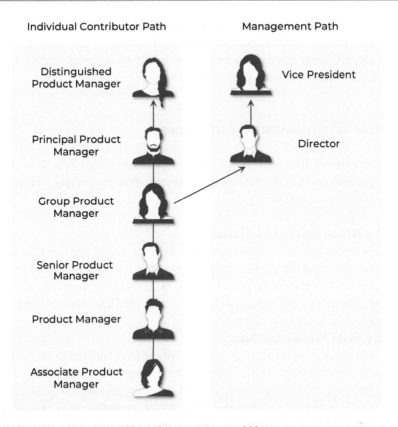

Fig. 20.5 Development stages. (With reference to Norton 2021)

- Artifacts: Visible aspects of the organizational culture that even outsiders can recognize. This includes office design, linguistic style, decoration, or clothing. A good example is Google's multi-colored bicycles in Mountain View.
- Shared values: Strategies, objectives and philosophies are made visible within the organization through mission statements, visions, and rules. These values serve as a guide when deciding whether or not actions are in keeping with the organization – take, for example, Amazon's frugality or Netflix's radical honesty (Hastings and Meyer 2020).
- Basic assumptions: These are at the core of an organizational culture. They include partially subconscious, shared beliefs and a common mode of perception. The basic assumptions shared by the members of the organization influence their every action and tend to be difficult to identify. A great example is the growth mindset referenced at Microsoft (Nadella et al. 2017).

The three levels of culture should be consistent with one another and with the organizational strategy, otherwise the competitive advantage of a functional organizational culture can turn into a disadvantage. Culture and strategy must not be at odds with one another. A sustainable, goal-oriented organizational culture complements a successful strategy. Conversely, a well-balanced organizational strategy is necessary for a healthy culture. A dysfunctional culture may be masked briefly by a strong product, but it will prove ineffective in the long term (Horowitz 2019).

20.4 Product Organization Archetypes

This section outlines five ways in which product organizations like those described above are put into practice. Each scenario represents different company objectives and product organization structures:

1. **Start-Up Before the Product-Market Fit**
   This is probably the most common way in which a digital product organization is established. After an initial phase with much ad-hoc and cross-sectional work, early signs of a product-market fit can be identified, resulting in founders and investors deciding to scale up. The company's objective is to stabilize structures and processes and establish organizational scalability.
2. **Start-Up in the Scaling-Up Phase**
   In general, start-ups in the scaling-up phase with several hundred to several thousand employees have already answered the question of product organization for themselves. The organization has clearly defined structures and processes, an established culture, and a certain degree of scaling up has taken place. Owing to the complex processes within a company of this size, the organization slows down in comparison to the early days of the start-up. In this phase, typical challenges include securing capacity for innovation, increasing efficiencies, and enabling further scaling up.
3. **Established Technology Companies**
   In established technology companies, including big-tech companies such as Facebook, Amazon, Netflix, and Google (FANG), the product organization has a deeply ingrained organizational and operational structure, and is defined in particular by the company culture. The main objective here is to guarantee ongoing renewal and maneuverability.
4. **Digital Transformation: Reorganization of the IT Department**
   When companies undergo transformation from a classic IT organization[1] headed up by a Chief Information Officer (CIO) to a modern IT organization with significantly broader skills in software development, the collaboration model for business units and

---

[1] Characteristics of a classic IT organization include project-oriented working, usually in accordance with the waterfall model, and the separation of the development and operation of an application.

Table 20.3 Change and adaptation process matrix

	Transformation into a product organization	Adaptations within a product organization
Incremental change	Suited to higher risk aversion and low to medium pressure to adapt	Suited to constant adaptations with regular experimentation
Wide-ranging, centrally controlled transformation	Suited to high pressure to adapt; enables high speed, but with high risk and possible friction	Suited to a high need for adaptation and low organizational maturity

specialist departments is redefined to improve how business and IT work together. This often involves (temporary) relocation of employees from business to IT and a switch to agile working methods at the team level. Products and platforms are identified and teams are assigned.

5. **Digital Transformation: New Digital Entity**
The second digital transformation variant is the foundation of a new digital entity, with a clearly defined business unit and employees from the field of software development. As above, a new collaboration model between IT and business is required. Technical profiles are deliberately removed from the classic IT environment to promote a much greater focus on the customer and a product and outcome mindset, in addition to increased efficiency and effectiveness.

20.5 Change and Adaptation Processes

The previous section described the situations in which product organizations occur, and some of the challenges that arise in those situations: establishing scalability, significantly increasing efficiency, and guaranteeing a capacity for innovation. But how do you structure the organization of a start-up when it is transitioning from the initial phase to a scaling-up phase? How do you turn a traditional organization into a modern product organization when planning a digital transformation, for example? These objectives can be achieved either through decentralized incremental change, or through a wide-ranging, centrally controlled transformation. Essentially, these are two distinct scenarios: one is transformation into a product organization, and the other is transformation within a product organization (see Table 20.3).

20.5.1 Transformation into a Product Organization

Changes to a company's structure, processes and culture, as defined in Sect. 20.3, are fundamental to the transformation of a traditional organization into a product organization.

- Structural changes: The organization must enable the cross-functional product teams to fulfil their responsibility to their product or value stream end-to-end as efficiently as possible. Outdated structures must be systematically removed. The objective of the structural change is to streamline communication, which reduces employees' mental load and gives them more time to carry out their work. To that end, interactions along the value stream are prioritized (Skelton and Pais 2019).
- Process changes: This is less about creating more efficient processes and more about prioritizing the following two questions as fundamental aspects of those processes: What shall we build? How shall we build it? The objective behind this transformation is minimizing risk and reducing the time to money (Moore and Cagan 2022).
- Cultural changes and change management: As explained in Sect. 20.3.3, the organizational culture must be aligned with the company's goals. A cultural transformation is essential for successful change processes and can only be achieved through dedicated, long-term change management

20.5.2 Transformation Within a Product Organization

Typically, organizational theory assumes a phased transformation model (an initial state is developed into a target state), as in Miles and Snow, for example (1984). Miles and Snow argue that a fit between the firm and its environment is necessary for organizational excellence, differentiating between strategy, processes, and structure. In this approach, strategy is the most important factor in successfully aligning an organization with its environment. Structure and processes must in turn follow the strategy, helping to simplify organizational movements towards external fit. Internal fit is achieved when, owing to the increased simplicity and optimized alignment, fewer coordination mechanisms arise in the processes and structure, which saves resources. Conversely, this means that changes in the structures and processes must never be considered separately from the strategy.

According to Miles and Snow, the prevailing conception is that in a longer, stable initial phase there is a misfit between the organization and its environment. This can be minimized through transformation, whereby operations move into a new, stable phase close to the optimum. However, in a volatile, uncertain, complex and ambiguous (VUCA) environment, these stable phases are at best short-lived, if they exist at all, which ultimately calls for continual, incremental adaptation into a modern product organization.

> **Example: Transformation of a Product Organization**
>
> One example of transformation within a product organization is the continual improvement of Amazon's leadership principles. These were first formulated and announced at Amazon in 2005. They then evolved into fundamental corporate guidelines. Over time, the principles have been continually expanded upon, amended, or replaced. For example, the 15th and 16th leadership principles, "Strive to be Earth's Best Employer" and "Success and Scale Bring Broad Responsibility", were added in 2021 in response to current developments. ◀

Leadership principles can be defined as an organization's core, publicly declared values. They shape the organization's entire culture and the decisions made within it. Given that they are firmly rooted in core processes, changing them has implications for the entire organization. The principles, or amendment of the principles, can therefore help to guide and influence an organization's continued improvement. Accordingly, strategic decisions must always be aligned with the leadership principles, and it is equally necessary to evaluate job applicants consistently in line with the principles (Bryar and Carr 2021; Jassy 2021).

20.6 Conclusion

Despite their countless differences, successful product organizations have certain characteristics in common: an outcome-focused approach, decentralization of decisions, risk mitigation through experimentation, a team focus, adaptability, and scalability. These shared characteristics are reinforced by corresponding structures, processes, roles and are ingrained in the company. All these elements, including the company culture, are taken as a competitive advantage and regularly adapted through incremental or targeted, wide-ranging transformations. There is no organizational blueprint that can simply be followed. Just as in the search for product-market fit, the optimal balance between structure, processes and culture must be determined iteratively for each product organization.

References

Bryar, C, and B. Carr. 2021. *Working backwards : Insights, stories, and secrets from inside Amazon*. New York: St. Martin's.
Cagan, M. 2014. Product vs. IT mindset. https://www.svpg.com/product-vs-it-mindset/.
Cagan, M. 2018. *Inspired: How to create products customers love*. San Francisco: Wiley.
Cagan, M., and C. Jones. 2020. *Empowered: Ordinary people, extraordinary products*. New Jersey: Wiley.
Doerr, J. 2018. *Measure what matters: How Google, bono and the gates rock the world with OKRs*. New York: Portfolio/Penguin.

Dunbar, R., and R. I. M. Dunbar. 1993. *Co-evolution of neocortex size, group size and language in humans.* London: Cambridge University Press.

Gilder, G. 1993. Metcalf's law and legacy. Forbes ASAP. Houston.

GitLab Inc. 2022a. What is DevOps? https://about.gitlab.com/topics/devops/.

GitLab Inc. 2022b. Data engineering. https://about.gitlab.com/job-families/finance/data-engineer/.

Hastings, R., and E. Meyer. 2020. *No rules rules.* New York: Penguin Press.

Horowitz, B. 2019. *What you do is who you are: How to create your business culture.* London: HarperCollins.

IBM. n. d. What is data science? https://www.ibm.com/topics/data-science#:~:text=Data%20science%20combines%20math%20and,decision%20making%20and%20strategic%20planning.

Jassy, A. 2021. Letter to shareholders. https://www.aboutamazon.com/news/company-news/2021-letter-to-shareholders.

Kniberg, H. 2014a. *Lean from the Trenches—Manage Large-Scale Projects with Kanban.* Dallas: The Pragmatic Bookshelf.

Kniberg, H. 2014b. Spotify engineering culture (part 1). https://engineering.atspotify.com/2014b/03/spotify-engineering-culture-part-1/.

Mehta. 2020. What's your shape? A product manager's guide to growing yourself and your team. https://www.ravi-mehta.com/product-manager-roles/.

Microsoft. n. d. SRE und DevOps. https://learn.microsoft.com/de-de/azure/site-reliability-engineering/articles/devops.

Miles, R. E., and C. C. Snow. 1984. Fit, failure and the hall of fame. *California Management Review* 26:10–28. https://doi.org/10.2307/41165078.

Miller, G. A. 1956. The magical number seven, plus or minus two: Some limits on our capacity for processing information. *Psychological Review* 63(2):81–97.

Moore, J., and M. Cagan. 2022. The transformation series. https://www.svpg.com/transformation-series/.

Nadella, S., G. Shaw, J. T. Nichols, and B. Gates. 2017. *Hit refresh: The quest to rediscover Microsoft's soul and imagine a better future for everyone.* London: HarperCollins.

Nambisan, S. 2017. Digital entrepreneurship: Toward a digital technology perspective of entrepreneurship. *Entrepreneurship Theory and Practice* 41(6):1029–1055.

Norton, K. 2021. Dual track PM ladders. https://www.bringthedonuts.com/newsletter/dual-track-product-manager-ladder.html.

Orosz, G. 2022. How big tech runs tech projects and the curious absence of scrum. https://blog.pragmaticengineer.com/project-management-at-big-tech/.

Osterling, M., and K. Martin. 2013. *Value stream mapping: How to visualize work and align leadership for organizational transformation.* McGraw-Hill.

Patton, J., and P. Economy. 2014. *User story mapping: Discover the whole story, build the right product.* Sebastopol: O'Reilly and Associates.

Perri, M. 2017. Product manager vs. product owner. https://melissaperri.com/blog/2017/06/29/product-manager-vs-product-owner.

Perri, M. 2019. Product operations: The fuel for winning product strategies. https://melissaperri.com/blog/2019/7/19/product-operations-the-fuel-for-winning-product-strategies.

Ries, E. 2011. *The lean startup: How today's entrepreneurs use continuous innovation to create radically successful businesses.* New York: Crown Business.

Schein, E. H. 1984. Coming to a new awareness of organizational culture. *Sloan Management Review* 25(2):3–16.

Schwaber, K., and J. Sutherland. 2020. Der Scrum Guide. Der gültige Leitfaden für Scrum: Die Spielregeln. https://scrumguides.org/docs/scrumguide/v2020/2020-Scrum-Guide-German.pdf.

Seiden, J. 2019. *Outcomes over output: Why customer behaviour is the key metric for business success.* Brooklyn: Sense & Respond Press.
Skelton, M., and M. Pais. 2019. *Team topologies: Organizing business and technology teams for fast flow.* Portland: IT Revolution.
Torres, T. 2021. *Continuous discovery habits: Discover products that create customer value and business.* Product Talk LLC. Bend.
Venkateswaran, M., C. T. Daniels, and M. Dickstein. 2021. Product organization structure: Which product management leadership model is right for your business? https://www.spencerstuart.com/research-and-insight/product-organization-structure.
Vernon, V. 2013. *Implementing domain-driven design.* Boston: Addison Wesley.
Yoo, Y., R. Boland, K. Lyytinen, and A. Majchrzak. 2012. Organizing for innovation in the digitized world. *Organization Science* 23(5):1398–1408.

Michael Schultheiß is a Senior Director of Product Management at McKinsey & Co. There, he builds digital products and, in particular, product organizations for clients from a wide variety of industries and regions. Before working as a consultant, he was a product leader at ZEIT/ZEIT ONLINE. He regularly serves as a lecturer or guest lecturer in product management at various universities and technical colleges.
Contact: michael_schultheiss@mckinsey.com

David Gehrke is a Research Assistant to Prof. Dr. Lutz Göcke, Chair of Digital Product Management at Nordhausen University of Applied Sciences, and Master's student at an IT subsidiary of an automotive group. After studying at the Kyungpook National University in South Korea, he worked as a Venture Architect and acted as a consultant in product support and orientation.
Contact: david.gehrke@hs-nordhausen.de

Lutz Göcke is a Professor of Digital Management at Nordhausen University of Applied Sciences. He is the initiator and head of the Digital Product Management course (B.A.), and the University Incubator for Entrepreneurship (HIKE) at said University. He teaches and researches digital innovation, business model innovations, and corporate entrepreneurship. Before joining the Nordhausen University of Applied Sciences, Lutz Göcke worked for a number of years as a digital product manager at Volkswagen AG.
Contact: lutz.goecke@hs-nordhausen.de

Choosing the "Right" Agile Framework for the Company

21

Stefan Roock

Abstract

After successful agile pilots (e.g., with Scrum), many companies wonder what agile approaches can look like for the company as a whole. All too often, they search for the one framework for everything: LeSS, Nexus, SAFe, Scrum@Scale, etc. This looks good on paper, but unnecessarily restricts the power of agility. This article discusses how companies can shape their agile journey to fully exploit the potential of agile thinking and working methods. It illustrates how maximum freedom and agility can harmonize with the necessary governance.

21.1 Introduction

When a company considers introducing agile working methods, the question of method quickly arises: Scrum, Kanban, Extreme Programming? Or think big with SAFe, LeSS, Nexus or the Spotify "model"?[1] However, this question is not useful for most companies

---

[1] An overview of common agile approaches can be found in Wolf, Roock, Zumbrägel (2023). A detailed description of Scrum can be found in Wolf and Roock (2021). Kanban is precisely described in Anderson (2011). Kent Beck described Extreme Programming in Beck (2004). Mathis (2018) describes SAFe, Larman, Vodde (2017) describe LeSS and Bittner, Kong, West (2018) describe Nexus. The Spotify "model" is described in Kniberg and Ivarsson (2012).

S. Roock (✉)
it-agile GmbH, Hamburg, Deutschland
e-mail: stefan.roock@it-agile.de

© The Author(s), under exclusive license to Springer Fachmedien Wiesbaden GmbH, part of Springer Nature 2024
S. Hoffmann (ed.), *Digital Product Management*,
https://doi.org/10.1007/978-3-658-44276-7_21

to answer, as they lack experience with agile approaches. Without this experiential knowledge, they cannot really assess which approach fits well with their own company.

Then external consultants with agile experience are often brought in to compensate for the lack of own experience. This can be very useful, but it does not solve the whole problem. After all, the external people hardly know the company. So on the one hand, we have the people in the company who know their own company well, but do not yet fully understand agility. On the other hand, we have external people who (hopefully) know agility well from their own experience, but do not really understand the company.

A way out of this dilemma is shown by *Safe-To-Fail experiments:* We look for a small experiment through which we can learn a lot about agile work in our own company and only take manageable risks. This clearly speaks in favor of starting with a pilot: a team or smaller project works with an agile approach. This generates the experiential knowledge needed to make a meaningful decision about the broader use of agility in the company.

Following Schwaber (2013), this article distinguishes between three ideal-typical stages of agility in the company (see Fig. 21.1):

1. **Single agile team:** The agile pilot is an example of this form. This approach can also be systematically used in the company beyond that. The company still works in a classical way and only uses agile methods in special situations for individual projects.
2. **Agile in complete product development:** The entire development is switched to agile or an agile development department is set up alongside the classic development.
3. **Agile company:** The entire company (or at least large parts of the company) works agile. The consequence is a network structure of interacting agile teams.

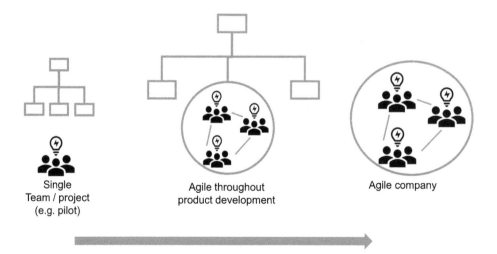

Fig. 21.1 Possible agile scenarios in the company

This article first discusses individual agile teams, then continues with the agile development department, and finally looks at agile companies.

21.2 The Appropriate Framework for the Agile Pilot

The question of the specific framework for the agile pilot should be answered by those who do the work, i.e., the team. External consultants with many years of agile experience can sketch the agile frameworks and the team decides by gut feeling what feels best. Then the team tries out the chosen framework and gathers its own experiences with it. Based on these experiences, the team adapts the framework or possibly even completely replaces it (see Fig. 21.2).

You cannot understand agility without having applied it. And if you still use the chosen method in the same way after several iterations as at the beginning, you have not yet understood agility.

After several adjustment cycles, it becomes clear which approach in which form is suitable for the team to achieve its own goals. Once this is the case, the pilot can be evaluated. Here, it should be openly and honestly reflected on what worked well and what was problematic (there are always things that are problematic). On this basis, it can then be decided whether and where agile work should be further spread in the company.

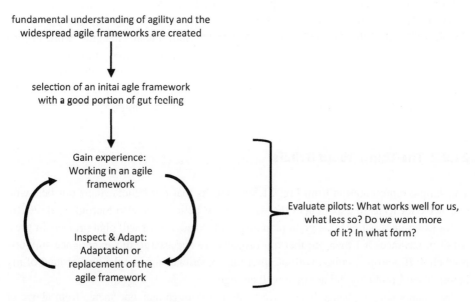

Fig. 21.2 Procedure for the agile pilot

21.2.1 Scrum vs. Kanban

Most pilots for individual teams use Scrum, followed by Kanban. In rare cases, Extreme Programming is used. This order is certainly due to the popularity of the frameworks, but also because they are well suited for pilots: Both Scrum and Kanban are easy to understand and the first steps can be taken relatively easily.

There is no formula to calculate which of the two approaches is better suited for your own context. But there are a few indicators that can help in the selection: Scrum is suitable when a new complex product is being developed or an existing product is to be substantially further developed. The Product Owner role in Scrum is intended to optimize the product benefit by prioritizing individual product requirements. Scrum therefore assumes that the value contribution of individual product features varies greatly. If this is not the case (e.g., for certain maintenance tasks), Scrum is less suitable.

Kanban, on the other hand, positions itself as an improvement process and not as a development method of its own. Thus, Kanban presupposes a somewhat functioning procedure that it can improve. It becomes difficult (though not impossible) if there is no development procedure at all or if a poorly functioning procedure needs to be "fixed" very quickly.

Unlike Scrum, Kanban does not require its own roles or meetings. It can therefore function more lightweight, e.g., also for maintenance or support IT settings. Since Kanban does not prescribe sprints, it can be used more easily in contexts where significantly faster reactions are necessary than a sprint cycle would allow.

Typically, your own Scrum or Kanban implementation evolves over time and adopts elements from the other "camp". For example, many Scrum teams integrate work-in-progress limits and Kanban implementations create roles that act similarly to Product Owner and Scrum Master. An outsider can therefore often not recognize from the lived process whether Scrum or Kanban was started with. This makes it clear that it is not about the mechanics of the chosen framework, but about the beliefs (aka mindset).

21.2.2 The Thing About Beliefs

The simple representation from Fig. 21.3 visualizes that our beliefs shape our behavior. Our behavior leads to experiences that support our beliefs (see also Sieroux et al. 2020). If, for example, I believe that good planning leads to success, I will plan projects in great detail in advance. If I then see that my projects are successful, this experience supports my belief. If a project fails, I will interpret this experience against the background of my belief: Then I probably did not plan well enough.

We cannot simply change beliefs. Certainly not through announcements from above or glossy posters with catchy slogans in the hallway. However, we can influence behavior and the interpretation of experiences (see Fig. 21.3, according to Sieroux et al. 2020): If we often enough make different experiences through new behavior, our beliefs change over time.

21 Choosing the "Right" Agile Framework for the Company

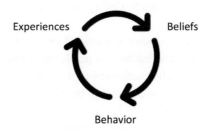

Fig. 21.3 Beliefs shape behavior

Agile frameworks are structural elements that "enforce" new behavior. This new behavior leads to new experiences. Through coaching, we can help to view these experiences from a new perspective (and not to bend them so that they fit the previous beliefs), see Fig. 21.4.

By going through this cycle several times, beliefs can change. Gradually, an agile mindset sets in and reproduces new, agile behavior. Once this point is reached, no agile framework is necessary anymore. People work agilely on their own. This also makes it clear why in companies that have been working agilely for many years, the typical agile frameworks are rarely found in their pure form.

However, one must not confuse cause and effect and prematurely adapt the agile framework—then there is a risk of bending the framework so that it still allows the old behavior. And then nothing actually changes; it's just called something different. We then also speak of "Scrum play-acting".

21.2.3 Agile Approach in Startups vs. Corporations

Startups bring different prerequisites than corporations. Startups are characterized by great dynamics on the edge of chaos; everything is constantly in flux. As soon as a double-digit number of people are working in the startup, structures are needed that provide

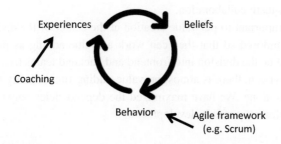

Fig. 21.4 Changing beliefs

sufficient stability and orientation so that everyone can work together in one direction. The challenge then is to maintain the flexibility and operational capability of the startup despite the additional structures.

Corporations come from the other extreme. Many corporations have developed excessive structures over decades that have a paralyzing effect. These companies need not more, but fewer structures. The challenge in this case is to avoid too much chaos by reducing structures. The currently well-running business should not be seriously endangered by the reduction of structures.

Agile frameworks can be useful in both scenarios. They can create the necessary structures for growth in startups and they can make corporations more responsive. Whether Scrum or Kanban is better suited does not depend significantly on whether it is a startup or a corporation. The indicators mentioned in the previous section weigh more heavily than the form of the company. However: In startups, the adjustment is easier than in corporations. Therefore, the demanding Extreme Programming or the very radical Naked Planning (see Sanders 2007) is more of an option in startups than in corporations.

21.3 Agile Work in Entire Product Development

If the agile pilot was successful, this success should of course also be rolled out to the rest of the company; in the first step to the complete product development.

Basically, the introduction of agile approaches for all teams in development does not differ from an agile pilot. From the outside, it is made clear what is to be achieved and why, and the teams choose the working methods and tools that seem suitable for them.

What is new are the cross-team topics. We do not achieve agility in the entire product development simply because all teams work agilely (see Leopold 2021). We must ensure that the individual teams, despite all their autonomy, continue to act in the company's interest, establish uniformity at the relevant points, and generate synergies.

21.3.1 Minimize Dependencies

In order to be able to use agility beyond individual teams, the belief must be unlearned that alignment can only be achieved through standardization. Instead, there needs to be a belief in the direction: With the right support, the teams will find the structures they need for effective cross-team collaboration.

For this, it is important to put value creation at the center of the discussion. First, the teams should be tailored so that they can work as value-adding as possible. A typical anti-pattern would be the division into frontend and backend teams (see Fig. 21.5).

With such a division, there is almost no value-adding functionality that can be developed by one team alone. We have maximized the dependencies between the teams and thus ensured the slowest possible development.

21 Choosing the "Right" Agile Framework for the Company

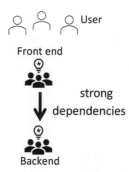

Fig. 21.5 Frontend and backend team: maximum dependencies

A better approach would be, for example, to divide the teams according to product areas, which each contain frontend and backend and are oriented towards the users. This reduces dependencies and increases the teams' ability to act (see Fig. 21.6).

If the teams are working on the same product, not all dependencies can be resolved. The teams cannot always work value-adding alone, but must cooperate with each other. The decision on how teams want to design their cooperation should again lie with the teams. To start with, it is often enough if the individual product areas call each other via interfaces. The teams can clarify among themselves who provides which interfaces and who uses them.

21.3.2 Managing Dependencies

In many contexts, overarching Kanban boards or Flight-Level systems (see Sieroux et al. 2020; Leopold 2021) have proven effective in creating a shared view of value creation. They visualize the collective progress in value creation and create a common dialogue space for the teams. In this space, they can decide how they want to deal with overarching problems.

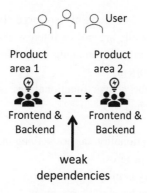

Fig. 21.6 Teams oriented towards value creation

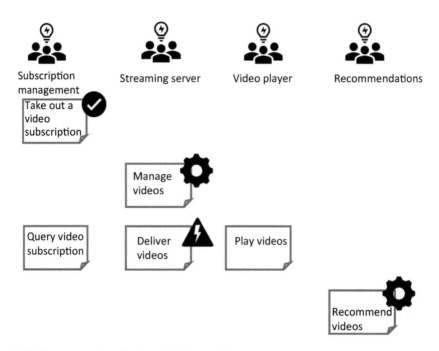

Fig. 21.7 Cross-team visualization of value creation

Figure 21.7 shows an example where we assume that we are a music streaming provider and now want to venture into video streaming. In this (greatly simplified) example, four teams are involved. The subscription management must be modified so that customers can subscribe to video subscriptions and the subscription management must be able to inform the other components whether an active video subscription exists. The streaming server must be expanded to manage and deliver videos. The video player must finally play the delivered videos. And last but not least, the recommendation component should recommend additional videos to customers based on their previous behavior.

The individual functionalities are certainly so large that they cannot be completed in a two-week iteration. The details are not of interest at this altitude. We assume that the teams are capable of appropriately breaking down the large functional blocks into smaller units and implementing them.

At this level, the state of the coarse functionalities is of interest. In the example shown, four states are distinguished:

1. No symbol: Work on the functionality has not yet begun.
2. Gear: The functionality is in progress
3. Checkmark: The functionality is fully developed.
4. Lightning: There is a problem we should talk about.

Representatives of the teams meet regularly and discuss the overall progress based on the visualization. In the example, there is a problem with the "Deliver Videos" functionality. Perhaps the implementation is more complex than thought. The team representatives could now decide that the "Recommendations" team pauses work on the "Recommend Videos" functionality and supports the streaming server team.

In addition to such ad-hoc measures, structural optimizations can also result from the discussions. For example, if coordination problems or similar bottlenecks become apparent again and again, teams could be merged or divided differently. This installs a continuous improvement process at the cross-team level.

21.3.3 Platforms

It may turn out that certain functionalities are needed by many teams. Then the dependencies between teams become complicated. One solution can be to copy the functionality into all using product areas. Another solution is to create a common platform where the basic functionalities are provided (see Fig. 21.8).

The platform approach may seem better than copying code. But this is often not the case. After all, managing a platform is a major challenge (see also Pichler 2020):

- Platforms often try to directly implement requirements of other teams. Then the platform quickly becomes a bottleneck and slows down product development instead of speeding it up.
- Platforms quickly put on fat: A lot of functionalities are integrated into the platform. This slows down the further development of the platform.
- Platforms are sometimes used to force other teams to do certain things. Then they limit the ability of the other teams to act.
- The members of the platform team must not lose touch with the working reality of the other teams. Otherwise, they develop chic, but unfortunately useless concepts in their "ivory tower".

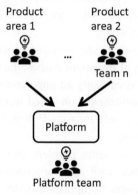

Fig. 21.8 Platform

Against this background, copying code should be considered a serious alternative (see also Steinacker 2014).

21.3.4 Caution with Top-Down Standardization

The classic way to create alignment is through top-down standardization, especially through scaling frameworks and tools. We are dealing here with a widespread management belief: Alignment needs standards. However, this urge for uniformity hinders agility. Often it is stipulated that all teams must work according to the same procedure (usually that of the pilot or a scaling framework SAFe®) and must use the same tool (e.g., Jira or Azure DevOps). Resistance from employees and loss of agility are often the result.

21.3.4.1 Resistance from Employees

Anyone who prescribes the same procedure and the same tool for the entire product development tramples on the idea of self-organization. After all, the point was that those who do the work decide how they do the work. They know best what they need to be able to work optimally value-adding:

> "Build projects around motivated individuals. Give them the environment and support they need and trust them to get the job done."
> "The best architectures, requirements, and designs emerge from self-organizing teams."
> (see: Agile Manifesto)

Enforcing self-organization by prescribing specific development frameworks and tools is at least incongruent with the principles of the Agile Manifesto. It should not be surprising that employees then exhibit behaviors that look like resistance. They often do not understand why the change is necessary and why the prescribed procedure and tool are particularly suitable for it.

Instead of uniform specifications, clarity is needed about the why of the change, success criteria, and appropriate support. First, employees must understand *why* a change is now necessary. Based on this clarity, we can talk about the direction of the change without prescribing the specific procedure. This can be done through *success criteria*: How do we recognize that the change was successful? The success criteria must be in a comprehensible context with the why.

For example, if the business side is very dissatisfied with IT because they have to wait too long for the implementation of important wishes, the satisfaction of the business side with the implementation speed is certainly an important success criterion. This could be supplemented by the average implementation speed weighted with the importance. This criterion can be easily and objectively measured. Within these criteria, the team should be allowed to find its own solution.

However, most teams face the same problem that we described above for companies: They have no experience with agile approaches and therefore lack the basis for an informed decision for a specific approach or for adapting the chosen approach.

Therefore, they need appropriate *support*. This can be done by an experienced consultant, through training, or simply by integrating experienced agile developers temporarily or permanently into the team.

The three aspects described do not guarantee that all participants are thrilled. However, it significantly reduces the potential for resistance as opportunities for participation are provided.

21.3.4.2 Loss of Agility

The second major problem is the loss of agility. If teams are prescribed procedures or tools, they cannot easily change or adapt them—even if the context requires it. Lengthy discussions and obtaining "permissions" are necessary, which is why not all teams actively pursue this arduous path. Why should they? Someone else apparently knew better how they can work well, and now this person should also know when and how a change in procedure is necessary.

21.3.5 Keep the Tools Away from Me

The larger the company, the greater the tool obsession. It may be hard to imagine in a corporation that you can work value-adding without cross-process tools. But it is very possible.

The teams should choose their work tools themselves. For one team, sticky notes on the wall or on digital whiteboards, like Miro, Mural, or Concept Board, may be suitable. Another team, on the other hand, might prefer to work with a ticket system, like Jira or Trello. And if a team realizes over time that it needs a different tool, it should be able to make the change easily itself.

The overarching needs of a company should be considered separately from its work tools. Especially when several teams are working on the same product, there needs to be overarching coordination. The means and tools used for this should then also be selected by the teams (usually through discussion between team representatives). So it could happen that larger development packages are defined in Jira, but each team maintains its derived user stories in its own form: sticky notes, Jira, etc.

The central tool specifications should be minimal. The larger the tool specifications, the harder it is for teams to adapt their working methods to changed context conditions. Every tool makes certain things easy and others difficult. A changed way of working often requires changed or new tools.

21.4 Agile Work throughout the Company

Real corporate agility requires agile work throughout the company—or at least in most of the company. To be fair, we must note that the authors of the Agile Manifesto probably did not have corporate agility in mind. The Agile Manifesto focuses on a single team in software development. Therefore, a brief definition of corporate agility is worthwhile:

"In a business context, agility is the ability of an organization to rapidly adapt to market and environmental changes in productive and cost-effective ways." (see Wikipedia 2022: "Business Agility")

So, at its core, it's about a company's adaptability to a changing context. It is not necessarily required that agile work is carried out everywhere in the company. Things that can be planned well do not need to be done agilely—this would be possible, but it is not efficient. And in the areas of the company where agile work is appropriate, not the same framework will be suitable everywhere (see argumentation above).

Furthermore, it is not sufficient for corporate agility that individual (or all) teams work agilely. They must collaborate across the board and the overarching structure must also be adaptable (see Hoffmann and Roock 2018). This brings with it two huge challenges:

1. *Autonomy and Alignment*: A structure is needed that gives the teams maximum freedom of action and still ensures that overarching goals can be achieved.
2. *Adaptable Structure*: The overarching structure itself must be adaptable. This is only possible at the necessary speed if it can happen without large-scale central reorganizations.

21.4.1 Autonomy and Alignment

We want capable teams that can quickly adapt to changing conditions. We achieve this by allowing the teams to make decentralized decisions, i.e., they have a high degree of autonomy. At the same time, we want the teams to pull together in the interest of the company. So, we desire alignment.

Autonomy and alignment initially seem like two poles of a tension field: More autonomy comes with less alignment and to achieve more alignment, we have to restrict autonomy.

However, the context can be designed in such a way that no tension field arises, but a coordinate system is spanned (see Fig. 21.9) and both alignment and autonomy can be achieved.

In the top left, we find *Command & Control*, where alignment is established through instructions and very little autonomy is possible. This paradigm is successful in *static* contexts, such as the majority of industrial mass production in the middle of the last century. In the increasingly dynamic business world, however, Command & Control is becoming less and less useful (see Drucker 2006; Bungay 2022).

We wish that despite decentralized decisions, alignment is maintained (top right in the diagram). In a military context, this is referred to as *Mission Command*. For this, it must be clear to all involved what the common goal is (the *What* and *Why* must be clear). They must understand the role they and everyone else play in achieving the goal.

21 Choosing the "Right" Agile Framework for the Company

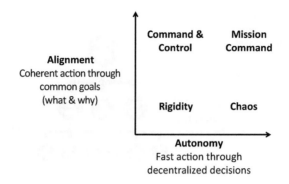

Fig. 21.9 Autonomy and Alignment. (Based on Bungay 2022)

And they must have the skills and permission to decide for themselves how to act in the respective situation.

When companies grant more autonomy, they often find that they do not end up with Mission Command. Instead, they move from top left to bottom right. Decisions are made more decentralized, but alignment to a common goal is missing. This results in *Chaos*. The cause is leadership behavior: The mechanisms that establish alignment in a Command & Control world (namely instruction and control) do not fit with decentralized decisions. A new leadership behavior must be learned so that the properties mentioned at Mission Command can be achieved.

Unfortunately, many companies do not make the necessary investments for this. And then the chaos is responded to with the classic alignment instruments. A lot of additional roles and meetings are introduced to establish alignment. We get alignment back, but sacrifice most of the speed and end up back at Command & Control.

For the sake of completeness, the area at the bottom left should also be mentioned: no alignment and no autonomy. This could be called rigidity and in the business world, this situation is rather rare. It would be an indication of management failure at all levels.

21.4.2 Adaptable Structure

No structure fits every context and the context—the market conditions—are changing faster and faster. Therefore, companies need adaptable structures. Ideally, the company structures organically adapt to what the market currently requires (see also Hoffmann and Roock 2018).

Two things are needed for this:

1. There must be contact with the market (especially with the customers) everywhere in the company so that it can be "sensed" what the market needs.
2. The necessary structural changes must be quickly and decentrally implementable.

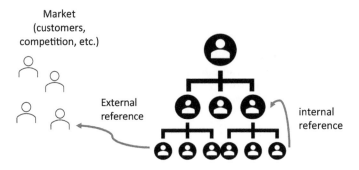

Fig. 21.10 Internal vs. External References

21.4.2.1 Market Contact Through External References

Market contact can be intensified if as many positions as possible in the company have direct market contact and orient themselves towards external references (instead of just internal references).

> "The external reference, that's what's happening in the market of customers, capital providers or even employees. The internal reference reflects what the company wants." (Vollmer 2017)

Customer wishes, customer satisfaction or even market dominance are external references. Utilization, productivity etc. are internal references, but also the organizational structure as a whole (see also Fig. 21.10).

Internal references encode what makes the company successful in the market. They are ideally the result of translating external references. Unfortunately, this translation process is sluggish and does not match the high market dynamics. As soon as the internal references are adjusted, the market has already changed again and new internal references are needed. A large amount of internal references thus hinders the company's adaptation to its environment. The stronger external references are anchored in the company, the faster the need for adaptation can be recognized.

A stronger external focus can be established in various ways. Possible examples are:

Instead (internal reference):	Better (external reference):
Teams are measured by how many features they implement	Teams are measured by how much value they have created from the customer's perspective (customer satisfaction can be a useful indicator)
Only internal stakeholders are present at the sprint review	Invite customers to the sprint review
Requirement managers or similar talk to customers and pass on written requirements to the development teams	Development teams interview customers and possibly observe at customers

Fig. 21.11 Sociocratic Basic Principles

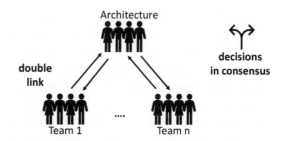

21.4.2.2 Company Adaptation with Sociocracy 3.0

For these adaptations to actually take place, the company structure must be able to change quickly. Here too, decentralized decisions are needed to adapt the local structure to the respective needs of the context. *Sociocracy* offers suitable models and tools for this[2]. Sociocracy pursues the goal of participatory organization and is based in its historical principles on double-linked circles and consent for decision-making (see Boeke 1945; Endenburg 2022). Circles are groups of people and form the basic building blocks of sociocratic companies. They are usually double-linked: A superior circle sends a leader to the subordinate circles and each subordinate circle sends a representative to the superior circle. Decisions in the circles are not made according to power or majority principle, but by consent. According to the consent principle, serious objections are used to improve proposals. The fact that someone does not like the proposal is not enough to prevent it. Through the double-linking and the consent principle, decisions can be made both participatively and quickly.

Figure 21.11 shows an example. There are a number of development teams that develop a software product as operational circles. To ensure a software architecture that allows effective collaboration of the individual software components, a superior "Architecture" circle was formed. Each development team sends a representative to the architecture circle and the architecture circle sends an architect to the development teams. The representatives of the development teams in the architecture circle bring the needs of their teams into the architecture decisions. The respective architect in the development team brings the decisions of the architecture circle into the development teams and ensures appropriate implementation. The consent decisions in the architecture circle ensure that the needs of the teams are sufficiently considered in architecture decisions.

Sociocracy 3.0 (S3) is the most modern sociocratic method and integrates agile principles and practices in particular (see Cumps 2021). S3 offers a large amount of patterns for the entire company at all levels. For our discussion, in addition to circles and consent, the concepts of tension, driver, and domain are particularly relevant.

---

[2] Holacracy offers similar concepts (see Robertson 2016).

A *tension* is a deviation of reality from an expectation. It always arises in people and is noticeable there through unpleasant emotions. This tension is examined and converted into a *driver*. The driver describes what the current situation is and what need the company has. Not every unpleasant emotion becomes a driver. You can also just have a bad day or bring private problems to work. Drivers are used to make things happen. Sometimes drivers can be dealt with by simply doing work (working *within the system*).

In the above example of the development teams and the architecture circle, a developer may have difficulty meeting a specific performance requirement when implementing a requirement. This will manifest itself in the developer as a tension (e.g., annoyance that he cannot meet a time commitment). The developer investigates this tension by offering a developer on his team support. Together they find out that the desired performance requirement cannot be met with the chosen architecture. They formulate a driver for this: "The desired performance requirement XYZ cannot be implemented with the chosen architecture. Since the performance requirement is essential for product success, the architecture must be adapted." The team's representative takes the driver to the architecture circle, where a response to the driver is made. In the case described, the architecture circle will probably adapt the architecture.

Sometimes, however, a driver also indicates that the company is structurally no longer well positioned for the requirements of the market. In this case, the driver often leads to an adjustment of the *domain* structure. A domain describes a task and responsibility area.

In our example, there is obviously the "Architecture" domain, for which the architecture circle is responsible. There are probably also domains for the individual components of the software product, for which the teams are responsible. There will probably also be a domain with overall product responsibility (see Fig. 21.12).

Now the problem could arise that there are always disagreements in the collaboration between the "Frontend" and "Backend" domains: The frontend team is often blocked because it has to wait for the backend team's work. The backend functionality often does not fit what is needed in the frontend and the revisions in the backend lead to waiting times in the frontend. This driver ends up in the "Product Responsibility" domain. There, it may be concluded that the separation between frontend and backend should be

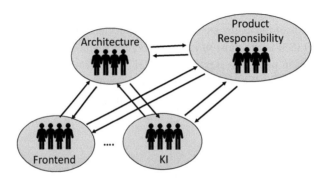

Fig. 21.12 Examples of domains

21 Choosing the "Right" Agile Framework for the Company

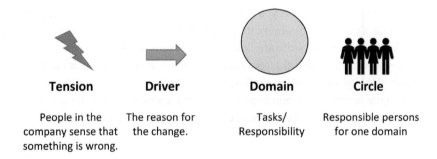

Fig. 21.13 Important S3 patterns for adaptable companies

abolished and the two domains are combined. This could then lead to the merged team "Frontend&Backend" becoming too large to work effectively. This leads to a new driver, which could then be dealt with directly by the "Frontend&Backend" team. The team could decide to form two teams to handle their domain, each consisting of frontend and backend developers.

The S3 patterns tension, driver, domain, and circle are shown in relation in Fig. 21.13.

If you play out this approach to the end, you end up with a company that no longer has fixed positions (e.g., purchasing department manager) but only flexible roles. There, someone might be the contact person for purchasing in the company; however, he has this role temporarily. Maybe we find out at some point that the person is needed more urgently elsewhere or that another person can fill the role better. And of course, it can happen that the purchasing domain no longer needs such a contact person or the entire domain is dissolved. Then the person takes on an important task elsewhere in the company.

For most companies, it would certainly be too big a step to implement S3 completely all at once. Such a big-bang approach would also completely contradict the argument of this chapter. S3 is based on the idea that the S3 patterns are used specifically where they provide a benefit—where one must respond to a business-relevant driver. In the end, this can lead to the entire company being structured according to S3. But this is by no means an inevitable consequence.

21.5 Summary

If there is no experience with agile development in the company yet, one should start with a manageable pilot. The pilot should ideally be implementable with just one team. Whether you choose Scrum, Kanban, or Extreme Programming for the pilot is not so important. What is more important is that you try something and learn from your own experience.

If the pilot was successful and you want more agility in the company, you need clarity about what effect you hope to achieve through agility. If you want more transparency and reliability in the delivery of software, it is sufficient to work with agile teams in development. If you want to make the company as a whole more agile to achieve business agility, agile thinking and working methods are needed in large parts of the company. In addition to agile teams, the interactions between the teams become relevant. They must adapt their behavior and also their structure to changed market requirements.

References

AgilesManifest. https://agilemanifesto.org/iso/de/manifesto.html.
Anderson, D. J. 2011. Kanban. dpunkt.verlag.
Beck, K., and C. Andres. 2004. *Extreme programming explained: Embrace change*. 2nd ed. Addison-Wesley Professional.
Bittner, K., P. Kong, and D. West. 2018. *Mit dem Nexus™ Framework Scrum skalieren*. dpunkt. verlag.
Boeke, K. 1945. Soziokratie: Demokratie, wie sie sein könnte. https://www.sociocracy.info/sociocracy-democracy-kees-boeke/.
Bungay, S. 2022. *The art of action: How leaders close the gaps between plans, actions and result*. Anniversary ed. Hodder and Stoughton Ltd.
Cumps, J. 2021. *Soziokratie 3.0—Der Roman*. dpunkt.verlag.
Endenburg, G. 2022. Die soziokratische Kreisorganisationsmethode. https://www.sociocracy.info/gerard-endenburg/.
Drucker, P. F. 2006. *The practice of management*. Reissue ed. Harper Business.
Hoffmann, J., and S. Roock. 2018. *Agile Unternehmen: Veränderungsprozesse gestalten, agile Prinzipien verankern, Selbstorganisation und neue Führungsstile etablieren*. dpunkt.verlag.
Kniberg, H., and A. Ivarsson. 2012. Scale Agile @ Spotify—with Tribes, Squads, Chapters & Guilds. https://blog.crisp.se/wp-content/uploads/2012/11/SpotifyScaling.pdf.
Larman, C., and B. Vodde. 2017. *Large-Scale Scrum: Scrum erfolgreich skalieren mit LeSS*. dpunkt.verlag.
Leopold, K. 2021. *Agilität neu denken: Mit Flight Levels zu echter Business-Agilität*. 2. edn. dpunkt.verlag.
Mathis, C. 2018. *SAFe—Das scaled agile framework*. 2. edn. dpunkt.verlag.
Pichler, R. 2020. Leveraging software platforms. https://www.romanpichler.com/blog/leveraging-software-platforms/Zuletzt.
Robertson, B. J. 2016. *Holacracy: Ein revolutionäres Management-System für eine volative Welt*. Vahlen.
Sanders, A. 2007. Naked planning explained—Kanban in the small. https://aaronsanders.co/naked-planning-explained-kanban-in-the-small/Zuletzt.
Schwaber, K., and J. Sutherland. 2013. *Software in 30 Tagen: Wie Manager mit Scrum Wettbewerbsvorteile für ihr Unternehmen schaffen*. dpunkt.verlag.
Sieroux, S., S. Roock, and H. Wolf. 2020. *Agile Leadership, Führungsmodelle, Führungsstile und das richtige Handwerkszeug für die agile Arbeitswelt*. dpunkt.verlag.
Steinacker, G. 2014. Scaling with Microservices and Vertical Decomposition. https://www.otto.de/jobs/technology/techblog/artikel/scaling-with-microservices-and-vertical-decomposition_2014-07-29.php.

Vollmer, L. 2017. Kundenservice vs. Firmenpolicy. 2017. https://www.capital.de/wirtschaft-politik/management-kundenservice-vs-unternehmenspolicy-kolumne-vollmer-8793.
Wikipedia. 2022. BusinessAgility. https://en.wikipedia.org/wiki/Business_agility.
Wolf, H., and S. Roock. 2021. *Scrum – verstehen und erfolgreich einsetzen.* 3rd revised edition. dpunkt.verlag.
Wolf, H., S. Roock, and S. Zumbrägel. 2023. *Agile Softwareentwicklung – Ein Überblick.* 5th ed. dpunkt.verlag.

Stefan Roock has been working with agile methodologies such as Extreme Programming, Scrum, and Kanban since 1999. Throughout his career, he has worked as a developer, Scrum Master, Product Owner and has helped many companies implement agility as a trainer and coach. He has accompanied agile transformations with hundreds and thousands of participants. Today, he focuses on Agile Leadership and Product Ownership.
Contact: stefan.roock@it-agile.de

Printed by Libri Plureos GmbH
in Hamburg, Germany